Software Architecture with C++

Design modern systems using effective architecture
concepts, design patterns, and techniques with C++20

Adrian Ostrowski
Piotr Gaczkowski

BIRMINGHAM - MUMBAI

Software Architecture with C++

Group Product Manager: Aaron Lazar
Publishing Product Manager: Richa Tripathi
Senior Editor: Rohit Singh
Content Development Editor: Kinnari Chohan
Technical Editor: Gaurav Gala
Copy Editor: Safis Editing
Project Coordinator: Deeksha Thakkar
Proofreader: Safis Editing
Indexer: Priyanka Dhadke
Production Designer: Aparna Bhagat

First published: April 2021

Production reference: 2210421

Published by Packt Publishing Ltd.
Livery Place
35 Livery Street
Birmingham
B3 2PB, UK.

ISBN 978-1-83855-459-0

www.packt.com

To Agnieszka, for all her love and support
To Mateusz, for being a great mentor
To my parents, for sparking the curiosity in me
To my friends, for not being hidden and for all they do

– Adrian Ostrowski

To Emilia, who tolerated me when I was writing this book; my parents, who encouraged me to learn coding; the mastermind group members who cheered me on in this journey; Hackerspace Trójmiasto, for positive vibes; IOD, for reminding me that I love writing; 255, for the workouts; and all the friends who shared the journey with me. Love you!

– Piotr Gaczkowski

Contributors

About the authors

Adrian Ostrowski is a modern C++ enthusiast interested in the development of both the C++ language itself and the high-quality code written in it. A lifelong learner with over a decade of experience in the IT industry and more than 8 years of experience with C++ specifically, he's always eager to share his knowledge. His past projects range from parallel computing, through fiber networking, to working on a commodity exchange's trading system. Currently, he's one of the architects of Intel and Habana's integration with machine learning frameworks.

In his spare time, Adrian used to promote music bands together with Piotr and has learned how to fly a glider. Currently, he likes riding his bicycle, going to music events, and browsing memes.

Piotr Gaczkowski has more than 10 years of experience in programming and practicing DevOps and uses his skills to improve people's lives. He likes building simple solutions to human problems, organizing cultural events, and teaching fellow professionals. Piotr is keen on automating boring activities and using his experience to share knowledge by conducting courses and writing articles about personal growth and remote work.

He has worked in the IT industry both in full-time positions and as a freelancer, but his true passion is music. When not making his skills useful at work, you can find him building communities.

About the reviewer

Andrey Gavrilin is a senior software engineer working for an international company that provides treasury management cloud solutions. He has an MSc degree in engineering (industrial automation) and has worked in different areas such as accounting and staffing, road data bank, web and Linux distribution development, and fintech. His interests include mathematics, electronics, embedded systems, full-stack web development, retro gaming, and retro programming.

Table of Contents

Section 2: The Design and Development of C++ Software

Preface

Modern C++ allows you to write high-performing applications in a high-level language without sacrificing readability and maintainability. There's more to software architecture than just language, though. We're going to show you how to design and build applications that are robust and scalable and that perform well.

Complete with step-by-step explanations of essential concepts, practical examples, and self-assessment questions, you will begin by understanding the importance of architecture, looking at a case study of an actual application.

You'll learn how to use established design patterns at the level of a single application, exploring how to make your applications robust, secure, performant, and maintainable. You'll then build higher-level services that connect multiple single applications using patterns such as service-oriented architecture, microservices, containers, and serverless technology.

By the end of this book, you will be able to build distributed services using modern C++ and associated tools to deliver solutions that your clients will recommend.

Are you interested in becoming a software architect or looking to learn more about modern trends in architecture? If so, this book should help you!

Who this book is for

Developers working with modern C++ will be able to put their knowledge to work with this practical guide to software architecture. The book takes a hands-on approach to implementation and associated methodologies that will have you up and running and productive in no time.

What this book covers

Chapter 1, *Importance of Software Architecture and Principles of Great Design*, looks at why we design software in the first place.

Chapter 2, *Architectural Styles*, covers the different approaches you can take in terms of architecture.

Chapter 3, *Functional and Nonfunctional Requirements*, explores understanding the needs of clients.

Chapter 4, *Architectural and System Design*, is all about creating effective software solutions.

Chapter 5, *Leveraging C++ Language Features*, gets you speaking native C++.

Chapter 6, *Design Patterns and C++*, focuses on modern C++ idioms and useful code constructs.

Chapter 7, *Building and Packaging*, is about getting code to production.

Chapter 8, *Writing Testable Code*, teaches you how to find bugs before the clients do.

Chapter 9, *Continuous Integration and Continuous Deployment*, introduces the modern way of automating software releases.

Chapter 10, *Security in Code and Deployment*, is where you will learn how to make sure it's hard to break your systems.

Chapter 11, *Performance*, looks at performance (of course!). C++ should be fast – can it be even faster?

Chapter 12, *Service-Oriented Architecture*, sees you building systems based on services.

Chapter 13, *Designing Microservices*, focuses on doing one thing only – designing microservices.

Chapter 14, *Containers*, gives you a unified interface to build, package, and run applications.

Chapter 15, *Cloud-Native Design*, goes beyond traditional infrastructure to explore cloud-native design.

To get the most out of this book

The code examples in this book are mostly written for GCC 10. They should work with Clang or Microsoft Visual C++ as well, though certain features from C++20 may be missing in older versions of the compilers. To get a development environment as close to the authors' as possible, we advise you to use Nix (https://nixos.org/download.html) and direnv (https://direnv.net/) in a Linux-like environment. These two tools should configure the compilers and supporting packages for you if you run direnv allow in a directory containing examples.

Without Nix and direnv, we can't guarantee that the examples will work correctly. If you're on macOS, Nix should work just fine. If you're on Windows, the Windows Subsystem for Linux 2 is a great way to have a Linux development environment with Nix.

To install both tools, you have to run the following:

```
# Install Nix
curl -L https://nixos.org/nix/install | sh
# Configure Nix in the current shell
. $HOME/.nix-profile/etc/profile.d/nix.sh
# Install direnv
nix-env -i direnv
# Download the code examples
git clone
https://github.com/PacktPublishing/Hands-On-Software-Architecture-with-Cpp.
git
# Change directory to the one with examples
cd Hands-On-Software-Architecture-with-Cpp
# Allow direnv and Nix to manage your development environment
direnv allow
```

After executing the preceding command, Nix should download and install all the necessary dependencies. This might take a while but it helps to ensure we're using exactly the same tools.

If you are using the digital version of this book, we advise you to type the code yourself or access the code via the GitHub repository (link available in the next section). Doing so will help you avoid any potential errors related to the copying and pasting of code.

Download the example code files

You can download the example code files for this book from GitHub at `https://github.com/PacktPublishing/Software-Architecture-with-Cpp`. In case there's an update to the code, it will be updated on the existing GitHub repository.

We also have other code bundles from our rich catalog of books and videos available at `https://github.com/PacktPublishing/`. Check them out!

Download the color images

We also provide a PDF file that has color images of the screenshots/diagrams used in this book. You can download it here: `https://static.packt-cdn.com/downloads/ 9781838554590_ColorImages.pdf`.

Conventions used

There are a number of text conventions used throughout this book.

`CodeInText`: Indicates code words in text, database table names, folder names, filenames, file extensions, pathnames, dummy URLs, user input, and Twitter handles. Here is an example: "The first two fields (`openapi` and `info`) are metadata describing the document."

A block of code is set as follows:

```
using namespace CppUnit;
using namespace std;
```

Bold: Indicates a new term, an important word, or words that you see onscreen. For example, words in menus or dialog boxes appear in the text like this. Here is an example: "Select **System info** from the **Administration** panel."

Warnings or important notes appear like this.

Tips and tricks appear like this.

Get in touch

Feedback from our readers is always welcome.

General feedback: If you have questions about any aspect of this book, mention the book title in the subject of your message and email us at customercare@packtpub.com.

Errata: Although we have taken every care to ensure the accuracy of our content, mistakes do happen. If you have found a mistake in this book, we would be grateful if you would report this to us. Please visit www.packtpub.com/support/errata, selecting your book, clicking on the Errata Submission Form link, and entering the details.

Piracy: If you come across any illegal copies of our works in any form on the Internet, we would be grateful if you would provide us with the location address or website name. Please contact us at copyright@packt.com with a link to the material.

If you are interested in becoming an author: If there is a topic that you have expertise in and you are interested in either writing or contributing to a book, please visit authors.packtpub.com.

Reviews

Please leave a review. Once you have read and used this book, why not leave a review on the site that you purchased it from? Potential readers can then see and use your unbiased opinion to make purchase decisions, we at Packt can understand what you think about our products, and our authors can see your feedback on their book. Thank you!

For more information about Packt, please visit packt.com.

1
Section 1: Concepts and Components of Software Architecture

This section introduces you to the basics of software architecture, demonstrating effective approaches to its design and documentation.

This section contains the following chapters:

- Chapter 1, *Importance of Software Architecture and Principles of Great Design*
- Chapter 2, *Architectural Styles*
- Chapter 3, *Functional and Nonfunctional Requirements*

1

Importance of Software Architecture and Principles of Great Design

The purpose of this introductory chapter is to show what role software architecture plays in software development. It will focus on the key aspects to keep in mind when designing the architecture of a C++ solution. We'll discuss how to design efficient code with convenient and functional interfaces. We'll also introduce a domain-driven approach for both code and architecture.

In this chapter, we'll cover the following topics:

- Understanding software architecture
- Learning the importance of proper architecture
- Exploring the fundamentals of good architecture
- Developing architecture using Agile principles
- The philosophy of C++
- Following the SOLID and DRY principles
- Domain-driven design
- Coupling and cohesion

Technical requirements

To play with the code from this chapter, you'll need the following:

- A Git client for checking out the repositories given shortly.
- A C++20-compliant compiler to compile all the snippets. Most of them are written in C++11/14/17, but concept support is required to experiment with the few that touch the subject.
- GitHub link for code snippets: `https://github.com/PacktPublishing/Software-Architecture-with-Cpp/tree/master/Chapter01`.
- GitHub link for GSL: `https://github.com/Microsoft/GSL`

Understanding software architecture

Let's begin by defining what software architecture actually is. When you create an application, library, or any software component, you need to think about how the elements you write will look and how they will interact with each other. In other words, you're designing them and their relations with their surroundings. Just like with urban architecture, it's important to think about the bigger picture to not end up in a haphazard state. On a small scale, every single building looks okay, but they don't combine into a sensible bigger picture – they just don't fit together well. This is what's called accidental architecture and it is one of the outcomes you want to avoid. However, keep in mind that whether you're putting your thoughts into it or not, when writing software you are creating an architecture.

So, what exactly should you be creating if you want to mindfully define the architecture of your solution? The Software Engineering Institute has this to say:

> *The software architecture of a system is the set of structures needed to reason about the system, which comprise software elements, relations among them, and properties of both.*

This means that in order to define an architecture thoroughly, we should think about it from a few perspectives instead of just hopping into writing code.

Different ways to look at architecture

There are several scopes that can be used to look at architecture:

- Enterprise architecture deals with the whole company or even a group of companies. It takes a holistic approach and is concerned about the strategy of whole enterprises. When thinking about enterprise architecture, you should be looking at how all the systems in a company behave and cooperate with each other. It's concerned about the alignment between business and IT.

- Solution architecture is less abstract than its enterprise counterpart. It stands somewhere in the middle between enterprise and software architecture. Usually, solution architecture is concerned with one specific system and the way it interacts with its surroundings. A solution architect needs to come up with a way to fulfill a specific business need, usually by designing a whole software system or modifying existing ones.

- Software architecture is even more concrete than solution architecture. It concentrates on a specific project, the technologies it uses, and how it interacts with other projects. A software architect is interested in the internals of the project's components.

- Infrastructure architecture is, as the name suggests, concerned about the infrastructure that the software will use. It defines the deployment environment and strategy, how the application will scale, failover handling, site reliability, and other infrastructure-oriented aspects.

Solution architecture is based on both software and infrastructure architectures to satisfy the business requirements. In the following sections, we will talk about both those aspects to prepare you for both small- and large-scale architecture design. Before we jump into that, let's also answer one fundamental question: why is architecture important?

Learning the importance of proper architecture

Actually, a better question would be: why is caring about your architecture important? As we mentioned earlier, regardless of whether you put conscious effort into building it or not, you will end up with some kind of architecture. If after several months or even years of development you still want your software to retain its qualities, you need to take some steps earlier in the process. If you won't think about your architecture, chances are it won't ever present the required qualities.

So, in order for your product to meet the business requirements and attributes such as performance, maintainability, scalability, or others, you need to take care of its architecture, and it is best if you do it as early as you can in the process. Let's now discuss two things that each good architect wants to protect their projects from.

Software decay

Even after you did the initial work and had a specific architecture in mind, you need to continuously monitor how the system evolves and whether it still aligns with its users' needs, as those may also change during the development and lifetime of your software. Software decay, sometimes also called erosion, occurs when the implementation decisions don't correspond to the planned architecture. All such differences should be treated as technical debt.

Accidental architecture

Failing to track if the development adheres to the chosen architecture or failing to intentionally plan how the architecture should look will often result in a so-called accidental architecture, and it can happen regardless of applying best practices in other areas, such as testing or having any specific development culture.

There are several anti-patterns that suggest your architecture is accidental. Code resembling a big ball of mud is the most obvious one. Having god objects is another important sign of this. Generally speaking, if your software is getting tightly coupled, perhaps with circular dependencies, but wasn't like that in the first place, it's an important signal to put more conscious effort into how the architecture looks.

Let's now describe what an architect must understand to deliver a viable solution.

Exploring the fundamentals of good architecture

It's important to know how to recognize a good architecture from a bad one, but it's not an easy task. Recognizing anti-patterns is an important aspect of it, but for an architecture to be good, primarily it has to support delivering what's expected from the software, whether it's about functional requirements, attributes of the solution, or dealing with the constraints coming from various places. Many of those can be easily derived from the architecture context.

Architecture context

The context is what an architect takes into account when designing a solid solution. It comprises requirements, assumptions, and constraints, which can come from the stakeholders, as well as the business and technical environments. It also influences the stakeholders and the environments, for example, by allowing the company to enter a new market segment.

Stakeholders

Stakeholders are all the people that are somehow involved with the product. Those can be your customers, the users of your system, or the management. Communication is a key skill for every architect and properly managing your stakeholder's needs is key to delivering what they expected and in a way they wanted.

Different things are important to different groups of stakeholders, so try to gather input from all those groups.

Your customers will probably care about the cost of writing and running the software, the functionality it delivers, its lifetime, time to market, and the quality of your solution.

The users of your system can be divided into two groups: end users and administrators. The first ones usually care about things such as the usability, user experience, and performance of the software. For the latter, more important aspects are user management, system configuration, security, backups, and recovery.

Finally, things that could matter for stakeholders working in management are keeping the development costs low, achieving business goals, being on track with the development schedule, and maintaining product quality.

Business and technical environments

Architecture can be influenced by the business side of the company. Important related aspects are the time to market, the rollout schedule, the organizational structure, utilization of the workforce, and investment in existing assets.

By technical environment, we mean the technologies already used in a company or those that are for any reason required to be part of the solution. Other systems that we need to integrate with are also a vital part of the technical environment. The technical expertise of the available software engineers is of importance here, too: the technological decisions an architect makes can impact staffing the project, and the ratio of junior to senior developers can influence how a project should be governed. Good architecture should take all of that into account.

Equipped with all this knowledge, let's now discuss a somewhat controversial topic that you'll most probably encounter as an architect in your daily work.

Developing architecture using Agile principles

Seemingly, architecture and Agile development methodologies are in an adversarial relationship, and there are many myths around this topic. There are a few simple principles that you should follow in order to develop your product in an Agile way while still caring about its architecture.

Agile, by nature, is iterative and incremental. This means preparing a big, upfront design is not an option in an Agile approach to architecture. Instead, a small, but still reasonable upfront design should be proposed. It's best if it comes with a log of decisions with the rationale for each of them. This way, if the product vision changes, the architecture can evolve with it. To support frequent release delivery, the upfront design should then be updated incrementally. Architecture developed this way is called evolutionary architecture.

Managing architecture doesn't need to mean keeping massive documentation. In fact, documentation should cover only what's essential as this way it's easier to keep it up to date. It should be simple and cover only the relevant views of the system.

There's also the myth of the architect as the single source of truth and the ultimate decision-maker. In Agile environments, it's the teams who are making decisions. Having said that, it's crucial that the stakeholders are contributing to the decision-making process – after all, their points of view shape how the solution should look.

An architect should remain part of the development team as often they're bringing strong technical expertise and years of experience to the table. They should also take part in making estimations and plan the architecture changes needed before each iteration.

In order for your team to remain Agile, you should think of ways to work efficiently and only on what's important. A good idea to embrace to achieve those goals is domain-driven design.

Domain-driven design

Domain-driven design, or DDD for short, is a term introduced by Eric Evans in his book of the same title. In essence, it's about improving communication between business and engineering and bringing the developers' attention to the domain model. Basing the implementation of this model often leads to designs that are easier to understand and evolve together with the model changes.

What has DDD got to do with Agile? Let's recall a part of the Agile Manifesto:

> **Individuals and interactions** over processes and tools
> **Working software** over comprehensive documentation
> **Customer collaboration** over contract negotiation
> **Responding to change** over following a plan
>
> — The Agile Manifesto

In order to make the proper design decisions, you must understand the domain first. To do so, you'll need to talk to people a lot and encourage your developer teams to narrow the gap between them and business people. The concepts in the code should be named after entities that are part of *ubiquitous language*. It's basically the common part of business experts' jargon and technical experts' jargon. Countless misunderstandings can be caused by each of these groups using terms that the other understands differently, leading to flaws in business logic implementations and often subtle bugs. Naming things with care and using terms agreed by both groups can mean bliss for the project. Having a business analyst or other business domain experts as part of the team can help a lot here.

If you're modeling a bigger system, it might be hard to make all the terms mean the same to different teams. This is because each of those teams really operates in a different context. DDD proposes the use of *bounded contexts* to deal with this. If you're modeling, say, an e-commerce system, you might want to think of the terms just in terms of a shopping context, but upon a closer look, you may discover that the inventory, delivery, and accounting teams actually all have their own models and terms.

Each of those is a different subdomain of your e-commerce domain. Ideally, each can be mapped to its own bounded context – a part of your system with its own vocabulary. It's important to set clear boundaries of such contexts when splitting your solution into smaller modules. Just like its context, each module has clear responsibilities, its own database schema, and its own code base. To help communicate between the teams in larger systems, you might want to introduce a context map, which will show how the terms from different contexts relate to each other:

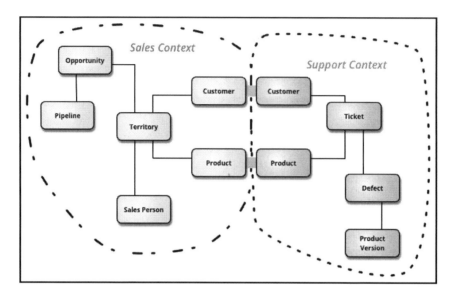

Figure 1.1 – Two bounding contexts with the matching terms mapped between them (image from one of Martin Fowler's articles on DDD: https://martinfowler.com/bliki/BoundedContext.html)

As you now understand some of the important project-management topics, we can switch to a few more technical ones.

The philosophy of C++

Let's now move closer to the programming language we'll be using the most throughout this book. C++ is a multi-paradigm language that has been around for a few decades now. During the years since its inception, it has changed a lot. When C++11 came out, Bjarne Stroustrup, the creator of the language, said that it felt like a completely new language. The release of C++20 marks another milestone in the evolution of this beast, bringing a similar revolution to how we write code. One thing, however, stayed the same during all those years: the language's philosophy.

In short, it can be summarized by three rules:

- There should be no language beneath C++ (except assembly).
- You only pay for what you use.
- Offer high-level abstractions at low cost (there's a strong aim for zero-cost).

Not paying for what you don't use means that, for example, if you want to have your data member created on the stack, you can. Many languages allocate their objects on the heap, but it's not necessary for C++. Allocating on the heap has some cost to it – probably your allocator will have to lock a mutex for this, which can be a big burden in some types of applications. The good part is you can easily allocate variables without dynamically allocating memory each time pretty easily.

High-level abstractions are what differentiate C++ from lower-level languages such as C or assembly. They allow for expressing ideas and intent directly in the source code, which plays great with the language's type safety. Consider the following code snippet:

```
struct Duration {
  int millis_;
};

void example() {
  auto d = Duration{};
  d.millis_ = 100;

  auto timeout = 1; // second
  d.millis_ = timeout; // ouch, we meant 1000 millis but assigned just 1
}
```

A much better idea would be to leverage the type-safety features offered by the language:

```
#include <chrono>

using namespace std::literals::chrono_literals;

struct Duration {
  std::chrono::milliseconds millis_;
};

void example() {
  auto d = Duration{};
  // d.millis_ = 100; // compilation error, as 100 could mean anything
  d.millis_ = 100ms; // okay
```

```
    auto timeout = 1s; // or std::chrono::seconds(1);
    d.millis_ =
        timeout; // okay, converted automatically to milliseconds
}
```

The preceding abstraction can save us from mistakes and doesn't cost us anything while doing so; the assembly generated would be the same as for the first example. That's why it's called a zero-cost abstraction. Sometimes C++ allows us to use abstractions that actually result in better code than if they were not used. One example of a language feature that, when used, could often result in such benefit is coroutines from C++20.

Another great set of abstractions, offered by the standard library, are algorithms. Which of the following code snippets do you think is easier to read and easier to prove bug-free? Which expresses the intent better?

```
// Approach #1
int count_dots(const char *str, std::size_t len) {
  int count = 0;
  for (std::size_t i = 0; i < len; ++i) {
    if (str[i] == '.') count++;
  }
  return count;
}

// Approach #2
int count_dots(std::string_view str) {
  return std::count(std::begin(str), std::end(str), '.');
}
```

Okay, the second function has a different interface, but even it if was to stay the same, we could just create `std::string_view` from the pointer and the length. Since it's such a lightweight type, it should be optimized away by your compiler.

Using higher-level abstractions leads to simpler, more maintainable code. The C++ language has strived to provide zero-cost abstractions since its inception, so build upon that instead of redesigning the wheel using lower levels of abstraction.

Speaking of simple and maintainable code, the next section introduces some rules and heuristics that are invaluable on the path to writing such code.

Following the SOLID and DRY principles

There are many principles to keep in mind when writing code. When writing object-oriented code, you should be familiar with the quartet of abstraction, encapsulation, inheritance, and polymorphism. Regardless of whether your writing C++ in a mostly object-oriented programming manner or not, you should keep in mind the principles behind the two acronyms: SOLID and DRY.

SOLID is a set of practices that can help you write cleaner and less bug-prone software. It's an acronym made from the first letters of the five concepts behind it:

- Single responsibility principle
- Open-closed principle
- Liskov substitution principle
- Interface segregation
- Dependency Inversion

We assume you already have the idea of how those principles relate to object-oriented programming, but since C++ is not always object-oriented, let's look at how they apply to different areas.

Some of the examples use dynamic polymorphism, but the same would apply to static polymorphism. If you're writing performance-oriented code (and you probably are if you chose C++), you should know that using dynamic polymorphism can be a bad idea in terms of performance, especially on the hot path. Further on in the book, you'll learn how to write statically polymorphic classes using the **Curiously Recurring Template Pattern** (**CRTP**).

Single responsibility principle

In short, the **Single Responsibility Principle** (**SRP**) means each code unit should have exactly one responsibility. This means writing functions that do one thing only, creating types that are responsible for a single thing, and creating higher-level components that are focused on one aspect only.

This means that if your class manages some type of resources, such as file handles, it should do only that, leaving parsing them, for example, to another type.

Often, if you see a function with "And" in its name, it's violating the SRP and should be refactored. Another sign is when a function has comments indicating what each section of the function (sic!) does. Each such section would probably be better off as a distinct function.

A related topic is the principle of least knowledge. In its essence, it says that no object should know no more than necessary about other objects, so it doesn't depend on any of their internals, for example. Applying it leads to more maintainable code with fewer interdependencies between components.

Open-closed principle

The **Open-Closed Principle (OCP)** means that code should be open for extension but closed for modification. Open for extension means that we could extend the list of types the code supports easily. Closed for modification means existing code shouldn't change, as this can often cause bugs somewhere else in the system. A great feature of C++ demonstrating this principle is `operator<<` of `ostream`. To extend it so that it supports your custom class, all you need to do is to write code similar to the following:

```
std::ostream &operator<<(std::ostream &stream, const MyPair<int, int>
    &mp) {
  stream << mp.firstMember() << ", ";
  stream << mp.secondMember();
  return stream;
}
```

Note that our implementation of `operator<<` is a free (non-member) function. You should prefer those to member functions if possible as it actually helps encapsulation. For more details on this, consult the article by Scott Meyers in the *Further reading* section at the end of this chapter. If you don't want to provide public access to some field that you wish to print to `ostream`, you can make `operator<<` a friend function, like so:

```
class MyPair {
// ...
  friend std::ostream &operator<<(std::ostream &stream,
    const MyPair &mp);
};
std::ostream &operator<<(std::ostream &stream, const MyPair &mp) {
  stream << mp.first_ << ", ";
  stream << mp.second_ << ", ";
  stream << mp.secretThirdMember_;
  return stream;
}
```

Note that this definition of OCP is slightly different from the more common one related to polymorphism. The latter is about creating base classes that can't be modified themselves, but are open for others to inherit from them.

Speaking of polymorphism, let's move on to the next principle as it is all about using it correctly.

Liskov substitution principle

In essence, the **Liskov Substitution Principle (LSP)** states that if a function works with a pointer or reference to a base object, it must also work with a pointer or reference to any of its derived objects. This rule is sometimes broken because the techniques we apply in source code do not always work in real-world abstractions.

A famous example is a square and a rectangle. Mathematically speaking, the former is a specialization of the latter, so there's an "is a" relationship from one to the other. This tempts us to create a Square class that inherits from the Rectangle class. So, we could end up with code like the following:

```
class Rectangle {
 public:
  virtual ~Rectangle() = default;
  virtual double area() { return width_ * height_; }
  virtual void setWidth(double width) { width_ = width; }
  virtual void setHeight(double height) { height_ = height; }
 private:
  double width_;
  double height_;
};

class Square : public Rectangle {
 public:
  double area() override;
  void setWidth(double width) override;
  void setHeight(double height) override;
};
```

How should we implement the members of the Square class? If we want to follow the LSP and save the users of such classes from surprises, we can't: our square would stop being a square if we called setWidth. We can either stop having a square (not expressible using the preceding code) or modify the height as well, thus making the square look different than a rectangle.

If your code violates the LSP, it's likely that you're using an incorrect abstraction. In our case, Square shouldn't inherit from Rectangle after all. A better approach could be making the two implement a GeometricFigure interface.

Since we are on the topic of interfaces, let's move on to the next item, which is also related to them.

Interface segregation principle

The interface segregation principle is just about what its name suggests. It is formulated as follows:

> *No client should be forced to depend on methods that it does not use.*

That sounds pretty obvious, but it has some connotations that aren't that obvious. Firstly, you should prefer more but smaller interfaces to a single big one. Secondly, when you're adding a derived class or are extending the functionality of an existing one, you should think before you extend the interface the class implements.

Let's show this on an example that violates this principle, starting with the following interface:

```
class IFoodProcessor {
 public:
  virtual ~IFoodProcessor() = default;
  virtual void blend() = 0;
};
```

We could have a simple class that implements it:

```
class Blender : public IFoodProcessor {
 public:
  void blend() override;
};
```

So far so good. Now say we want to model another, more advanced food processor and we recklessly tried to add more methods to our interface:

```
class IFoodProcessor {
 public:
  virtual ~IFoodProcessor() = default;
  virtual void blend() = 0;
  virtual void slice() = 0;
  virtual void dice() = 0;
};

class AnotherFoodProcessor : public IFoodProcessor {
 public:
  void blend() override;
```

```
    void slice() override;
    void dice() override;
};
```

Now we have an issue with the `Blender` class as it doesn't support this new interface – there's no proper way to implement it. We could try to hack a workaround or throw `std::logic_error`, but a much better solution would be to just split the interface into two, each with a separate responsibility:

```
class IBlender {
 public:
   virtual ~IBlender() = default;
   virtual void blend() = 0;
};

class ICutter {
 public:
   virtual ~ICutter() = default;
   virtual void slice() = 0;
   virtual void dice() = 0;
};
```

Now our `AnotherFoodProcessor` can just implement both interfaces, and we don't need to change the implementation of our existing food processor.

We have one last SOLID principle left, so let's learn about it now.

Dependency inversion principle

Dependency inversion is a principle useful for decoupling. In essence, it means that high-level modules should not depend on lower-level ones. Instead, both should depend on abstractions.

C++ allows two ways to inverse the dependencies between your classes. The first one is the regular, polymorphic approach and the second uses templates. Let's see how to apply both of them in practice.

Assume you're modeling a software development project that is supposed to have frontend and backend developers. A simple approach would be to write it like so:

```
class FrontEndDeveloper {
 public:
   void developFrontEnd();
};
```

```cpp
class BackEndDeveloper {
 public:
  void developBackEnd();
};

class Project {
 public:
  void deliver() {
    fed_.developFrontEnd();
    bed_.developBackEnd();
  }
 private:
  FrontEndDeveloper fed_;
  BackEndDeveloper bed_;
};
```

Each developer is constructed by the `Project` class. This approach is not ideal, though, since now the higher-level concept, `Project`, depends on lower-level ones – modules for individual developers. Let's see how applying dependency inversion using polymorphism changes this. We can define our developers to depend on an interface as follows:

```cpp
class Developer {
 public:
  virtual ~Developer() = default;
  virtual void develop() = 0;
};

class FrontEndDeveloper : public Developer {
 public:
  void develop() override { developFrontEnd(); }
 private:
  void developFrontEnd();
};

class BackEndDeveloper : public Developer {
 public:
  void develop() override { developBackEnd(); }
 private:
  void developBackEnd();
};
```

Now, the `Project` class no longer has to know the implementations of the developers. Because of this, it has to accept them as constructor arguments:

```cpp
class Project {
 public:
  using Developers = std::vector<std::unique_ptr<Developer>>;
  explicit Project(Developers developers)
```

```
      : developers_{std::move(developers)} {}

  void deliver() {
    for (auto &developer : developers_) {
      developer->develop();
    }
  }

private:
  Developers developers_;
};
```

In this approach, `Project` is decoupled from the concrete implementations and instead depends only on the polymorphic interface named `Developer`. The "lower-level" concrete classes also depend on this interface. This can help you shorten your build time and allows for much easier unit testing – now you can easily pass mocks as arguments in your test code.

Using dependency inversion with virtual dispatch comes at a cost, however, as now we're dealing with memory allocations and the dynamic dispatch has overhead on its own. Sometimes C++ compilers can detect that only one implementation is being used for a given interface and will remove the overhead by performing devirtualization (often you need to mark the function as `final` for this to work). Here, however, two implementations are used, so the cost of dynamic dispatch (commonly implemented as jumping through **virtual method tables**, or **vtables** for short) must be paid.

There is another way of inverting dependencies that doesn't have those drawbacks. Let's see how this can be done using a variadic template, a generic lambda from C++14, and `variant`, either from C++17 or a third-party library such as Abseil or Boost. First are the developer classes:

```
class FrontEndDeveloper {
 public:
  void develop() { developFrontEnd(); }
 private:
  void developFrontEnd();
};

class BackEndDeveloper {
 public:
  void develop() { developBackEnd(); }
 private:
  void developBackEnd();
};
```

Now we don't rely on an interface anymore, so no virtual dispatch will be done. The `Project` class will still accept a vector of `Developers`:

```
template <typename... Devs>
class Project {
 public:
  using Developers = std::vector<std::variant<Devs...>>;

  explicit Project(Developers developers)
      : developers_{std::move(developers)} {}

  void deliver() {
    for (auto &developer : developers_) {
      std::visit([](auto &dev) { dev.develop(); }, developer);
    }
  }

 private:
  Developers developers_;
};
```

If you're not familiar with `variant`, it's just a class that can hold any of the types passed as template parameters. Because we're using a variadic template, we can pass however many types we like. To call a function on the object stored in the variant, we can either extract it using `std::get` or use `std::visit` and a callable object – in our case, the generic lambda. It shows how duck-typing looks in practice. Since all our developer classes implement the `develop` function, the code will compile and run. If your developer classes would have different methods, you could, for instance, create a function object that has overloads of `operator()` for different types.

Because `Project` is now a template, we have to either specify the list of types each time we create it or provide a type alias. You can use the final class like so:

```
using MyProject = Project<FrontEndDeveloper, BackEndDeveloper>;
auto alice = FrontEndDeveloper{};
auto bob = BackEndDeveloper{};
auto new_project = MyProject{{alice, bob}};
new_project.deliver();
```

This approach is guaranteed to not allocate separate memory for each developer or use a virtual table. However, in some cases, this approach results in less extensibility, since once the variant is declared, you cannot add another type to it.

As the last thing to mention about dependency inversion, we'd like to note that there is a similarly named idea called dependency injection, which we even used in our examples. It's about injecting the dependencies through constructors or setters, which can be beneficial to code testability (think about injecting mock objects, for example). There are even whole frameworks for injecting dependencies throughout whole applications, such as Boost.DI. Those two concepts are related and often used together.

The DRY rule

DRY is short for "don't repeat yourself." It means you should avoid code duplication and reuse when it's possible. This means you should extract a function or a function template when your code repeats similar operations a few times. Also, instead of creating several similar types, you should consider writing a template.

It's also important not to reinvent the wheel when it's not necessary, that is, not to repeat others' work. Nowadays there are dozens of well-written and mature libraries that can help you with writing high-quality software faster. We'd like to specifically mention a few of them:

- Boost C++ Libraries (`https://www.boost.org/`)
- Facebook's Folly (`https://github.com/facebook/folly`)
- Electronic Arts' EASTL (`https://github.com/electronicarts/EASTL`)
- Bloomberg's BDE (`https://github.com/bloomberg/bde`)
- Google's Abseil (`https://abseil.io/`)
- The Awesome Cpp list (`https://github.com/fffaraz/awesome-cpp`) with dozens more

Sometimes duplicating code can have its benefits, however. One such scenario is developing microservices. Of course, it's always a good idea to follow DRY inside a single microservice, but violating the DRY rule for code used in multiple services can actually be worth it. Whether we're talking about model entities or logic, it's easier to maintain multiple services when code duplication is allowed.

Imagine having multiple microservices reusing the same code for an entity. Suddenly one of them needs to modify one field. All the other services now have to be modified as well. The same goes for dependencies of any common code. With dozens or more microservices that have to be modified because of changes unrelated to them, it's often easier for maintenance to just duplicate the code.

Since we're talking about dependencies and maintenance, let's proceed to the next section, which discusses a closely related topic.

Coupling and cohesion

Coupling and cohesion are two terms that go hand in hand in software. Let's see what each of them means and how they relate to each other.

Coupling

Coupling is a measure of how strongly one software unit depends on other units. A unit with high coupling relies on many other units. The lower the coupling, the better.

For example, if a class depends on private members of another class, it means they're tightly coupled. A change in the second class would probably mean that the first one needs to be changed as well, which is why it's not a desirable situation.

To weaken the coupling in the preceding scenario, we could think about adding parameters for the member functions instead of directly accessing other classes' private members.

Another example of tightly coupled classes is the first implementation of the `Project` and developer classes in the dependency inversion section. Let's see what would happen if we were to add yet another developer type:

```cpp
class MiddlewareDeveloper {
 public:
   void developMiddleware() {}
};

class Project {
 public:
   void deliver() {
     fed_.developFrontEnd();
     med_.developMiddleware();
     bed_.developBackEnd();
   }

 private:
   FrontEndDeveloper fed_;
   MiddlewareDeveloper med_;
   BackEndDeveloper bed_;
};
```

It looks like instead of just adding the `MiddlewareDeveloper` class, we had to modify the public interface of the `Project` class. This means they're tightly coupled and that this implementation of the `Project` class actually breaks the OCP. For comparison, let's now see how the same modification would be applied to the implementation using dependency inversion:

```
class MiddlewareDeveloper {
 public:
  void develop() { developMiddleware(); }

 private:
  void developMiddleware();
};
```

No changes to the `Project` class were required, so now the classes are loosely coupled. All we needed to do was to add the `MiddlewareDeveloper` class. Structuring our code this way allows for smaller rebuilds, faster development, and easier testing, all with less code that's easier to maintain. To use our new class, we only need to modify the calling code:

```
using MyProject = Project<FrontEndDeveloper, MiddlewareDeveloper,
BackEndDeveloper>;
auto alice = FrontEndDeveloper{};
auto bob = BackEndDeveloper{};
auto charlie = MiddlewareDeveloper{};
auto new_project = MyProject{{alice, charlie, bob}};
new_project.deliver();
```

This shows coupling on a class level. On a larger scale, for instance, between two services, the low coupling can be achieved by introducing techniques such as message queueing. The services wouldn't then depend on each other directly, but just on the message format. If you're having a microservice architecture, a common mistake is to have multiple services use the same database. This causes coupling between those services as you cannot freely modify the database schema without affecting all the microservices that use it.

Let's now move on to cohesion.

Cohesion

Cohesion is a measure of how strongly a software unit's elements are related. In a highly cohesive system, the functionality offered by components in the same module is strongly related. It feels like such components just belong together.

On a class level, the more fields a method manipulates, the more cohesive it is to the class. This means that the most commonly spotted low-cohesion data types are those big monolithic ones. When there's too much going on in a class, it most probably is not cohesive and breaks the SRP, too. This makes such classes hard to maintain and bug-prone.

Smaller classes can be incohesive as well. Consider the following example. It may seem trivial, but posting real-life scenarios, often hundreds if not thousands of lines long, would be impractical:

```
class CachingProcessor {
 public:
  Result process(WorkItem work);
  Results processBatch(WorkBatch batch);
  void addListener(const Listener &listener);
  void removeListener(const Listener &listener);

 private:
  void addToCache(const WorkItem &work, const Result &result);
  void findInCache(const WorkItem &work);
  void limitCacheSize(std::size_t size);
  void notifyListeners(const Result &result);
  // ...
};
```

We can see that our processor actually does three types of work: the actual work, the caching of the results, and managing listeners. A common way to increase cohesion in such scenarios is to extract a class or even multiple ones:

```
class WorkResultsCache {
 public:
  void addToCache(const WorkItem &work, const Result &result);
  void findInCache(const WorkItem &work);
  void limitCacheSize(std::size_t size);
 private:
  // ...
};

class ResultNotifier {
 public:
  void addListener(const Listener &listener);
  void removeListener(const Listener &listener);
  void notify(const Result &result);
 private:
  // ...
};

class CachingProcessor {
```

```
public:
  explicit CachingProcessor(ResultNotifier &notifier);
  Result process(WorkItem work);
  Results processBatch(WorkBatch batch);
private:
  WorkResultsCache cache_;
  ResultNotifier notifier_;
  // ...
};
```

Now each part is done by a separate, cohesive entity. Reusing them is now possible without much hassle. Even making them a template class should require little work. Last but not least, testing such classes should be easier as well.

Putting this on a component or system level is straightforward – each component, service, and system you design should be concise and focus on doing one thing and doing it right:

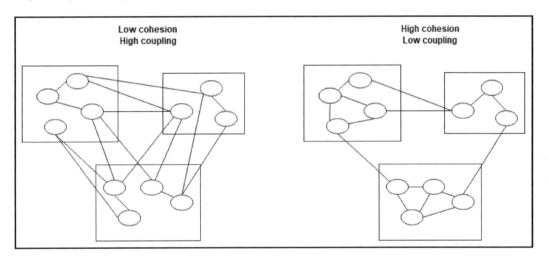

Figure 1.2 – Coupling versus cohesion

Low cohesion and high coupling are usually associated with software that's difficult to test, reuse, maintain, or even understand, so it lacks many of the quality attributes usually desired to have in software.

Those terms often go together because often one trait influences the other, regardless of whether the unit we talk about is a function, class, library, service, or even a whole system. To give an example, usually, monoliths are highly coupled and low cohesive, while distributed services tend to be at the other end of the spectrum.

This concludes our introductory chapter. Let's now summarize what we've learned.

Summary

In this chapter, we discussed what software architecture is and why it's worth caring about it. We've shown what happens when architecture is not updated along with the changing requirements and implementation and how to treat architecture in an Agile environment. Then we moved on to some core principles of the C++ language.

We learned that many terms from software development can be perceived differently in C++ because C++ allows more than writing object-oriented code. Finally, we discussed terms such as coupling and cohesion.

You should now be able to point out many design flaws in code reviews and refactor your solutions for greater maintainability, as well as being less bug-prone as a developer. You can now design class interfaces that are robust, self-explanatory, and complete.

In the next chapter, we will learn about the different architectural approaches or styles. We will also learn about how and when we can use them to gain better results.

Questions

1. Why care about software architecture?
2. Should the architect be the ultimate decision-maker in an Agile team?
3. How is the SRP related to cohesion?
4. In what phases of a project's lifetime can it benefit from having an architect?
5. What's the benefit of following the SRP?

Further reading

1. Eric Evans, *Domain-Driven Design: Tackling Complexity in the Heart of Software*
2. Scott Meyers, *How Non-member Functions Improve Encapsulation*, `https://www.drdobbs.com/cpp/how-non-member-functions-improve-encapsu/184401197`

Architectural Styles 2

This chapter introduces the different architectural approaches or styles. Each section will discuss a different approach to designing software with its pros and cons, as well as describe when and how to apply it to reap its benefits. We'll begin this chapter by comparing stateful and stateless architectures. Next, we'll go from monolith systems, through various types of service-oriented designs, all the way to microservices. Then, we'll start to look at architectural styles from different angles by describing event-based systems, layered systems, and finally, modular designs.

Once you have completed this chapter, you'll be familiar with the following topics:

- Deciding between stateful and stateless approaches
- Understanding monoliths—why they should be avoided, and recognizing exceptions
- Understanding services and microservices
- Exploring event-based architecture
- Understanding layered architecture
- Learning module-based architecture

Technical requirements

You will need to know what a software service is and be able to read code in C++11.

The code from this chapter can be found at the following GitHub page: `https://github.com/PacktPublishing/Software-Architecture-with-Cpp/tree/master/Chapter02`.

Deciding between stateful and stateless approaches

Stateful and stateless are two opposite ways to write software, each with their own pros and cons.

As the name suggests, stateful software's behavior depends on its internal state. Let's take a web service, for instance. If it remembers its state, the consumer of the service can send less data in each request, because the service remembers the context of those requests. However, saving on the request size and bandwidth has a hidden cost on the web service's side. If the user sends many requests at the same time, the service now has to synchronize its work. As multiple requests could change the state, at the same time, not having synchronization could lead to data races.

If the service was stateless, however, then each request coming to it would need to contain all the data needed to process it successfully. This means that the requests would get bigger and use up more bandwidth, but on the other hand, it would allow for better performance and scaling of the service. If you're familiar with functional programming, you would probably find stateless services intuitive. Processing each request can be understood as a call to a pure function. In fact, many of the advantages that stateless programming provides stem from its functional programming roots. Mutable state is the enemy of concurrent code. Functional programming relies on immutable values, even if this means making copies instead of modifying existing objects. Thanks to this, each thread can work independently and no data races are possible.

Since there are no race conditions, no locks are required as well, which can be an enormous boost in terms of performance. No locks also mean that you will no longer need to deal with deadlocks. Having pure functions means that your code will be easier to debug, too, since you don't have any side effects. Not having side effects, in turn, is also helpful for compilers, as optimizing code without side effects is a much easier task and can be performed more aggressively. Yet another benefit of writing code in a functional manner is that the sources you write tend to be more terse and expressive, especially when compared to code that heavily depends on the **Gang of Four (GoF)** design patterns.

This doesn't necessarily mean that if bandwidth is not an issue, you should always go with stateless. Those decisions can be made on many levels, from single classes or functions to whole applications.

Take classes, for example. If you're modeling, say, a `Consultant`, it makes sense that the class would contain fields such as the consultant's name, contact data, hourly rate, current and past projects, and whatnot. It is natural for it to be stateful. Now, imagine that you need to calculate the pay they receive for their work. Should you create a `PaymentCalculator` class? Should you add a member or a free function to calculate this? If you go with the class approach, should you pass a `Consultant` as a constructor parameter or a method argument? Should the class have properties such as allowances?

Adding a member function to calculate the pay would break the **Single Responsibility Principle (SRP)**, as now the class would then have two responsibilities: calculating the pay and storing the consultant's data (state). This means introducing a free function or a separate class for this purpose should be preferred to having such hybrid classes.

Should there be a state in such a class in the first place? Let's discuss the different approaches to our `PaymentCalculator` class.

One approach would be to expose the properties required for calculation purposes:

```
class PaymentCalculator;
{
 public:
   double calculate() const;

   void setHours(double hours);
   void setHourlyRate(double rate);
   void setTaxPercentage(double tax);
 private:
   double hours_;
   double netHourlyRate_;
   double taxPercentage_;
};
```

This approach has two cons. The first is that it's not thread-safe; a single instance of such a `PaymentCalculator` class cannot be used in multiple threads without locks. The second is that once our calculations become more complicated, the class will probably start duplicating more fields from our `Consultant` class.

To eliminate the duplication, we could rework our class to store a `Consultant` instance like this:

```
class PaymentCalculator {
 public:
   double calculate() const;

   void setConsultant(const Consultant &c);
```

```
    void setTaxPercentage(double tax);

  private:
   gsl::not_null<const Consultant *> consultant_;
   double taxPercentage_;
};
```

Note that since we cannot rebind references easily, we're using a helper class from the **Guideline Support Library (GSL)** to store a rebindable pointer in a wrapper that automatically ensures we're not storing a null value.

This approach still has the disadvantage of not being thread-safe. Can we do any better? It turns out that we can make the class thread-safe by making it stateless:

```
class PaymentCalculator {
 public:
   static double calculate(const Consultant &c, double taxPercentage);
};
```

If there is no state to manage, it doesn't really matter if you decide to create free functions (perhaps in a distinct namespace) or group them as static functions of a class, as we did in the preceding snippet. In terms of classes, it's useful to distinguish between value (entity) types and operation types, as mixing them can lead to SRP violations.

Stateless and stateful services

The same principles that we discussed for classes can be mapped to higher-level concepts, for instance, microservices.

What does a stateful service look like? Let's take FTP as an example. If it's not anonymous, it requires the user to pass a username and password to create a session. The server stores this data to identify the user as still connected, so it's constantly storing state. Each time the user changes the working directory, the state gets updated. Each change done by the user is reflected as a change of state, even when they disconnect. Having a stateful service means that depending on the state, you can be returned different results for two identically looking GET requests. If the server loses the state, your requests can even stop processing correctly.

Stateful services can also have issues with incomplete sessions or unfinished transactions and added complexity. How long should you keep the sessions open? How can you verify whether the client has crashed or disconnected? When should we roll back any changes made? While you can come up with answers to those questions, it's usually easier to rely on the consumers of your service communicating with it in a dynamic, "intelligent" way. Since they'll be maintaining some kind of state on their own, having a service that also maintains the state is not only unnecessary but often wasteful.

Stateless services, as the REST ones described later in the book, take the opposite approach. Each request must contain all the data required in order for it to be successfully processed, so two identical idempotent requests (such as GET) will cause identical replies. This is assuming the data stored on the server doesn't change, but data is not necessarily the same thing as state. All that matters is that each request is self-contained.

Statelessness is fundamental in modern internet services. The HTTP protocol is stateless, while many service APIs, for example, Twitter's, are stateless as well. REST, which Twitter's API relies on, is designed to be functionally stateless. The whole concept behind this acronym, **Representational State Transfer** (**REST**), carries the notion that all the state required for processing the request must be transferred within it. If this is not the case, you can't say you have a RESTful service. There are, however, some exceptions to the rule, driven by practical needs.

If you're building an online store, you probably want to store information pertaining to your customers, such as their order history and shipping addresses. The client on the customer's side probably stores an authentication cookie, while the server will probably store some user data in a database. The cookie replaces our need for managing a session, as it'd be done in a stateful service.

Keeping sessions on the server side is a bad approach for services for several reasons: they add a lot of complexity that could be avoided, they make bugs harder to replicate, and most importantly, they don't scale. If you'd want to distribute the load to another server, chances are you'd have trouble replicating the sessions with the load and synchronizing them between servers. All session information should be kept on the client's side.

This means that if you wish to have a stateful architecture, you need to have a good reason to. Take the FTP protocol, for instance. It has to replicate the changes both on the client side and server side. The user only authenticates to a single, specific server, in order to perform single-stated data transfers. Compare this with services such as Dropbox, where the data is often shared between users and the file access is abstracted away through an API, to see why a stateless model would suit this case better.

Understanding monoliths—why they should be avoided, and recognizing exceptions

The simplest architectural style in which you can develop your application is a monolithic one. This is why many projects are started using this style. A monolithic application is just one big block, meaning that functionally distinguishable parts of the application, such as dealing with I/O, data processing, and the user interface, are all interwoven instead of being in separate architectural components. Another notable example of this architectural style is the Linux kernel. Note that the kernel being monolithic does not stop it from being modular.

It can be easier to deploy such a monolithic application than a multi-component one as there is simply one thing that needs to be deployed. It can also be easier to test, as end-to-end testing just requires that you launch a single component. Integration is easier too since, as well as scaling your solution, you can just add more instances behind a load balancer. With all those advantages, why would anyone dread this architectural style? It turns out that despite those advantages, there are also many drawbacks.

The scalability offered sounds nice in theory, but what if your application has modules with different resource requirements? How about needing to scale just one module from your application? The lack of modularity, an inherent property of monolithic systems, is the source of many flaws associated with this architecture.

What's more, the longer you develop a monolithic application, the more problems you'll have in maintaining it. It's a challenge to keep the internals of such an application loosely coupled, as it's so easy to just add yet another dependency between its modules. As such an application grows, it becomes harder and harder to understand it, so the development process will most probably slow down over time because of the added complexity. It can also be hard to maintain **Design-Driven Development**'s (DDD) bounded contexts when developing monoliths.

Having one big application has drawbacks regarding the deployment and execution sides as well. It will take a lot longer to start such an application than it would take to start more, smaller services. And regardless of what you change in the application, you might not like that it forces you to redeploy the whole application at once. Now, imagine that one of your developers introduces a resource leak in the application. If the leaky code is executed over and over, it will not only bring down its single aspect of the app's functionality, it can also bring down the rest of the application as well.

If you're a fan of using bleeding-edge technologies in your project, a monolithic style doesn't bring any great news either. Since you now need to migrate your whole application at once, it's harder to update any libraries or frameworks.

The preceding explanation suggests that a monolithic architecture is only good for simple and small applications. There is, however, one more situation where it could actually be a good idea to use it. If you care about performance, having a monolith can sometimes help you to squeeze more from your app in terms of latency or throughput when compared to microservices. Inter-process communication will always incur some overhead, which monolithic applications don't need to pay. If you're interested in measurements, see the paper listed in the *Further reading* section of this chapter.

Understanding services and microservices

Because of the drawbacks of monolithic architectures, other approaches have emerged. A common idea is to split your solution into multiple services that communicate with each other. You can then split the development between different teams, each taking care of a separate service. The boundaries of each team's work are clear, unlike in the monolithic architecture style.

A **service-oriented architecture**, or **SOA** for short, means that the business functions are modularized and presented as separate services for the consumer applications to use. Each service should have a self-describing interface and hide any implementation details, such as the internal architecture, technologies, or the programming language used. This allows for multiple teams to develop the services however they like, meaning that under the hood, each can use what suits their needs best. If you have two teams of developers, one proficient in C# and one in C++, they can develop two services that can easily communicate with one another.

Advocates of SOA came up with a manifesto prioritizing the following:

- Business value over technical strategy
- Strategic goals over project-specific benefits
- Intrinsic interoperability over custom integration
- Shared services over purpose-specific implementations
- Flexibility over optimization
- Evolutionary refinement over pursuit of initial perfection

Even though this manifesto doesn't bind you to a specific tech stack, or implementation, or type of services, the two most common types of services are SOAP and REST. Aside from those, recently, there's a third one that has been growing in popularity: gRPC-based. You can find out more about these in the chapters on services-oriented architecture and microservices.

Microservices

As the name suggests, microservices is a software development pattern where an application is split as a collection of loosely-coupled services that communicate using lightweight protocols. The microservices pattern is similar to the UNIX philosophy stating that a program should only have one purpose. According to UNIX philosophy, advanced problems are solved by composing such programs into UNIX pipelines. Similarly, microservice-based systems are composed of many microservices and supporting services.

Let's start with an overview of the pros and cons of this architectural style.

Benefits and disadvantages of microservices

The small size of services in a microservice architecture means that they're faster to develop, deploy, and understand. As the services are built independently of each other, the time necessary to compile their new versions can be drastically reduced. Thanks to this, it is easier to employ rapid prototyping and development when dealing with this architectural style. This, in turn, makes it possible to reduce the lead-time, meaning that business requirements can be introduced and evaluated much quicker.

Some other benefits of a microservice-based approach include the following:

- Modularity, which is inherent to this architectural style.
- Better testability.
- Flexibility when replacing system parts (such as single services, databases, message brokers, or cloud providers).
- Integration with legacy systems: it is not necessary to migrate an entire application, just the parts that require current development.
- Enabling distributed development: independent development teams can work on multiple microservices in parallel.
- Scalability: a microservice may be scaled independently of the others.

On the other hand, here are some disadvantages of microservices:

- They require a mature DevOps approach and reliance on CI/CD automation.
- They are harder to debug, and require better monitoring and distributed tracing.
- Additional overhead (in terms of auxiliary services) may outweigh the benefits for smaller applications.

Let's now discuss what are the characteristics of services written in this architectural style.

Characteristics of microservices

Since the microservice style is fairly recent, there is no single definition for microservices. According to Martin Fowler, there are several essential characteristics of microservices, which we will describe next:

- Each service should be an independently replaceable and upgradeable component. This is connected to easier deployment and loose coupling between the services, as opposed to components being libraries in a monolithic application. In the latter case, when you replace one library, you often have to redeploy the whole application.
- Each service should be developed by a cross-functional team, focused on a specific business capability. Ever heard of Conway's law?

    "Any organization that designs a system (defined broadly) will produce a design whose structure is a copy of the organization's communication structure."

    – Melvyn Conway, 1967

    If you don't have cross-functional teams, you end up with software silos. The lack of communication that comes with them will make you constantly jump through hurdles to successfully deliver.

- Each service should be a product, which is owned by the development team throughout its lifetime. This stays in contrast to the project mentality, where you develop software and just pass it on for someone to maintain.

- Services should have smart endpoints and use dump pipes, not the other way around. This stands in contrast to traditional services, which often rely on the logic of an **Enterprise Service Bus** (**ESB**), which often manages the routing of messages and transforms them according to business rules. In microservices, you achieve cohesiveness by storing the logic in the service and avoid coupling with messaging components. Using "dumb" message queues, such as ZeroMQ, can help with this goal.

- Services should be governed in a decentralized way. Monoliths are usually written using one specific technology stack. When they're being split into microservices, each one can choose whatever suits its own specific needs best. Governing and assuring that each microservice runs 24/7 is done by a team responsible for this specific service instead of a central department. Companies such as Amazon, Netflix, and Facebook follow this approach and observe that making developers responsible for the flawless execution of their services in production helps to ensure high quality.

- Services should manage their data in a decentralized way. Instead of having one database for all of them, each microservice can choose a database that best matches its needs. Having decentralized data can lead to some challenges with handling updates, but allows for better scaling. This is why microservices often coordinate in a transaction-free manner and offer eventual consistency.

- The infrastructure used by services should be managed automatically. To deal with dozens of microservices in an efficient manner, you need to have Continuous Integration and Continuous Delivery in place, as otherwise, deploying your services will be hell. Automated runs of all your tests will save you lots of time and trouble. Implementing Continuous Deployment on top of that will shorten the feedback loop and allow your customers to use your new features faster, too.

- Microservices should be prepared for the failure of other services that they depend on. In a distributed deployment environment with so many moving parts, it's normal for some of them to break from time to time. Your services should be able to handle such failures gracefully. Patterns such as Circuit Breaker or Bulkhead (described later in the book) can help to achieve this. To make your architecture resilient, it's also critical to be able to bring failing services back up efficiently or even to know ahead of time that they're going to crash. Real-time monitoring of latency, throughput, and resource usage is essential for this. Get to know Netflix's Simian Army toolkit as it's invaluable for creating a resilient architecture.

- Architectures based on microservices should be ready to constantly evolve. You should design microservices and the cooperation between them in a manner that allows for easy replacement of a single microservice, or sometimes even groups of them. It's tricky to design the services properly, especially since some of the complexity that was once in the code of one bigger module can now be present as complex communication schemes between services, where it's harder to manage – so-called Spaghetti Integration. This means the experience and skill set of the architect plays a more important role than with traditional services or a monolithic approach.

On top of that, here are some other characteristics shared by many (but not all) microservices:

- Using separate processes that communicate over network protocols
- Using technology-agnostic protocols (such as HTTP and JSON)
- Keeping services small and with a low runtime overhead

Now, you should have a good understanding of what the characteristics of microservice-based systems are, so let's see how this approach compares with other architectural styles.

Microservices and other architectural styles

Microservices may be used as an architectural pattern on their own. However, they are often combined with other architectural choices, such as cloud-native computing, serverless applications, and mostly with lightweight application containers.

Service-oriented architectures bring loose coupling and high cohesion. Microservices can do it too, when applied correctly. However, it can be somewhat challenging because it requires good intuition to partition the system into the usually vast amount of microservices.

There are more similarities between microservices and their bigger cousins as they, too, can have SOAP-, REST-, or gRPC-based messaging and use technologies such as message queues for being event-driven. They also have well-known patterns to help with achieving the required quality attributes, such as fault tolerance (for example, through the isolation of faulty components), but in order to have an efficient architecture, you must decide on your approach to elements such as API gateways, service registries, load balancing, fault tolerance, monitoring, configuration management, and, of course, the technology stack to use.

Scaling microservices

Microservices scale differently to monolithic applications. In monoliths, the entire functionality is handled by a single process. Scaling the application means replicating this process across different machines. Such scaling doesn't take into account which of the functionalities are heavily used and which do not require additional resources.

With microservices, each functional element is handled as a separate service, which means a separate process. In order to scale a microservices-based application, only the parts that require more resources can be replicated to different machines. Such an approach makes it easier to better use the available resources.

Transitioning to microservices

Most companies have some kind of existing monolithic code that they don't want to immediately rewrite using microservices, but still want to transition to this kind of architecture. In such cases, it's possible to adapt microservices incrementally, by adding more and more services that interact with the monolith. You can create new functionalities as microservices or just cut out some parts of the monolith and create microservices out of them.

More details regarding microservices, including how to build your own from scratch, are available in Chapter 13, *Designing Microservices*.

Exploring event-based architecture

Event-based systems are those whose architecture revolves around processing events. There are components that generate events, the channels through which the events propagate, and the listeners who react to them, potentially triggering new events too. It's a style that promotes asynchrony and loose coupling, which makes it a good way to increase performance and scalability, as well as an easy solution to deploy.

With those advantages, there are also some challenges to solve. One of them is the complexity to create a system of this type. All the queues must be made fault-tolerant so that no events are lost in the middle of being processed. Processing transactions in a distributed way is also a challenge on its own. Using the Correlation ID pattern to track events between processes, along with monitoring techniques, can save you hours of debugging and scratching your head.

Examples of event-based systems include stream processors and data integrations, as well as systems aiming for low latency or high scalability.

Let's now discuss common topologies used in such systems.

Common event-based topologies

The two main topologies of event-driven architectures are broker-based and mediator-based. Those topologies differ in how the events flow through the system.

The mediator topology is best used when processing an event that requires multiple tasks or steps that can be performed independently. All events produced initially land in the mediator's event queue. The mediator knows what needs to be done in order to handle the event, but instead of performing the logic itself, dispatches the event to appropriate event processors through each processor's event channel.

If this reminds you of how business processes flow, then you've got good intuition. You can implement this topology in **Business Process Management (BPM)** or **Business Process Execution Language (BPEL)**. However, you can also implement it using technologies such as Apache Camel, Mule ESB, and others:

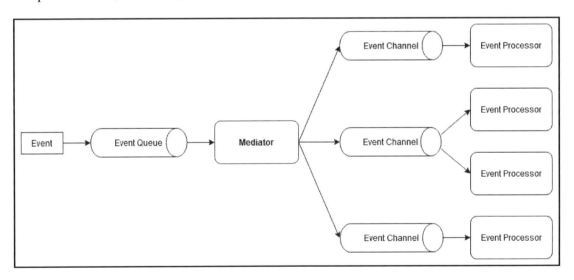

Figure 2.1 – The mediator topology

A broker, on the other hand, is a lightweight component that contains all the queues and doesn't orchestrate the processing of an event. It can require that the recipients subscribe to specific kinds of events and then simply forwards all the ones that are interesting for them. Many message queues rely on brokers, for example, ZeroMQ, which is written in C++ and aims for zero waste and low latency:

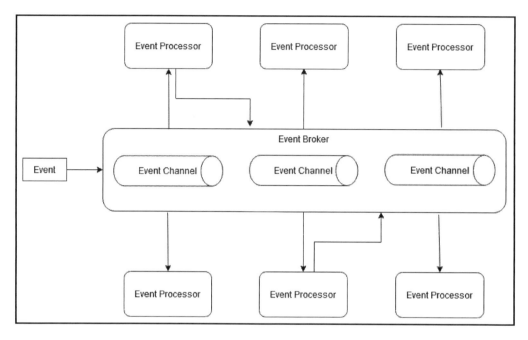

Figure 2.2 – The broker topology

Now that you know the two common topologies used in event-based systems, let's learn about a powerful architectural pattern using events at its core.

Event sourcing

You can think of events as notifications that contain additional data for the notified services to process. There is, however, another way to think of them: a change of state. Think how easy it would be to debug issues with your application logic if you'd be able to know the state in which it was when the bug occurred and what change was requested of it. That's one benefit of event sourcing. In essence, it captures all the changes that happen to the system by simply recording all the events in the sequence they happened.

Often, you'll find that the service no longer needs to persist its state in a database, as storing the events somewhere else in the system is enough. Even if it does, it can be done asynchronously. Another benefit that you derive from event sourcing is a complete audit log for free:

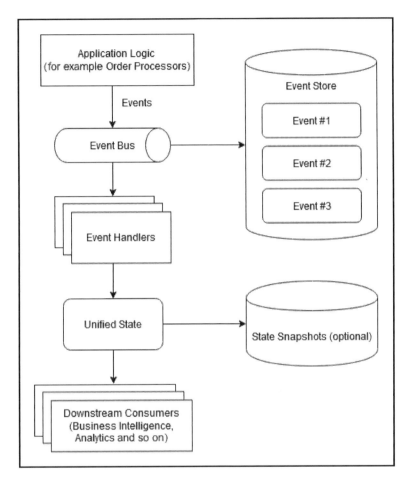

Figure 2.3 – Event sourcing architecture. Providing a unified view of the application state can allow for consuming it and creating periodic snapshots for faster recovery

Thanks to the reduced need for data synchronization, event-sourced systems often offer low latency, which makes them a good fit for trading systems and activity trackers, among others.

Let's now learn about another popular architectural style.

Understanding layered architecture

If your architecture starts to look like spaghetti or you just want to prevent it, having your components structured in layers may help. Remember Model-View-Controller? Or maybe similar patterns, such as Model-View-ViewModel or Entity-Control-Boundary? Those are all typical examples of a layered architecture (also called N-tier architecture if the layers are physically separated from each other). You can structure code in layers, you can create layers of microservices, or apply this pattern to other areas where you think it could bring its benefits. Layering provides abstraction and the separation of concerns, and this is the main reason why it's being introduced. However, it can also help reduce complexity, while improving modularity, reusability, and maintainability of your solution.

A real-world example would be in self-driving cars, where layers can be used to hierarchically make decisions: the lowest layer would handle the car's sensors, then another layer would deal with single features consuming the sensor data, and on top of that one, there could be another one to ensure that all the features result in safe behavior. When sensors are replaced in another model of the car, only the lowest layer will need to be replaced.

A layered architecture is often pretty easy to implement since most developers already know the notion of layers – they simply need to develop several layers and stack them as in the following diagram:

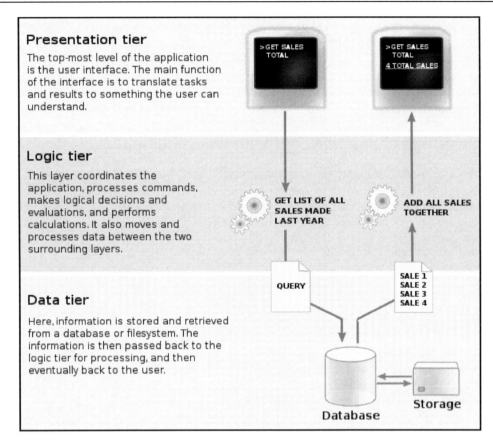

Figure 2.4 – An example of a 3-tiered architecture using a textual interface in the presentation layer

The challenge with creating an efficient layered architecture lays in specifying stable, well-defined interfaces between the layers. Often, you can have several layers on top of one. For instance, if you have a layer for domain logic, it can be a base for a presentation layer and a layer for providing APIs to other services.

This doesn't mean that layering is always a good thing. With microservices, there are two main scenarios where layering emerges. The first is when you want to separate one group of services from another. For instance, you could have a fast-changing layer to engage with your business partners, with content that changes frequently, and another business capabilities-oriented layer. The latter is not being changed at such a fast pace and is using stable technologies. Separating those two makes sense. There's also a notion that less stable components should rely on more stable components, so it's easy to see that you could have two layers here with the customer-facing one depending on the business capabilities.

The other scenario is when layers are created to reflect the communication structure of the organization (hello again, Conway's law). This will probably reduce communication between the teams, which can result in a decrease in innovation as now the teams won't know the internals or ideas of each other that well.

Let's now discuss another example of a layered architecture often used with microservices—Backends for Frontends.

Backends for Frontends

It's not uncommon to see many frontends that rely on the same backend. Let's say you have a mobile application and a web application, both using the same backend. It may be a good design choice at first. However, once the requirements and usage scenarios of those two applications diverge, your backend will require more and more changes, serving just one of the frontends. This can lead to the backend having to support competing requirements, like two separate ways to update the data store or different scenarios for providing data. Simultaneously, the frontends start to require more bandwidth to communicate with the backend properly, which also leads to more battery usage in mobile apps. At this point, you should consider introducing a separate backend for each frontend.

This way, you can think of a user-facing application as being a single entity having two layers: the frontend and the backend. The backend can depend on another layer, consisting of downstream services. Refer to the following diagram:

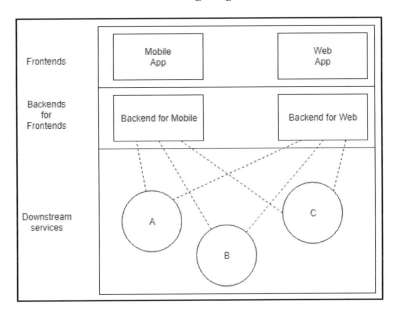

Figure 2.5 – The Backends for Frontends pattern

The drawback of using **Backends for Frontends (BFFs)** is that some code must be duplicated. As long as this speeds up development and is not a burden in the long term, it's OK. But it also means that you should be on the watch for possibilities to aggregate duplicated logic in a downstream service. Sometimes, introducing a service just to aggregate similar calls can help solve duplication issues. Often, if you have many frontends, some can still share a backend and not cause it to have competing requirements. If you're creating mobile applications for iOS and Android, for instance, you could think of reusing the same backend for those, and having separate ones for web and/or desktop applications.

Learning module-based architecture

 In this section, by modules, we mean software components that can be loaded and unloaded in runtime. For C++20's modules, refer to `Chapter 5`, *Leveraging C++ Language Features*.

If you've ever needed to run a component with as little downtime as possible, but for any reason couldn't apply the usual fault-tolerance patterns, such as redundant copies of your service, making this component module-based can come to save your day. Or you may just be attracted by a vision of a modular system with versioning of all the modules, with an easy lookup of all the available services, along with the decoupling, testability, and enhancing teamwork that module-based systems can cause. All of this is why **Open Service Gateway Initiative (OSGi)** modules were created for Java and got ported to C++ in more than a few frameworks. Examples of architectures using modules include IDEs such as Eclipse, **Software Defined Networking (SDN)** projects such as OpenDaylight, or home automation software such as OpenHAB.

OSGi also allows for automatic dependency management between modules, controlling their initialization and unloading, as well as controlling their discovery. Since it's service-oriented, you can think of using OSGi services as something akin to having tiny (micro?) services in one "container". This is why one of the C++ implementations is named C++ Micro Services. To see them in action, refer to their *Getting Started* guide from the *Further reading* section.

One interesting concept adopted by the C++ Micro Services framework is a new way to deal with singletons. The `GetInstance()` static function will, instead of just passing a static instance object, return a service reference obtained from the bundled context. So effectively, singleton objects will get replaced by services that you can configure. It can also save you from the static deinitialization fiasco, where multiple singletons that depend on each other have to unload in a specific order.

Summary

In this chapter, we've discussed the various architectural styles that you can encounter in the wild and apply to your software. We've discussed monolithic architecture, went through service-oriented architecture, moved onto microservices, and discussed the various ways in which they can provide external interfaces and interact with each other. You learned how to write RESTful services and how to create a resilient and easy-to-maintain microservice architecture.

We've also shown how to create simple clients to consume equally simple services. Later on, we discussed various other approaches to architecture: an event-driven one, a runtime module-based one, and showed where layering can be spotted and why. You now know how to implement event sourcing and recognize when to use BFFs. Moreover, you now know how architecture styles can help you achieve several quality attributes and what challenges this can bring.

In the next chapter, you'll learn how to know which of those attributes are important in a given system.

Questions

1. What are the traits of a RESTful service?
2. What toolkit can you use to aid you in creating a resilient distributed architecture?
3. Should you use centralized storage for your microservices? Why/why not?
4. When should you write a stateful service instead of a stateless one?
5. How does a broker differ from a mediator?
6. What is the difference between an N-tier and an N-layer architecture?
7. How should you approach replacing a monolith with a microservice-based architecture?

Further reading

- Flygare, R., and Holmqvist, A. (2017). *Performance characteristics between monolithic and microservice-based systems (Dissertation)*. Retrieved from `http://urn.kb.se/resolve?urn=urn:nbn:se:bth-14888`
- Engelen, Robert. (2008). *A framework for service-oriented computing with C and C++ web service components*. ACM Trans. Internet Techn. 8. 10.1145/1361186.1361188
- Fowler, Martin. *Microservices – A definition of this new architectural term*. Retrieved from `https://martinfowler.com/articles/microservices.html#MicroservicesAndSoa`
- *Getting Started – C++ Micro Services documentation*. Retrieved from `http://docs.cppmicroservices.org/en/stable/doc/src/getting_started.html`

3
Functional and Nonfunctional Requirements

As an architect, it is important for you to recognize which requirements are significant for the architecture and why. This chapter will teach you about the various requirements of a solution—functional and nonfunctional. Functional requirements are those that tell you what your solution should do. On the other hand, nonfunctional ones are those that tell you how your solution should be.

In this chapter, we'll cover the following topics:

- Understanding the types of requirements
- Recognizing architecturally significant requirements
- Gathering requirements from various sources
- Documenting requirements
- Documenting architecture
- Choosing the right views to document
- Generating documentation

By the end of this chapter, you will have learned how to recognize and categorize both types of requirements and how to create documentation that describes them in a clear manner.

Technical requirements documentation from sources, you must have

To replicate our steps to generate documentation from sources, you must have CMake, Doxygen, Sphinx, m2r2 and Breathe installed. We're using the ReadTheDocs Sphinx theme, so please install it as well. Feel free to use the latest versions of the tools mentioned.

You can find the related code at `https://github.com/PacktPublishing/Software-Architecture-with-Cpp/tree/master/Chapter03`.

Understanding the types of requirements

While creating a software system, you should constantly ask yourself whether what you're making is what your customers need. Many times, they won't even know what requirement fulfills their needs best. It's the role of a successful architect to discover the requirements of the product and to make sure they are being met. There are three distinct types of requirements that you need to consider: functional requirements, quality attributes, and constraints. Let's have a look at each of these.

Functional requirements

The first group is the functional requirements. These are the ones that define what your system should do, or what functionality it should offer.

 Remember that functionality does not always influence architecture, so you'll have to keep an eye on which of those requirements will actually dictate what your solution will look like.

Often, if a functional requirement has some qualities that must be met, it can become architecturally significant. Consider an app for merchants and visitors of the Dominican Fair, an annual event with music, various arts, and shops, happening in the city of Gdańsk. A few examples of functional requirements for it could be the following:

- *As a shopkeeper, I want to filter orders that contain a specific product.*
- *Clicking the Subscribe button adds the customer to a list of notified watchers of a selected merchant.*

The first of those requirements tells us we'll have to have a component for tracking orders and products with search capabilities. Depending on how exactly the UI should appear and what scale our app should be, we could just add a simple page to our app, or it could require features such as Lucene or Elasticsearch. This means that we could be looking at an **Architecturally Significant Requirement (ASR)**, one that can influence our architecture.

The second example is even more straightforward; now we know we need to have a service for subscribing and sending notifications. This is definitely an architecturally significant functional requirement. Let's now look at some **Non-Functional Requirements (NFRs)** that can also be ASRs.

By the way, the first requirement is actually given as a user story. User stories are requirements given in the following format: "*As a <role>, I can/want to <capability>, so that <benefit>*." This is a common way to phrase requirements and can help stakeholders and developers find common ground and communicate better.

Nonfunctional requirements

Instead of focusing on what functionality your system should have, nonfunctional requirements focus on how well and under which conditions the system should perform said functionality. This group consists of two main subgroups: **Quality Attributes (QAs)** and **constraints**.

Quality attributes

Quality attributes (QAs) are the traits of your solution, such as performance, maintainability, and user-friendliness. There are dozens, if not hundreds, of different qualities your software can have. Try to focus just on the important ones instead of listing all that come to your mind when choosing which ones your software should have. Examples of quality attribute requirements include the following:

- The system will respond in under 500 ms for 99.9% of all requests under usual load (don't forget to specify what the usual load is or will be).
- The website will not store customer credit card data used in the payment process (an example of confidentiality).
- When updating the system, if updating any component fails, the system will be rolled back to a state prior to the update (survivability).
- As a user of Windows, macOS, and Android, I want to be able to use the system from all of them (portability; try to understand whether it's needed to support platforms such as desktop, mobile, and/or web).

While catching functional requirements in a backlog is pretty straightforward, we cannot say the same regarding quality attribute requirements. Fortunately, there are a few ways you could approach this:

- Some of them can be expressed in the **Definition of done** or **Acceptance criteria** for your tasks, stories, and releases.
- Others can be expressed directly as user stories, as shown in the last example previously.
- You can also check them as part of design and code reviews and create automated tests for some of them.

Constraints

Constraints are the non-negotiable decisions that you must follow while delivering the project. Those can be design decisions, technological ones, or even political (regarding people or organizational matters). Two other common constraints are **time** and **budget**. Examples of constraints could be as follows:

- *The team will never grow beyond four developers, one QA engineer, and one sysadmin.*
- *Since our company leverages Oracle DB in all its current products, the new product must use it too so we can make the most of our expertise.*

nonfunctional requirements are always going to influence your architecture. It's essential not to over-specify them, as having *false positives* will be a constant burden during product development. It's equally important to not under-specify them as this can later come out in missed sales opportunities or failing to comply with regulatory bodies' requirements.

In the next section, you will learn how to strike a balance between those two extremes and to focus on just those requirements that really matter in your specific case.

Recognizing architecturally significant requirements

When designing a software system, it's common to deal with dozens or hundreds of various requirements. In order to make sense of them and come up with a good design, you need to know which of them are important and which could be implemented regardless of your design decisions, or even dismissed. You should learn how to recognize the most important ones so you can focus on them first and deliver the most value in the shortest possible time.

You should prioritize requirements using two metrics: the business value and the impact on architecture. Those that will be high on both scales are most important and should be dealt with as a matter of priority. If you come up with too many such requirements, you should revisit your prioritization scheme. If it doesn't help, it might be that the system just isn't achievable.

ASRs are those that have a measurable impact on your system's architecture. They can be both functional and nonfunctional. How can you identify which ones are actually significant? If the absence of a specific requirement were to allow you to create a different architecture, you are looking at an ASR. Late discovery of such requirements will often cost you both time and money, as you'll need to redesign some part of your system, if not the whole solution. You can only hope it won't cost you other resources and your reputation, too.

It's a common mistake to start by applying concrete technologies to your architecture from the very beginning of your architectural work. We strongly suggest that you first gather all the requirements, focus on the ones significant for the architecture, and only then decide what technologies and technology stacks to build your project on.

Since it's that important to recognize ASRs, let's talk about a few patterns that can help you with this.

Indicators of architectural significance

If you have a requirement to integrate with any external system, this is most likely going to influence your architecture. Let's go through some common indicators that a requirement is an ASR:

- **Needing to create a software component to handle it**: Examples include sending emails, pushing notifications, exchanging data with the company's SAP server, or using a specific data storage.
- **Having a significant impact on the system**: Core functionality often defines what your system should look like. Cross-cutting concerns, such as authorization, auditability, or having transactional behavior, are other good examples.
- **Being hard to achieve**: Having low latency is a great example: unless you think of it early in development, it can be a long battle to achieve it, especially if you suddenly realize you can't really afford to have garbage collections when you're on your hot path.

- **Forcing trade-offs when satisfying certain architectures**: Perhaps your design decision will even need to compromise some requirements in favor of other, more important ones if the cost is too high. It's a good practice to log such decisions somewhere and to notice that you're dealing with ASRs here. If any requirement constrains you or limits the product in any way, it's very likely significant for the architecture. If you want to come up with the best architecture given many trade-offs, then be sure to read about the **Architecture Trade-off Analysis Method (ATAM)**, which you can read about under one of the links in the *Further reading* section.

Constraints and the environment your application will run in can also impact your architecture. Embedded apps need to be designed in a different way to those running in the cloud, and apps being developed by less-experienced developers should probably use a simple and safe framework instead of using one with a steep learning curve or developing their own.

Hindrances in recognizing ASRs and how to deal with them

Contrary to intuition, many architecturally significant requirements are difficult to spot at first glance. This is caused by two factors: they can be hard to define and even if they're described, this can be done vaguely. Your customers might not yet be clear about what they need, but you should still be proactive in asking questions to steer clear of any assumptions. If your system is to send notifications, you must know whether those are real time or whether a daily email will suffice, as the former could require you to create a publisher-subscriber architecture.

In most cases, you'll need to make some assumptions since not everything is known upfront. If you discover a requirement that challenges your assumptions, it might be an ASR. If you assume you can maintain your service between 3 a.m. and 4 a.m. and you realize your customers from a different time zone will still need to use it, it will challenge your assumption and likely change the product's architecture.

What's more, people often tend to treat quality attributes vaguely during the earlier phases of projects, especially less-experienced or less-technical individuals. On the other hand, that's the best moment to address such ASRs, as the cost of implementing them in the system is the lowest.

It's worth noting, however, that many people, when specifying requirements, like to use vague phrases without actually thinking it through. If you were designing a service similar to Uber, some examples could be: *when receiving a DriverSearchRequest, the system must reply with an AvailableDrivers message fast*, or *the system must be available 24/7*.

Upon asking questions, it often turns out that 99.9% monthly availability is perfectly fine, and *fast* is actually a few seconds. Such phrases always require clarification, and it's often valuable to know the rationale behind them. Perhaps it is just someone's subjective opinion, not backed by any data or business needs. Also, note that in the request and response case, the quality attribute is hidden inside another requirement, making it even harder to catch.

Finally, requirements being architecturally significant for one system aren't necessarily of the same importance to another, even if those systems serve similar purposes. Some will become more important over time, once the system grows and starts to communicate with more and more other systems. Others may become important once the needs for the product change. This is why there's no silver bullet in telling which of your requirements will be ASRs, and which won't.

Equipped with all this knowledge on how to distinguish the important requirements from the rest, you know *what* to look for. Let's now say a few words about *where* to look.

Gathering requirements from various sources

Now that you know what requirements to focus on, let's discuss a few techniques for gathering these requirements.

Knowing the context

When mining requirements, you should take into account the broader context. You must identify what potential problems may have a negative impact on your product in the future. Those risks often come from the outside. Let's revisit our Uber-like service scenario. An example risk for your service could be a potential change in legislation: you should be aware that some countries may try to change the law to remove you from their market. Uber's way to mitigate those risks is to have local partners cope with regional limitations.

Future risks aside, you must also be aware of current issues, such as the lack of subject matter experts in the company, or heavy competition on the market. Here's what you can do:

- Be aware of and note any assumptions being made. It's best to have a dedicated document for tracking those.
- Ask questions to clarify or eliminate your assumptions, if possible.
- You need to consider the dependencies inside your project, as they can influence the development schedule. Other useful areas are the business rules that shape the day-to-day behavior of the company, as your product will likely need to adhere to and possibly enhance those.
- Moreover, if there's enough data relating to the users or the business, you should try to mine it to get insights and find useful patterns that can help with making decisions regarding the future product and its architecture. If you already have some users but are unable to mine data, it's often useful to just observe how they behave.

Ideally, you could record them when they perform their daily tasks using the currently deployed systems. This way, you could not only automate parts of their work but also change their workflow to a more efficient one entirely. However, remember that users don't like changing their habits, so it's better to introduce changes gradually where possible.

Knowing existing documentation

Existing documents can be a great source of information, even though they can also have their issues. You should reserve some time to at least get familiar with all the existing documents related to your work. Chances are that there are some requirements hidden in them. On the other hand, keep in mind that the documentation is never perfect; highly likely it will lack some significant information. You should also be prepared for it to be outdated. There is never one source of truth when it comes to architecture, so aside from reading documents, you should have lots of discussions with the people involved. Nonetheless, reading documents can be a great way of preparing yourself for such discussions.

Knowing your stakeholders

To be a successful architect, you must learn to communicate with business people as requirements come, directly or indirectly, from them. Whether they're from your company or a customer, you should get to know the context of their business. For instance, you must know the following:

- What drives the business?
- What goals does the company have?
- What specific objectives will your product help to achieve?

Once you are aware of this, it will be much easier to establish a common ground with many people coming from management or executives, as well as gathering more specific requirements regarding your software. If the company cares about the privacy of its users, for instance, it can have a requirement to store as little data about its users as possible and to encrypt it using a key stored only on a user's device. Often, if such requirements come from the company culture, it will be too obvious for some employees to even articulate them. Knowing the context of the business can help you to ask proper questions and help the company in return.

Having said that, remember that your stakeholders can, and will, have needs that aren't necessarily directly reflected in the company's objectives. They can have their own ideas for functionality to provide or metrics that the software should achieve. Perhaps a manager promised his employees a chance to learn a new technology or work with a specific one. If this project is important for their career, they can be a strong ally and even convince others as to your decisions.

Another important group of stakeholders is the people responsible for deploying your software. They can come with their own subgroup of needs, called transition requirements. Examples of those include user and database migration, infrastructure transition, or data conversion, so don't forget to reach out to them to gather these as well.

Gathering requirements from stakeholders

At this point, you should have a list of stakeholders with their roles and contact information. Now it's time to make use of it: be sure to make time to talk with each stakeholder about what they need from the system and how they envision it. You can hold interviews such as 1:1 meetings or group ones. When talking with your stakeholders, help them to make informed decisions – show the potential outcomes of their answers on the end product.

It's common for stakeholders to say that all of their requirements are equally important. Try to persuade them to prioritize their requirements according to the value they bring to their business. Certainly, there will be some mission-critical requirements, but most probably, the project won't fail if a bunch of others won't be delivered, not to mention any nice-to-haves that will land on your requirements wish list.

Aside from interviews, you can also organize workshops for them, which could work like brainstorming sessions. In such workshops, once the common ground is established and everybody knows why they're taking part in such a venture, you can start asking everyone for as many usage scenarios as they can think of. Once these have been established, you can proceed with consolidating similar ones, after which you should prioritize and, finally, refine all the stories. Workshops are not just about functional requirements; each usage scenario can have a quality attribute assigned as well. After refining, all the quality attributes should be measurable. The final thing to note is this: you don't need to bring all stakeholders into such events, as they can sometimes take more than a day, depending on the size of the system.

Now that you know how to mine for requirements using various techniques and sources, let's discuss how to pour your findings into well-crafted documents.

Documenting requirements

Once you're done with the steps described previously, it's time to put all the requirements you've gathered and refine them together in a single document. It doesn't matter what form the document will take and how you will manage it. What matters is that you have a document that puts all the stakeholders on the same page with regard to what is required from the product and what value each requirement brings.

Requirements are produced and consumed by all stakeholders, and a broad set of them will need to read your document. This means that you should write it so that it brings value for people of various technical skills from customers, salespeople, and marketers, through designers and project managers, to software architects, developers, and testers.

Sometimes it makes sense to prepare two versions of the document, one for the people closest to the business side of the project, and another, a more technical one, for the development team. However, usually, it's enough to just have one document written to be understandable by everyone, with sections (sometimes single paragraphs) or whole chapters meant to cover the more technical details.

Let's now take a tour of what sections could go into your requirements document.

Documenting the context

A requirements document should act as one of the entry points for people getting on board with your project: it should outline the purpose of your product, who will use it, and how it can be used. Before design and development, the product team members should read it to have a clear idea of what they'll actually work on.

The context section should provide an overview of the system – why it's being built, what business goals is it trying to accomplish, and what key functionality it will deliver.

You can describe a few typical user personas, such as *John the CTO*, or *Ann the driver*, to give the readers a better chance to think about the users of the system as actual human beings and know what to expect from them.

All those things described in the *Knowing the context* section should also be summarized as parts of this context section, or sometimes even given separate sections in the document. The context and scope sections should provide all the information required by most non-project stakeholders. They should be concise and precise.

The same goes for any open questions you may want to research and decide on later. For each decision you make, it's best to note the following:

- What the decision itself was
- Who made it and when
- What rationale stands behind it

Now that you know how to document the context of your project, let's learn how to properly describe its scope too.

Documenting the scope

This section should define what's in the scope of the project, as well as what is beyond the scope. You should provide a rationale for why the scope is defined in a particular way, especially when writing about things that won't make the cut.

This section should also cover the high-level functional and nonfunctional requirements, but details should go into the subsequent sections of the document. If you're familiar with Agile practices, just describe epics and bigger user stories here.

If you or your stakeholders have any assumptions regarding the scope, you should mention those here. If the scope is subject to change due to any issues or risks, you should also write some words about it, and similarly for any trade-offs you had to make.

Documenting functional requirements

Each requirement should be precise and testable. Consider this example: "The system will have a ranking system for the drivers." How would you create tests against it? It's better to create a section for the ranking system and specify the precise requirements for it there.

Consider this other example: If there's a free driver close to the rider, they should be notified of the incoming ride request. What if there's more than one driver available? What maximum distance can we still describe as being *close*?

This requirement is both imprecise and lacking parts of the business logic. We can only hope that the case where there are no free drivers is covered by another requirement.

In 2009, Rolls Royce developed its **Easy Approach to Requirements Syntax (EARS)**, to help cope with this. In EARS, there are five basic types of requirements, which should be written in a different way and serve different purposes. They can be later combined to create more complex requirements. Those basic ones are as follows:

- **Ubiquitous requirement**: "The $SYSTEM shall $REQUIREMENT," for example, the application will be developed in C++.
- **Event-driven**: "When $TRIGGER $OPTIONAL_PRECONDITION the $SYSTEM shall $REQUIREMENT," for example, "When an order arrives, the gateway will produce a NewOrderEvent.
- **Unwanted behavior**: "If $CONDITION, then the $SYSTEM shall $REQUIREMENT," for example if the processing of the request takes longer than 1 second, the tool will display a progress bar.
- **State-driven**: "While $STATE, the $SYSTEM shall $REQUIREMENT," for example, while a ride is taking place, the app will display a map to help the driver navigate to the destination.
- **Optional feature**: "Where $FEATURE, the $SYSTEM shall $REQUIREMENT," for example, where A/C is present, the app will let the user set the temperature through the mobile application.

An example of a more complex requirement would be: When using a dual-server setup, if the backup server doesn't hear from the primary one for 5 seconds, it should try to register itself as a new primary server.

You don't need to use EARS, but it can help if you struggle with ambiguous, vague, overly complex, untestable, omissive, or otherwise badly worded requirements. Whatever way or wording you choose, be sure to use a concise model, which is based on common syntax and uses predefined keywords. It's also good practice to assign an identificator for each requirement you list, so you'll have an easy way to refer to them.

When it comes to more detailed requirements formats, it should have the following fields:

- **ID or Index**: To easily identify a specific requirement.
- **Title**: You can use the EARS template here.
- **Detailed Description**: You can put whatever information you find relevant here, for example, user stories.
- **Owner**: Who this requirement serves. This can be the product owner, the sales team, legal, IT, and so on.
- **Priority**: Pretty self-explanatory.
- **Deliver By**: If this requirement is needed for any key date, you can note it here.

Now that we know how to document functional requirements, let's discuss how you should approach documenting the nonfunctional ones.

Documenting nonfunctional requirements

Each quality attribute, such as performance or scalability, should have its own section in your document, with specific, testable requirements listed. Most of the QAs are measurable, so having specific metrics can do a world of good to resolve future questions. You can also have a separate section about the constraints that your project has.

With regard to wording, you can use the same EARS template to document your NFRs. Alternatively, you can also specify them as user stories using the personas that you defined in the context of this chapter.

Managing the version history of your documentation

You can take one of the two following approaches: either create a version log inside the document or use an external versioning tool. Both have their pros and cons, but we recommend going with the latter approach. Just like you use a version control system for your code, you can use it for your documentation. We're not saying you must use a Markdown document stored in a Git repo, but that's a perfectly valid approach as long as you're also generating a **business people-readable** version of it, be it a web page or a PDF file. Alternatively, you can just use online tools, such as RedmineWikis, or Confluence pages, which allow you to put a meaningful comment describing what's been changed on each edit you publish and to view the differences between versions.

If you decided to take a revision log approach, it's usually a table that includes the following fields:

- **Revision**: A number identifying which iteration of the document the changes were introduced at. You can also add tags for special revisions, such as *the first draft*, if you so wish.
- **Updated by**: Who made the change.
- **Reviewed by**: Who reviewed the change.
- **Change description**: A *commit message* for this revision. It states what changes have taken place.

Documenting requirements in Agile projects

Many proponents of Agile would claim that documenting all the requirements is simply a waste of time as they will probably change anyway. However, a good approach is to treat them similarly to items in your backlog: the ones that will be developed in the upcoming sprints should be defined in more detail than the ones that you wish to implement later. Just like you won't split your epics into stories and stories into tasks before it's necessary, you can get away with having just roughly described, less granular requirements until you're certain that you need them implemented.

 Note who or what was the source of a given requirement so that you'll know how who can provide you with necessary input for refining it in the future.

Let's take our Dominican Fair, for example. Say in the next sprint, we'll be building the shop page for a visitor to view, and in the sprint after that one, we'll be adding a subscription mechanism. Our requirements could look like the following:

ID	Priority	Description	Stakeholders
DF-42	P1	The shop's page must show the shop's inventory, with a photo and price for each item.	Josh, Rick
DF-43	P2	The shop's page must feature a map with the shop's location.	Josh, Candice
DF-44	P2	Customers must be able to subscribe to shops.	Steven

As you can see, the first two items relate to the feature we'll be doing next. so they are described in more detail. Who knows, maybe before the next sprint, the requirement about subscriptions will be dropped, so it doesn't make sense to think about every detail of it.

There are cases, on the other hand, that would still require you to have a complete list of requirements. If you need to deal with external regulators or internal teams such as auditing, legal, or compliance, chances are they'll still require a well-written physical document from you. Sometimes just handing them a document containing work items extracted from your backlog is OK. It's best to communicate with such stakeholders just like with any other ones: gather their expectations to know the minimum viable documentation that satisfies their needs.

What's important about documenting requirements is to have an understanding between you and the parties proposing specific requirements. How can this be achieved? Once you have a draft ready to go, you should show your documentation to them and gather feedback. This way, you'll know what was ambiguous, unclear, or missing. Even if it takes a few iterations, it will help you have a common ground with your stakeholders, so you'll gain more confidence that you're building the right thing.

Other sections

It's a good idea to have a links and resources section in which you point to stuff such as the issue tracker boards, artifacts, CI, the source repo, and whatever else you'll find handy. Architectural, marketing, and other kinds of documents can also be listed here.

If needed, you can also include a glossary.

You now know how to document your requirements and related information. Let's now say a few words about documenting the designed system.

Documenting architecture

Just as you should document your requirements, you should also document the emerging architecture. It's certainly not just for the sake of having documentation: it should help each person involved in the project to be more productive by making them better understand what's required from them and from the final product. Not all diagrams you'll make will be useful for everyone, but you should create them from the perspective of their future readers.

There's a multitude of frameworks to document your vision and many of them serve specific fields, project types, or architectural scopes. If you're interested in documenting enterprise architecture, for instance, you could be interested in TOGAF. This is an acronym for *The Open Group Architecture Framework*. It relies on four domains, namely the following:

- Business architecture (strategy, organization, key processes, and governance)
- Data architecture (logical and physical data management)
- Application architecture (blueprints for individual systems)
- Technical architecture (hardware, software, and network infrastructure)

Such grouping is useful if you document your software in the scope of the whole company or even broader ones. Other similar-scale frameworks include those developed by the **British Ministry of Defence (MODAF)** and the **American equivalent (DoDAF)**.

If you're not documenting enterprise architectures, and especially if you're just starting on your architectural self-development path, you'll probably be more interested in other frameworks, such as the 4+1 and C4 models.

Understanding the 4+1 model

The 4+1 view model was created by Philippe Kruchten in 1995. The author then claimed it is intended for "describing the architecture of software-intensive systems, based on the use of multiple, concurrent views." Its name comes from the views it consists of.

This model is widely known since it has been on the market for so long and does its job. It's well suited for bigger projects and while it can be used for small- and medium-sized ones as well, it can also turn out too complex for their needs (especially if they're written in an Agile way). If that's your case, you should try out the C4 model described in the next section.

A downside to the 4+1 model is that it uses a fixed set of views, while a pragmatic approach to document architecture would be to choose views based on the specifics of your project (more on that later).

A nice upside, on the other hand, is how the views link together, especially when it comes to scenarios. At the same time, each stakeholder can easily get the parts of the model relevant to them. This brings us to how the model appears:

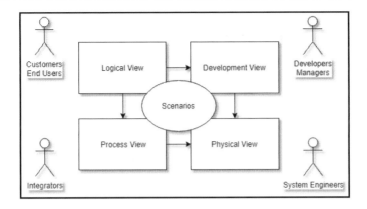

Figure 3.1 – An overview of the 4+1 model

Actors in the preceding diagram are the ones most interested in their corresponding views. All the views can be represented using different kinds of **Unified Modeling Language (UML)** diagrams. Let's now discuss each view:

- **The logical view** shows how functionality is provided to users. It shows the system's components (objects) and how they interact with each other. Most commonly, it consists of class and state diagrams. If you have thousands of classes or just want to better show the interactions between them, you should also have communication or sequence diagrams, both being parts of our next view:

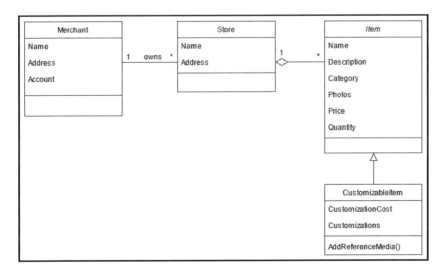

Figure 3.2 – Class diagrams can be used to show what types we plan to have, along with their relations

- **The process view** revolves around the system's runtime behavior. It shows processes, the communication between them, and interactions with external systems. It's represented by activity and interaction diagrams. This view addresses many NFRs, including concurrency, performance, availability, and scalability:

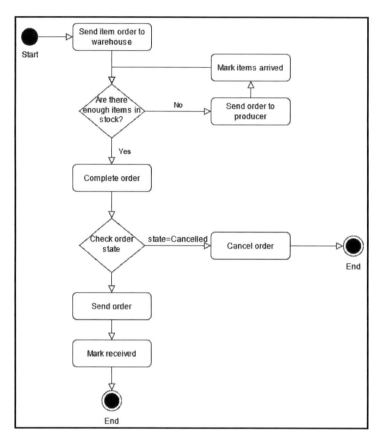

Figure 3.3 – Activity diagrams are graphical representations of workflows and processes

- **The development view** is for decomposing into subsystems and revolves around software organization. Reuse, tooling constraints, layering, modularization, packaging, execution environments – this view can represent them by showing a building-block decomposition of the system. It does so by using components and package diagrams:

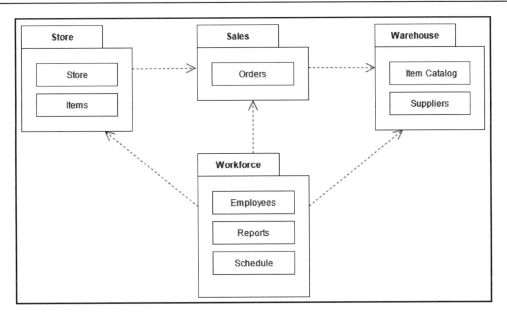

Figure 3.4 – Package diagrams can show the parts of a system from a higher perspective, as well as dependencies or relations between specific components

- **The physical view** is used to map software to hardware using deployment diagrams. Aimed at system engineers, it can cover a subset of NFRs concerned with the hardware, for example, communication:

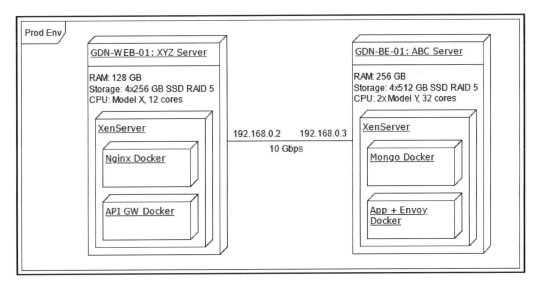

Figure 3.5 – Deployment diagrams demonstrate the hardware on which each software component will run. It can also be used to pass on information regarding the network

- **The scenarios** are gluing all the other views together. Represented by use case diagrams, these can be useful for all stakeholders. This view shows whether the system does what it should and that it is consistent. When all other views are finished, the scenario view can be redundant. However, all the other views wouldn't be possible without usage scenarios. This view shows the system from a high level, while the other views go into the details:

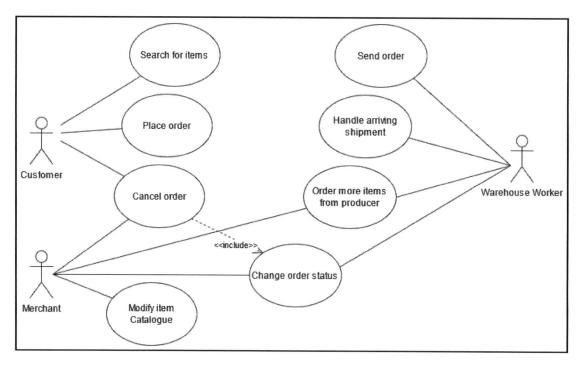

Figure 3.6 – Use case diagrams show how specific actors interact with the system and how the interactions relate to each other

Each of those views is interconnected with the others and often they must coexist to show the full picture. Let's think about expressing concurrency. It can't be done using only the logical view, as it's more expressive to map them to tasks and processes; we need the process view. On the other hand, the processes will be mapped to physical, often distributed, nodes. This means we'll need to effectively document it in three views, each of which will be relevant for a specific group of stakeholders. Other connections between the views include the following:

- Both logical and process views are used in analysis and design to conceptualize the product.

- Development and deployment in conjunction describe how the software is packaged and when each package will get deployed.
- The logical and development views show how the functionality is reflected in the source code.
- The process and deployment views are meant to collectively describe NFRs.

Now that you're familiar with the 4+1 model, let's discuss another one, which is simple, yet extremely effective: the C4 model. We hope using it will be a blast (pun intended).

Understanding the C4 model

The C4 model is a great fit for small- to medium-sized projects. It's easy to apply, as it's quite simple and it doesn't rely on any predefined notation. If you want to start diagramming using it, you can try out Tobias Shochguertel's c4-draw.io plugin (`https://github.com/tobiashochguertel/c4-draw.io`) for the free online drawing tool – draw.io (`https://www.draw.io/`).

In the C4 model, there are four main types of diagram, namely the following:

- Context
- Container
- Component
- Code

Just like zooming in and out using a map, you can use those four types to show more details of a particular code region or "zoom out" to show more about the interactions and surroundings of either a specific module or even the whole system.

The system context is a great starting point for looking at the architecture, as it shows the system as a whole, surrounded by its users and other systems that it interacts with. You can take a look at an example C4 context diagram here:

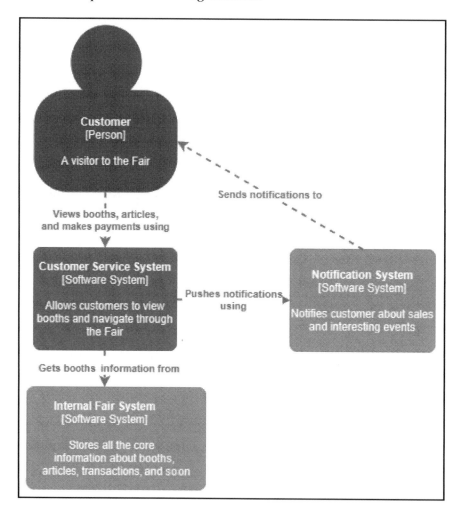

Figure 3.7 – A C4 context diagram

As you can see, it shows the "big picture," so it shouldn't focus on specific technologies or protocols. Instead, think of it as a diagram that could also be shown to non-technical stakeholders. Just by looking at the diagram, it should be clear that there's one actor involved (the human-shaped depiction of the customer), who interacts with one of the components of our solution, namely, the customer service system. This system, on the other hand, interacts with two more, with each of the interactions described along with the arrows.

The context diagram we described is used to provide an overview of the system with few details. Let's now look at the other diagrams one by one:

- **Container diagram**: This one is for showing the overview of the system internals. If your system uses a database, offers services, or just consists of certain applications, this diagram will show it. It can also show the major technology choices for the containers. Note that containers don't mean Docker containers; although each is a separately runnable and deployable unit, this diagram type is not about deployment scenarios. The container view is meant for technical people but isn't limited to the development team only. Architects, as well as operations and support, are the intended audience, too.
- **Component diagram**: If you want more details about a specific container, this is where the component diagram comes into play. It shows how the components inside a selected container interact with each other, as well as with elements and actors outside the container. By looking at this diagram, you can learn about the responsibilities of each component and what technology it's being built with. The intended audience for component diagrams is mostly focused around a specific container and consists of the development team and the architect.
- **Code diagrams**: We finally come to code diagrams, which emerge when you zoom in to a specific component. This view consists mostly of UML diagrams, including class, entity-relationship, and others, and ideally should be created automatically from source code by standalone tools and IDEs. You should definitely not make such diagrams for each component in your system; instead, focus on making them for the most important ones in a way that allows them to actually tell the reader what you wanted to tell. This means that less can be more in such diagrams, so you should omit unnecessary elements from code diagrams. In many systems, especially smaller ones, this class of diagram is omitted. The target audience is the same as in the case of component diagrams.

You may find the C4 model lacking some specific views. If you're wondering how to demonstrate how your system should be deployed, for instance, you might be interested to learn that aside from the main diagrams, there are also a few supplementary ones. One of them is the deployment diagram, which you can see next. It shows how containers in your system are mapped to nodes in your infrastructure. In general, it's a simpler version of UML's deployment diagram:

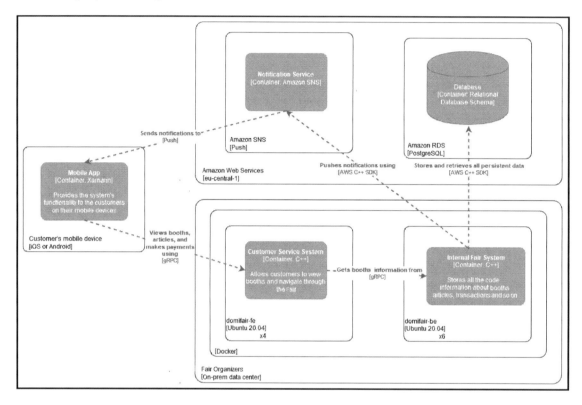

Figure 3.8 – A C4 deployment diagram

Speaking of UML diagrams with regard to the C4 model, you might also wonder why it puts such little effort into presenting the system's use cases. If that's your case, then you should think about supplementing the preceding models with either the use case diagram from UML or perhaps think about introducing some sequence diagrams.

When documenting architecture, it's more important what you document and what knowledge you share than to follow a specific hard set of rules. Choose whatever tools suit your needs the best.

Documenting architecture in Agile projects

In Agile environments, your approach to documenting architecture should be similar to the one about documenting requirements. First and foremost, consider who will be reading the materials you prepare to be sure you're describing the right things in the right way. Your documentation doesn't need to be a lengthy Word document. You can use presentations, wiki pages, single diagrams, or even recordings from meetings when someone describes the architecture.

What is important is to gather feedback on the documented architecture. Again, in the same way, as with the documented requirements, it's important to reiterate the documents with your stakeholders to know where to improve them. Even though this may seem like you're wasting time, if done properly, it should save you some time in terms of delivering the product. Good enough documentation should help newcomers to start being productive faster and guide more familiar stakeholders down the road. If you just discuss the architecture at some meetings, chances are, a quarter later, no one will remember why you made the decisions you made and whether they will remain valid in the ever-changing, Agile landscape.

Reiteration is important when creating documentation because most probably there will be some misunderstanding of an important detail or two. Other times, you or your stakeholders will gain more knowledge and decide to change things. Be prepared to go through the document at least a few times before it will be considered mature and done. Often, a few conversations over IM, phone, or in-person will help you finish it quicker and address any follow-ups that could arise, so prefer those to emails or other asynchronous ways of communication.

Choosing the right views to document

Architecture is way too complex a topic to be described by a single big diagram. Imagine you're the architect of a building. To design the whole thing, you'd need separate diagrams for different aspects: one for plumbing, another one for electricity and other cables, and so on. Each of those diagrams would show a different view of the project. The same goes for software architecture: you need to present the software from different perspectives, aimed at different stakeholders.

Moreover, if you were building a smart house, chances are you would draw some plan of the devices you want to place around. Although not all projects will require such views, since it plays a role in your project, it may be worth adding it. The same approach is also valid for architecture: if you find a different view valuable to the document, you should do it. So, how do you know which views could be valuable? You can try to perform the following steps:

1. Start with the views from either the 4+1 model or the C4 model.
2. Ask your stakeholders what is essential for them to have documented and think about modifying your set of views.
3. Choose views that will help you to evaluate whether the architecture meets its objectives and that all the ASRs are satisfied. Read the first paragraph of each of the views from the next sections to check whether they suit your needs.

If you're still not sure which views to document, here's a set of tips:

Try to just pick the most important views, because when there are too many of them, the architecture will become too hard to follow. A good set of views should not only showcase the architecture but also expose the technical risks to the project.

There are a few things you should think about when choosing what views you should describe in your documentation. We'll describe them shortly here, but if you're interested, you should grab *Rozanski and Woods'* book mentioned in the *Further reading* section.

Functional view

If your software is being developed as part of a bigger system, especially with teams that don't communicate on a daily basis, you should include a functional view (as in the 4+1 model).

One important and often overlooked aspect of documenting your architecture is the definition of the interfaces you provide, despite it being one of the most important things to describe. Whether it's an interface between two of your components or an entry point for the outside world, you should take the time to document it clearly, describing the semantics of objects and calls, as well as usage examples (which you can sometimes reuse as tests).

Another great benefit of including a functional view in your documentation is that it clarifies the responsibilities between components of your system. Each team developing the system should understand where the boundaries are and who's responsible for developing which functionality. All requirements should be explicitly mapped to components to eliminate gaps and duplicated work.

 An important thing to note here is to avoid overloading your functional view. If it gets messy, no one will want to read it. If you're starting to describe infrastructure on it, consider adding a deployment view. If you end up having a *God object* in your models, try to rethink the design and split it into smaller, more cohesive pieces.

One last important note about the functional view: try to keep each diagram you include on one level of abstraction. On the other hand, don't make it too vague by choosing an overly abstract level; ensure that every element is properly defined and understood by the interested parties.

Information view

If your system has non-straightforward needs with regard to information, its processing flow, management process, or storage, perhaps it's a good idea to include this kind of view.

Take the most important, data-rich entities and demonstrate how they flow through the system, who owns them, and who the producers and consumers are. It may be useful to mark how long certain data remains "fresh" and when it can be safely discarded, what the expected latency for it to arrive at certain points of the system is, or how to deal with identifiers if your system works in a distributed environment. If your system manages transactions, this process, along with any rollbacks, should also be clear to your stakeholders. Techniques for transforming, sending, and persisting data can also be important for some of them. If you are operating in the financial domain or have to deal with personal data, you most probably must obey some regulations, so describe how your system plans to tackle this.

The structure of your data can be diagrammed using UML class models. Remember to be clear about the format of your data, especially if it flows between two different systems. NASA lost the $125 million-worth Mars Climate Orbiter, which it co-developed with Lockheed Martin, because they used different units unknowingly, so keep an eye out for data inconsistencies between systems.

The processing flow of your data can use UML's activity model, and to show the life cycle of information, a state diagram can be used.

Concurrency view

If running many concurrent units of execution is an important aspect of your product, consider adding a concurrency view. It can show what issues and bottlenecks you may have (unless that sounds too detailed). Other good reasons to include it are the reliance on interprocess communication, having a non-straightforward task structure, concurrent state management, synchronization, or task failure handling logic.

Use whatever notation you want for this view, as long as it captures the units of execution and their communication. Assign priorities to your processes and threads, if necessary, and then analyze any potential issues, such as deadlocks or contention. You can use state diagrams to show the possible states and their transitions for important units of execution (waiting for queries, executing a query, distributing results, and so on).

If you're not sure about the need to introduce concurrency to your system, a good rule of thumb is *don't*. And if you must, strive for a simple design. Debugging concurrency issues is never easy and always long, so if possible, try to optimize what you have first instead of just throwing more threads at the problem at hand.

If, by looking at your diagram, you're worried about resource contention, try to replace locks on big objects with more locks, but finer-grained, use lightweight synchronization (sometimes atomics are enough), introduce optimistic locking, or reduce what's shared (creating an additional copy of some data in a thread and processing it can be faster than sharing access to the only copy).

Development view

If you're building a big system with lots of modules, and you need to structure your code, have system-wide design constraints, or if you want to share some common aspects between parts of your system, presenting the solution from a development viewpoint should benefit you, along with software developers and testers.

A package diagram of the development view can be handy to show where different modules in your system are located, what their dependencies are, and other related modules (for example, residing in the same software layer). It doesn't need to be a UML diagram – even boxes and lines would do. If you plan for a module to be replaceable, this kind of diagram can show you what other software packages can be affected.

Tactics to increase reuse in your system, such as creating your own runtime framework for components, or tactics for increasing the coherence of your systems, such as a common approach to authentication, logging, internationalization, or other kinds of processing, are all part of the development view. If you see any common parts of the system, document it to be sure that all developers see them too.

A common approach to code organization, building, and configuration management should also go into this section of your documentation. If all this sounds like a lot to document, then focus on the most important parts and cover the rest just briefly, if at all.

Deployment and operational views

If you have a non-standard or complex deployment environment, such as specific needs with regard to hardware, third-party software or networking requirements, consider documenting it in a separate deployment section, aimed at system administrators, developers, and testers.

If necessary, cover the following things:

- The amount of memory required
- The CPU thread count (with or without hyperthreading)
- Pinning and affinity with regard to NUMA nodes
- Specialist networking equipment requirements, such as switches that mark packages to measure latency and throughput in a black-box manner
- The networking topology
- The estimated bandwidth required
- Storage requirements for your app
- Any third-party software that you plan to use

Once you have the requirements, you can map them to specific hardware and put them into a runtime platform model. You can use a UML deployment diagram with stereotypes if you desire formal modeling. This should show your processing nodes and client nodes, online and offline storage, network links, specialized hardware, such as firewalls or FPGA or ASIC devices, and a mapping between functional elements and the nodes they'll run on.

If you have non-straightforward networking needs, you can add another diagram showing the networking nodes and the connections between them.

If you depend on specific technologies (including specific versions of software), it's a good idea to list them to see whether there are any compatibility issues between the software you use. Sometimes, two third-party components will require the same dependency, but in different versions.

If you have a specific installation and upgrade plan in your head, it might be a good idea to write a few words about it. Things such as A/B testing, blue-green deployments, or any particular container magic that your solution will rely on should be clear to everyone involved. Data migration plans should also be covered, if needed, including how long the migration can take and when it could be scheduled.

Any plans for configuration management, performance monitoring, operational monitoring, and control, as well as backup strategies, can all be things worth describing. You'll probably want to create a few groups, identify the dependencies of each, and define the approach for each such group. If you can think about any probable errors that may occur, have a plan to detect and recover from them.

A few notes to the support team can also go into this section: what support is required by which stakeholder group, what classes of incidents you plan to have, how to escalate, and what each level of support will be responsible for.

It's best to engage early with the operational staff and create diagrams specifically for them in order to keep them engaged.

Now that we've discussed how to create documentation about your system and its requirements manually, let's switch to documenting your APIs in an automated manner.

Generating documentation

As engineers, we don't like manual labor. This is why, if something can be automated and save us work, it most likely will be. With all this effort to create good enough documentation, having the possibility to automate at least parts of the work can actually be bliss.

Generating requirements documentation

If you're creating a project from scratch, it can be hard to generate documentation out of thin air. However, sometimes it's possible to generate documentation if you have nothing but the requirements in an appropriate tool. If you're using JIRA, for instance, a starting point would be to just export all items from an issue navigator view. You can use whatever filter you like and get printouts just for those items. If you don't like the default set of fields or just feel this is not what you're looking for, you can try out one of JIRA's plugins for requirements management. They allow a whole lot more than to just export requirements; for example, **R4J (Requirements for Jira)** allows you to create whole hierarchies of requirements, trace them, manage changes and propagate them through your whole project, perform impact analyses of any requirements changes, and, of course, export using user-defined templates. Many such tools will also aid you in creating test suites for your requirements, but none that we saw were free.

Generating diagrams from code

If you want to get to know your code structure without taking an initial deep dive into the sources, you might be interested in tools that generate diagrams from code.

One such tool is CppDepend. It enables you to create various dependency diagrams between different parts of your sources. What's more, it allows you to query and filter the code based on various parameters. Whether you want to just grasp how the code is structured, discover what the dependencies are between different software components and how tightly they're coupled, or want to quickly locate parts with the most technical debt, you might be interested in this tool. It's proprietary, but offers a fully functional trial.

Some diagramming tools allow you to create code from class diagrams and class diagrams from code. Enterprise Architect enables you to take your class and interface diagrams and generate code in multiple languages. C++ is one of these, and allows UML class diagrams to be generated directly from source code. Another tool that can do that is Visual Paradigm.

Generating (API) documentation from code

To help others navigate your existing code and use the APIs you provide, a good idea is to provide documentation generated from the comments in your code. There's no better place for such documentation than just right next to the functions and data types it describes, and this helps a lot in keeping them in sync.

A de facto standard tool for writing such documentation is Doxygen. Its positives are that it's fast (especially for big projects and HTML document generation), the generator has some built-in correctness checks (for example, for partially documented parameters in a function – a good marker to check whether the documentation is still up to date), and it allows the navigation of class and file hierarchies. Its disadvantages include not being able to do a full-text search, less than ideal PDF generation, and an interface some may find cumbersome.

Fortunately, the usability flaws can be remediated by using another popular tool for documentation. If you've ever read any Python documentation, you have probably stumbled upon Sphinx. It has a fresh-looking and usable interface and uses reStructuredText as a markup language. The good news is that there's a bridge between those two, so you can take XML generated from Doxygen and use it in Sphinx. This bridging software is called Breathe.

Let's now see how to set it up in your project. Let's assume we keep our sources in `src`, public headers in `include`, and documentation in `doc`. First, let's create a `CMakeLists.txt` file:

```
cmake_minimum_required(VERSION 3.10)

project("Breathe Demo" VERSION 0.0.1 LANGUAGES CXX)

list(APPEND CMAKE_MODULE_PATH "${CMAKE_CURRENT_LIST_DIR}/cmake")
add_subdirectory(src)
add_subdirectory(doc)
```

We've set requirements on the CMake version supported by our project, specified its name, version, and the languages used (in our case, it's just C++), and added the `cmake` directory to the path under which CMake looks for its include files.

In the `cmake` subdirectory, we'll create one file, `FindSphinx.cmake`, which we'll use just as the name suggests, since Sphinx doesn't offer one already:

```
find_program(
  SPHINX_EXECUTABLE
  NAMES sphinx-build
  DOC "Path to sphinx-build executable")

# handle REQUIRED and QUIET arguments, set SPHINX_FOUND variable
include(FindPackageHandleStandardArgs)
find_package_handle_standard_args(
  Sphinx "Unable to locate sphinx-build executable" SPHINX_EXECUTABLE)
```

Now, CMake will look for our Sphinx build tool and, if found, will set appropriate CMake variables to mark the Sphinx package as found. Next, let's create our sources to generate the documentation. Let's have an `include/breathe_demo/demo.h` file:

```
#pragma once

// the @file annotation is needed for Doxygen to document the free
// functions in this file
/**
 * @file
 * @brief The main entry points of our demo
 */

/**
 * A unit of performable work
 */
struct Payload {
  /**
   * The actual amount of work to perform
   */
  int amount;
};

/**
   @brief Performs really important work
   @param payload the descriptor of work to be performed
 */
void perform_work(struct Payload payload);
```

Note the comment syntax. Doxygen recognizes it while parsing our header file so that it knows what to put in the generated documentation.

Now, let's add a corresponding `src/demo.cpp` implementation for our header:

```
#include "breathe_demo/demo.h"

#include <chrono>
#include <thread>

void perform_work(Payload payload) {
  std::this_thread::sleep_for(std::chrono::seconds(payload.amount));
}
```

No Doxygen comments here. We prefer to document our types and functions in the header files since they're the interface to our library. The source files are just implementation and they don't add anything new to the interface.

Aside from the preceding files, we also need a simple `CMakeLists.txt` file in `src`:

```
add_library(BreatheDemo demo.cpp)
target_include_directories(BreatheDemo PUBLIC
  ${PROJECT_SOURCE_DIR}/include)
target_compile_features(BreatheDemo PUBLIC cxx_std_11)
```

Here, we specify the source files for our target, the directory with the header files for it, and the required C++ standard to compile against.

Now, let's move to the `doc` folder, where the magic happens; first, its `CMakeLists.txt` file, beginning with a check to establish whether Doxygen is available and omitting generation if so:

```
find_package(Doxygen)
if (NOT DOXYGEN_FOUND)
  return()
endif()
```

If Doxygen is not installed, we'll just skip documentation generation. Note also the `return()` call, which will exit the current CMake list file, a not-that-widely-known, but nevertheless useful, trick.

Next, assuming Doxygen was found, we need to set some variables to steer the generation. We want just the XML output for Breathe, so let's set the following variables:

```
set(DOXYGEN_GENERATE_HTML NO)
set(DOXYGEN_GENERATE_XML YES)
```

To force relative paths, use `set(DOXYGEN_STRIP_FROM_PATH ${PROJECT_SOURCE_DIR}/include)`. If you have any implementation details to hide, you can do this using `set(DOXYGEN_EXCLUDE_PATTERNS "*/detail/*")`. OK, since we have all the variables set, let's now generate:

```
# Note: Use doxygen_add_docs(doxygen-doc ALL ...) if you want your
# documentation to be created by default each time you build. Without the #
keyword you need to explicitly invoke building of the 'doc' target.
doxygen_add_docs(doxygen-doc ${PROJECT_SOURCE_DIR}/include COMMENT
                "Generating API documentation with Doxygen")
```

Here, we call a CMake function specifically written for using Doxygen. We define a target, `doxygen-doc`, which we'll need to explicitly invoke to generate our docs on demand, just like the comment says.

Now we need to create a Breathe target to consume what we got from Doxygen. We can use our `FindSphinx` module to this end:

```
find_package(Sphinx REQUIRED)
configure_file(${CMAKE_CURRENT_SOURCE_DIR}/conf.py.in
                ${CMAKE_CURRENT_BINARY_DIR}/conf.py @ONLY)
add_custom_target(
  sphinx-doc ALL
  COMMAND ${SPHINX_EXECUTABLE} -b html -c ${CMAKE_CURRENT_BINARY_DIR}
          ${CMAKE_CURRENT_SOURCE_DIR} ${CMAKE_CURRENT_BINARY_DIR}
  WORKING_DIRECTORY ${CMAKE_CURRENT_BINARY_DIR}
  COMMENT "Generating API documentation with Sphinx"
  VERBATIM)
```

First, we invoke our module. Then, we fill in a Python configuration file with variables from our project for Sphinx to use. We create a `sphinx-doc` target that will generate HTML files as its output and will print a line in the build's output when doing so.

Finally, let's force CMake to call Doxygen each time we generate Sphinx docs: `add_dependencies(sphinx-doc doxygen-doc)`.

If you wish to have more targets for documentation, it may be useful to introduce some CMake functions that will handle documentation-related targets for you.

Let's now see what lies inside our `conf.py.in` file, used to steer our feline tool. Let's create it and let it point Sphinx to Breathe:

```
extensions = [ "breathe", "m2r2" ]
breathe_projects = { "BreatheDemo": "@CMAKE_CURRENT_BINARY_DIR@/xml" }
breathe_default_project = "BreatheDemo"

project = "Breathe Demo"
author = "Breathe Demo Authors"
copyright = "2021, Breathe Demo Authors"
version = "@PROJECT_VERSION@"
release = "@PROJECT_VERSION@

html_theme = 'sphinx_rtd_theme'
```

As you can see from the preceding listing, we set the extensions for Sphinx to use, the name of the documented project, and a few other related variables. Note `@NOTATION@`, used by CMake to fill in the output file with the value of appropriate CMake variables. Finally, we tell Sphinx to use our ReadTheDocs theme (`sphinx_rtd_theme`).

The final pieces of the puzzle are reStructuredText files, which define what to include where in the docs. First, let's create an `index.rst` file, containing a table of contents and a few links:

```
Breathe Demo
============

Welcome to the Breathe Demo documentation!

.. toctree::
 :maxdepth: 2
 :caption: Contents:

Introduction <self>
 readme
 api_reference
```

The first link points to this page, so we can get back to it from other ones. We'll display `Introduction` as the label. Other names point to other files with the `.rst` extension. Since we're including the M2R2 Sphinx extension, we can include our `README.md` file in the docs, which can save you some duplication. The contents of the `readme.rst` file are simply `.. mdinclude:: ../README.md`. Now for the last part: merging Doxygen's output. This is done in the `api_reference.rst` file using just the following command:

```
API Reference
=============

.. doxygenindex::
```

So we just named the reference page as we liked and specified that the Doxygen-generated docs should be listed here, and that's all! Just build the `sphinx-doc` target and you'll get a page looking like so:

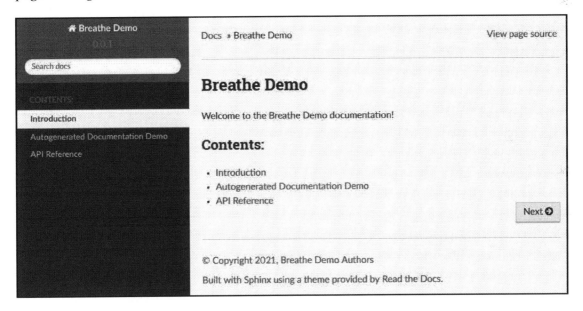

Figure 3.9 – The main page of our documentation, consolidating both the generated and manually written parts

And when we look at the API docs page, it should look like this:

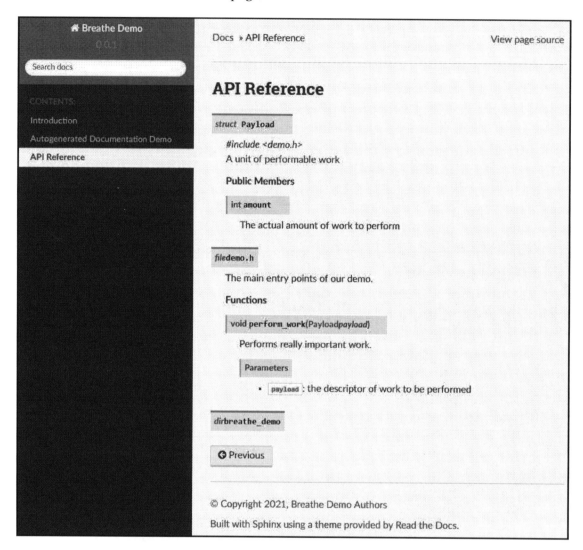

Figure 3.10 – The automatically generated API documentation

As you can see, the documentation was automatically generated for our `Payload` type with each of its members, as well as for the free `perform_work` function, including each of its parameters, and was grouped based on the file that defines them. Neat!

Summary

In this chapter, you got to know all the essentials regarding requirements and documentation. You learned how to gather requirements successfully and how to identify the most important ones. You can now prepare lean and useful documentation that shows only what's important in a view-oriented manner. You are able to distinguish between different types and styles of diagrams and use the one that suits your needs the best. Last, but not least, you are now able to automatically generate aesthetic documentation.

In the next chapter, you'll learn about useful architectural design patterns that will help you fulfill your system's requirements. We'll discuss various patterns and how to apply them to provide many important quality attributes, both on a single-component scale in distributed systems.

Questions

1. What are quality attributes?
2. What sources should be used when gathering requirements?
3. How can you tell whether a requirement is architecturally significant?
4. When is development view documentation useful?
5. How can you automatically check whether your code's API documentation is out of date?
6. How can you indicate on a diagram that a given process is handled by different components of the system?

Further reading

1. *Evaluate the Software Architecture using ATAM*, JC Olamendy, blog post: `https://johnolamendy.wordpress.com/2011/08/12/evaluate-the-software-architecture-using-atam/`
2. **EARS**: *The Easy Approach to Requirements Syntax*, John Terzakis, Intel Corporation, conference talk from the ICCGI conference: `https://www.iaria.org/conferences2013/filesICCGI13/ICCGI_2013_Tutorial_Terzakis.pdf`
3. Eoin Woods and Nick Rozanski, *Software Systems Architecture: Working With Stakeholders Using Viewpoints and Perspectives*

2
Section 2: The Design and Development of C++ Software

This section presents techniques for creating effective software solutions with C++. It demonstrates techniques for solving common challenges and avoiding pitfalls when designing, developing, and building C++ code. The techniques come from the C++ language itself, as well as design patterns, tools, and build systems.

This section contains the following chapters:

- Chapter 4, *Architectural and System Design*
- Chapter 5, *Leveraging C++ Language Features*
- Chapter 6, *Design Patterns and C++*
- Chapter 7, *Building and Packaging*

4
Architectural and System Design

Patterns help us deal with complexity. At the level of a single software component, you can use software patterns such as the ones described by the four authors of the book (better known as the *Gang of Four*) *Design Patterns: Elements of Reusable Object-Oriented Software*. When we move higher up and start looking at the architecture between different components, knowing when and how to apply architectural patterns can go a long way.

There are countless such patterns that are useful for different scenarios. In fact, to even get to know all of them, you would need to read more than just one book. That being said, we selected several patterns for this book, suited for achieving various architectural goals.

In this chapter, we'll introduce you to a few concepts and fallacies related to architectural design; we'll show when to use the aforementioned patterns and how to design high-quality components that are easy to deploy.

The following topics will be covered in this chapter:

- The different service models and when to use each of them
- How to avoid the fallacies of distributed computing
- The outcomes of the CAP theorem and how to achieve eventual consistency
- Making your system fault-tolerant and available
- Integrating your system
- Achieving performance at scale
- Deploying your system
- Managing your APIs

By the end of this chapter, you'll know how to design your architecture to provide several important qualities, such as fault tolerance, scalability, and deployability. Before that, let's first learn about two inherent aspects of distributed architectures.

Technical requirements

The code from this chapter requires the following tools to build and run:

- Docker
- Docker Compose

The source code snippets from the chapter can be found at `https://github.com/PacktPublishing/Software-Architecture-with-Cpp/tree/master/Chapter04`.

Understanding the peculiarities of distributed systems

There are many types of different software systems, each of them suited for different scenarios, built for different needs, and using different sets of assumptions. Writing and deploying a classical, standalone desktop application is nothing like writing and deploying a microservice that needs to communicate with many others over a network.

In this section, we'll go through the various models that you can use to deploy your software, the common mistakes that people should avoid when creating distributed systems, and some of the compromises people need to make to create such systems successfully.

Different service models and when to use them

Let's first start with service models. When designing a bigger system, you need to decide how much of the infrastructure you will manage versus how much you can build upon existing building blocks. Sometimes, you might want to leverage existing software without the need to manually deploy an app or back up data, for example, by using Google Drive through its API as storage for your app. Other times, you can rely on an existing cloud platform such as Google's App Engine to deploy your solution without the need to worry about providing a language runtime or databases. If you can decide to deploy everything in your own way, you can either leverage an infrastructure from a cloud provider or use your company's one.

Let's discuss the different models and where each can be useful.

On-premises model

The classical way, and the only way available in the pre-cloud era, is to just deploy everything on your own premises. You need to buy all the hardware and software required and make sure it will provide enough capacity for your needs. If you're working for a start-up company, this may be a big upfront cost. Along with the growth of your userbase, you need to buy and set up more resources so that your service can deal even with the occasional spikes in load. All this means you need to predict the growth of your solution and act proactively, as there's no way you could just automatically scale depending on the current load.

Even in the cloud era, deploying on-premises is still useful and often spotted in the wild. Sometimes you're dealing with data that shouldn't, or even can't, leave your company's premises, either due to data privacy issues or compliance ones. Other times, you need to have as little latency as possible and you need your own data center to do so. Sometimes you may calculate the costs and decide that in your case, on-premises will be cheaper than a cloud solution. Last, but not least, your company might just already have an existing data center that you can use.

Deploying on-premises doesn't mean you need to have a monolith system. Often, companies have their own private clouds deployed on-premises. This helps to cut costs by better utilization of the available infrastructure. You can also mix a private cloud solution with one of the other service models, which can be useful when you need that extra capacity from time to time. This is called a **hybrid deployment** and is offered by all major cloud providers as well as provided by OpenStack's Omni project.

Infrastructure as a Service (IaaS) model

Speaking of other models, the most basic cloud service model is called **Infrastructure as a Service (IaaS)**. It's also the most similar to on-premises: you can think of IaaS as a way to have a virtual data center. As the name suggests, the cloud provider offers you a slice of the infrastructure they host, which consists of three types of resources:

- Compute, such as virtual machines, containers, or bare-metal machines (excluding operating systems)
- Networking, which aside from the network itself includes DNS servers, routing, and firewalls
- Storage, including backup and recovery capabilities

It's still up to you to provide all the software: operating systems, middleware, and your applications.

IaaS can be used in scenarios ranging from hosting websites (might be cheaper than traditional web hosting), through storage (for example, Amazon's S3 and Glacier services), to high-performance computing and big data analysis (requires huge computing power). Some companies use it to quickly set up and purge test and development environments when needed.

Using IaaS instead of on-premises infrastructure can be a cheap way to test new ideas while saving you the time needed for configuration.

If your service observes spikes in usage, for example, during the weekends, you might want to leverage your cloud's automatic scaling capabilities: scale up when needed and scale back down later to save money.

IaaS solutions are offered by all the popular cloud service providers.

A similar concept, sometimes thought of as a subset of IaaS, is **Containers as a Service (CaaS)**. In CaaS, instead of bare-metal systems and virtual machines, the service provides you with containers and orchestration capabilities that you can use to build your own container clusters. CaaS offerings can be found with Google Cloud Platform and AWS, among others.

Platform as a Service (PaaS) model

If the infrastructure itself is not enough for your needs, you can use the **Platform as a Service (PaaS)** model instead. In this model, the cloud service provider manages not only the infrastructure (just like in IaaS), but also the operating systems, any required middleware, and the runtime – the platform that you will deploy your software on.

Often a PaaS solution will provide you with app versioning capabilities, service monitoring and discovery, database management, business intelligence, and even development tools.

With PaaS, you're covered throughout the whole development pipeline: from building and testing to deploying, updating, and managing your service. However, PaaS solutions are more costly than IaaS offerings. On the other hand, with the whole platform provided, you can cut the costs and time to develop parts of your software and easily provide the same setup for development teams scattered around the globe.

All main cloud providers have their own offerings, for example, Google App Engine or Azure App Service. There are also independent ones, such as Heroku.

Aside from the more generic PaaS, there's also **Communications Platform as a Service (CPaaS)**, in which you're provided with the whole communications backend, including audio and video, which you can integrate into your solution. This technology allows you to easily provide video-enabled help desks or just integrate live chats into your apps.

Software as a Service (SaaS) model

Sometimes you might not want to develop a software component on your own and just want to use an existing one. **Software as a Service (SaaS)** basically gives you a hosted application. With SaaS, you don't need to worry about either the infrastructure or the platform built upon it, and not even about the software itself. The provider is responsible for installing, running, updating, and maintaining the whole software stack, as well as backups, licensing, and scaling.

There's quite a variety to what software you can get in the SaaS model. Examples vary from office suites such as Office 365 and Google Docs to messaging software such as Slack, through **Customer Relationship Management (CRM)** systems, and span even to gaming solutions such as cloud gaming services, allowing you to play resource-hungry video games hosted on the cloud.

Usually, to access such services, all you need is a browser, so this can be a great step in providing remote work capabilities for your employees.

You can create your own SaaS applications and provide them to users either by deploying them however you like, or through means such as AWS Marketplace.

Function as a Service (FaaS) model and serverless architecture

With the advent of cloud-native, another model that is growing in popularity is **Function as a Service (FaaS)**. It can be helpful if you want to achieve a serverless architecture. With FaaS, you get a platform (similarly to PaaS) on which you can run short-lived applications, or functions.

With PaaS, you typically always need to have at least one instance of your service running, while in FaaS you can run them only when they're actually needed. Running your function can make the time to handle requests longer (measured in seconds; you need to launch the function after all). However, some of those requests can be cached to reduce both the latency and costs. Speaking about costs, FaaS can get way more expensive than PaaS if you run the functions for a long time, so you must do the math when designing your system.

If used correctly, FaaS abstracts away the servers from the developers, can reduce your costs, and can provide you with better scalability, as it can be based on events, not resources. This model is commonly used for running prescheduled or manually triggered tasks, processing batches or streams of data, and handling incoming, not-so-urgent requests. A few popular providers of FaaS are AWS Lambda, Azure Functions, and Google Cloud Functions.

Now that we've covered the common service models in the cloud, let's discuss some of the wrong assumptions people make when designing distributed systems.

Avoiding the fallacies of distributed computing

When people new to distributed computing begin their journey with designing such systems, they tend to forget or ignore a few aspects of such systems. Although they were first noticed back in the 90s, they remain current today.

The fallacies are discussed in the following sub-sections. Let's have a quick rundown on each of them.

The network is reliable

Networking equipment is designed for long years of flawless operation. Despite that, many things can still cause packet loss, ranging from power outages through poor wireless networking signal, configuration errors, someone tripping over a cable, or even animals biting through wires. For instance, Google had to protect their underwater cables with Kevlar because they were being bitten by sharks (yes, really). You should always assume that data can get lost somewhere over the network. Even if that doesn't happen, software issues can still occur on the other side of the wire.

To fend off such issues, be sure you have a policy for automatically retrying failed network requests and a way to handle common networking issues. When retrying, try to not overload the other party and not commit the same transaction multiple times. You can use a message queue to store and retry sending for you.

Patterns such as circuit breaker, which we'll show later in this chapter, can also help. Oh, and be sure to not just wait infinitely, hogging up resources with each failed request.

Latency is zero

Both the network and the services you're running have to take some time to respond even under normal conditions. Occasionally they'll have to take longer, especially when being under a bigger-than-average load. Sometimes instead of a few milliseconds, your requests can take seconds to complete.

Try to design your system so it doesn't wait on too many fine-grained remote calls, as each such call can add to your total processing time. Even in a local network, 10,000 requests for 1 record will be much slower than 1 request for 10,000 records. To reduce network latency, consider sending and handling requests in bulk. You can also try to hide the cost of small calls by doing other processing tasks while waiting for their results.

Other ways to deal with latency are to introduce caches, push the data in a publisher-subscriber model instead of waiting for requests, or deploy closer to the customers, for example, by using **Content Delivery Networks (CDNs)**.

Bandwidth is infinite

When adding a new service to your architecture, make sure you take note of how much traffic it's going to use. Sometimes you might want to reduce the bandwidth by compressing the data or by introducing a throttling policy.

This fallacy also has to do with mobile devices. If the signal is weak, often the network will become the bottleneck. This means the amount of data a mobile app uses should generally be kept low. Using the *Backends for Frontends* pattern described in `Chapter 2`, *Architectural Styles*, can often help save precious bandwidth.

If your backend needs to transfer lots of data between some components, try to make sure such components are close together: don't run them in separate data centers. With databases, this often boils down to better replication. Patterns such as CQRS (discussed later in this chapter) are also handy.

The network is secure

This is a dangerous fallacy. A chain is only as strong as its weakest link, and unfortunately, there are many links in distributed systems. Here are a few ways to make those links stronger:

- Be sure to always apply security patches to every component that you use, to your infrastructure, operating systems, and other components.

- Train your personnel and try to protect your system from the human factor; sometimes it's a rogue employee that compromises a system.
- If your system will be online, it will get attacked, and it's possible that a breach will happen at one point. Be sure to have a written plan on how to react to such events.
- You might have heard about the defense in depth principle. It boils down to having different checks for different parts of your system (your infrastructure, your applications, and so on) so that when a breach happens, its range, and the associated damage, will be limited.
- Use firewalls, certificates, encryption, and proper authentication.

For more on security, refer to `Chapter 10`, *Security in Code and Deployment*.

Topology doesn't change

This one became especially true in the microservices era. Autoscaling and the emergence of the *cattle, not pets* approach to managing infrastructure mean that the topology will constantly change. This can affect latency and bandwidth, so some of this fallacy's outcomes are the same as the ones described earlier.

Fortunately, the mentioned approach also comes with guidelines on how to effectively manage your *herd* of servers. Relying on hostnames and DNS instead of hardcoding IPs is a step in the right direction, and service discovery, described later in this book, is another one. A third, even bigger, step is to always assume your instances can fail and automate reacting to such scenarios. Netflix's *Chaos Monkey tool* can also help you test your preparedness.

There is one administrator

The knowledge about distributed systems, due to their nature, is often distributed itself. Different people are responsible for the development, configuration, deployment, and administration of such systems and their infrastructure. Different components are often upgraded by different people, not necessarily in sync. There's also the so-called bus factor, which in short is the risk factor for a key project member being hit by a bus.

How do we deal with all of this? The answer consists of a few parts. One of them is the DevOps culture. By facilitating close collaboration between development and operations, people share the knowledge about the system, thus reducing the bus factor. Introducing continuous delivery can help with upgrading the project and keeping it always up.

Try to model your system to be loosely coupled and backward compatible, so upgrades of components don't require other components to be upgraded too. An easy way to decouple is by introducing messaging between them, so consider adding a queue or two. It will help you with downtime during upgrades as well.

Finally, try to monitor your system and gather logs in a centralized place. Decentralization of your system shouldn't mean you now need to manually look at logs at a dozen different machines. The **ELK (Elasticsearch, Logstash, Kibana)** stack is invaluable for this. Grafana, Prometheus, Loki, and Jaeger are also very popular, especially with Kubernetes. If you're looking for something more lightweight than Logstash, consider Fluentd and Filebeat, especially if you're dealing with containers.

Transport cost is zero

This fallacy is important for planning your project and its budget. Building and maintaining a network for a distributed system costs both time and money, regardless of whether you deploy on-premises or in the cloud – it's just a matter of when you pay the cost. Try to estimate the costs of the equipment, the data to be transferred (cloud providers charge for this), and the required manpower.

If you're relying on compression, be wary that while this reduces networking costs, it can increase the price for your compute. In general, using binary APIs such as gRPC-based will be cheaper (and faster) than JSON-based ones, and those are still cheaper than XML. If you send images, audio, or video, it's a must to estimate how much this will cost you.

The network is homogeneous

Even if you plan what hardware to have and what software to run on your network, it's easy to end up with at least some heterogeneity. A slightly different configuration on some of the machines, a different communication protocol used by that legacy system that you need to integrate with, or different mobile phones sending requests to your system are just a few examples of this. Another one is extending your on-premises solution by using additional workers in the cloud.

Try to limit the number of protocols and formats used, strive to use standard ones, and avoid vendor lock-in to ensure your system can still communicate properly in such heterogeneous environments. Heterogeneity can also mean differences in resiliency. Try to use the circuit breaker pattern along with retries to handle this.

Now that we've discussed all the fallacies, let's discuss yet another pretty important aspect of distributed architectures.

CAP theorem and eventual consistency

To design successful systems that spread across more than one node, you need to know and use certain principles. One of them is the **CAP theorem**. It's about one of the most important choices you need to make when designing a distributed system and owes its name to the three properties a distributed system can have. They are as follows:

- **Consistency**: Every read would get you the data after the most recent write (or an error).
- **Availability**: Every request will get a non-error response (without the guarantee that you'll get the most recent data).
- **Partition tolerance**: Even if a network failure occurs between two nodes, the system as a whole will continue working.

In essence, the theorem states that you can pick at most two of those three properties for a distributed system.

As long as the system operates properly, it looks like all three of the properties can be satisfied. However, as we know from looking at the fallacies, the network is unreliable, so partitions will occur. In such cases, a distributed system should still operate properly. This means the theorem actually makes you choose between delivering partition tolerance and consistency (that is CP), or partition tolerance and availability (that is AP). Usually, the latter is the better choice. If you want to choose CA, you have to remove the network entirely and be left with a single-node system.

If under a partition, you decide to deliver consistency, you will have to either return an error or risk timeouts when waiting for the data to be consistent. If you choose availability over consistency, you risk returning stale data – the latest writes might be unable to propagate across the partition.

Both those approaches are suited for different needs. If your system requires atomic reads and writes, for instance, because a customer could lose their money, go with CP. If your system must continue operating under partitions, or you can allow eventual consistency, go with AP.

Okay, but what is eventual consistency? Let's discuss the different levels of consistency to understand this.

In a system offering strong consistency, each write is synchronously propagated. This means all reads will always see the latest writes, even at the cost of higher latency or lower availability. This is the type that relational DBMSes offer (based on ACID guarantees) and is best suited for systems that require transactions.

In a system offering eventual consistency, on the other hand, you only guarantee that after a write, reads will eventually see the change. Usually, *eventually* means in a couple of milliseconds. This is due to the asynchronous nature of data replication in such systems, as opposed to the synchronous propagation from the previous paragraph. Instead of providing ACID guarantees, for example, using an RDBMS, here we have BASE semantics, often provided by NoSQL databases.

For a system to be asynchronous and eventually consistent (as AP systems often are), it's needed to have a way to solve state conflicts. A common way to do so is to exchange updates between instances and choose either the first or the last write as the accepted one.

Let's now discuss two related patterns that can help in achieving eventual consistency.

Sagas and compensating transactions

The saga pattern is useful when you need to perform distributed transactions.

Before the microservice era, if you had one host with one database, you could rely on the database engine to do the transaction for you. With multiple databases on one host, you could use **Two-Phase Commits (2PCs)** to do so. With 2PCs, you would have a coordinator, who would first tell all the databases to prepare, and once they all report being ready, it would tell them all to commit the transaction.

Now, as each microservice likely has its own database (and it should if you want scalability), and they're spanned all over your infrastructure, you can no longer rely on simple transactions and 2PCs (losing this ability often means you no longer want an RDBMS, as NoSQL databases can be much faster).

Instead, you can use the saga pattern. Let's demonstrate it in an example.

Imagine you want to create an online warehouse that tracks how much supply it has and allows payment by credit cards. To process an order, above all other services, you need three: one for processing the order, one for reserving the supplies, and one for charging the card.

Now, there are two ways the saga pattern can be implemented: **choreography-based** (also called **event-based**) and **orchestration-based** (also called **command-based**).

Choreography-based sagas

In the first case, the first part of the saga would be the order processing service sending an event to the supply service. This one would do its part and send another event to the payment service. The payment service would then send yet another event back to the order service. This would complete the transaction (the saga), and the order could now be happily shipped.

If the order service would want to track the state of the transaction, it would simply need to listen to all those events as well.

Of course, sometimes the order would be impossible to complete, and a rollback would need to happen. In this case, each step of the saga would need to be rolled back separately and carefully, as other transactions could run in parallel, for example, modifying the supply state. Such rollbacks are called **compensating transactions**.

This way of implementing the saga pattern is pretty straightforward, but if there any many dependencies between the involved services it might be better to use the *orchestration* approach. Speaking of which, let's now say a few words about this second approach to sagas.

Orchestration-based sagas

In this case, we'll need a message broker to handle communication between our services, and an orchestrator that would coordinate the saga. Our order service would send a request to the orchestrator, which would then send commands to both the supply and payment services. Each of those would then do their part and send replies back to the orchestrator, through a reply channel available at the broker.

In this scenario, the orchestrator has all the logic needed to, well, orchestrate the transaction, and the services themselves don't need to be aware of any other services taking part in the saga.

If the orchestrator is sent a message that one of the services failed, for example, if the credit card has expired, it would then need to start the rollback. In our case, it would again use the broker to send an appropriate rollback command to specific services.

Okay, that's enough about eventual consistency for now. Let's now switch to other topics related to availability.

Making your system fault tolerant and available

Availability and fault tolerance are software qualities that are at least somewhat important for every architecture. What's the point of creating a software system if the system can't be reached? In this section, we'll learn what exactly those terms mean and a few techniques to provide them in your solutions.

Calculating your system's availability

Availability is the percentage of the time that a system is up, functional, and reachable. Crashes, network failures, or extremely high load (for example, from a DDoS attack) that prevents the system from responding can all affect its availability.

Usually, it's a good idea to strive for as high a level of availability as possible. You may stumble upon the term *counting the nines*, as availability is often specified as 99% (two nines), 99.9% (three), and so on. Each additional nine is much harder to obtain, so be careful when making promises. Take a look at the following table to see how much downtime you could afford if you specified it on a monthly basis:

Downtime/month	Uptime
7 hours 18 minutes	99% ("two nines")
43 minutes 48 seconds	99.9% ("three nines")
4 minutes 22.8 seconds	99.99% ("four nines")
26.28 seconds	99.999% ("five nines")
2.628 seconds	99.9999% ("six nines")
262.8 ms	99.99999% ("seven nines")
26.28 ms	99.999999% ("eight nines")
2.628 ms	99.9999999% ("nine nines")

A common practice for cloud applications is to provide a **Service-Level Agreement (SLA)**, which specifies how much downtime can occur per a given period of time (for example, a year). An SLA for your cloud service will strongly depend on the SLAs of the cloud services you build upon.

To calculate a compound availability between two services that need to cooperate, you should just multiply their uptimes. This means if you have two services with 99.99% availability, their compound availability will be 99.99% * 99.99% = 99.98%. To calculate the availability of redundant services (such as two independent regions), you should multiply their unavailability. For instance, if two regions have 99.99% availability, their total unavailability will be (100% – 99.99%) * (100% – 99.99%) = 0.01% * 0.01% = 0.0001%, so their compound availability is 99.9999%.

Unfortunately, it's impossible to provide 100% availability. Failures do occur from time to time, so let's learn how to make your system tolerate them.

Building fault-tolerant systems

Fault tolerance is a system's ability to detect such failures and to handle them gracefully. It's essential that your cloud-based services are resilient, as due to the nature of the cloud, many different things can suddenly go south. Good fault tolerance can help your service's availability.

Different types of issues require different handling: from prevention, through detection, to minimizing the impact. Let's start with common ways to avoid having a single point of failure.

Redundancy

One of the most basic preventions is introducing **redundancy**. Similar to how you can have a spare tire for your car, you can have a backup service that takes over when your primary server goes down. This stepping-in is also known as **failover**.

How does the backup server know when to step in? One way to implement this is by using the heartbeat mechanism described in the *Detecting faults* section.

To make the switch faster, you can send all the messages that are going into the primary server also to the backup one. This is called a **hot standby**, as opposed to a cold one – initializing from zero. A good idea in such a case is to stay one message behind, so if a *poisoned* message kills the primary server, the backup one can simply reject it.

The preceding mechanism is called an **active-passive** (or **master-slave**) failover, as the backup server doesn't handle incoming traffic. If it did, we would have an **active-active** (or **master-master**) failover. For more on active-active architectures, refer to the last link in the *Further reading* section.

Be sure you don't lose any data when the failover happens. Using a message queue with backing storage may help with this.

Leader election

It's also important for both the servers to know which one is which – if both start behaving as primary instances, you'll likely be in trouble. Choosing the primary server is called the leader election pattern. There are a few ways to do so, for example, by introducing a third-party arbiter, by racing to take exclusive ownership of a shared resource, by choosing the instance with the lowest rank, or by using algorithms such as bully election or token ring election.

Leader election is also an essential part of the next related concept: achieving consensus.

Consensus

If you want your system to operate even when network partitions happen or some instances of your service experience faults, you need a way for your instances to reach consensus. They must agree what values to commit and often in what order. A simple approach is by allowing each instance to vote on the correct state. However, in some cases this is not enough to reach a consensus correctly or at all. Another approach would be to elect a leader and let it propagate its value. Because it's not easy to implement such algorithms by hand, we'd recommend using popular industry-proven consensus protocols such as Paxos and Raft. The latter is growing in popularity as it is simpler and easier to understand.

Let's now discuss another way to prevent your system from faulting.

Replication

This one is especially popular with databases, and it helps with scaling them, too. **Replication** means you will run a few instances of your service in parallel with duplicated data, all handling incoming traffic.

Don't confuse replication with sharding. The latter doesn't require any data redundancy, but can often bring you great performance at scale. If you're using Postgres, we recommend you try out Citus (`https://www.citusdata.com`).

In terms of databases, there are two ways you can replicate.

Master-slave replication

In this scenario, all the servers are able to perform read-only operations, but there's only one master server that can also write. The data is replicated from the master, through the slaves, either in a one-to-many topology or using a tree topology. If the master fails, the system can still operate in read-only mode until this fault is remediated.

Multi-master replication

You can also have a system with multiple master servers. If there are two servers, you have a *master-master replication* scheme. If one of the servers dies, the others can still operate normally. However, now you either need to synchronize the writes or provide looser consistency guarantees. Also, you need to provide a **load balancer**.

Examples of such replication include Microsoft's Active Directory, OpenLDAP, Apache's CouchDB, or Postgres-XL.

Let's now discuss two ways to prevent faults caused by too high a load.

Queue-based load leveling

This tactic is aimed at reducing the impact of sudden spikes in your system's load. Flooding a service with requests can cause performance issues, reliability ones, and even dropping valid requests. Once again, queues are there to save the day.

To implement this pattern, we just need to introduce a queue for the incoming requests to be added asynchronously. You can use Amazon's SQS, Azure's Service Bus, Apache Kafka, ZeroMQ, or other queues to achieve that.

Now, instead of having spikes in incoming requests, the load will get averaged. Our service can grab the requests from the said queue and process them without even knowing that the load was increased. Simple as that.

If your queue is performant and your tasks can be parallelized, a side benefit of this pattern would be better scalability.

Also, if your service isn't available, the requests will still get added into the queue for said service to process when it recovers, so this may be a way to help with bumping the availability.

If the requests come infrequently, consider implementing your service as a function that runs only when there are items in the queue to save costs.

Keep in mind that when using this pattern, the overall latency will increase by the addition of the queue. Apache Kafka and ZeroMQ should yield low latency, but if that's a deal-breaker, there's yet another way to deal with increased load.

Back pressure

If the load remains high, chances are you'll have more tasks than you're able to handle. This can cause cache misses and swapping if the requests will no longer fit into memory, as well as dropping requests and other nasty things. If you expect a heavy load, applying back pressure might be a great way to deal with it.

In essence, back pressure means that instead of putting more pressure on our service with each incoming request, we push back into the caller so it needs to handle the situation. There are a few different ways to do so.

For instance, we can block our thread that receives network packets. The caller will then see that it is unable to push the request to our service – instead, we push the pressure up the stream.

Another way is to recognize greater load and simply return an error code, for example, 503. You can model your architecture so that this is done for you by another service. One such service is the Envoy Proxy (`https://envoyproxy.io`), which can come in handy on many other occasions too.

Envoy can apply back pressure based on predefined quotas, so your service will actually never get overloaded. It can also measure the time it takes to process requests and apply back pressure only if it goes above a certain threshold. There are many other cases for which a variety of error codes will get returned. Hopefully, the caller has a plan on what to do if the pressure goes back on them.

Now that we know how to prevent faults, let's learn how to detect them once they occur.

Detecting faults

Proper and fast fault detection can save you a lot of trouble, and often money. There are many ways to detect faults tailored to different needs. Let's go over a selection of them.

Sidecar design pattern

Since we were discussing Envoy, it might be worth saying that it's an example of the **sidecar design pattern**. This pattern is useful in many more cases than just error prevention and detection, and Envoy is a great example of this.

In general, sidecars allow you to add a number of capabilities to your services without the need to write additional code. Similarly, as a physical sidecar can be attached to a motorcycle, a software sidecar can be attached to your service – in both cases extending the offered functionality.

How can a sidecar be helpful in detecting faults? First of all, by providing health checking capabilities. When it comes to passive health checking, Envoy can detect whether any instance in a service cluster has started behaving badly. This is called **outlier detection**. Envoy can look for consecutive 5XX error codes, gateway failures, and so on. Aside from detecting such faulty instances, it can eject them so the overall cluster remains healthy.

Envoy also offers active health checking, meaning it can probe the service itself instead of just observing its reactions to incoming traffic.

Throughout this chapter, we'll show a few other usages for the sidecar pattern in general, and Envoy in particular. Let's now discuss the next mechanism of fault detection.

Heartbeat mechanism

One of the most common ways of fault detection is through the **heartbeat mechanism**. A **heartbeat** is a signal or a message that is sent on regular intervals (usually a few seconds) between two services.

If a few consecutive heartbeats are missing, the receiving service can consider the sending service *dead*. In the case of our primary-backup service pair from a few sections previously, this can cause a failover to happen.

When implementing a heartbeat mechanism, be sure that it's reliable. False alarms can be troublesome, as the services may get confused, for example, about which one should be the new master. A good idea might be to provide a separate endpoint just for heartbeats, so it won't be as easily affected by the traffic on the regular endpoints.

Leaky bucket counter

Another way to detect faults is by adding a so-called **leaky bucket** counter. With each error, the counter would get incremented, and after a certain threshold is reached (the bucket is full), a fault would get signaled and handled. In regular time intervals, the counter would get decreased (hence, leaky bucket). This way, the situation would only be considered a fault if many errors occurred in a short time period.

This pattern can be useful if in your case it's normal to sometimes have errors, for instance, if you're dealing with networking.

Now that we know how to detect faults, let's learn what to do once they happen.

Minimizing the impact of faults

It takes time to detect an ongoing fault, and it takes even more of this precious resource to resolve it. This is why you should strive to minimize the impact of faults. Here are a few ways that can help.

Retrying the call

When your application calls another service, sometimes the call will fail. The simplest remedy for such a case is to just retry the call. If the fault was transient and you don't retry, that fault will likely get propagated through your system, making more damage than it should. Implementing an automated way to retry such calls can save you a lot of hassle.

Remember our sidecar proxy, Envoy? Turns out it can perform the automatic retries on your behalf, saving you from doing any changes to your sources.

For instance, see this example configuration of a retry policy that can be added to a route in Envoy:

```
retry_policy:
  retry_on: "5xx"
  num_retries: 3
  per_try_timeout: 2s
```

This will make Envoy retry calls if they return errors such as the 503 HTTP code or gRPC errors that map to 5XX codes. There will be three retries, each considered failed if not finished within 2 seconds.

Avoiding cascading failures

We mentioned that without retries the error will get propagated, causing a cascade of failures throughout the system. Let's now show more ways to prevent this from happening.

Circuit breaker

The **circuit breaker pattern** is a very useful tool for this. It allows us to quickly notice that a service is unable to process requests, so the calls to it can be short-circuited. This can happen both close to the callee (Envoy provides such a capability), or on the caller side (with the additional benefit of shaving off time from the calls). In Envoy's case, it can be as simple as adding the following to your config:

```
circuit_breakers:
  thresholds:
    - priority: DEFAULT
      max_connections: 1000
      max_requests: 1000
      max_pending_requests: 1000
```

In both cases, the load caused by the calls to the service may drop, which in some cases can help the service return to normal operation.

How do we implement a circuit breaker on the caller side? Once you've made a few calls, and, say, your leaky bucket overflows, you can just stop making new calls for a specified period of time (for example, until the bucket no longer overflows). Simple and effective.

Bulkhead

Another way to limit fault from spreading is taken straight from the stockyards. When building ships, you usually don't want the ship to get full of water if a hole breaks in the hull. To limit the damage of such holes, you would partition the hull into bulkheads, each of which would be easy to isolate. In this case, only the damaged bulkhead would get filled with water.

The same principle applies to limiting the fault impact in software architecture. You can partition your instances into groups, and you can assign the resources they use into groups as well. Setting quotas can also be considered an example of this pattern.

Separate bulkheads can be created for different groups of users, which can be useful if you need to prioritize them or provide a different level of service to your critical consumers.

Geodes

The last way we'll show is called **Geodes**. The name comes from geographical nodes. It can be used when your service is deployed in multiple regions.

If a fault occurs in one region, you can just redirect the traffic to other, unaffected regions. This will of course make the latency much higher than if you'd made calls to other nodes in the same data center, but usually redirecting less critical users to remote regions is a much better choice than just failing their calls entirely.

Now that you know how to provide availability and fault tolerance through your system's architecture, let's discuss how to integrate its components together.

Integrating your system

A distributed system is not just isolated instances of your applications running unaware of the existing world. They constantly communicate with each other and have to be properly integrated together to provide the most value.

Much was already said on the topic of integration, so in this section, we'll try to showcase just a handful of patterns for effective integration of both entirely new systems, as well as new parts of the system that needs to coexist with other existing parts, often legacy ones.

To not make this chapter be a whole book on its own, let's start this section with a recommendation of an existing one. If you're interested in integration patterns, especially focused on messaging, then Gregor Hohpe and Bobby Woolf's *Enterprise Integration Patterns* book is a must-read for you.

Let's take a brief look at two patterns covered by this book.

Pipes and filters pattern

The first integration pattern that we'll discuss is called **pipes and filters**. Its purpose is to decompose a big processing task into a series of smaller, independent ones (called **filters**), which you can then connect together (using pipes, such as message queues). This approach gives you scalability, performance, and reusability.

Assume you need to receive and process an incoming order. You can do it in one big module, so you don't need extra communication, but the different functions of such a module would be hard to test and it would be harder to scale them well.

Instead, you can split the order processing into separate steps, each handled by a distinct component: one for decoding, one for validating, another one for the actual processing of the order, and then yet another one for storing it somewhere. With this approach, you can now independently perform each of those steps, easily replace or disable them if needed, and reuse them for processing different types of input messages.

If you want to process multiple orders at the same time, you can also pipeline your processing: while one thread validates a message, another thread decodes the next one, and so on.

The downside is that you need to use synchronized queues as your pipes, which introduces some overhead.

To scale one step of your processing, you might want to use this pattern along with the next one on our list.

Competing consumers

The idea of competing consumers is simple: you have an input queue (or a messaging channel) and a few instances of consumers that fetch and process items from the queue concurrently. Each of the consumers can process the message, so they compete with each other to be the receiver.

This way, you get scalability, free load balancing, and resilience. With the addition of the queue, you now also have the **queue-based load leveling pattern** in place.

This pattern integrates effortlessly with priority queues if you need to shave latency from a request or just want a specific task submitted to your queue to be performed in a more urgent manner.

 This pattern can get tricky to use if the ordering is important. The order in which your consumers receive and finish to process messages may vary, so make sure that either this doesn't impact your system, or you find a way to reorder the results later on. If you need to process messages in sequence, you might not be able to use this pattern.

Let's now see a few more patterns, this time to help us integrate with existing systems.

Transitioning from legacy systems

Developing a system from scratch can be a blissful experience. Development instead of maintenance and a possibility to use a bleeding-edge technology stack – what's not to like? Unfortunately, that bliss often ends when integrating with an existing, legacy system starts. Fortunately, though, there are some ways to ease that pain.

Anti-corruption layer

Introducing an **anti-corruption layer** can help your solution in painless integration with a legacy system that has different semantics. This additional layer is responsible for communication between those two sides.

Such a component allows your solution to be designed with more flexibility – without the need to compromise your technology stack nor architectural decisions. To achieve that requires only a minimal set of changes in the legacy system (or none, if the legacy system doesn't need to make calls to the new system).

For instance, if your solution is based on microservices, the legacy system can just communicate with the anti-corruption layer instead of locating and reaching each microservice directly. Any translations (for example, due to outdated protocol versions) are also done in the additional layer.

Keep in mind that adding such a layer can introduce latency and has to satisfy quality attributes for your solution, for example, scalability.

Strangler pattern

The **strangler pattern** allows the gradual migration from a legacy system to a new one. While the anti-corruption layer we just looked at is useful for communication between the two systems, the strangler pattern is meant for providing services from both to the outside world.

Early in the migration process, the strangler facade will route most of the requests into the legacy system. During the migration, more and more calls can be forwarded into the new one, while *strangling* the legacy system more and more, limiting the functionality it offers. As the final step of the migration, the strangler, along with the legacy system, can be retired – the new system will now provide all the functionality:

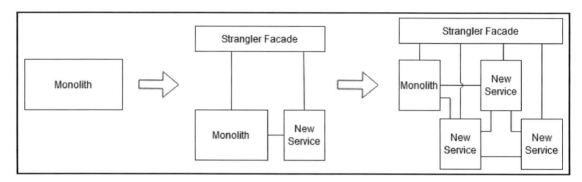

Figure 4.1 – The strangling of a monolith. After the migration, the strangler can still be used as an entry point, or adapter, for legacy requests

This pattern can be overkill for small systems and can get tricky if the datastore should be shared or is for event-sourced systems. When adding it to your solution, be sure to plan for achieving the proper performance and scalability.

Speaking of those two attributes, let's now discuss a few things that help achieve them.

Achieving performance at scale

When designing C++ applications, performance is usually a key factor. While using the language can go a long way in the scope of a single application, the proper high-level design is also essential to achieving optimal latency and throughput. Let's discuss a few crucial patterns and aspects.

CQRS and event sourcing

There are many ways to scale compute but scaling data access can be tricky. However, it's often necessary when your userbase grows. **Command-query responsibility segregation (CQRS)** is a pattern that can help here.

Command-query responsibility segregation

In traditional CRUD systems, both reads and writes are performed using the same data model and the data flows the same way. The titular segregation basically means to treat queries (reads) and commands (writes) in two separate ways.

Many applications have a strongly biased ratio of reads to writes – there's usually a lot more reading from the database than updating it in a typical app. This means making the reads as fast as possible can yield better performance: reads and writes can now be optimized and scaled separately. Other than that, introducing CQRS can help if many writes are competing with each other, or if a track of all the writes needs to be maintained, or if a set of your API users should have read-only access.

Having separate models for reads and writes can allow having different teams to work on both sides. The developers working on the read side of things don't need to have a deep understanding of the domain, which is required to perform updates properly. When they make a request, they get a **data transfer object** (**DTO**) from a thin read layer in just one simple call instead of going through the domain model.

If you're not aware of what a DTO is, think of returning item data from the database. If the caller asks for a list of items, you could provide them with an `ItemOverview` object containing just the names and thumbnails of items. On the other hand, if they want items for a specific store, you could also provide a `StoreItem` object containing a name, more pictures, a description, and a price. Both `ItemOverview` and `StoreItem` are DTOs, grabbing data from the same `Item` objects in the database.

The read layer can reside either on top of the data storage used for writes, or it can be a different data storage that gets updated via events as you can see in the following figure:

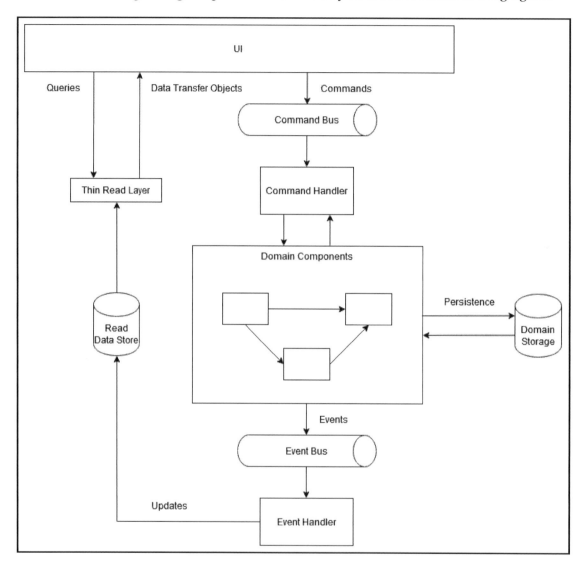

Figure 4.2 – CQRS with event sourcing

Using the approach pictured here, you can create as many different commands as you like, each having its own handler. Usually, the commands are asynchronous and don't return any values to the caller. Each handler uses domain objects and persists the changes done. After doing that, events are published, which event handlers can use to update the storage used by read operations. Continuing our last example, item data queries would grab information from a database updated by events such as `ItemAdded` or `ItemPriceChanged`, which could be triggered by commands such as `AddItem` or `ModifyItem`.

Using CQRS allows us to have different data models for read and write operations. For instance, you can create stored procedures and materialized views to speed up reads. Using different types of storage (SQL and NoSQL) for the read and domain stores can also be beneficial: one efficient way to persist data is to use an Apache Cassandra cluster while using Elasticsearch is a great way to search through the stored data quickly.

Aside from the preceding pros, CQRS also has its cons. Due to the complexity it introduces, it's usually not a good fit for small or less requiring architectures. It's often useful to apply it only to the parts of your system where it would bring the biggest benefits. You should also notice that updating the read store after the domain store means that now we have eventual consistency instead of strong consistency.

Command-query separation

CQRS is actually based on a simpler idea introduced long ago in the Eiffel programming language (the same one that introduced contracts). **Command-query separation (CQS)** is a principle that devises to separate API calls into, well, commands and queries – just like in CQRS, but regardless of the scale. It plays really well with objective programming and imperative programming in general.

If your function's name starts with a *has*, *is*, *can*, or a similar word, it should be just a query and not modify the underlying state or have any side effects. This brings two great benefits:

- **Much easier reasoning about the code**: It's clear that such functions are semantically just *reads*, never *writes*. This can make looking for a change of state much easier when debugging.
- **Reduce heisenbugs**: If you have ever had to debug an error that manifested in a release build, but not in the debug one (or the other way around), you have dealt with a heisenbug. It's rarely something pleasurable. Many such errors can be caused by assert calls that modify the state. Following CQS eliminates such bugs.

Similarly to asserts, if you want to have contracts (pre- and post-conditions), it's super important to only use queries in them. Otherwise disabling some contract checks could also lead to heisenbugs, not to mention how counterintuitive it would be.

Let's now say a few more words about event sourcing.

Event sourcing

As introduced in Chapter 2, *Architectural Styles*, event sourcing means that instead of always storing the whole state of your application, possibly dealing with conflicts during updates, you can just store the changes that happened to your application's state. Using event sourcing can boost your app's performance by eliminating concurrent updates and allowing all interested parties to perform gradual changes to their state. Saving the history of the operations done (for example, market transactions) can allow easier debugging (by replaying them later) and auditing. This also brings more flexibility and extensibility to the table. Some domain models can get much simpler when event sourcing is introduced.

One cost of event sourcing is being eventually consistent. Another one is slowing down the startup of your application – unless you make periodic snapshots of the state or can use the read-only store as in CQRS, discussed in the previous section.

Okay, enough of CQRS and related patterns. Let's now move on to another hot topic when it comes to performance (no pun intended): caching.

Caching

Proper usage of caches can yield better performance, lower latency, reduce the server load (and thus, costs of running in the cloud), and help with scalability concerns (fewer servers required) – what's not to like?

 If you're here for tips on CPU caches, you can find them in Chapter 11, *Performance*.

Caching is a big topic, so we'll only cover a few aspects of it here.

Caching works by simply storing the data that is read most often in non-persistent storage with fast access times. There are many different types of caches:

- **Client-side caches**: For storing data specifically for a given customer, often placed on the client's machine or browser.
- **Web server caches**: For speeding up reading from web pages, for instance, through HTTP accelerators such as Varnish that can cache the web server responses.
- **Database caches**: Many database engines have built-in, tunable caching.
- **Application caches**: For speeding up your application, which can now read data from a cache instead of reaching out to its database.
- **CDNs can be treated as caches too**: For serving content from a location close to the user in order to reduce latency.

Some types of caches can be replicated or deployed in clusters to provide performance at scale. An alternative can also be to shard them: similarly to as you would shard databases, you can use different instances of your caches for distinct parts of your data.

Let's now go through the different approaches to updating the data in the cache. After all, no one likes to be served stale data.

Updating caches

There are a few approaches to keeping the cached data fresh. Whether it's you who decided how to update cached items or another company, it's worth knowing them. In this section, we'll discuss their pros and cons.

Write-through approach

If you require strong consistency, synchronously updating both the database and the cache is the valid approach for you. This approach protects you from data loss: if data became visible to a user, it means it is already written to the database. A downside of write-through caches is that the latency to perform the update is bigger than in other approaches.

Write-behind approach

An alternative approach, also known as **write-back**, is to provide the user with just access to the cache. When the user performs an update, the cache will then queue the incoming update, which will then be asynchronously executed, thus updating the database. The obvious downside here is that if something goes wrong, the data can never be written. It's also not as easy to implement as the other approaches. The upside, however, is the lowest latency as seen by the user.

Cache-aside

This last approach, also called **lazy loading,** is about filling the cache on-demand. In this case, data access looks as follows:

1. A call to the cache is made to check whether the value is already there. If so, just return it.
2. Reach the main data store or service that provides the value.
3. Store the value in the cache and return it to the user.

This type of caching is often done using Memcached or Redis. It can be really fast and efficient – the cache only contains data that was requested.

However, if data that is not in the cache is often requested, the preceding three calls can increase the latency noticeably. To mitigate this for cache restarts, the cache can be primed (initialized) with selected data from the persistent store.

The items in the cache can also become stale, so it's best to set a time-to-live for each entry. If the data is to be updated, it can happen in a write-through manner by removing the record from the cache and updating it in the database. Take care when using multi-level caches with just a time-based update policy (for instance, as in DNS caches). This may lead to using stale data for long periods of time.

We've discussed the types of caches and strategies to update them, so that's enough about caches for now. Let's move on to a different aspect of providing scalable architectures.

Deploying your system

Even though deploying services sounds easy, there's a lot of things to think about if you take a closer look. This section will describe how to perform efficient deployments, configure your services after installing them, check that they stay healthy after being deployed, and how to do it all while minimizing downtime.

The sidecar pattern

Remember Envoy from earlier in this chapter? It's a very useful tool for efficient application development. Instead of embedding infrastructure services such as logging, monitoring, or networking into your application, you can deploy the Envoy proxy along with your app, just like a sidecar would be *deployed* next to a motorbike. Together, they can do much more than the app without the sidekick (another name for this pattern).

Using a sidecar can speed up development, as many of the functionality it brings would need to be developed independently by each of your microservices. Because it's separate from your application, a sidecar can be developed using any programming language you find best for the job. The sidecar, along with all the functionality it provides, can be maintained by an independent team of developers and updated independently from your main service.

Because sidecars reside right next to the app they enhance, they can use local means of inter-process communication. Usually, it's fast enough and much faster than communicating from another host, but remember that it can sometimes be too big a burden.

Even if you deploy a third-party service, deploying your selected sidecar next to it can still provide value: you can monitor the resource usage and the condition of both the host and the service, as well as tracing requests throughout your distributed system. Sometimes it's also possible to reconfigure the service dynamically based on its condition, via editing the config file or a web interface.

Deploying a service with tracing and a reverse proxy using Envoy

Let's now use Envoy as a front proxy for our deployment. Start by creating Envoy's configuration file, in our case named `envoy-front_proxy.yaml`, with the address of our proxy:

```
static_resources:
  listeners:
  - address:
      socket_address:
        address: 0.0.0.0
        port_value: 8080
    traffic_direction: INBOUND
```

We've specified that Envoy is going to listen for incoming traffic on port 8080. Later in the config, we'll route it to our service. Now, let's specify that we'd like to handle HTTP requests using our set of service instances and adding some tracing capabilities on top. First, let's add an HTTP endpoint:

```
filter_chains:
  - filters:
      - name: envoy.filters.network.http_connection_manager
        typed_config:
          "@type":
type.googleapis.com/envoy.extensions.filters.network.http_connection_manage
r.v3.HttpConnectionManager
```

Now, let's specify that requests should have IDs assigned and be traced by a distributed tracing system, Jaeger:

```
generate_request_id: true
tracing:
  provider:
    name: envoy.tracers.dynamic_ot
    typed_config:
      "@type":
type.googleapis.com/envoy.config.trace.v3.DynamicOtConfig
        library: /usr/local/lib/libjaegertracing_plugin.so
        config:
          service_name: front_proxy
          sampler:
            type: const
            param: 1
          reporter:
            localAgentHostPort: jaeger:6831
          headers:
            jaegerDebugHeader: jaeger-debug-id
            jaegerBaggageHeader: jaeger-baggage
            traceBaggageHeaderPrefix: uberctx-
          baggage_restrictions:
            denyBaggageOnInitializationFailure: false
            hostPort: ""
```

We'll create IDs for requests and use the OpenTracing standard (DynamicOtConfig) with the native Jaeger plugin. The plugin will report to a Jaeger instance running under the specified address and add the specified headers.

We also need to specify that all traffic (see the `match` section) from all domains shall be routed into our service cluster:

```
codec_type: auto
stat_prefix: ingress_http
route_config:
  name: example_route
  virtual_hosts:
    - name: front_proxy
      domains:
        - "*"
      routes:
        - match:
            prefix: "/"
          route:
            cluster: example_service
          decorator:
            operation: example_operation
```

We'll define our `example_service` cluster in a second. Note that each request coming to the cluster will be marked by a predefined operation decorator. We also need to specify what router address to use:

```
http_filters:
- name: envoy.filters.http.router
  typed_config: {}
use_remote_address: true
```

Now we know how to handle and trace the requests, so what's left is to define the clusters we used. Let's start with our service's cluster:

```
clusters:
  - name: example_service
    connect_timeout: 0.250s
    type: strict_dns
    lb_policy: round_robin
    load_assignment:
      cluster_name: example_service
      endpoints:
        - lb_endpoints:
            - endpoint:
                address:
                  socket_address:
                    address: example_service
                    port_value: 5678
```

Each cluster can have multiple instances (endpoints) of our service. Here, if we decide to add more endpoints, the incoming requests will be load-balanced using the round-robin strategy.

Let's also add an admin interface:

```
admin:
  access_log_path: /tmp/admin_access.log
  address:
    socket_address:
      address: 0.0.0.0
      port_value: 9901
```

Let's now place the config inside a container that will run Envoy using a Dockerfile, which we named `Dockerfile-front_proxy`:

```
FROM envoyproxy/envoy:v1.17-latest

RUN apt-get update && \
    apt-get install -y curl && \
    rm -rf /var/lib/apt/lists/*
RUN curl -Lo -
https://github.com/tetratelabs/getenvoy-package/files/3518103/getenvoy-cent
os-jaegertracing-plugin.tar.gz | tar -xz && mv libjaegertracing.so.0.4.2
/usr/local/lib/libjaegertracing_plugin.so

COPY envoy-front_proxy.yaml /etc/envoy/envoy.yaml
```

We also downloaded the Jaeger native plugin that we used in our Envoy config.

Now let's specify how to run our code in several containers using Docker Compose. Create a `docker-compose.yaml` file, starting with the front proxy service definition:

```
version: "3.7"

services:
  front_proxy:
    build:
      context: .
      dockerfile: Dockerfile-front_proxy
    networks:
      - example_network
    ports:
      - 12345:12345
      - 9901:9901
```

We use our Dockerfile here, a simple network, and we expose two ports from the container on the host: our service and the admin interface. Let's now add the service our proxy will direct to:

```
example_service:
  image: hashicorp/http-echo
  networks:
    - example_network
  command: -text "It works!"
```

In our case, the service will just display a predefined string in a simple web server.

Now, let's run Jaeger in another container, exposing its port to the outside world:

```
jaeger:
  image: jaegertracing/all-in-one
  environment:
    - COLLECTOR_ZIPKIN_HTTP_PORT=9411
  networks:
    - example_network
  ports:
    - 16686:16686
```

The last step will be to define our network:

```
networks:
  example_network: {}
```

And we're done. You can now run the service using `docker-compose up --build` and point your browser to the endpoints we specified.

Using a sidecar proxy has one more benefit: even if your service will die, the sidecar is usually still alive and can respond to external requests while the main service is down. The same applies when your service is redeployed, for example, because of an update. Speaking of which, let's learn how to minimize the related downtime.

Zero-downtime deployments

There are two common ways to minimize the risk of downtime during deployments: **blue-green deployments** and **canary releases**. You can use the Envoy sidecar when introducing any of those two.

Blue-green deployments

Blue-green deployments can help you minimize both the downtime and the risk related to deploying your app. To do so, you'll need two identical production environments, called *blue* and *green*. While green serves the customers, you can perform the update in the blue one. Once the update was made, the services were tested, and all looks stable, you can switch the traffic so it now flows to the updated (blue) environment.

If any issues are spotted in the blue environment after the switch, the green one is still there – you can just switch them back. The users probably won't even notice any changes, and because both the environments are up and running, no downtime should be visible during the switch. Just make sure you won't lose any data during the switch (for example, transactions made in the new environment).

Canary releases

The simplest way to not have all your service instances fail after an update is often, well, not updating all of them at once. That's the key idea behind the incremental variant of blue-green deployments, also called a **canary release**.

In Envoy, you could put the following in the `routes` section of your config:

```
- match:
    prefix: "/"
  route:
    weighted_clusters:
      clusters:
      - name: new_version
        weight: 5
      - name: old_version
        weight: 95
```

You should also remember to define the two clusters from the preceding snippet, the first one with the old version of your service:

```
clusters:
  - name: old_version
    connect_timeout: 0.250s
    type: strict_dns
    lb_policy: round_robin
    load_assignment:
      cluster_name: old_version
      endpoints:
        - lb_endpoints:
            - endpoint:
```

```
        address:
          socket_address:
            address: old_version
            port_value: 5678
```

The second cluster will run the new version:

```
  - name: new_version
    connect_timeout: 0.250s
    type: strict_dns
    lb_policy: round_robin
    load_assignment:
      cluster_name: new_version
      endpoints:
        - lb_endpoints:
            - endpoint:
                address:
                  socket_address:
                    address: new_version
                    port_value: 5678
```

When an update gets deployed, the new version of a service will only be seen and used by a small fraction (here: 5%) of your users. If the updated instances remain stable and no checks and verifications fail, you can gradually update more and more hosts in several steps, until all of them are switched to a new version. You can do it either by updating the config files by hand or by using the admin endpoint. Voila!

Let's now move on to the last deployment pattern that we'll cover here.

External configuration store

If you're deploying a simple application, it can be okay to just deploy its configuration along with it. However, when you want to have a more complex deployment with many application instances, it can quickly become a burden to redeploy a new version of the app just to reconfigure it. At the same time, manual configuration changes are a no-go if you want to treat your services like cattle, not pets. Introducing an external configuration store can be an elegant way to overcome such hurdles.

In essence, your apps can grab their configuration from said store instead of just relying on their local config files. This allows you to provide common settings for multiple instances and tune parameters for some of them, while having an easy and centralized way to monitor all your configs. If you want an arbiter to decide which nodes will be master nodes and which will serve as backup ones, an external config store can provide the instances with such information. It's also useful to implement a configuration update procedure so that your instances can be easily reconfigured during operation. You can use ready solutions such as Firebase Remote Config, leverage the Java-based Netflix Archaius, or write a configuration store on your own leveraging cloud storage and change notifications.

Now that we've learned some useful deployment patterns, let's move to another important topic when it comes to high-level design: APIs.

Managing your APIs

Proper APIs are essential for the success of your development team and product. We can divide this topic into two smaller ones: system-level APIs and component-level APIs. In this section, we'll discuss handling APIs on the first of those levels, while the next chapter will present you with tips on the second.

Aside from managing objects, you'll also want to manage your whole API. If you want to introduce policies regarding API usage, control access to said API, gather performance metrics and other analytical data, or just charge your customers based on their use of your interfaces, **API management (APIM)** is the solution you're looking for.

Typically a set of APIM tools consists of these components:

- **An API gateway**: A single entry point for all users of an API. More on this in the next section.
- **Reporting and analytics**: To monitor the performance and latency of your APIs, resources consumed, or data sent. Such tools can be leveraged to detect trends in usage, know which parts of the API and which components behind them are performance bottlenecks, or what SLAs are reasonable to offer and how to improve them.
- **A portal for developers**: To help them get up to speed with your API quickly, and to subscribe to your APIs at all.
- **A portal for administrators**: To manage policies, users, and package APIs into sellable products.
- **Monetization**: To charge your customers based on how they use your APIs and to aid related business processes.

APIM tools are provided both by cloud providers and independent parties, for example, NGINX's Controller or Tyk.

When designing APIs for a given cloud, get to know the good practices the cloud provider usually documents. For instance, you can find common design patterns for Google Cloud Platform in the *Further reading* section. In their case, lots of the practices revolve around using Protobufs.

Choosing the right way to consume APIs can take you a long way. The most simple way to file requests to your servers is by connecting to the services directly. While easy to set up and okay for small apps, it can lead to performance issues down the road. An API consumer will likely need to call a few different services, leading to high latency. Proper scalability is also impossible to achieve using this approach.

A better approach is to use an API gateway. Such gateways are often an essential part of an APIM solution, but can also be used on their own.

API gateways

An API gateway is an entry point for clients who want to use your API. It can then route the incoming requests into a specific instance or cluster of services. This can simplify your client code, as it no longer needs to know all the backend nodes, or how they cooperate with each other. All a client needs to know is the address of an API gateway — the gateway will handle the rest. Thanks to hiding the backend architecture from the client, it can be easily remodeled without even touching the client's code.

The gateway can aggregate multiple parts of your system's API into one, and then use **layer-7 routing** (for example, based on the URL) to a proper part of your system. Layer-7 routing is offered by both cloud providers themselves, as well as tools such as Envoy.

As with many patterns described in this chapter, always consider whether it's worth it to add more complexity by introducing another pattern to your architecture. Think about how adding it will affect your availability, fault tolerance, and performance if they matter to you. After all, a gateway usually is just a single node, so try to not make it a bottleneck or a single point of failure.

The Backends for Frontends pattern we mentioned a few chapters earlier can be thought of as a variant of the API gateway pattern. In the Backends for Frontends case, each frontend connects to its own gateway.

Now that you know how system design relates to API design, let's summarize what we've discussed in the last sections.

Summary

In this chapter, we've learned quite a lot of stuff. You now know when to apply which service model and how to avoid the common pitfalls of designing distributed systems. You've learned about the CAP theorem and what practical outcomes it has for distributed architectures. You can now run transactions in such systems successfully, reduce their downtime, prevent issues, and gracefully recover from errors. Dealing with unusually high load is no longer black magic. Integrating parts of your system, even legacy ones, with your newly designed parts is also something you're able to perform. You now also have some tricks up your sleeve to increase the performance and scalability of your system. Deploying and load balancing your system are also demystified, so you can now perform them efficiently. Last but not least, discovering services and designing and managing their APIs are all things that you have now learned to perform. Nice!

In the next chapter, we'll learn how you can use specific C++ features to travel on the road to excellent architecture in a more pleasant and efficient way.

Questions

1. What is event sourcing?
2. What are the practical consequences of the CAP theorem?
3. What can you use Netflix's Chaos Monkey for?
4. Where can caching be applied?
5. How do you prevent your app from going down when a whole data center does?
6. Why use an API Gateway?
7. How can Envoy help you to achieve various architectural goals?

Further reading

- Microsoft Azure cloud design patterns: `https://docs.microsoft.com/en-us/azure/architecture/patterns/`
- Common design patterns for cloud APIs by Google: `https://cloud.google.com/apis/design/design_patterns`
- Microsoft REST API guidelines: `https://github.com/microsoft/api-guidelines/blob/vNext/Guidelines.md`
- Envoy Proxy's *Getting Started* page: `https://www.envoyproxy.io/docs/envoy/latest/start/start`
- Active-active application architectures with MongoDB: `https://developer.mongodb.com/article/active-active-application-architectures`

5
Leveraging C++ Language Features

The C++ language is a unique beast. It's used in a plethora of cases, varying from creating firmware and operating systems, desktop and mobile applications, to server software, frameworks, and services. C++ code runs on all kinds of hardware, is massively deployed on compute clouds, and can even be found in outer space. Such success wouldn't have been possible without the broad set of features this multi-paradigm language has.

This chapter describes how to leverage what the C++ language offers so that we can achieve safe and performant solutions. We will demonstrate the best industry practices for type safety, avoiding memory issues, and creating efficient code in an equally efficient manner. We will also teach you how to use certain language features when designing APIs.

In this chapter, we'll cover the following topics:

- Managing resources and avoiding leaks
- Moving computations from runtime to compile time
- Leveraging the power of safe types
- Creating easy to read and performant code
- Dividing code into modules

During this journey, you'll learn about the features and techniques that are available in various standards of C++, ranging from C++98 all the way to C++20. This will include declarative programming, RAII, `constexpr`, templates, concepts, and modules. Without further ado, let's begin this journey.

Technical requirements

You will need the following tools to build the code in this chapter:

- A compiler that supports C++20 (GCC 11+ is recommended)
- CMake 3.15+

The source code for this chapter can be found at `https://github.com/PacktPublishing/Software-Architecture-with-Cpp/tree/master/Chapter05`.

Designing great APIs

Although C++ allows you to use the well-known object-oriented APIs that you may be familiar with if you write code in so-called coffee-based languages, it has some other tricks up its sleeves. We'll mention a few of them in this section.

Leveraging RAII

What's the main difference between a C API and a C++ one? Usually, it's not about polymorphism or having classes per se, but about an idiom called RAII.

RAII stands for **Resource Acquisition Is Initialization**, but it's actually more about releasing resources than acquiring them. Let's take a look at a similar API written in C and C++ to show this feature in action:

```
struct Resource;

// C API
Resource* acquireResource();
void releaseResource(Resource *resource);

// C++ API
using ResourceRaii = std::unique_ptr<Resource, decltype(&releaseResource)>;
ResourceRaii acquireResourceRaii();
```

The C++ API is based on the C one, but this doesn't always need to be the case. What's important here is that in the C++ API, there's no need for a separate function to free our precious resource. Thanks to the RAII idiom, it's done automatically once a `ResourceRaii` object goes out of scope. This takes the burden of manual resource management away from the user, and the best part is that it comes at no extra cost.

What's more, we didn't need to write any class of our own – we just reused the standard library's `unique_ptr`, which is a lightweight pointer. It ensures that the object it manages will always be freed, and it will always be freed exactly once.

Since we're managing some special kinds of resources and not memory, we had to use a custom deleter type. Our `acquireResourceRaii` function would need to pass the actual pointer to the `releaseResource` function. The C API itself doesn't need to be exposed to the user if you only want to consume it from C++.

An important thing to note here is that RAII is not just for managing memory: you can use it to easily handle ownership of any resource, such as locks, file handles, database connections, and anything else that should be released once its RAII wrappers go out of scope.

Specifying the interfaces of containers in C++

Implementations of the standard library are great places to search for idiomatic and performant C++ code. For instance, if you want to read some really interesting template code, you should give `std::chrono` a shot, as it demonstrates some useful techniques and has a fresh approach to this. A link to libstdc++'s implementation can be found in the *Further reading* section.

When it comes to other places of the library, even a quick peek at its containers shows that their interfaces tend to differ from their counterparts in other programming languages. To show this, let's take a look at a pretty straightforward class from the standard library, `std::array`, and analyze it bit by bit:

```
template <class T, size_t N>
struct array {
 // types:
 typedef T& reference;
 typedef const T& const_reference;
 typedef /*implementation-defined*/ iterator;
 typedef /*implementation-defined*/ const_iterator;
 typedef size_t size_type;
 typedef ptrdiff_t difference_type;
 typedef T value_type;
 typedef T* pointer;
 typedef const T* const_pointer;
 typedef reverse_iterator<iterator> reverse_iterator;
 typedef reverse_iterator<const_iterator> const_reverse_iterator;
```

The first thing you can see when you start reading the class definition is that it creates aliases for some types. This is common across the standard containers, and the names of those aliases are the same in many of them. This happens for a few reasons. One of them is the rule of least surprise – having it this way reduces the time developers spend scratching their heads and trying to understand what you meant and how a specific alias was named. Another reason is that the users of your class and library writers will often depend on such type traits when they're writing their own code. If your container won't provide such aliases, it will make using it with some standard utilities or type traits harder, so the users of your APIs will have to work around this or even use a completely different class.

Having such type aliases can be useful even if you're not using them in your templates. It's not uncommon to rely on those types for function parameters and class member fields, so always remember to provide them if you're writing a class that other people could use. For instance, if you're writing an allocator, many of its consumers will rely on specific type aliases being present.

Let's see what the array class will bring us:

```
// no explicit construct/copy/destroy for aggregate type
```

So, the next interesting thing about `std::array` is that it has no definition of a constructor, including copy/move constructors; assign operators; or destructors. It's simply because having those wouldn't add any value. Often, adding such members when it's not necessary is actually harmful to performance. With a non-defaulted constructor (and `T() {}` is already non-defaulted, as opposed to `T() = default;`), your class is no longer trivial nor trivially constructible, which prevents the compiler from making optimizations to it.

Let's see what other declarations our class has:

```
constexpr void fill(const T& u);
constexpr void swap(array<T, N>&) noexcept(is_nothrow_swappable_v<T&>);
```

Now, we can see two member functions, including a member swap. Often, it's profitable to not rely on the default behavior of `std::swap` and to provide our own. For instance, in the case of `std::vector`, the underlying storage is swapped as a whole instead of each element being swapped. When you're writing a member swap function, be sure to also introduce a free function named `swap` so that it can be detected via **argument-dependent lookup (ADL)**. It could just call your member's `swap` function.

One more thing regarding the swap function that's worth mentioning is that it's conditionally `noexcept`. If the stored type can be swapped without throwing exceptions, the array's swap will be `noexcept` as well. Having a non-throwing swap can help you achieve strong exception safety guarantees in copy operations for classes that are storing our type as a member.

As shown in the following code block, now comes a big set of functions that show us another important aspect of many classes – their iterators:

```
// iterators:
constexpr iterator begin() noexcept;
constexpr const_iterator begin() const noexcept;
constexpr iterator end() noexcept;
constexpr const_iterator end() const noexcept;

constexpr reverse_iterator rbegin() noexcept;
constexpr const_reverse_iterator rbegin() const noexcept;
constexpr reverse_iterator rend() noexcept;
constexpr const_reverse_iterator rend() const noexcept;

constexpr const_iterator cbegin() const noexcept;
constexpr const_iterator cend() const noexcept;
constexpr const_reverse_iterator crbegin() const noexcept;
constexpr const_reverse_iterator crend() const noexcept;
```

Iterators are vital for every container. If you don't provide iterator access for your class, you won't be able to use it in range-based for loops and it won't be compatible with all the useful algorithms from the standard library. This doesn't mean that you need to write your own iterator types – you could just use a simple pointer if your storage is contiguous. Providing `const` iterators can help you use your class in an immutable manner, and providing reverse iterators can help with enabling more use cases for your container.

Let's see what comes next:

```
// capacity:
constexpr size_type size() const noexcept;
constexpr size_type max_size() const noexcept;
constexpr bool empty() const noexcept;

// element access:
constexpr reference operator[](size_type n);
constexpr const_reference operator[](size_type n) const;
constexpr const_reference at(size_type n) const;
constexpr reference at(size_type n);
constexpr reference front();
constexpr const_reference front() const;
```

```
constexpr reference back();
constexpr const_reference back() const;

constexpr T * data() noexcept;
constexpr const T * data() const noexcept;
private:
// the actual storage, like T elements[N];
};
```

Following the iterators, we have a few ways to inspect and modify the container's data. In the case of `array`, all of them are `constexpr`. This means that if we were to write some compile-time code, we could use our array class. We'll look at this in more detail later in this chapter, in the *Moving computations at compile time* section.

Finally, we made it through the whole definition of our `array`. Its interface doesn't end there, however. Starting with C++17, after a type definition, you can spot lines similar to the following:

```
template<class T, class... U>
  array(T, U...) -> array<T, 1 + sizeof...(U)>;
```

Such statements are called **deduction guides**. They're part of a feature called **Class Template Argument Deduction (CTAD)**, which was introduced in C++17. It allows you to omit the template parameters when you're declaring a variable. It's handy for `array` because now, you can just write the following:

```
auto ints = std::array{1, 2, 3};
```

However, it could be even handier for more complex types, such as maps, as follows:

```
auto legCount = std::unordered_map{ std::pair{"cat", 4}, {"human", 2},
{"mushroom", 1} };
```

There is, however, a catch here: we needed to specify that we're passing the key-value pair when we passed the first argument (note that we also used a deduction guide for it).

Since we're on the topic of interfaces, let's point to some other aspects of them.

Using pointers in interfaces

The types that you use in your interfaces matter a lot. Even if there's documentation, a good API should still be intuitive at a glance. Let's see how different approaches to passing resource parameters to a function can suggest different things to the API consumer.

Consider the following function declarations:

```
void A(Resource*);
void B(Resource&);
void C(std::unique_ptr<Resource>);
void D(std::unique_ptr<Resource>&);
void E(std::shared_ptr<Resource>);
void F(std::shared_ptr<Resource>&);
```

When should you use which of those functions?

Since smart pointers are now the standard way to deal with resources, A and B should be left for simple parameter passing and shouldn't be used if you don't do anything with the ownership of the passed objects. A should only be used for a single resource. For example, if you want to pass multiple instances, you could use a container, such as `std::span`. If you know the object you want to pass is not null, it's best to pass it by using a reference, such as a const reference. You can also consider passing by value if the object is not too big.

A good rule of thumb regarding functions C to F is that you should only pass smart pointers as arguments if you want to manipulate the pointers themselves; for example, for transferring ownership.

The C function takes a `unique_ptr` by value. This means it's a resource sink. In other words, it consumes and then frees the resource. Note that just by selecting a specific type, the interface expresses its intent clearly.

The D function should only be used if you want to pass in a `unique_ptr` containing one resource and receive another resource in the same `unique_ptr` as an out parameter. It's not a good idea to have such a function for simply passing a resource since it requires that the caller stores it specifically in a `unique_ptr`. In other words, if you think about passing a `const unique_ptr<Resource>&`, just pass a `Resource*` (or `Resource&`) instead.

The E function is meant for sharing resource ownership with the callee. Passing a `shared_ptr` by value can be relatively costly, as it is required to increment its reference counters. However, in this case, passing `shared_ptr` by value is okay, since a copy must be made somewhere if the callee really wants to become a shared owner.

The F function is similar to D and should only be used when you want to manipulate the `shared_ptr` instance and propagate the change through this in/out parameter. If you're unsure if the function should take ownership or not, consider passing a `const shared_ptr&`.

Specifying preconditions and postconditions

It's not uncommon for a function to have some requirements regarding its parameters. Each requirement should be stated as a precondition. If a function guarantees that its result has some properties – for example, it is non-negative – the function should make that clear as well. Some developers resort to placing comments to inform others about this, but it doesn't really enforce the requirement in any way. Placing if statements is better, but hides the reason for the check. Currently, the C++ standard still doesn't offer a way to deal with this (contracts were first voted into the C++20 standard, just to be removed later on). Fortunately, libraries such as Microsoft's **Guideline Support Library** (GSL) provide their own checks.

Let's assume that, for whatever reason, we're writing our own queue implementation. The push member function could look like this:

```
template<typename T>
T& Queue::push(T&& val) {
 gsl::Expects(!this->full());
 // push the element
 gsl::Ensures(!this->empty());
}
```

Note that the user doesn't even need access to the implementation to be sure that some checks are in place. The code is also self-documenting as it's clear what the function requires and what the result will be.

Leveraging inline namespaces

In systems programming, oftentimes, you're not always just writing code against an API; often, you need to care about ABI compatibility as well. A famous ABI break happened when GCC released its fifth version, with one of the major changes being the change of the class layout of std::string. This meant that libraries working with older GCC versions (or still using the new ABI in newer versions, which is still a thing in recent GCC releases) would not work with code written using a later ABI. In the case of an ABI break, if you receive a linker error, you can consider yourself lucky. In some cases, such as mixing NDEBUG code with debug code, you'll likely get memory corruption if a class only has members available in one such configuration' for instance, special members being added for better debugging.

Some memory corruptions, which are often hard to debug, can easily be turned into linker errors with the use of C++11's inline namespaces. Consider the following code:

```
#ifdef NDEBUG
inline namespace release {
#else
inline namespace debug {
#endif

struct EasilyDebuggable {
// ...
#ifndef NDEBUG
// fields helping with debugging
#endif
};

} // end namespace
```

Because the preceding code uses inline namespaces, the users won't see a difference between the two build types when you're declaring objects of this class: all declarations from an inline namespace are visible in the surrounding scope. The linker, however, will end up with different symbol names, which will cause the linker to fail if it tries to link incompatible libraries, giving us the ABI safety we're looking for and a nice error message mentioning the inline namespace.

For more tips on providing safe and elegant ABIs, please see *Arvid Norberg's The ABI Challenge* talk from *C++Now* 2019, which is linked in the *Further reading* section.

Leveraging std::optional

Going back from ABIs to APIs, let's mention one more type that we omitted when we were designing great APIs earlier in this book. The hero of this section can save the day when it comes to optional parameters for functions as it can help your types have components that may or may not hold value, and it can also be used for designing clean interfaces or as a replacement for pointers. This hero is called std::optional and was standardized in C++17. If you can't use C++17, you can still find it in Abseil (absl::optional), or find a very similar version from Boost (boost::optional). A big plus of using those classes is that they express the intent very clearly, which helps with writing clean and self-documenting interfaces. Let's see it in action.

Optional function parameters

We'll start by passing arguments to functions that can, but may not, hold value. Have you ever stumbled upon a function signature similar to the following?

```
void calculate(int param); // If param equals -1 it means "no value"

void calculate(int param = -1);
```

Sometimes, it's just too easy to pass a -1 by mistake when you didn't want to if `param` was calculated somewhere else in code – perhaps where it was even a valid value. How about the following signature?

```
void calculate(std::optional<int> param);
```

This time, it's much clearer what to do if you don't want to pass a `value`: just pass an empty optional. The intent is clear, and -1 can still be used as a valid value instead of you having to give it any special meaning in a type-unsafe manner.

That's just one usage of our optional template. Let's see some others.

Optional function return values

Just like with accepting special values to signify the *no value* of a parameter, a function can sometimes return *no value*. Which of the following would you prefer?

```
int try_parse(std::string_view maybe_number);
bool try_parse(std::string_view maybe_number, int &parsed_number);
int *try_parse(std::string_view maybe_number);
std::optional<int> try_parse(std::string_view maybe_number);
```

How can you tell what value the first function will return in case of errors? Or will it throw an exception instead of returning a magic value? Moving on to the second signature, it looks like `false` will be returned if there is an error, but it's still easy to just forget to check it and read `parsed_number` directly, potentially causing trouble. In the third case, while it's relatively safe to assume a `nullptr` will be returned on errors and an integer in case of success, it's now unclear if the returned `int` should be freed.

With the last signature, it's clear by just looking at it that an empty value will be returned in case of errors and that there's nothing else that needs to be done. It's simple, understandable, and elegant.

Optional return values can also be used to just mark a *no value* being returned, not necessarily that an error had occurred. Having said that, let's move on to our last use case for optionals.

Optional class members

Achieving coherence in a class state is not always an easy task. For instance, sometimes, you want to have a member or two that can simply not be set. Instead of creating another class for such a case (which increases code complexity) or reserving a special value (which is easy to pass unnoticed), you can use an optional class member. Consider the following type:

```
struct UserProfile {
  std::string nickname;
  std::optional <std::string> full_name;
  std::optional <std::string> address;
  std::optional <PhoneNumber> phone;
};
```

Here, we can see which fields are necessary and which ones don't need to be filled. The same data could be stored using empty strings, but this wouldn't be clearly visible just from the struct's definition. Another alternative would be to use `std::unique_ptr's`, but then we would lose data locality, which is often essential for performance. For such cases, `std::optional` can be of great value. It should definitely be a part of your toolbox when you want to design clean and intuitive APIs.

This knowledge can help you provide high-quality and intuitive APIs. There's one more thing you can do to improve them further that will also help you write less buggy code by default. We will discuss this in the next section.

Writing declarative code

Are you familiar with imperative versus declarative coding styles? The former is when your code tells the machine *how* to achieve what you want step by step. The latter is when you tell the machine just *what* you want to achieve. Certain programming languages favor one over the other. For instance, C is imperative, while SQL is declarative, just like many functional languages. Some languages allow you to mix the styles – think of LINQ in C#.

C++ is a flexible beast that allows you to write code in both ways. Is there one you should prefer? It turns out that when you're writing declarative code, usually a higher level of abstraction is kept, which leads to fewer bugs and easier-to-spot errors. So, how can we write C++ declaratively? There are two main tactics to apply.

The first one is to write functional-style C++, which is where you prefer a pure-functional style (no side effects of functions) if possible. Instead of writing loops by hand, you should try using standard library algorithms. Consider the following code:

```
auto temperatures = std::vector<double>{ -3., 2., 0., 8., -10., -7. };
// ...
for (std::size_t i = 0; i < temperatures.size() - 1; ++i) {
    for (std::size_t j = i + 1; j < temperatures.size(); ++j) {
        if (std::abs(temperatures[i] - temperatures[j]) > 5)
            return std::optional{i};
    }
}
return std::nullopt;
```

Now, compare the preceding code with the following snippet, which does the same:

```
auto it = std::ranges::adjacent_find(temperatures,
                                     [](double first, double second) {
    return std::abs(first - second) > 5);
});
if (it != std::end(temperatures))
    return std::optional{std::distance(std::begin(temperatures), it)};
return std::nullopt);
```

Both snippets return the last day that had a relatively stable temperature. Which one of those would you rather read? Which one is easier to understand? Even if you're not that familiar with C++ algorithms now, after encountering them a few times in code, they just feel simpler, safer, and cleaner than hand-crafted loops. That's because they often are.

The second tactic for writing declarative code in C++ is already somewhat present in the previous snippet. You should prefer using declarative APIs, such as the one from the ranges library. And although no range views were used in our snippet, they can make a lot of difference. Consider the following snippet:

```
using namespace std::ranges;
auto is_even = [](auto x) { return x % 2 == 0; };
auto to_string = [](auto x) { return std::to_string(x); };
auto my_range = views::iota(1)
    | views::filter(is_even)
    | views::take(2)
```

```
        | views::reverse
        | views::transform(to_string);
    std::cout << std::accumulate(begin(my_range), end(my_range), ""s) << '\n';
```

This is a great example of declarative coding: you just specify what should happen, not how. The preceding code takes the first two even numbers, reverses their order, and prints them as a string, thus printing the famous answer to life, the universe, and everything: 42. All of this is done in an intuitive and easily modifiable way.

Showcasing a featured items gallery

Enough with the toy examples, though. Remember our Dominican Fair application from Chapter 3, *Functional and Nonfunctional Requirements*? Let's write a component that will select and display a few featured items from the stores that a customer saved as their favorites. This can be pretty handy when we're writing a mobile app, for example.

Let's start with a mostly C++17 implementation, which we'll update to C++20 throughout this chapter. This will include adding support for ranges.

First, let's start with some code for obtaining information about the current user:

```
using CustomerId = int;

CustomerId get_current_customer_id() { return 42; }
```

Now, let's add the store owners:

```
struct Merchant {
    int id;
};
```

The stores also need to have items in them:

```
struct Item {
    std::string name;
    std::optional<std::string> photo_url;
    std::string description;
    std::optional<float> price;
    time_point<system_clock> date_added{};
    bool featured{};
};
```

Some items may not have photos or prices, which is why we used std::optional for those fields.

Next, let's add some code that describes our items:

```
std::ostream &operator<<(std::ostream &os, const Item &item) {
  auto stringify_optional = [](const auto &optional) {
    using optional_value_type =
        typename std::remove_cvref_t<decltype(optional)>::value_type;
    if constexpr (std::is_same_v<optional_value_type, std::string>) {
      return optional ? *optional : "missing";
    } else {
      return optional ? std::to_string(*optional) : "missing";
    }
  };

  auto time_added = system_clock::to_time_t(item.date_added);

  os << "name: " << item.name
     << ", photo_url: " << stringify_optional(item.photo_url)
     << ", description: " << item.description
     << ", price: " << std::setprecision(2)
     << stringify_optional(item.price)
     << ", date_added: "
     << std::put_time(std::localtime(&time_added), "%c %Z")
     << ", featured: " << item.featured;
  return os;
}
```

First, we created a helper lambda for converting our `optionals` into strings. Since we only want to use it in our << operator, we defined it inside it.

Note how we used C++14's generic lambdas (the auto parameter), along with C++17's `constexpr` and the `is_same_v` type trait, so that we have a different implementation when we're dealing with an optional `<string>` versus other cases. Achieving the same pre-C++17 would require writing templates with overloads, resulting in more complicated code:

```
enum class Category {
  Food,
  Antiques,
  Books,
  Music,
  Photography,
  Handicraft,
  Artist,
};
```

Finally, we can define the store itself:

```
struct Store {
    gsl::not_null<const Merchant *> owner;
    std::vector<Item> items;
    std::vector<Category> categories;
};
```

What's worth noting here is the use of the `gsl::not_null` template from the Guidelines Support Library, which signals that the owner will always be set. Why not use just a plain old reference? That's because we may want our store to be moveable and copyable. Using a reference would hinder that.

Now that we have those building blocks, let's define how to get a customer's favorite stores. For simplicity, let's assume we're dealing with hardcoded stores and merchants instead of creating code to deal with external data stores.

First, let's define a type alias for the stores and begin our function definition:

```
using Stores = std::vector<gsl::not_null<const Store *>>;

Stores get_favorite_stores_for(const CustomerId &customer_id) {
```

Next, let's hardcode some merchants, as follows:

```
static const auto merchants = std::vector<Merchant>{{17}, {29}};
```

Now, let's add a store with some items, as shown here:

```
static const auto stores = std::vector<Store>{
    {.owner = &merchants[0],
     .items =
         {
             {.name = "Honey",
              .photo_url = {},
              .description = "Straight outta Compton's apiary",
              .price = 9.99f,
              .date_added = system_clock::now(),
              .featured = false},
             {.name = "Oscypek",
              .photo_url = {},
              .description = "Tasty smoked cheese from the Tatra
                              mountains",
              .price = 1.23f,
              .date_added = system_clock::now() - 1h,
              .featured = true},
         },
     .categories = {Category::Food}},
```

Leveraging C++ Language Features

```
      // more stores can be found in the complete code on GitHub
  };
```

Here, we introduced our first C++20 feature. You might not be familiar with the `.field = value;` syntax unless you've coded in C99 or newer. Starting from C++20, you can use this notation (officially called designated initializers) to initialize aggregate types. It's more constrained than in C99 because the order is important, although it has some other minor differences. Without those initializers, it can be hard to understand which value initializes which field. With them, the code is more verbose but easier to comprehend, even for people unfamiliar with programming.

Once we've defined our stores, we can write the last part of our function, which will do the actual lookup:

```
  static auto favorite_stores_by_customer =
      std::unordered_map<CustomerId, Stores>{{42, {&stores[0],
&stores[1]}}};
  return favorite_stores_by_customer[customer_id];
}
```

Now that we have our stores, let's write some code to obtain the featured items for those stores:

```
using Items = std::vector<gsl::not_null<const Item *>>;

Items get_featured_items_for_store(const Store &store) {
  auto featured = Items{};
  const auto &items = store.items;
  for (const auto &item : items) {
    if (item.featured) {
      featured.emplace_back(&item);
    }
  }
  return featured;
}
```

The preceding code was for obtaining items from one store. Let's also write a function that will obtain items from all the given stores:

```
Items get_all_featured_items(const Stores &stores) {
  auto all_featured = Items{};
  for (const auto &store : stores) {
    const auto featured_in_store = get_featured_items_for_store(*store);
    all_featured.reserve(all_featured.size() + featured_in_store.size());
    std::copy(std::begin(featured_in_store), std::end(featured_in_store),
              std::back_inserter(all_featured));
  }
```

```
        return all_featured;
    }
```

The preceding code uses `std::copy` to insert elements into a vector, with memory preallocated by the reserve call.

Now that we have a way to obtain interesting items, let's sort them by "freshness" so that the most recently added ones will appear first:

```
void order_items_by_date_added(Items &items) {
    auto date_comparator = [](const auto &left, const auto &right) {
        return left->date_added > right->date_added;
    };
    std::sort(std::begin(items), std::end(items), date_comparator);
}
```

As you can see, we leveraged `std::sort` with a custom comparator. If you like, you could also force the same type for both `left` and `right`. To do so in a generic manner, let's use another C++20 feature: template lambdas. Let's apply them to the preceding code:

```
void order_items_by_date_added(Items &items) {
    auto date_comparator = []<typename T>(const T &left, const T &right) {
        return left->date_added > right->date_added;
    };
    std::sort(std::begin(items), std::end(items), date_comparator);
}
```

The `T` type for the lambda will be deduced just like it would for any other template.

The last two parts that are missing are the actual rendering code and the main function to glue it all together. In our example case, rendering will be as simple as printing to an `ostream`:

```
void render_item_gallery(const Items &items) {
    std::copy(
        std::begin(items), std::end(items),
        std::ostream_iterator<gsl::not_null<const Item *>>(std::cout, "\n"));
}
```

In our case, we just copy each element to the standard output and insert a newline between the elements. Using `copy` and an `ostream_iterator` allows you to handle the element's separators for yourself. This can be handy in some cases; for instance, if you don't want a comma (or a newline, in our case) after the last element.

Finally, our main function will look like this:

```
int main() {
  auto fav_stores = get_favorite_stores_for(get_current_customer_id());

  auto selected_items = get_all_featured_items(fav_stores);

  order_items_by_date_added(selected_items);

  render_item_gallery(selected_items);
}
```

Voila! Feel free to run the code to see how it prints our featured items:

```
name: Handmade painted ceramic bowls, photo_url:
http://example.com/beautiful_bowl.png, description: Hand-crafted and hand-
decorated bowls made of fired clay, price: missing, date_added: Sun Jan  3
12:54:38 2021 CET, featured: 1
name: Oscypek, photo_url: missing, description: Tasty smoked cheese from
the Tatra mountains, price: 1.230000, date_added: Sun Jan  3 12:06:38 2021
CET, featured: 1
```

Now that we're done with our base implementation, let's see how we can improve it by using some new language features from C++20.

Introducing standard ranges

Our first addition will be the ranges library. As you may recall, it can help us achieve elegant, simple, and declarative code. For brevity, first, we will pull in the ranges namespace:

```
#include <ranges>

using namespace std::ranges;
```

We'll leave the code-defining merchants, items, and stores as-is. Let's start our modifications by using the get_featured_items_for_store function:

```
Items get_featured_items_for_store(const Store &store) {
  auto items = store.items | views::filter(&Item::featured) |
              views::transform([](const auto &item) {
                return gsl::not_null<const Item *>(&item);
              });
  return Items(std::begin(items), std::end(items));
}
```

As you can see, making a range out of a container is straightforward: just pass it to a pipe operator. Instead of our hand-crafted loop to filter featured elements, we can use the `views::filter` expression, passing it a member pointer as the predicate. Due to the magic of `std::invoke` under the hood, this will correctly filter out all items that have our Boolean data member set to `false`.

Next, we need to convert each item into a `gsl::not_null` pointer so that we can avoid unnecessary item copies. Finally, we return a vector of such pointers, the same as in our base code.

Now, let's see how we can use the preceding function to obtain all the featured items from all our stores:

```
Items get_all_featured_items(const Stores &stores) {
  auto all_featured = stores | views::transform([](auto elem) {
                        return get_featured_items_for_store(*elem);
                      });

  auto ret = Items{};
  for_each(all_featured, [&](auto elem) {
    ret.reserve(ret.size() + elem.size());
    copy(elem, std::back_inserter(ret));
  });
  return ret;
}
```

Here, we created a range from all the stores and transformed them using the function we created in the previous step. Because we needed to dereference each element first, we used a helper lambda. Views are lazily evaluated, so each transform will be done only when it is about to be consumed. This can sometimes save you lots of time and computations: assuming you would only want the first N items, you can skip the unnecessary calls to `get_featured_items_for_store`.

Once we have our lazy view, similar to our base implementation, we can reserve space in the vector and copy items there from each nested vector in the `all_featured` view. Range algorithms are more concise to use if you take the whole container. Look how copy doesn't require us to write `std::begin(elem)` and `std::end(elem)`.

Now that we have our items, let's simplify our sorting code by using ranges to process them:

```
void order_items_by_date_added(Items &items) {
  sort(items, greater{}, &Item::date_added);
}
```

Again, you can see how ranges can help you write more concise code. The preceding copy and the sort here are both range *algorithms*, as opposed to *views*. They are eager and allow you to use projections. In our case, we just passed another member of our item class so that it can be used for comparison when sorting. Effectively, each item will be projected as just its `date_added`, which will then be compared using `greater{}`.

But wait – our items are actually `gsl::not_null` pointers to `Item`. How does this work? It turns out that our projection will dereference the `gsl::not_null` pointer first because of the cleverness of `std::invoke`. Neat!

The last change that we can make is in our "rendering" code:

```
void render_item_gallery([[maybe_unused]] const Items &items) {
  copy(items,
       std::ostream_iterator<gsl::not_null<const Item *>>(std::cout,
"\n"));
}
```

Here, ranges just help us remove some boilerplate code.

When you run our updated version of the code, you should get the same output as in the base case.

If you were expecting more from ranges than just concise code, there's good news: they can be used even more efficiently in our case.

Reducing memory overhead and increasing performance using ranges

You already know that using lazy evaluation in `std::ranges::views` can help with performance by eliminating unnecessary compute. It turns out we can also use ranges to reduce the memory overhead in our example. Let's revisit our code for obtaining featured items from a store. It can be shortened down to the following:

```
auto get_featured_items_for_store(const Store &store) {
  return store.items | views::filter(&Item::featured) |
         views::transform(
             [](const auto &item) { return gsl::not_null(&item); });
}
```

Note that our function no longer returns items, instead relying on C++14's auto return type deduction. In our case, instead of returning a vector, our code will return a lazy view.

Let's learn how to consume this for all stores:

```
Items get_all_featured_items(const Stores &stores) {
  auto all_featured = stores | views::transform([](auto elem) {
                    return get_featured_items_for_store(*elem);
                  }) |
                  views::join;
  auto as_items = Items{};
  as_items.reserve(distance(all_featured));
  copy(all_featured, std::back_inserter(as_items));
  return as_items;
}
```

Now, because our preceding function returns a view instead of the vector, we end up with a view of views after calling `transform`. This means we can use yet another standard view called join to join our nested views into just one that's unified.

Next, we use `std::ranges::distance` to preallocate space in our destination vector, after which we make our copy. Some ranges are sized, in which case you could call `std::ranges::size` instead. The resulting code has just one call to `reserve`, which should give us a nice performance boost.

This concludes introducing ranges to our code. Since we ended this section on a performance-related note, let's talk about one more topic that's important for this aspect of C++ programming.

Moving computations at compile time

Starting with the advent of modern C++ in the early 2000s, C++ programming became more about computing things during compilation instead of deferring them to runtime. It's much cheaper to detect errors during compilation than to debug them later on. Similarly, it's much faster to have the result ready before the program is started instead of calculating it later on.

At first, there was template metaprogramming, but with C++11 onward, each new standard brought additional features for compile-time compute: be it type traits, constructs such as `std::enable_if` or `std::void_t`, or C++20's `consteval` for computing stuff only at compile time.

One feature that improved over the years was the `constexpr` keyword and its related code. C++20 really improved and extended `constexpr`. Now, you can not only write regular simple `constexpr` functions thanks to the previous standards (quite an improvement from C++11's single-expression ones), but you can also use dynamic allocations and exceptions inside them, not to mention `std::vector` and `std::string`!

There's more: even virtual functions can now be `constexpr`: overload resolution happens as usual, but if a given one is `constexpr`, it can get called at compile time.

Yet another improvement was made to standard algorithms. Their non-parallel versions are all ready for you to use in your compile-time code. Consider the following example, which can be used to check if a given merchant is present in a container:

```cpp
#include <algorithm>
#include <array>

struct Merchant { int id; };

bool has_merchant(const Merchant &selected) {
    auto merchants = std::array{Merchant{1}, Merchant{2}, Merchant{3},
                        Merchant{4}, Merchant{5}};
    return std::binary_search(merchants.begin(), merchants.end(), selected,
                        [](auto a, auto b) { return a.id < b.id; });
}
```

As you can see, we're doing a binary search for an array of merchants, sorted by their IDs.

To gain insight into the code and its performance, we recommend that you take a quick look at the assembly that this code generates. Along with the advent of compile-time computations and chasing performance, one of the invaluable tools that was developed was the `https://godbolt.org` site. It can be used to quickly play with code to see how different architectures, compilers, flags, library versions, and implementations influence the generated assembly.

We tested the preceding code using GCC trunk (before GCC 11 was officially released) with −O3 and `--std=c++2a`. In our case, we checked the generated assembly with the following code:

```cpp
int main() { return has_merchant({4}); }
```

You can see the few dozens of assembly lines using the following Godbolt: `https://godbolt.org/z/PYMTYx`.

But wait – you could say that *there's a function call in the assembly, so maybe we could inline it so it can be optimized better?* That would be a valid point. Often, this helps a lot, although now, we just get the assembly inlined (see: `https://godbolt.org/z/hPadxd`).

So, now, try changing the signature to the following:

```
constexpr bool has_merchant(const Merchant &selected)
```

`constexpr` functions are implicitly inline, so we removed that keyword. If we look into the assembly, we will see that some magic happened: the search was optimized away! As you can see at `https://godbolt.org/z/v3hj3E`, all the assembly that was left was as follows:

```
main:
        mov     eax, 1
        ret
```

The compiler optimized our code so that the only thing left is our pre-computed result being returned. That's pretty impressive, isn't it?

Helping the compiler help you by using const

Compilers can optimize pretty well, even if you don't give them `inline` or `constexpr` keywords, as in the preceding example. One thing that helps them achieve performance for you is marking variables and functions as `const`. Perhaps even more importantly, it also helps you avoid making mistakes in your code. Many languages have immutable variables by default, which can lead to fewer bugs, code that's easier to reason about, and often faster multi-threaded performance.

Even though C++ has mutable variables by default and you need to explicitly type `const`, we encourage you to do so. It can really help you stop making tricky typos related to modifying a variable that you shouldn't.

Using `const` (or `constexpr`) code is part of a bigger philosophy called type safety. Let's say a few words about it.

Leveraging the power of safe types

C++ relies heavily on mechanisms that help you write type-safe code. Language constructs such as explicit constructors and conversion operators have been baked into the language for a long time. More and more safe types are being introduced to the standard library. There's `optional` to help you avoid referencing empty values, `string_view` to help you avoid going out of a range, and `any` as a safe wrapper for any type, just to name a few. Moreover, with its zero-cost abstractions, it's recommended that you create your own types that are useful and hard or impossible to misuse.

Often, using C-style constructs can lead to type-unsafe code. One example would be C-style casts. They can resolve to a `const_cast`, `static_cast`, `reinterpret_cast`, or one of these two combined with a `const_cast`. Accidentally writing to a `const` object that was `const_cast` is undefined behavior. So is reading memory returned from a `reinterpret_cast<T>`, if T was not the original type of the object (C++20's `std::bit_cast` can help here). Both of those cases are much easier avoided if C++ casts are used.

C was perhaps too permissive when it came to types. Fortunately, C++ introduces many type-safe alternatives to problematic C constructs. There are streams and `std::format` instead of `printf` et al., and there's `std::copy` and other similar algorithms instead of the unsafe `memcpy`. Finally, there are templates instead of functions taking a void * (and paying a price in terms of performance). With C++, templates get even more type safety through a feature called concepts. Let's see how we can improve our code by using them.

Constraining template parameters

The first way concepts can improve your code is by making it more generic. Do you remember the cases where you needed to change the container type in one place, which caused a cascade of changes in other places too? If you weren't changing the container to one with totally different semantics and that you had to use in a different way, that means your code may not have been generic enough.

On the other hand, have you ever written a template or sprinkled `auto` over your code and later wondered if your code would break if someone changed the underlying type?

Concepts are all about putting the right level of constraints onto the types you're operating on. They constrain what types your template can match, and are checked at compile time. For instance, let's say you write the following:

```
template<typename T>
void foo(T& t) {...}
```

Now, you can write the following instead:

```
void foo(std::swappable auto& t) {...}
```

Here, `foo()` must be passed a type that supports `std::swap` to work.

Do you recall some templates that matched just too many types? Previously, you could use `std::enable_if`, `std::void_t`, or `if constexpr` to constrain them. However, writing `enable_if` statements was a bit cumbersome and could slow down your compilation times. Here, concepts come to the rescue once more due to their conciseness and how they express their intent clearly.

There are a few dozen standard concepts in C++20. Most of them live in the `<concepts>` header and can be divided into four categories:

- Core language concepts, such as `derived_from`, `integral`, `swappable`, and `move_constructible`
- Comparison concepts, such as `boolean-testable`, `equality_comparable_with`, and `totally_ordered`
- Object concepts, such as `movable`, `copyable`, `semiregular`, and `regular`
- Callable concepts, such as `invokable`, `predicate`, and `strict_weak_order`

Additional ones are defined in the `<iterator>` header. These can be divided into the following categories:

- Indirect callable concepts, such as `indirect_binary_predicate` and `indirectly_unary_invocable`
- Common algorithm requirements, such as `indirectly_swappable`, `permutable`, `mergeable`, and `sortable`

Finally, a dozen can be found in the `<ranges>` header. Examples include `range` (duh), `contiguous_range`, and `view`.

If that's not enough for your needs, you can declare your own concepts similarly to how the standard defines the ones we just covered. For instance, the `movable` concept is implemented like so:

```
template <class T>
concept movable = std::is_object_v<T> && std::move_constructible<T> &&
std::assignable_from<T&, T> && std::swappable<T>;
```

Furthermore, if you look at `std::swappable`, you'll see the following:

```
template<class T>
concept swappable = requires(T& a, T& b) { ranges::swap(a, b); };
```

This means a type, T, will be `swappable` if `ranges::swap(a, b)` compiles for two references of this type.

> When defining your own concepts, be sure that you cover the semantic requirements for them. Specifying and using a concept when defining an interface is a promise that's made to the consumers of that interface.

Often, you can go with the so-called shorthand notation in declarations for brevity:

```
void sink(std::movable auto& resource);
```

For readability and type safety, it's recommended that you use `auto` together with a concept to constrain the type and let your readers know the kind of object they're dealing with. Code written in this manner will retain the perks of auto-like genericity. You can use this in both regular functions and lambdas.

A great bonus of using concepts is shorter error messages. It's not uncommon to cut a few dozens and dozens of lines about one compilation error down to just a few lines. Yet another bonus is that you can overload on concepts.

Now, let's go back to our Dominican Fair example. This time, we'll add some concepts to see how they can improve our implementation.

First, let's make `get_all_featured_items` return just a range of items. We can do so by adding the concept to the return type, like so:

```
range auto get_all_featured_items(const Stores &stores);
```

So far, so good. Now, let's add yet another requirement to this type that will be enforced when we call `order_items_by_date_added`: our range must be sortable. `std::sortable` has already been defined for a range iterator, but for our convenience, let's define a new concept called `sortable_range`:

```
template <typename Range, typename Comp, typename Proj>
concept sortable_range =
    random_access_range<Range> &&std::sortable<iterator_t<Range>, Comp,
Proj>;
```

Similar to its standard library counterpart, we can accept a comparator and a projection (which we introduced with ranges). Our concept is satisfied by (will be matched by) types that satisfy the `random_access_range` concept, as well as having an iterator that satisfies the aforementioned sortable concept. It's as simple as that.

When defining concepts, you can also use the `requires` clause to specify additional constraints. For instance, if you want our range to store elements with a `date_added` member only, you could write the following:

```
template <typename Range, typename Comp>
concept sortable_indirectly_dated_range =
    random_access_range<Range> &&std::sortable<iterator_t<Range>, Comp> &&
requires(range_value_t<Range> v) { { v->date_added }; };
```

However, in our case, we don't need to constrain the type that much, as you should leave some flexibility when you're using concepts and define them so that it will make sense to reuse them.

What's important here is that you can use the `requires` clause to specify what code should be valid to call on your type when it meets the requirements for a concept. If you want, you can specify constraints on the type that's returned by each subexpression; for instance, to define something incrementable, you could use the following:

```
requires(I i) {
  { i++ } -> std::same_as<I>;
}
```

Now that we have our concept, let's redefine the `order_items_by_date_added` function:

```
void order_items_by_date_added(
    sortable_range<greater, decltype(&Item::date_added)> auto &items) {
  sort(items, greater{}, &Item::date_added);
}
```

Now, our compiler will check if any range we pass to it is a sortable one and contains a `date_added` member that can be sorted using `std::ranges::greater{}`.

If we were to use the more constrained concept here, the function would look like this:

```
void order_items_by_date_added(
    sortable_indirectly_dated_range<greater> auto &items) {
  sort(items, greater{}, &Item::date_added);
}
```

Finally, let's redo our rendering function:

```
template <input_range Container>
requires std::is_same_v<typename Container::value_type,
                        gsl::not_null<const Item *>> void
render_item_gallery(const Container &items) {
  copy(items,
       std::ostream_iterator<typename Container::value_type>(std::cout,
"\n"));
}
```

Here, you can see that a concept name can be used instead of the `typename` keyword in a template declaration. One line below this, you can see that the `requires` keyword can also be used to further constrain the appropriate types based on their traits. This can be handy if you don't want to specify a new concept.

That's it for concepts. Now, let's write some modular C++ code.

Writing modular C++

The last big feature of C++ we'll discuss in this chapter is modules. They are yet one more addition to C++20 that has a great impact on building and partitioning code.

C++ has used `#include` for a really long time now. However, this textual form of dependency inclusion has its flaws, as listed here:

- Due to the need to process lots of text (even a `Hello World` after preprocessing is around half a million lines of code), it's slow. This leads to **one-definition rule (ODR)** violations.
- The order of your `includes` matters, but it shouldn't. This one is twice as bad as the preceding one as it also leads to cyclic dependencies.

- Finally, it's hard to encapsulate stuff that just needs to be in header files. Even if you put some stuff in a detailed namespace, someone will use it, as Hyrum's law predicts.

Fortunately, this is when modules enter the game. They should solve the aforementioned flaws, bringing a great speedup to build times and better C++ scalability when it comes to building. With modules, you only export what you want to export, which results in good encapsulation. Having a specific order of dependency inclusion is no longer an issue too, as the order of imports doesn't matter.

 Unfortunately, at the time of writing, compiler support for modules is still only partially done. This is why we decided to just showcase what was already available in GCC 11. Sadly, this means that stuff such as module partitions won't be covered here.

Each module, after compilation, will be compiled to not only the object file but also a module interface file. This means that instead of parsing a file with all of its dependencies, compilers can quickly know what types and functions a given module contains. All you need to do is to type the following:

```
import my_module;
```

You can use it once `my_module` has been compiled and available. The module itself should be defined in a `.cppm` file, but those are still not supported by CMake. You might be better off just naming them `.cpp` for the time being.

Without further ado, let's return to our Dominican Fair example and show how to use them in practice.

First, let's create our first module for the customer code, starting with the following directive:

```
module;
```

This statement marks that from this point on, everything will be private in this module. This marks a good place to put your includes and other content that won't be exported.

Next, we must specify the name of the exported module:

```
export module customer;
```

This will be the name we'll use to import the module later. This line must come before the exported contents. Now, let's specify what our module will actually export, prefixing the definitions with the `export` keyword:

```
export using CustomerId = int;

export CustomerId get_current_customer_id() { return 42; }
```

And done! Our first module is ready to be used. Let's create another one for the merchant:

```
module;

export module merchant;

export struct Merchant {
  int id;
};
```

Pretty similar to our first module, here, we specified the name and the type to be exported (as opposed to a type alias and a function for the first one). You can export other definitions, such as templates, too. It gets tricky with macros, though, as you need to import `<header_file>` for them to be visible.

By the way, a good advantage of modules is that they don't allow macros to propagate to imported modules. This means that when you write code such as the following, the module won't have `MY_MACRO` defined:

```
#define MY_MACRO
import my_module;
```

It helps to have determinism in modules as it protects you from breaking code in other modules.

Now, let's define a third module for our stores and items. We won't discuss exporting other functions, enums, and other types as it won't differ from the previous two modules. What's interesting is how the module file starts. First, let's include what we need in our private module section:

```
module;

#include <chrono>
#include <iomanip>
#include <optional>
#include <string>
#include <vector>
```

In C++20, standard library headers are not modules yet, but this will likely change in the near future.

Now, let's see what happens next:

```
export module store;

export import merchant;
```

This is the interesting part. Our store module imports the merchant module we defined previously and then reexports it as part of the store's interface. This can be handy if your module is a facade for other ones, such as in module partitions in the near future (also part of C++20). When available, you will be able to split your module across multiple files. One of them could contain the following:

```
export module my_module:foo;

export template<typename T> foo() {}
```

As we discussed previously, it would then be exported by the main file of your module as follows:

```
export module my_module;

export import :foo;
```

This concludes modules and the big C++ features that we planned for this chapter. Let's summarize what we've learned.

Summary

In this chapter, we learned about many C++ features and their impact on writing concise, expressive, and performant C++ code. We learned about providing proper C++ component interfaces. You're now able to apply principles such as RAII to write elegant code that's free from resource leaks. You also know how to leverage types such as `std::optional` to express your intent better in your interfaces.

Next, we demonstrated how to use features such as generic and template lambdas, as well as `if constexpr` for writing less code that will work with many types. You're now also able to define objects in a clear manner using designated initializers.

Afterward, you learned how to write simple code in a declarative style using standard ranges, how to write code that can be executed at both compile time and runtime using `constexpr`, and how to write more constrained templated code using concepts.

Finally, we demoed how to write modular code with C++ modules. In the next chapter, we'll discuss how to design C++ code so that we can build upon the available idioms and patterns.

Questions

1. How can we ensure that each file that our code will open will be closed when it's not being used anymore?
2. When should you use "naked" pointers in C++ code?
3. What is a deduction guide?
4. When should you use `std::optional` and `gsl::not_null`?
5. How are range algorithms different than views?
6. How can you constrain your type by doing more than just specifying the concept's name when you're defining a function?
7. How is `import X` different than `import <X>`?

Further reading

- *C++ Core Guidelines*, the section on *Concepts*: https://isocpp.github.io/CppCoreGuidelines/CppCoreGuidelines#Rt-concepts
- libstdc++'s implementation of `std::chrono`: https://code.woboq.org/gcc/libstdc++-v3/include/std/chrono.html

6
Design Patterns and C++

C++ is not just an object-oriented language, and it doesn't just offer dynamic polymorphism, so design in C++ is not just about the Gang of Four patterns. In this chapter, you will learn about the commonly used C++ idioms and design patterns and where to use them.

The following topics will be covered in this chapter:

- Writing idiomatic C++
- Curiously recurring template pattern
- Creating objects
- Tracking state and visiting objects in C++
- Dealing with memory efficiently

That's quite a list! Let's not waste time and jump right in.

Technical requirements

The code from this chapter requires the following tools to build and run:

- A compiler supporting C++20
- CMake 3.15+

The source code snippets from the chapter can be found at `https://github.com/PacktPublishing/Software-Architecture-with-Cpp/tree/master/Chapter06`.

Writing idiomatic C++

If you're familiar with object-oriented programming languages, you must have heard of the Gang of Four's design patterns. While they can be implemented in C++ (and often are), this multi-paradigm language often takes a different approach for achieving the same goals. If you want to beat the performance of the so-called coffee-based languages such as Java or C#, sometimes paying the cost of virtual dispatch is too much. In many cases, you'll know upfront what types you'll deal with. If that happens, you can often write more performant code using the tools available both in the language and in the standard library. Out of many, there's a group that we will start this chapter with – the language idioms. Let's start our journey by looking at a few of them.

By definition, an idiom is a construct that recurs in a given language, an expression that's specific to the language. "Native speakers" of C++ should know its idioms by intuition. We already mentioned smart pointers, which are one of the most common ones. Let's now discuss a similar one.

Automating scope exit actions using RAII guards

One of the most powerful expressions in C++ is the brace closing a scope. This is the place where destructors get called and the RAII magic happens. To tame this spell, you don't need to use smart pointers. All you need is an RAII guard – an object that, when constructed, will remember what it needs to do when destroyed. This way, regardless of whether the scope exits normally or by an exception, the work will happen automatically.

The best part – you don't even need to write an RAII guard from scratch. Well-tested implementation already exists in various libraries. If you're using GSL, which we mentioned in the previous chapter, you can use `gsl::finally()`. Consider the following example:

```
using namespace std::chrono;

void self_measuring_function() {
  auto timestamp_begin = high_resolution_clock::now();

  auto cleanup = gsl::finally([timestamp_begin] {
    auto timestamp_end = high_resolution_clock::now();
    std::cout << "Execution took: " <<
duration_cast<microseconds>(timestamp_end - timestamp_begin).count() << "
us";
  });
```

```
  // perform work
  // throw std::runtime_error{"Unexpected fault"};
}
```

Here, we take a timestamp at the start of the function and another one at the end. Try running this example and see how uncommenting the `throw` statement affects the execution. In both cases, our RAII guard will properly print the execution time (assuming the exception is caught somewhere).

Let's now discuss a few more popular C++ idioms.

Managing copyability and movability

When designing a new type in C++, it's important to decide whether it should be copyable and movable. Even more important is implementing those semantics for a class correctly. Let's discuss those issues now.

Implementing non-copyable types

There are cases when you don't want your class to be copied. Classes that are very expensive to copy are one example. Another would be those subject to error due to slicing. In the past, a common way to prevent such objects from copying was by using the non-copyable idiom:

```
struct Noncopyable {
  Noncopyable() = default;
  Noncopyable(const Noncopyable&) = delete;
  Noncopyable& operator=(const Noncopyable&) = delete;
};

class MyType : NonCopyable {};
```

Note, however, that such a class is also not movable, although it's easy to not notice it when reading the class definition. A better approach would be to just add the two missing members (the move constructor and move assignment operator) explicitly. As a rule of thumb, when declaring such special member functions, always declare all of them. This means that from C++11 onward, the preferred way would be to write the following:

```
struct MyTypeV2 {
  MyTypeV2() = default;
  MyTypeV2(const MyTypeV2 &) = delete;
  MyTypeV2 & operator=(const MyTypeV2 &) = delete;
  MyTypeV2(MyTypeV2 &&) = delete;
```

```
    MyTypeV2 & operator=(MyTypeV2 &&) = delete;
};
```

This time, the members were defined directly in the target type without the helper `NonCopyable` type.

Adhering to the rules of three and five

There's one more thing to mention when discussing special member functions: if you don't delete them and are providing your own implementations, most probably you need to define all of them, including the destructor, too. This was called the rule of three in C++98 (due to the need to define three functions: the copy constructor, the copy assignment operator, and the destructor) and since C++11's move operations, it is now replaced by the rule of five (the two additional ones being the move constructor and the move assignment operator). Applying these rules can help you avoid resource management issues.

Adhering to the rule of zero

If, on the other hand, you're good to go with just the default implementations of all special member functions, then just don't declare them at all. This is a clear sign that you want the default behavior. It's also the least confusing. Consider the following type:

```
class PotentiallyMisleading {
public:
  PotentiallyMisleading() = default;
  PotentiallyMisleading(const PotentiallyMisleading &) = default;
  PotentiallyMisleading &operator=(const PotentiallyMisleading &) =
default;
  PotentiallyMisleading(PotentiallyMisleading &&) = default;
  PotentiallyMisleading &operator=(PotentiallyMisleading &&) = default;
  ~PotentiallyMisleading() = default;

private:
  std::unique_ptr<int> int_;
};
```

Even though we defaulted all the members, the class is still non-copyable. That's because it has a `unique_ptr` member that is non-copyable itself. Fortunately, Clang will warn you about this, but GCC does not by default. A better approach would be to apply the rule of zero and instead write the following:

```
class RuleOfZero {
    std::unique_ptr<int> int_;
};
```

Now we have less boilerplate code and by looking at the members, it's easier to notice that it does not support copying.

There's one more important idiom to know about when it comes to copying that you'll get to know in a minute. Before that happens, we shall touch on yet another idiom, which can (and should) be used to implement the first one.

Using hidden friends

In essence, hidden friends are non-member functions defined in the body of the type that declares them as a friend. This makes such functions impossible to call in ways other than by using **Argument-Dependent Lookup (ADL)**, effectively making them hidden. Because they reduce the number of overloads a compiler considers, they also speed up compilation. A bonus of this is that they provide shorter error messages than their alternatives. Their last interesting property is that they cannot be called if an implicit conversion should happen first. This can help you avoid such accidental conversions.

Although friends in C++ are generally not recommended, things look differently for hidden friends; if the advantages from the previous paragraph don't convince you, you should also know that they should be the preferred way of implementing customization points. Now, you're probably wondering what those customization points are. Briefly speaking, they are callables used by the library code that the user can specialize in for their types. The standard library reserves quite a lot of names for those, such as `begin`, `end`, and their reverse and `const` variations, `swap`, `(s)size`, `(c)data`, and many operators, among others. If you decide to provide your own implementation for any of those customization points, it had better behave as the standard library expects.

Okay, enough theory for now. Let's see how to provide a customization point specialization using a hidden friend in practice. For example, let's create an oversimplified class to manage arrays of types:

```cpp
template <typename T> class Array {
public:
  Array(T *array, int size) : array_{array}, size_{size} {}

  ~Array() { delete[] array_; }

  T &operator[](int index) { return array_[index]; }
  int size() const { return size_; }

  friend void swap(Array &left, Array &right) noexcept {
    using std::swap;
    swap(left.array_, right.array_);
    swap(left.size_, right.size_);
  }

private:
  T *array_;
  int size_;
};
```

As you can see, we defined a destructor, which means we should provide other special member functions too. We implement them in the next section, using our hidden friend `swap`. Note that despite being declared in the body of our `Array` class, this `swap` function is still a non-member function. It accepts two `Array` instances and doesn't have access to this.

Using the `std::swap` line makes the compiler first look for `swap` functions in the namespaces of the swapped members. If not found, it will fall back to `std::swap`. This is called the *two-step ADL and fallback idiom*, or *two-step* for short, because we first make `std::swap` visible, and then call `swap`. The `noexcept` keyword tells the compiler that our `swap` function does not throw, which allows it to generate faster code in certain situations. Aside from `swap`, always mark your default and move constructors with this keyword too for the same reason.

Now that we have a `swap` function, let's use it to apply another idiom to our `Array` class.

Providing exception safety using the copy-and-swap idiom

As we mentioned in the previous section, because our `Array` class defines a destructor, according to the rule of five, it should also define other special member functions. In this section, you'll learn about an idiom that lets us do this without boilerplate, while also adding strong exception safety as a bonus.

If you're not familiar with the exception safety levels, here's a quick recap of the levels your functions and types can offer:

- **No guarantee**: This is the most basic level. No guarantees are made about the state of your object after an exception is thrown while it's being used.
- **Basic exception safety**: Side effects are possible, but your object won't leak any resources, will be in a valid state, and will contain valid data (not necessarily the same as before the operation). Your types should always offer at least this level.
- **Strong exception safety**: No side effects will happen. The object's state will be the same as before the operation.
- **No-throw guarantee**: Operations will always succeed. If an exception is thrown during the operation, it will be caught and handled internally so the operation does not throw exceptions outside. Such operations can be marked as `noexcept`.

So, how can we kill these two birds with one stone and write no-boilerplate special members while also providing strong exception safety? It's pretty easy, actually. As we have our `swap` function, let's use it to implement the assignment operators:

```
Array &operator=(Array other) noexcept {
  swap(*this, other);
  return *this;
}
```

In our case, a single operator suffices for both the copy and move assignments. In the copy case, we take the parameter by value, so this is where a temporary copy is being made. Then, all we need to do is swap the members. We have not only achieved strong exception safety but were also able to not throw from the assignment operator's body. However, an exception can still be thrown right before the function gets called, when the copy happens. In the case of the move assignment, no copy is made as taking by value will just take the moved object.

Now, let's define the copy constructor:

```
Array(const Array &other) : array_{new T[other.size_]},
size_{other.size_} {
```

```
        std::copy_n(other.array_, size_, array_);
    }
```

This guy can throw depending on `T` and because it allocates memory. Now, let's define the move constructor too:

```
    Array(Array &&other) noexcept
        : array_{std::exchange(other.array_, nullptr)},
    size_{std::exchange(other.size_, 0)} {}
```

Here, we use `std::exchange` so that our members get initialized and `other`'s members get cleaned up, all on the initialization list. The constructor is declared `noexcept` for performance reasons. For instance, `std::vector` can move their elements when they grow only if they're `noexcept` move-constructible, and will copy otherwise.

That's it. We've created an `array` class providing strong exception safety with little effort and no code duplication.

Let's now tackle yet another C++ idiom, which can be spotted in a few places in the standard library.

Writing niebloids

Niebloids, named after Eric Niebler, are a type of function object that the standard uses for customization points from C++17 onward. With the introduction of standard ranges described in Chapter 5, *Leveraging C++ Language Features*, their popularity started to grow, but they were first proposed by Niebler back in 2014. **Their purpose is to disable ADL where it's not wanted so overloads from other namespaces are not considered by the compiler.** Remember the *two-step idiom* from the previous sections? Because it's inconvenient and easy to forget, the notion of *customization point objects* was introduced. In essence, these are function objects performing the *two-step* for you.

If your libraries should provide customization points, it's probably a good idea to implement them using niebloids. All the customization points in the standard library introduced in C++17 and later are implemented this way for a reason. Even if you just need to create a function object, still consider using niebloids. They offer all the good parts of ADL while reducing the drawbacks. They allow specialization and together with concepts they give you a way to customize the overload set of your callables. They also allow better customization of algorithms, all at the slight cost of writing a bit more verbose code than usual.

In this section, we'll create a simple range algorithm that we'll implement as a niebloid. Let's call it `contains` as it will simply return a Boolean value denoting whether a given element is found in the range or not. First, let's create the function object itself, starting with the declaration of its iterator-based call operator:

```
namespace detail {
struct contains_fn final {
   template <std::input_iterator It, std::sentinel_for<It> Sent, typename T,
            typename Proj = std::identity>
   requires std::indirect_binary_predicate<
       std::ranges::equal_to, std::projected<It, Proj>, const T *> constexpr
bool
   operator()(It first, Sent last, const T &value, Proj projection = {})
const {
```

It looks verbose, but all this code has a purpose. We make our struct `final` to aid the compiler in generating more efficient code. If you look at the template parameters, you'll see an iterator and a sentinel – the basic building blocks of each standard range. The sentinel is often an iterator, but it can be any semiregular type that can be compared with the iterator (a semiregular type is copyable and default-initializable). Next, T is the type of element to search for, while `Proj` denotes a projection – an operation to apply to each range element before comparison (the default of `std::identity` simply passes its input as output).

After the template parameters, there come the requirements for them; the operator requires that we can compare the projected value and the searched-for value for equality. After those constraints, we simply specify the function parameters.

Let's now see how it's implemented:

```
      while (first != last && std::invoke(projection, *first) != value)
         ++first;
      return first != last;
   }
```

Here, we simply iterate over the elements, invoking the projection on each element and comparing it with the searched-for value. We return `true` if found and `false` otherwise (when `first == last`).

The preceding function would work even if we didn't use standard ranges; we also need an overload for ranges. Its declaration can be as follows:

```
template <std::ranges::input_range Range, typename T,
          typename Proj = std::identity>
requires std::indirect_binary_predicate<
    std::ranges::equal_to,
    std::projected<std::ranges::iterator_t<Range>, Proj>,
    const T *> constexpr bool
operator()(Range &&range, const T &value, Proj projection = {}) const {
```

This time, we take a type satisfying the `input_range` concept, the element value, and the type of projection as template parameters. We require that the range's iterator after calling the projection can be compared for equality with objects of type `T`, similarly as before. Finally, we use the range, the value, and the projection as our overload's parameters.

The body of this operator will be pretty straightforward, too:

```
    return (*this)(std::ranges::begin(range), std::ranges::end(range),
value,
                   std::move(projection));
  }
};
}  // namespace detail
```

We simply call the previous overload using an iterator and sentinel from the given range, while passing the value and our projection unchanged. Now, for the last part, we need to provide a `contains` niebloid instead of just the `contains_fn` callable:

```
inline constexpr detail::contains_fn contains{};
```

By declaring an inline variable named `contains` of type `contains_fn`, we allow anyone to call our niebloid using the variable name. Now, let's call it ourselves to see whether it works:

```
int main() {
  auto ints = std::ranges::views::iota(0) | std::ranges::views::take(5);

  return contains(ints, 42);
}
```

And that's it. Our ADL-inhibiting functor works as intended.

If you think all of this is a tad too verbose, then you might be interested in `tag_invoke`, which might become part of the standard at some point in the future. Refer to the *Further reading* section for a paper on this topic and a YouTube video that explains ADL, niebloids, hidden friends, and `tag_invoke` nicely.

Let's now move on to yet another useful C++ idiom.

Policy-based design idiom

Policy-based design was first introduced by Andrei Alexandrescu in his excellent *Modern C++ Design* book. Although published in 2001, many ideas showed in it are still used today. We recommend reading it; you can find it linked in the *Further reading* section at the end of this chapter. The policy idiom is basically a compile-time equivalent of the Gang of Four's Strategy pattern. If you need to write a class with customizable behavior, you can make it a template with the appropriate policies as template parameters. A real-world example of this could be standard allocators, passed as a policy to many C++ containers as the last template parameter.

Let's return to our `Array` class and add a policy for debug printing:

```
template <typename T, typename DebugPrintingPolicy = NullPrintingPolicy>
class Array {
```

As you can see, we can use a default policy that won't print anything. `NullPrintingPolicy` can be implemented as follows:

```
struct NullPrintingPolicy {
  template <typename... Args> void operator()(Args...) {}
};
```

As you can see, regardless of the arguments given, it won't do anything. The compiler will completely optimize it out, so no overhead will be paid when the debug printing feature is not used.

If we want our class to be a bit more verbose, we can use a different policy:

```
struct CoutPrintingPolicy {
  void operator()(std::string_view text) { std::cout << text << std::endl;
  }
};
```

This time, we'll simply print the text passed to the policy to `cout`. We also need to modify our class to actually use our policy:

```
Array(T *array, int size) : array_{array}, size_{size} {
    DebugPrintingPolicy{}("constructor");
}

Array(const Array &other) : array_{new T[other.size_]},
size_{other.size_} {
    DebugPrintingPolicy{}("copy constructor");
    std::copy_n(other.array_, size_, array_);
}

// ... other members ...
```

We simply call the policy's `operator()`, passing the text to be printed. Since our policies are stateless, we can instantiate it each time we need to use it without extra cost. An alternative could also be to just call a static function from it.

Now, all we need to do is to instantiate our `Array` class with the desired policy and use it:

```
Array<T, CoutPrintingPolicy>(new T[size], size);
```

One drawback of using compile-timed policies is that the template instantiations using different policies are of different types. This means more work is required to, for instance, assign from a regular `Array` class to one with `CoutPrintingPolicy`. To do so, you would need to implement assignment operators as template functions with the policy as the template parameter.

Sometimes an alternative to using policies is to use traits. As an example, take `std::iterator_traits`, which can be used to use various information about iterators when writing algorithms that use them. An example could be `std::iterator_traits<T>::value_type`, which can work for both custom iterators defining a `value_type` member, and simple ones such as pointers (in which case `value_type` would refer to the pointed-to type).

Enough about policy-based design. Next on our list is a powerful idiom that can be applied in multiple scenarios.

Curiously recurring template pattern

Despite having *pattern* in its name, the **Curiously Recurring Template Pattern (CRTP)** is an idiom in C++. It can be used to implement other idioms and design patterns and to apply static polymorphism, to name a few areas. Let's start with this last one as we'll cover the others later on.

Knowing when to use dynamic versus static polymorphism

When mentioning polymorphism, many programmers will think of dynamic polymorphism, where the information needed to perform a function call is gathered at runtime. In contrast to this, static polymorphism is about determining the calls at compile time. An advantage of the former is that you can modify the list of types at runtime, allowing extending your class hierarchies through plugins and libraries. The big advantage of the second is that it can get better performance if you know the types upfront. Sure, in the first case you can sometimes expect your compiler to devirtualize your calls, but you cannot always count on it doing so. However, in the second case, you can get longer compilation times.

Looks like you cannot win in all cases. Still, choosing the right type of polymorphism for your types can go a long way. If performance is at stake, we strongly suggest you consider static polymorphism. CRTP is an idiom that can be used to apply it.

Many design patterns can be implemented in one way or another. As the cost of dynamic polymorphism is not always worth it, the Gang of Four design patterns are often not the best solution in C++. If your type hierarchy should be extended at runtime, or compile times are a much bigger issue than performance for you (and you don't plan on using modules any time soon), then the classical implementations of the Gang of Four patterns may be a good fit. Otherwise, you can try to implement them using static polymorphism or by applying simpler C++-focused solutions, some of which we describe in this chapter. It's all about choosing the best tool for the job.

Implementing static polymorphism

Let's now implement our statically polymorphic class hierarchy. We'll need a base template class:

```
template <typename ConcreteItem> class GlamorousItem {
public:
```

```
    void appear_in_full_glory() {
      static_cast<ConcreteItem *>(this)->appear_in_full_glory();
    }
};
```

The template parameter for the base class is the derived class. This may seem odd at first, but it allows us to `static_cast` to the correct type in our interface function, in this case, named `appear_in_full_glory`. We then call the implementation of this function in a derived class. Derived classes could be implemented like so:

```
class PinkHeels : public GlamorousItem<PinkHeels> {
public:
  void appear_in_full_glory() {
    std::cout << "Pink high heels suddenly appeared in all their beauty\n";
  }
};

class GoldenWatch : public GlamorousItem<GoldenWatch> {
public:
  void appear_in_full_glory() {
    std::cout << "Everyone wanted to watch this watch\n";
  }
};
```

Each of these classes derives from our `GlamorousItem` base class using itself as the template argument. Each also implements the required function.

Note that, as opposed to dynamic polymorphism, the base class in CRTP is a template, so you'll get a different base type for each of your derived classes. This means you can't easily create a container of your `GlamorousItem` base class. What you can do, however, is several things:

- Store them in a tuple.
- Create a `std::variant` of your derived classes.
- Add one common class to wrap all instantiations of `Base`. You can use a variant for this one as well.

In the first case, we could use the class as follows. First, create the tuple of instances of base:

```
template <typename... Args>
using PreciousItems = std::tuple<GlamorousItem<Args>...>;

auto glamorous_items = PreciousItems<PinkHeels, GoldenWatch>{};
```

Our type-aliased tuple will be able to store any glamorous items. Now, all we need to do is to call the interesting function:

```
std::apply(
    []<typename... T>(GlamorousItem<T>... items) {
        (items.appear_in_full_glory(), ...); },
    glamorous_items);
```

Because we're trying to iterate a tuple, the easiest way to do so is to call `std::apply`, which invokes the given callable on all the elements of the given tuple. In our case, the callable is a lambda that accepts only `GlamorousItem` base class. We use fold expressions, introduced in C++17, to ensure our function will be called for all elements.

If we were to use a variant instead of a tuple, we'd need to use `std::visit`, like so:

```
using GlamorousVariant = std::variant<PinkHeels, GoldenWatch>;
auto glamorous_items = std::array{GlamorousVariant{PinkHeels{}},
GlamorousVariant{GoldenWatch{}}};
for (auto& elem : glamorous_items) {
    std::visit([]<typename T>(GlamorousItem<T> item){
item.appear_in_full_glory(); }, elem);
}
```

The `std::visit` function basically takes the variant and calls the passed lambda on the object stored in it. Here, we create an array of our glamorous variants, so we can just iterate over it like over any other container, visiting each variant with the appropriate lambda.

If you find it not intuitive to write from the interface user's perspective, consider this next approach, which wraps the variant into yet another class, in our case called `CommonGlamorousItem`:

```
class CommonGlamorousItem {
public:
    template <typename T> requires std::is_base_of_v<GlamorousItem<T>, T>
    explicit CommonGlamorousItem(T &&item)
        : item_{std::forward<T>(item)} {}
private:
    GlamorousVariant item_;
};
```

To construct our wrapper, we use a forwarding constructor (`templated T&&` being its parameter). We then forward instead of moving to create the `item_` wrapped variant, as this way we only move r-value inputs. We also constrain the template parameters, so on one hand, we only wrap the `GlamorousItem` base class and on the other, our template is not used as a move or copy constructor.

We also need to wrap our member function:

```
void appear_in_full_glory() {
  std::visit(
      []<typename T>(GlamorousItem<T> item) {
          item.appear_in_full_glory(); },
      item_);
}
```

This time, the `std::visit` call is an implementation detail. The user can use this wrapper class in the following way:

```
auto glamorous_items = std::array{CommonGlamorousItem{PinkHeels{}},
                                  CommonGlamorousItem{GoldenWatch{}}};
for (auto& elem : glamorous_items) {
  elem.appear_in_full_glory();
}
```

This approach lets the user of the class write easy-to-understand code, but still keep the performance of static polymorphism.

To offer a similar user experience, albeit with worse performance, you can also use a technique called type erasure, which we'll discuss next.

Interlude – using type erasure

Although type erasure isn't related to CRTP, it fits in nicely with our current example, which is why we're showing it here.

The type erasure idiom is about hiding the concrete type under a polymorphic interface. A great example of this approach can be found in Sean Parent's talk *Inheritance Is The Base Class of Evil* from the *GoingNative 2013* conference. We highly recommend you watch it in your spare time; you can find a link to it in the *Further reading* section. In the standard library, you can find it in `std::function`, `std::shared_ptr's deleter`, or `std::any`, among others.

The convenience of use and flexibility comes at a price – this idiom needs to use pointers and virtual dispatch, which makes the mentioned utilities from the standard library bad to use in performance-oriented use cases. Beware.

To introduce type erasure to our example, we no longer need CRTP. This time, our `GlamorousItem` class will wrap dynamically polymorphic objects in a smart pointer:

```
class GlamorousItem {
public:
  template <typename T>
  explicit GlamorousItem(T t)
      : item_{std::make_unique<TypeErasedItem<T>>(std::move(t))} {}

  void appear_in_full_glory() { item_->appear_in_full_glory_impl(); }

private:
  std::unique_ptr<TypeErasedItemBase> item_;
};
```

This time, we store a pointer to base (`TypeErasedItemBase`), which will point to derived wrappers for our items (`TypeErasedItem<T>`s). The base class can be defined as follows:

```
struct TypeErasedItemBase {
  virtual ~TypeErasedItemBase() = default;
  virtual void appear_in_full_glory_impl() = 0;
};
```

Each derived wrapper needs to implement this interface, too:

```
template <typename T> class TypeErasedItem final : public
TypeErasedItemBase {
  public:
    explicit TypeErasedItem(T t) : t_{std::move(t)} {}
    void appear_in_full_glory_impl() override { t_.appear_in_full_glory();
}

  private:
    T t_;
};
```

The base class's interface is implemented by calling the function from the wrapped object. Note that the idiom is called "type erasure" because the `GlamorousItem` class doesn't know what `T` it is actually wrapping. The `information` type gets erased when the item gets constructed, but it all works because `T` implements the required methods.

The concrete items can be implemented in a simpler manner, as shown next:

```
class PinkHeels {
public:
  void appear_in_full_glory() {
    std::cout << "Pink high heels suddenly appeared in all their beauty\n";
```

```
    }
};

class GoldenWatch {
public:
  void appear_in_full_glory() {
    std::cout << "Everyone wanted to watch this watch\n";
  }
};
```

This time, they don't need to inherit from any base. All we need is duck typing – if it quacks like a duck, it's probably a duck. And if it can appear in full glory, it's probably glamorous.

Our type-erased API can be used as follows:

```
auto glamorous_items =
    std::array{GlamorousItem{PinkHeels{}}, GlamorousItem{GoldenWatch{}}};
for (auto &item : glamorous_items) {
  item.appear_in_full_glory();
}
```

We just create an array of our wrappers and iterate over it, all using simple, value-based semantics. We find it the most pleasant to use, as the polymorphism is hidden from the caller as an implementation detail.

However, a big drawback of this approach is, as we mentioned before, poor performance. Type erasure comes at a price, so it should be used sparingly and definitely not in the hot path.

Now that we've described how to wrap and erase types, let's switch to discussing how to create them.

Creating objects

In this section, we'll discuss common solutions to problems related to object creation. We'll discuss various types of object factories, go through builders, and touch on composites and prototypes. However, we'll take a slightly different approach than the Gang of Four when describing their solutions. They proposed complex, dynamically polymorphic class hierarchies as proper implementations of their patterns. In the C++ world, many patterns can be applied to real-world problems without introducing as many classes and the overhead of dynamic dispatch. That's why in our case, the implementations will be different and in many cases simpler or more performant (although more specialized and less "generic" in the Gang of Four sense). Let's dive right in.

Using factories

The first type of creational patterns we'll discuss here are factories. They're useful when the object construction can be done in a single step (a pattern useful if it cannot be covered right after factories), but when the constructor just isn't good enough on its own. There are three types of factories – factory methods, factory functions, and factory classes. Let's introduce them one by one.

Using factory methods

Factory methods, also called the *named constructor idiom*, are basically member functions that call a private constructor for you. When do we use them? Here are a few scenarios:

- **When there are many different ways to construct an object, which would make errors likely**. For example, imagine constructing a class for storing different color channels for a given pixel; each channel is represented by a one-byte value. Using just a constructor would make it too easy to pass the wrong order of channels, or values meant for a different color palette entirely. Also, switching the pixel's internal representation of colors would get tricky pretty fast. You could argue that we should have different types representing colors in those different formats, but often, using a factory method is a valid approach as well.
- **When you want to force the object to be created on the heap or in another specific memory area**. If your object takes up loads of space on the stack and you're afraid you'll run out of stack memory, using a factory method is a solution. The same if you require all instances to be created in some area of memory on a device, for instance.
- **When constructing your object can fail, but you cannot throw exceptions**. You should use exceptions instead of other methods of error handling. When used properly, they can yield cleaner and better-performing code. However, some projects or environments require that exceptions are disabled. In such cases, using a factory method will allow you to report errors happening during construction.

A factory method for the first case we described could look as follows:

```
class Pixel {
public:
  static Pixel fromRgba(char r, char b, char g, char a) {
    return Pixel{r, g, b, a};
  }
  static Pixel fromBgra(char b, char g, char r, char a) {
    return Pixel{r, g, b, a};
```

```
    }

    // other members

private:
    Pixel(char r, char g, char b, char a) : r_(r), g_(g), b_(b), a_(a) {}
    char r_, g_, b_, a_;
}
```

This class has two factory methods (actually, the C++ standard doesn't recognize the term *method*, calling them *member functions* instead): `fromRgba` and `fromBgra`. Now it's harder to make a mistake and initialize the channels in the wrong order.

Note that having a private constructor effectively inhibits any class from inheriting from your type, as without access to its constructor, no instances can be created. If that's your goal and not a side effect, however, you should prefer to just mark your class as final.

Using factory functions

As opposed to using factory member functions, we can also implement them using non-member ones. This way, we can provide better encapsulation, as described by Scott Meyers in his article linked in the *Further reading* section.

In the case of our `Pixel`, we could also create a free function to fabricate its instances. This way, our type could have simpler code:

```
struct Pixel {
    char r, g, b, a;
};

Pixel makePixelFromRgba(char r, char b, char g, char a) {
    return Pixel{r, g, b, a};
}

Pixel makePixelFromBgra(char b, char g, char r, char a) {
    return Pixel{r, g, b, a};
}
```

Using this approach makes our design conform to the open-closed principle described in Chapter 1, *Importance of Software Architecture and Principles of Great Design*. It's easy to add more factory functions for other color palettes without the need to modify the `Pixel` struct itself.

This implementation of `Pixel` allows the user to initialize it by hand instead of using one of our provided functions. If we want, we can inhibit this behavior by changing the class declaration. Here's how it could look after the fix:

```
struct Pixel {
  char r, g, b, a;

private:
  Pixel(char r, char g, char b, char a) : r(r), g(g), b(b), a(a) {}
  friend Pixel makePixelFromRgba(char r, char g, char b, char a);
  friend Pixel makePixelFromBgra(char b, char g, char r, char a);
};
```

This time, our factory functions are friends of our class. However, the type is no longer an aggregate, so we can no longer use aggregate initialization (`Pixel{}`), including designated initializers. Also, we gave up on the open-closed principle. The two approaches offer different trade-offs, so choose wisely.

Choosing the return type of a factory

Yet another thing you should choose when implementing an object factory is the actual type it should return. Let's discuss the various approaches.

In the case of `Pixel`, which is a value type and not a polymorphic one, the simplest approach works the best – we simply return by value. If you produce a polymorphic type, return it by a smart pointer (**never** use a naked pointer for this as this will yield memory leaks at some point). If the caller should own the created object, usually returning it in `unique_ptr` to the base class is the best approach. In the not-so-common cases where your factory and the caller must both own the object, use `shared_ptr` or another reference-counted alternative. Sometimes it's enough that the factory keeps track of the object but doesn't store it. In such cases, store `weak_ptr` inside the factory and return `shared_ptr` outside.

Some C++ programmers would argue that you should return specific types using an out parameter, but that's not the best approach in most cases. In the case of performance, returning by value is usually the best choice, as compilers will not make extra copies of your object. If the issue is with the type being non-copyable, from C++17 onward, the standard specifies where copy elision is mandatory, so returning such types by value is usually not an issue. If your function returns multiple objects, use a pair, tuple, struct, or container.

If something goes wrong during construction, you have several choices:

- Return `std::optional` of your type if there's no need to provide error messages to the caller.
- Throw an exception if errors during construction are rare and should be propagated.
- Return `absl::StatusOr` of your type if errors during construction are common (see Abseil's documentation for this template in the *Further reading* section).

Now that you know what to return, let's discuss our last type of factories.

Using factory classes

Factory classes are types that can fabricate objects for us. They can help decouple polymorphic object types from their callers. They can allow for using object pools (in which reusable objects are kept so that you don't need to constantly allocate and free them) or other allocation schemes. Those are just a few examples of how they can be useful. Let's take a closer look at yet another one. Imagine you need to create different polymorphic types based on input parameters. In some cases, a polymorphic factory function such as the one shown next is not enough:

```
std::unique_ptr<IDocument> open(std::string_view path) {
    if (path.ends_with(".pdf")) return std::make_unique<PdfDocument>();
    if (name == ".html") return std::make_unique<HtmlDocument>();

    return nullptr;
}
```

What if we wanted to open other kinds of documents as well, such as OpenDocument text files? It may be ironic to discover that the preceding open factory is not open for extension. It might not be a big issue if we own the codebase, but if the consumers of our library need to register their own types, this can be an issue. To solve it, let's use a factory class that will allow registering functions to open different kinds of documents, as shown next:

```
class DocumentOpener {
public:
  using DocumentType = std::unique_ptr<IDocument>;
  using ConcreteOpener = DocumentType (*)(std::string_view);

private:
  std::unordered_map<std::string_view, ConcreteOpener> openerByExtension;
};
```

The class doesn't do much yet, but it has a map from extensions to functions that should be called to open files of given types. Now we'll add two public member functions. The first one will register new file types:

```
void Register(std::string_view extension, ConcreteOpener opener) {
  openerByExtension.emplace(extension, opener);
}
```

Now we have a way of filling the map. The second new public function will open the documents using an appropriate opener:

```
DocumentType open(std::string_view path) {
  if (auto last_dot = path.find_last_of('.');
      last_dot != std::string_view::npos) {
    auto extension = path.substr(last_dot + 1);
    return openerByExtension.at(extension)(path);
  } else {
    throw std::invalid_argument{"Trying to open a file with no
extension"};
  }
}
```

Basically, we extract the extension from the file path, throw an exception if it's empty, and if not, we look for an opener in our map. If found, we use it to open the given file, and if not, the map will throw another exception for us.

Now we can instantiate our factory and register custom file types such as the OpenDocument text format:

```
auto document_opener = DocumentOpener{};

document_opener.Register(
    "odt", [](auto path) -> DocumentOpener::DocumentType {
      return std::make_unique<OdtDocument>(path);
    });
```

Notice that we're registering a lambda because it can be converted to our `ConcreteOpener` type, which is a function pointer. However, if our lambda had state, this wouldn't be the case. In such a situation, we would need to use something to wrap us up. One such thing could be `std::function`, but the drawback of this would be the need to pay the cost of type erasure each time we would want to run the function. In the case of opening files, that's probably okay. If you need better performance, however, consider using a type such as `function_ref`.

An example implementation of this utility proposed to the C++ standard (not yet accepted) can be found on Sy Brand's GitHub repo referred to in the *Further reading* section.

Okay, now that we have our opener registered in the factory, let's use it to open a file and extract some text out of it:

```
auto document = document_opener.open("file.odt");
std::cout << document->extract_text().front();
```

And that's all! If you want to provide the consumers of your library with a way to register their own types, they must have access to your map at runtime. You can either provide them with an API to reach it or make the factory static and allow them to register from anywhere in the code.

That does it for factories and building objects in a single step. Let's discuss another popular pattern to be used if factorys aren't a good fit.

Using builders

Builders are similar to factories, a creational pattern coming from the Gang of Four. Unlike factories, they can help you build more complex objects: those that cannot be built in a single step, such as types assembled from many separate parts. They also provide you with a way to customize the construction of objects. In our case, we'll skip designing complex hierarchies of builders. Instead, we'll show how a builder can help. We'll leave implementing hierarchies to you, as an exercise.

Builders are needed when an object cannot be produced in a single step, but having a fluent interface can just make them pleasant to use if the single step is not trivial. Let's demonstrate creating fluent builder hierarchies using CRTP.

In our case, we'll create a CRTP, `GenericItemBuilder`, that we'll use as our base builder, and `FetchingItemBuilder`, which will be a more specialized one that can fetches data using a remote address if that's a supported feature. Such specializations can even live in different libraries, for instance, consuming different APIs that may or may not be available at build time.

For demo purposes, we'll build instances of our `Item` struct from Chapter 5, *Leveraging C++ Language Features*:

```
struct Item {
  std::string name;
  std::optional<std::string> photo_url;
  std::string description;
  std::optional<float> price;
  time_point<system_clock> date_added{};
  bool featured{};
};
```

If you want, you can enforce that `Item` instances are built using a builder by making the default constructor private and making the builders friends:

```
template <typename ConcreteBuilder> friend class GenericItemBuilder;
```

Our builder's implementation can be started as follows:

```
template <typename ConcreteBuilder> class GenericItemBuilder {
public:
  explicit GenericItemBuilder(std::string name)
      : item_{.name = std::move(name)} {}
protected:
  Item item_;
```

Although it's generally not recommended to create protected members, we want our descendant builders to be able to reach our item. An alternative would be to use just the public methods of our base builder in derived ones.

We take the name in the builder's constructor, as it's a single input coming from the user that needs to be set when we create our item. This way, we make sure that it will be set. An alternative would be to check whether it's okay at the final stage of building, when the object is being released to the user. In our case, the build step can be implemented as follows:

```
Item build() && {
  item_.date_added = system_clock::now();
  return std::move(item_);
}
```

We enforce that the builder is "consumed" when this method is called; it must be an r-value. This means we can either use the builder in one line or move it in the last step to mark its end of work. We then set the creation time for our item and move it outside of the builder.

Our builder's API could offer functions such as the following:

```
ConcreteBuilder &&with_description(std::string description) {
  item_.description = std::move(description);
  return static_cast<ConcreteBuilder &&>(*this);
}

ConcreteBuilder &&marked_as_featured() {
  item_.featured = true;
  return static_cast<ConcreteBuilder &&>(*this);
}
```

Each of them returns the concrete (derived) builder object as an r-value reference. Perhaps counterintuitively, this time such a return type should be preferred to returning by value. This is to avoid unnecessary copies of `item_` when building. On the other hand, returning by an l-value reference could lead to dangling references and would make calling `build()` harder because the returned l-value reference wouldn't match the expected r-value one.

The final builder type could look as follows:

```
class ItemBuilder final : public GenericItemBuilder<ItemBuilder> {
  using GenericItemBuilder<ItemBuilder>::GenericItemBuilder;
};
```

It's just a class that reuses the constructors from our generic builder. It can be used as follows:

```
auto directly_loaded_item = ItemBuilder{"Pot"}
                              .with_description("A decent one")
                              .with_price(100)
                              .build();
```

As you can see, the final interface can be called using function chaining and the method names make the whole invocation fluent to read, hence the name *fluent interfaces*.

What if we were to not load each item directly, but rather use a more specialized builder that could load parts of the data from a remote endpoint? We could define it as follows:

```
class FetchingItemBuilder final
    : public GenericItemBuilder<FetchingItemBuilder> {
public:
  explicit FetchingItemBuilder(std::string name)
      : GenericItemBuilder(std::move(name)) {}

  FetchingItemBuilder&& using_data_from(std::string_view url) && {
    item_ = fetch_item(url);
    return std::move(*this);
```

```
        }
    };
```

We also use CRTP to inherit from our generic builder and also enforce giving us a name. This time, however, we extend the base builder with our own function to fetch the contents and put them in the item we're building. Thanks to CRTP, when we call a function from our base builder, we'll get the derived one returned, which makes the interface much easier to use. It can be called in the following manner:

```
auto fetched_item =
    FetchingItemBuilder{"Linen blouse"}
        .using_data_from("https://example.com/items/linen_blouse")
        .marked_as_featured()
        .build();
```

All nice and dandy!

Builders can also come in handy if you need to always create immutable objects. As the builder has access to private members of the class, it can modify them, even if the class doesn't provide any setters for them. That's of course not the only case when you can benefit from using them.

Building with composites and prototypes

A case where you would need to use a builder is when creating a composite. A composite is a design pattern in which a group of objects is treated as one, all sharing the same interface (or the same base type). An example would be a graph, which you could compose out of subgraphs, or a document, which could nest other documents. When you would call print() on such an object, all its sub-objects would get their print() functions called in order to print the whole composite. The builder pattern can be useful for creating each sub-object and composing them all together.

Prototype is yet another pattern that can be used for object construction. If your type is very costly to create anew, or you just want to have a base object to build upon, you might want to use this pattern. It boils down to providing a way to clone your object, which you could later either use on its own or modify so it becomes what it should be. In the case of a polymorphic hierarchy, just add clone() like so:

```
class Map {
public:
    virtual std::unique_ptr<Map> clone() const;
    // ... other members ...
};
```

```
class MapWithPointsOfInterests {
public:
    std::unique_ptr<Map> clone() override const;
    // ... other members ...
private:
    std::vector<PointOfInterest> pois_;
};
```

Our `MapWithPointsOfInterests` object could clone the points too, so we don't need to re-add each of them manually. This way, we can have some default provided to the end user when they create their own map. Note also that in some cases, instead of using a prototype, a simple copy constructor would suffice.

We have now covered object creation. We touched on variants along the way, so why not revisit them (pun intended) to see how else they can help us?

Tracking state and visiting objects in C++

State is a design pattern meant to help change the behavior of an object when its internal state changes. The behavior for different states should be independent of each other so that adding new states doesn't affect the current ones. The simple approach of implementing all the behavior in the stateful object doesn't scale and is not open for extension. Using the state pattern, new behavior can be added by introducing new state classes and defining the transitions between them. In this section, we'll show a way to implement states and a state machine leveraging `std::variant` and statically polymorphic double dispatch. In other words, we'll build a finite state machine by joining the state and visitor patterns in a C++ way.

First, let's define our states. In our example, let's model the states of a product in a store. They can be as follows:

```
namespace state {

struct Depleted {};

struct Available {
  int count;
};

struct Discontinued {};
} // namespace state
```

Our states can have properties of their own, such as the count of items left. Also, as opposed to dynamically polymorphic ones, they don't need to inherit from a common base. Instead, they are all stored in one variant, as shown next:

```
using State = std::variant<state::Depleted, state::Available,
state::Discontinued>;
```

Aside from states, we also need events for state transitions. Check the following code:

```
namespace event {

struct DeliveryArrived {
   int count;
};

struct Purchased {
   int count;
};

struct Discontinued {};

} // namespace event
```

As you can see, our events can also have properties and don't inherit from a common base. Now, we need to implement the transitions between the states. This can be done as follows:

```
State on_event(state::Available available, event::DeliveryArrived
delivered) {
   available.count += delivered.count;
   return available;
}

State on_event(state::Available available, event::Purchased purchased) {
   available.count -= purchased.count;
   if (available.count > 0)
     return available;
   return state::Depleted{};
}
```

If a purchase is made, the state can change, but it can also stay the same. We can also use templates to handle several states at once:

```
template <typename S> State on_event(S, event::Discontinued) {
   return state::Discontinued{};
}
```

If an item gets discontinued, it doesn't matter what state it was in. Okay, let's now implement the last supported transition:

```
State on_event(state::Depleted depleted, event::DeliveryArrived delivered)
{
   return state::Available{delivered.count};
}
```

The next piece of the puzzle we need is a way to define multiple call operators in one object generically so that the best matching overload can be called. We'll use it later to call the transitions we just defined. Our helper can look as follows:

```
template<class... Ts> struct overload : Ts... { using Ts::operator()...; };
template<class... Ts> overload(Ts...) -> overload<Ts...>;
```

We create an `overload` struct that will provide all the call operators passed to it during construction, using variable templates, a fold expression, and a class template argument deduction guide. For a more in-depth explanation of this, along with an alternative way of implementing visitation, refer to Bartłomiej Filipek's blog post in the *Further reading* section.

We can now start implementing the state machine itself:

```
class ItemStateMachine {
public:
   template <typename Event> void process_event(Event &&event) {
      state_ = std::visit(overload{
         [&](const auto &state) requires std::is_same_v<
            decltype(on_event(state, std::forward<Event>(event))), State> {
            return on_event(state, std::forward<Event>(event));
         },
         [](const auto &unsupported_state) -> State {
            throw std::logic_error{"Unsupported state transition"};
         }
      },
      state_);
   }

private:
   State state_;
};
```

Our `process_event` function will accept any of our defined events. It will call an appropriate `on_event` function using the current state and the passed event and switch to the new state. If an `on_event` overload is found for the given state and event, the first lambda will get called. Otherwise, the constraint won't be satisfied and the second, more generic overload will get called. This means if there's an unsupported state transition, we'll just throw an exception.

Now, let's provide a way to report the current state:

```
std::string report_current_state() {
    return std::visit(
        overload{[](const state::Available &state) -> std::string {
                    return std::to_string(state.count) +
                    " items available";
                },
                [](const state::Depleted) -> std::string {
                    return "Item is temporarily out of stock";
                },
                [](const state::Discontinued) -> std::string {
                    return "Item has been discontinued";
                }},
        state_);
}
```

Here, we use our overload to pass three lambdas, each returning a report string generated by visiting our state object.

We can now call our solution:

```
auto fsm = ItemStateMachine{};
std::cout << fsm.report_current_state() << '\n';
fsm.process_event(event::DeliveryArrived{3});
std::cout << fsm.report_current_state() << '\n';
fsm.process_event(event::Purchased{2});
std::cout << fsm.report_current_state() << '\n';
fsm.process_event(event::DeliveryArrived{2});
std::cout << fsm.report_current_state() << '\n';
fsm.process_event(event::Purchased{3});
std::cout << fsm.report_current_state() << '\n';
fsm.process_event(event::Discontinued{});
std::cout << fsm.report_current_state() << '\n';
// fsm.process_event(event::DeliveryArrived{1});
```

Upon running, this will yield the following output:

```
Item is temporarily out of stock
3 items available
1 items available
3 items available
Item is temporarily out of stock
Item has been discontinued
```

That is, unless you uncomment the last line with the unsupported transition, in which case an exception will be thrown at the end.

Our solution is much more performant than dynamic polymorphism-based ones, although the list of supported states and events is constrained to those provided at compile time. For more information on states, variants, and the various ways of visitations, see Mateusz Pusz's talk from CppCon 2018, also listed in the *Further reading* section.

Before we close this chapter, one last thing we'd like for you to learn about is handling memory. Let's begin our last section.

Dealing with memory efficiently

Even if you don't have very limited memory, it's a good idea to look at how you use it. Usually, memory throughput is the performance bottleneck of modern-day systems, so it's always important to make good use of it. Performing too many dynamic allocations can slow down your program and lead to memory fragmentation. Let's learn a few ways to mitigate those issues.

Reducing dynamic allocations using SSO/SOO

Dynamic allocations can sometimes cause you other trouble than just throwing when you construct objects despite not having enough memory. They often cost you CPU cycles and can cause memory fragmentation. Fortunately, there is a way to protect against it. If you've ever used `std::string` (post GCC 5.0), you most probably used an optimization called **Small String Optimization** (SSO). This is one example of a more general optimization named **Small Object Optimization** (SSO), which can be spotted in types such as Abseil's InlinedVector. The main idea is pretty straightforward: if the dynamically allocated object is small enough, it should be stored inside the class that owns it instead of being dynamically allocated. In `std::string`'s case, usually, there's a capacity, length, and the actual string to store. If the string is short enough (in GCC's case, on 64-bit platforms, it's 15 bytes), it will be stored in some of those members.

Storing objects in place instead of allocating them somewhere else and storing just the pointer has one more benefit: less pointer chasing. Each time you need to reach to data stored behind a pointer, you increase the pressure on the CPU caches and risk needing to fetch data from the main memory. If this is a common pattern, it can influence the overall performance of your app, especially if the pointed-to addresses aren't guessed by the CPU's prefetcher. Using techniques such as SSO and SOO are invaluable in reducing those issues.

Saving memory by herding COWs

If you used GCC's `std::string` before GCC 5.0, you might have used a different optimization called **Copy-On-Write (COW)**. The COW string implementation, when it had multiple instances created with the same underlying character array, was actually sharing the same memory address for it. When the string was written to, the underlying storage was copied — hence the name.

This technique helped save memory and keep the caches hot, and often offered solid performance on a single thread. Beware of using it in multi-threaded contexts, though. The need for using locks can be a real performance killer. As with any performance-related topic, it's best to just measure whether in your case it's the best tool for the job.

Let's now discuss a feature of C++17 that can help you achieve good performance with dynamic allocations.

Leveraging polymorphic allocators

The feature we're talking about is polymorphic allocators. To be specific, the `std::pmr::polymorphic_allocator` and the polymorphic `std::pmr::memory_resource` class that the allocator uses to allocate memory.

In essence, it allows you to easily chain memory resources to make the best use of your memory. Chains can be as simple as one resource that reserves a big chunk and distributes it, falling back to another that simply calls `new` and `delete` if it depletes memory. They can also be much more complex: you can build a long chain of memory resources that handle pools of different sizes, offer thread-safety only when needed, bypass the heap and go for the system's memory directly, return you the last freed chunk of memory to provide cache hotness, and do other fancy stuff. Not all of these capabilities are offered by the standard polymorphic memory resources, but thanks to their design, it's easy to extend them.

Let's first tackle the topic of memory arenas.

Using memory arenas

A memory arena, also called a region, is just a large chunk of memory that exists for a limited time. You can use it to allocate smaller objects that you use for the lifetime of the arena. Objects in the arena can be either deallocated as usual or erased all at once in a process called *winking out*. We'll describe it later on.

Arenas have several great advantages over the usual allocations and deallocations – they increase performance because they limit the memory allocations that need to grab upstream resources. They also reduce fragmentation of memory, because any fragmentation that would happen will happen inside the arena. Once an arena's memory is released, the fragmentation is no more as well. A great idea is to create separate arenas per thread. If only a single thread uses an arena, it doesn't need to use any locking or other thread-safety mechanisms, reducing thread contention and giving you a nice boost in performance.

If your program is single-threaded, a low-cost solution to increase its performance could be as follows:

```
auto single_threaded_pool = std::pmr::unsynchronized_pool_resource();
std::pmr::set_default_resource(&single_threaded_pool);
```

The default resource if you won't set any explicitly will be `new_delete_resource`, which calls `new` and `delete` each time just like regular `std::allocator` does, and with all the thread-safety it provides (and costs).

If you use the preceding code snippet, all the allocations done using `pmr` allocators would be done with no locks. You still need to actually use the `pmr` types, though. To do so with standard containers, for instance, you need to simply pass `std::pmr::polymorphic_allocator<T>` as the allocator template parameter. Many standard containers have `pmr`-enabled type aliases. The two variables created next are of the same type and both will use the default memory resource:

```
auto ints = std::vector<int,
std::pmr::polymorphic_allocator<int>>(std::pmr::get_default_resource());
auto also_ints = std::pmr::vector<int>{};
```

The first one gets the resource passed explicitly, though. Let's now go through the resources available in `pmr`.

Using the monotonic memory resource

The first one we'll discuss is `std::pmr::monotonic_buffer_resource`. It's a resource that only allocates memory and doesn't do anything on deallocation. It will only deallocate memory when the resource is destructed or on an explicit call to `release()`. This, connected with no thread safety, makes this type extremely performant. If your application occasionally needs to perform a task that does lots of allocations on a given thread, then releases all the objects used at once afterward, using monotonic resources will yield great gains. It's also a great base building block for chains of resources.

Using pool resources

A common combo of two resources is to use a pool resource on top of a monotonic buffer resource. The standard pool resources create pools of different-sized chunks. There are two types in `std::pmr`, `unsynchronized_pool_resource` for use when only one thread allocates and deallocates from it and `synchronized_pool_resource` for multi-threaded use. Both should provide you with much better performance compared to the global allocator, especially when using the monotonic buffer as their upstream resource. If you wonder how to chain them, here's how:

```
auto buffer = std::array<std::byte, 1 * 1024 * 1024>{};
auto monotonic_resource =
    std::pmr::monotonic_buffer_resource{buffer.data(), buffer.size()};
auto pool_options = std::pmr::pool_options{.max_blocks_per_chunk = 0,
    .largest_required_pool_block = 512};
auto arena =
    std::pmr::unsynchronized_pool_resource{pool_options,
&monotonic_resource};
```

We create a 1 MB buffer for the arena to reuse. We pass it to a monotonic resource, which is then passed to an unsynchronized pool resource, creating a simple yet efficient chain of allocators that won't call new until all the initial buffer is used up.

You can pass a `std::pmr::pool_options` object to both the pool types to limit the max count of blocks of a given size (`max_blocks_per_chunk`) or the size of the largest block (`largest_required_pool_block`). Passing 0 causes the implementation's default to be used. In the case of GCC's library, the actual blocks per chunk differ depending on the block size. If the max size is exceeded, the pool resource will allocate directly from its upstream resource. It also goes to the upstream resource if the initial memory was depleted. In this case, it allocates geometrically growing chunks of memory.

Writing your own memory resource

If the standard memory resources don't suit all your needs, you can always create a custom one quite simply. For instance, a good optimization that not all standard library implementations offer is to keep track of the last chunks of a given size that were released and return them back on the next allocations of given sizes. This Most Recently Used cache can help you increase the hotness of data caches, which should help your app's performance. You can think of it as a set of LIFO queues for chunks.

Sometimes you might also want to debug allocations and deallocations. In the following snippet, I have written a simple resource that can help you with this task:

```
class verbose_resource : public std::pmr::memory_resource {
  std::pmr::memory_resource *upstream_resource_;
public:
  explicit verbose_resource(std::pmr::memory_resource *upstream_resource)
    : upstream_resource_(upstream_resource) {}
```

Our verbose resource inherits from the polymorphic base resource. It also accepts an upstream resource, which it will use for actual allocations. It has to implement three private functions – one for allocating, one for deallocating, and one for comparing instances of the resource itself. Here's the first one:

```
private:
  void *do_allocate(size_t bytes, size_t alignment) override {
    std::cout << "Allocating " << bytes << " bytes\n";
    return upstream_resource_->allocate(bytes, alignment);
  }
```

All it does is print the allocation size on the standard output and then use the upstream resource to allocate memory. The next one will be similar:

```
void do_deallocate(void *p, size_t bytes, size_t alignment) override {
  std::cout << "Deallocating " << bytes << " bytes\n";
  upstream_resource_->deallocate(p, bytes, alignment);
}
```

We log how much memory we deallocate and use the upstream to perform the task. Now the last required function is stated next:

```
[[nodiscard]] bool
do_is_equal(const memory_resource &other) const noexcept override {
  return this == &other;
}
```

We simply compare the addresses of the instances to know whether they're equal. The `[[nodiscard]]` attribute helps us be sure that the caller actually consumes the returned value, which can help us avoid accidental misuse of our function.

That's it. For a powerful feature such as the `pmr` allocators, the API isn't that complex now, isn't it?

Aside from tracking allocations, we can also use `pmr` to guard us against allocating when we shouldn't.

Ensuring there are no unexpected allocations

The special `std::pmr::null_memory_resource()` will throw an exception when anyone tries to allocate memory using it. You can safeguard from performing any allocations using `pmr` by setting it as the default resource as shown next:

```
std::pmr::set_default_resource(null_memory_resource());
```

You can also use it to limit allocation from the upstream when it shouldn't happen. Check the following code:

```
auto buffer = std::array<std::byte, 640 * 1024>{}; // 640K ought to be
enough for anybody
auto resource = std::pmr::monotonic_buffer_resource{
    buffer.data(), buffer.size(), std::pmr::null_memory_resource()};
```

If anybody tries to allocate more than the buffer size we set, `std::bad_alloc` would be thrown.

Let's move on to our last item in this chapter.

Winking out memory

Sometimes not having to deallocate the memory, as the monotonic buffer resource does, is still not enough for performance. A special technique called *winking* out can help here. Winking out objects means that they're not only not deallocated one by one, but their constructors aren't called too. The objects simply evaporate, saving time that would normally be spent calling destructors for each object and their members (and their members...) in the arena.

NOTE: This is an advanced topic. Be careful when using this technique, and only use it if the possible gain is worth it.

This technique can save your precious CPU cycles, but it's not always possible to use it. Avoid winking out memory if your objects handle resources other than memory. Otherwise, you will get resource leaks. The same goes if you depend on any side effects the destructors of your objects would have.

Let's now see winking out in action:

```cpp
auto verbose = verbose_resource(std::pmr::get_default_resource());
auto monotonic = std::pmr::monotonic_buffer_resource(&verbose);
std::pmr::set_default_resource(&monotonic);

auto alloc = std::pmr::polymorphic_allocator{};
auto *vector = alloc.new_object<std::pmr::vector<std::pmr::string>>();
vector->push_back("first one");
vector->emplace_back("long second one that must allocate");
```

Here, we created a polymorphic allocator by hand that'll use our default resource – a monotonic one that logs each time it reaches upstream. To create objects, we'll use a C++20 addition to `pmr`, the `new_object` function. We create a vector of strings. We can pass the first one using `push_back`, because it's small enough to fit into the small-string buffer we have thanks to SSO. The second string would need to allocate a string using the default resource and only then pass it to our vector if we used `push_back`. Emplacing it causes the string to be constructed inside the vector's functions (not before the call), so it will use the vector's allocator. Finally, we don't call the destructors of allocated objects anywhere, and just deallocate everything at once, when we exit the scope. This should give us hard-to-beat performance.

That was the last item on our list for this chapter. Let's summarize what we've learned.

Summary

In this chapter, we went through various idioms and patterns used in the C++ world. You should now be able to write fluent, idiomatic C++. We've demystified how to perform automatic cleanup. You can now write safer types that properly move, copy, and swap. You learned how to use ADL to your advantage both with compilation times and writing customization points. We discussed how to choose between static and dynamic polymorphism. We also learned how to introduce policies to your types, when to use type erasure, and when not.

What's more, we discussed how to create objects using factories and fluent builders. Moreover, using memory arenas for this is also no longer arcane magic. So is writing state machines using tools such as variants.

We did all that as well as touching on extra topics down the road. Phew! The next stop on our journey will be about building your software and packaging it.

Questions

1. What are the rules of three, five, and zero?
2. When do we use niebloids versus hidden friends?
3. How can arrays interfaces be improved to be more production-ready?
4. What are fold expressions?
5. When shouldn't you use static polymorphism?
6. How can we save on one more allocation in the winking out example?

Further reading

1. *tag_invoke: A general pattern for supporting customisable functions*, Lewis Baker, Eric Niebler, Kirk Shoop, ISO C++ proposal, `https://wg21.link/p1895`
2. *tag_invoke :: niebloids evolved*, Gašper Ažman for the Core C++ Conference, YouTube video, `https://www.youtube.com/watch?v=oQ26YL0J6DU`
3. *Inheritance Is The Base Class of Evil*, Sean Parent for the GoingNative 2013 Conference, Channel9 video, `https://channel9.msdn.com/Events/GoingNative/2013/Inheritance-Is-The-Base-Class-of-Evil`

4. *Modern C++ Design*, Andrei Alexandrescu, Addison-Wesley, 2001

5. *How Non-Member Functions Improve Encapsulation*, Scott Meyers, Dr. Dobbs article, `https://www.drdobbs.com/cpp/how-non-member-functions-improve-encapsu/184401197`

6. *Returning a Status or a Value*, Status User Guide, Abseil documentation, `https://abseil.io/docs/cpp/guides/status#returning-a-status-or-a-value`

7. `function_ref`, GitHub repository, `https://github.com/TartanLlama/function_ref`

8. *How To Use std::visit With Multiple Variants*, Bartłomiej Filipek, post on Bartek's coding blog, `https://www.bfilipek.com/2018/09/visit-variants.html`

9. CppCon 2018: Mateusz Pusz, *Effective replacement of dynamic polymorphism with std::variant*, YouTube video, `https://www.youtube.com/watch?v=gKbORJtnVu8`

Building and Packaging

As an architect, you will need to know about all the elements that make up the build process. This chapter will explain all the elements that make up the build process. From compiler flags to automation scripts and beyond, we will guide you to the point where each possible module, service, and artifact is versioned and stored in a central location ready for deployment. We will mainly focus on CMake.

In this chapter, you'll learn about the following:

- What compiler flags you should consider using
- How to create build systems based on Modern CMake
- How to build reusable components
- How to use external code in CMake cleanly
- How to create DEB and RPM packages, as well as NSIS installers, using CPack
- How to use the Conan package manager for installing your dependencies and for creating your own packages

After reading this chapter, you'll know how to write state-of-the-art code for building and packaging your project.

Technical requirements

To replicate the examples from this chapter, you should install a recent version of **GCC** and **Clang, CMake 3.15** or higher, **Conan**, and **Boost 1.69**.

The source code snippets from the chapter can be found at `https://github.com/PacktPublishing/Software-Architecture-with-Cpp/tree/master/Chapter07`.

Getting the most out of compilers

Compilers are one of the most important tools in every programmer's workshop. That's why getting to know them well can help you out in many different ways, on countless occasions. In this section, we'll describe a few tips to use them effectively. This will only touch the tip of the iceberg as whole books can be written about these tools and their vast variety of available flags, optimizations, functionalities, and other specifics. GCC even has a wiki page with a list of books about compilers! You can find it in the *Further reading* section at the end of this chapter.

Using multiple compilers

One of the things you should consider in your build process is using multiple compilers instead of just one, the reason being the several benefits that come with it. One of them is that they can detect different issues with your code. For instance, MSVC has signedness checks enabled by default. Using several compilers can help with potential portability issues you may encounter in the future, especially when a decision is made to also compile your code on a different OS, such as moving from Linux to Windows or the other way. To make such efforts at no cost, you should strive to write portable, ISO C++-compliant code. One of the benefits of **Clang** is that it strives for compliance with the C++ standards more than GCC. If you're using **MSVC**, try adding the `/permissive-` option (available since Visual Studio 17; enabled by default for projects created using version 15.5+). For **GCC**, try not to use the GNU variants when choosing the C++ standard for your code (for example, prefer `-std=c++17` to `-std=gnu++17`). If performance is your goal, being able to build your software with a wide range of compilers will also allow you to pick the one that will offer the fastest binaries for your specific use cases.

Regardless of which compiler you choose for your release builds, consider using Clang for development. It runs on macOS, Linux, and Windows, supports the same set of flags as GCC, and aims to provide the fastest build times and concise compilation errors.

If you're using CMake, you have two common ways to add another compiler. One is to pass the appropriate compilers when invoking CMake, like so:

```
mkdir build-release-gcc
cd build-release-gcc
cmake .. -DCMAKE_BUILD_TYPE=Release -DCMAKE_C_COMPILER=/usr/bin/gcc -
DCMAKE_CXX_COMPILER=/usr/bin/g++
```

It's also possible to just set CC and CXX before invoking CMake, but those variables are not honored on all platforms (such as macOS).

Another approach is to use toolchain files. It's probably an overkill if you just need to use a different compiler, but it's the go-to solution when you want to cross-compile. To use a toolchain file, you should pass it as a CMake argument: –
DCMAKE_TOOLCHAIN_FILE=toolchain.cmake.

Reducing build times

Every year, programmers spend countless hours waiting for their builds to complete. Reducing build times is an easy way to improve the productivity of whole teams, so let's discuss a few approaches to doing it.

Using a fast compiler

One of the simplest ways to have faster builds is sometimes to upgrade your compiler. For instance, by upgrading Clang to 7.0.0, you could shave up to 30% off of build times using **Precompiled Header (PCH)** files. Since Clang 9, it has gained the -ftime-trace option, which can provide you with information on the compilation times of all the files it processes. Other compilers have similar switches, too: check out GCC's -ftime-report or MSVC's /Bt and /d2cgsummary. Often you can get faster compiles by switching the compiler, which is especially useful on your development machine; for example, Clang usually compiles code faster than GCC.

Once you have a fast compiler, let's take a look at what it needs to compile.

Rethinking templates

Different parts of the compilation process take a different amount of time to complete. This is especially important for compile-time constructs. One of Odin Holmes' interns, Chiel Douwes, created the so-called Rule of Chiel based on benchmarking the compile-time costs of various template operations. This, and other type-based template metaprogramming tricks, can be seen in the *Type Based Template Metaprogramming is Not Dead* lecture by Odin Holmes. From fastest to slowest, they are as follows:

- Looking up a memoized type (for example, a template instantiation)
- Adding a parameter to an alias call
- Adding a parameter to a type

- Calling an alias
- Instantiating a type
- Instantiating a function template
- Using **SFINAE (Substitution Failure Is Not an Error)**

To demonstrate this rule, consider the following code:

```
template<bool>
 struct conditional {
     template<typename T, typename F>
     using type = F;
 };

 template<>
 struct conditional<true> {
     template<typename T, typename F>
     using type = T;
 };

 template<bool B, typename T, typename F>
 using conditional_t = conditional<B>::template type<T, F>;
```

It defines a `conditional` **template alias, which stores a type that resolves as** T **if condition** B **is true, and to** F **otherwise. The traditional way to write such a utility would be as follows:**

```
template<bool B, class T, class F>
 struct conditional {
     using type = T;
 };

 template<class T, class F>
 struct conditional<false, T, F> {
     using type = F;
 };

 template<bool B, class T, class F>
 using conditional_t = conditional<B,T,F>::type;
```

However, this second way is slower to compile than the first because it relies on creating template instances instead of type aliases.

Let's now take a look at what tools and their features you can use to keep compile times low.

Leveraging tools

A common technique that can make your builds faster is to use a **single compilation unit build,** or **unity build**. It won't speed up every project, but it may be worth a shot if there's plenty of code in your header files. Unity builds work by just including all your .cpp files in one translation unit. Another similar idea is to use pre-compiled headers. Plugins such as Cotire for CMake will handle both of these techniques for you. CMake 3.16 also adds native support for unity builds, which you can enable either for one target, `set_target_properties(<target> PROPERTIES UNITY_BUILD ON)`, or globally by setting `CMAKE_UNITY_BUILD` to `true`. If you just want PCHs, you might want to take a look into CMake 3.16's `target_precompile_headers`.

> If you feel like you are including too much in your C++ files, consider using a tool named **include-what-you-use** to tidy them up. Preferring forward declaring types and functions to including header files can also go a long way in reducing the compilation times.

If your project takes forever to link, there are some ways to deal with this as well. Using a different linker, such as LLVM's LLD or GNU's Gold, can help a lot, especially since they allow multi-threaded linking. If you can't afford to use a different linker, you can always experiment with flags such as -fvisibility-hidden or -fvisibility-inlines-hidden and mark only the functions you want to have visible in your shared library with an appropriate annotation in the source code. This way, the linker will have less work to perform. If you're using link-time optimization, try to only do that for the builds that are performance-critical: those that you plan to profile and those meant for production. Otherwise, you'll probably just waste your developers' time.

If you're using CMake and aren't tied to a specific generator (for example, CLion requires using the `Code::Blocks` generator), you can replace the default Make generator with a faster one. **Ninja** is a great one to start with as it was created specifically to reduce build times. To use it, just pass -G Ninja when invoking CMake.

There are still two more great tools that will surely give you a boost. One of them is **Ccache**. It's a tool that runs its cache of C and C++ compilation outputs. If you're trying to build the same thing twice, it will get the results from the cache instead of running the compilation. It keeps the statistics, such as cache hits and misses, can remember the warnings that it should emit when compiling a specific file, and has many configuration options that you can store in the ~/.ccache/ccache.conf file. To obtain its statistics, just run ccache --show-stats.

The second tool is **IceCC** (or Icecream). It's a fork of distcc, essentially a tool to distribute your builds across hosts. With IceCC, it's easier to use a custom toolchain. It runs the iceccd daemon on each host and an icecc-scheduler service that manages the whole cluster. The scheduler, unlike in distcc, makes sure to only use the idle cycles on each machine, so you won't end up overloading other people's workstations.

To use both IceCC and Ccache for your CMake builds, just add `-DCMAKE_C_COMPILER_LAUNCHER="ccache;icecc"` `-DCMAKE_CXX_COMPILER_LAUNCHER="ccache;icecc"` to your CMake invocation. If you're compiling on Windows, instead of the last two tools, you could use clcache and Incredibuild or look for other alternatives.

Now that you know how to build fast, let's move on to another important topic.

Finding potential code issues

Even the quickest builds aren't worth much if your code has bugs. There are dozens of flags to warn you of potential issues in your code. This section will try to answer which ones you should consider enabling.

First, let's start with a slightly different matter: how not to get warned about issues with code from other libraries. Getting warned about issues that you can't really fix isn't useful. Fortunately, there are compiler switches to disable such warnings. In GCC, for instance, you have two types of `include` files: regular (passed using `-I`) and system ones (passed using `-isystem`). If you specify a directory using the latter, you won't get warnings from the headers it contains. MSVC has an equivalent for `-isystem`: `/external:I`. Additionally, it has other flags to handle external includes, such as `/external:anglebrackets`, which tells the compiler to treat all files included using angle brackets as external ones, thus disabling warnings for them. You can specify a warning level for external files. You can also keep warnings coming from template instantiations caused by your code using `/external:templates-`. If you're looking for a portable way to mark `include` paths as system/external ones, and you're using CMake, you can add the `SYSTEM` keyword to a `target_include_directories` directive.

Speaking of portability, if you want to be conformant to a C++ standard (and you should), consider adding –pedantic to your compile options for GCC or Clang, or the /permissive- option for MSVC. This way, you'll get informed about every non-standard extension that you might be using. If you're using CMake, add the following line for each of your targets, set_target_properties(<target> PROPERTIES CXX_EXTENSIONS OFF), to disable compiler-specific extensions.

If you're using MSVC, strive to compile your code with /W4, since it enables most of the important warnings. For GCC and Clang, try to use –Wall –Wextra –Wconversion –Wsign-conversion. The first one, despite its name, enables only some common warnings. The second, however, adds another bunch of warnings. The third one is based on the tips from a great book by Scott Meyers, titled *Effective C++* (it's a set of good warnings, but check that it's not too noisy for your needs). The last two are about type conversions and signedness conversions. All those flags together create a sane safety net, but you can, of course, look for more flags to enable. Clang has a –Weverything flag. Try to periodically run a build with it to discover new, potential warnings that could be worth enabling in your codebase. You might be surprised at how many messages you get with this flag, although enabling some of the warning flags might not be worth the hassle. An MSVC alternative is named /Wall. Take a look at the following tables to see some other interesting options that are not enabled by the preceding 9:

GCC/Clang:

Flag	Meaning
–Wduplicated–cond	Warn when the same condition is used in if and else–if blocks.
–Wduplicated–branches	Warn if both branches contain the same source code.
–Wlogical–op	Warn when operands in logical operations are the same and when a bitwise operator should be used instead.
–Wnon–virtual–dtor	Warn when a class has virtual functions but not a virtual destructor.
–Wnull–dereference	Warn about null dereferences. This check may be inactive in unoptimized builds.
–Wuseless–cast	Warn when casting to the same type.
–Wshadow	A whole family of warnings about declarations that shadow other, previous declarations.

MSVC:

Flag	Meaning
/w44640	Warn on non-thread-safe static member initialization.

One last thing worth mentioning is the question: to -Werror (or /WX on MSVC) or not to -Werror? This really depends on your personal preferences as issuing errors instead of warnings has its pros and cons. On the plus side, you won't let any of your enabled warnings slip by. Your CI build will fail and your code won't compile. When running multi-threaded builds, you won't lose any warnings in the quickly passing compilation messages. However, there are some minuses too. You won't be able to upgrade your compiler if it enables any new warnings or just detects more issues. The same goes for dependencies, which can deprecate some functions they provide. You won't be able to deprecate anything in your code if it's used by other parts of your project. Fortunately, you can always use a mixed solution: strive to compile with -Werror, but disable it when you need to do the things it inhibits. This requires discipline, as if any new warnings are to slip in, you may have a hard time eliminating them.

Using compiler-centric tools

Nowadays, compilers allow you to do much more with them than a few years back. This is owing to the introduction of LLVM and Clang. By providing APIs and a modular architecture allowing easy reuse, caused tools such as sanitizers, automatic refactoring, or code completion engines to flourish. You should consider taking advantage of what this compiler infrastructure offers you. Use clang-format to ensure all the code in your code base conforms to a given standard. Consider adding pre-commit hooks using the pre-commit tool to reformat new code before commit. You can also add Python and CMake formatters to the mix. Statically analyze the code using clang-tidy – a tool that actually understands your code instead of just reasoning about it. There's a ton of different checks this tool can perform for you, so be sure to customize the list and options to your specific needs. You can also run nightly or weekly tests of your software with sanitizers enabled. This way, you can detect threading issues, undefined behavior, memory access, management issues, and more. Running tests using debug builds can also be of value if your release builds have assertions disabled.

If you think that more could be done, you can consider writing your own code refactorizations using Clang's infrastructure. There's already a clang-rename tool if you want to see how to create an LLVM-based tool of your own. Additional checks and fix-its for clang-tidy are also not that hard to create, and they can save you hours of manual labor.

You can integrate many tools into your building process. Let's now discuss the heart of the process: the build system.

Abstracting the build process

In this section, we'll delve into CMake scripts, the de facto standard build system generator used for C++ projects worldwide.

Introducing CMake

What does it mean that CMake is a build system generator and not a build system per se? Simply that CMake can be used to generate various types of build systems. You can use it to generate Visual Studio projects, Makefile projects, Ninja-based ones, Sublime, Eclipse, and a few others.

CMake comes with a set of other tools, such as CTest for executing tests and CPack for packaging and creating setup programs. CMake itself allows exporting and installing targets too.

CMake's generators can be either single-configuration, such as Make or NMAKE, or multi-configuration, such as Visual Studio. For single-configuration ones, you should pass the `CMAKE_BUILD_TYPE` flag when running the generation for the first time in a folder. For instance, to configure a debug build, you could run `cmake <project_directory> -DCMAKE_BUILD_TYPE=Debug`. Other predefined configurations are `Release`, `RelWithDebInfo` (release with debug symbols), and `MinSizeRel` (release optimized for minimum binary size). To keep your source directories clean, always create a separate build folder and run CMake generation from there.

Although it's possible to add your own build type, you should really strive not to do so, as this makes using some IDEs much harder and doesn't scale. A much better option is to use, well, `option`.

CMake files can be written in two styles: an obsolete one, based on variables, and a target-based Modern CMake style. We'll focus just on the latter here. Try to avoid setting things through global variables, as this causes issues when you want to reuse your targets.

Creating CMake projects

Each CMake project should have the following lines in their top-level `CMakeLists.txt` file:

```
cmake_minimum_required(VERSION 3.15...3.19)

project(
    Customer
    VERSION 0.0.1
    LANGUAGES CXX)
```

Setting a minimum and a maximum supported version is important as it influences how CMake will behave by setting policies. You can also set them manually if needed.

The definition of our project specifies its name, version (which will be used to populate a few variables), and the programming languages that CMake will use to build the project (which populates many more variables and finds the required tools).

A typical C++ project has the following directories:

- `cmake`: For CMake scripts
- `include`: For public headers, usually with a subfolder named after the project
- `src`: For source files and private headers
- `test`: For tests

You can use the CMake directory to store your custom CMake modules. To have easy access to scripts from this directory, you can add it to CMake's `include()` search path like so:

```
list(APPEND CMAKE_MODULE_PATH "${CMAKE_CURRENT_LIST_DIR}/cmake"
```

When including CMake modules, you can omit the `.cmake` suffix. This means `include(CommonCompileFlags.cmake)` is equal to just `include(CommonCompileFlags)`.

Distinguishing between CMake directory variables

Navigating through the directories in CMake has a common pitfall that not everyone is aware of. When writing CMake scripts, try to distinguish between the following built-in variables:

- PROJECT_SOURCE_DIR: The directory where the project command was last called from a CMake script.
- PROJECT_BINARY_DIR: Like the preceding one, but for the build directory tree.
- CMAKE_SOURCE_DIR: Top-level source directory (this may be in another project that just adds ours as a dependency/subdirectory).
- CMAKE_BINARY_DIR: Like CMAKE_SOURCE_DIR, but for the build directory tree.
- CMAKE_CURRENT_SOURCE_DIR: The source directory corresponding to the currently processed CMakeLists.txt file.
- CMAKE_CURRENT_BINARY_DIR: The binary (build) directory matching CMAKE_CURRENT_SOURCE_DIR.
- CMAKE_CURRENT_LIST_DIR: The directory of CMAKE_CURRENT_LIST_FILE. It can be different from the current source directory if the current CMake script was included from another one (common for CMake modules that are included).

Having cleared that up, let's now start navigating through those directories.

In your top-level CMakeLists.txt file, you will probably want to call add_subdirectory(src) so that CMake will process that directory.

Specifying CMake targets

In the src directory, you should have another CMakeLists.txt file, this time probably defining a target or two. Let's add an executable for a customer microservice for the Dominican Fair system we mentioned earlier in the book:

```
add_executable(customer main.cpp)
```

Source files can be specified as in the preceding code line or added later using target_sources.

A common CMake antipattern is the use of globs to specify source files. A big drawback of using them is that CMake will not know if a file was added until it reruns generation. A common consequence of that is that if you pull changes from a repository and simply build, you can miss compiling and running new unit tests or other code. Even if you used globs with CONFIGURE_DEPENDS, the build time will get longer because globs must be checked as part of each build. Besides, the flag may not work reliably with all generators. Even the CMake authors discourage using it in favor of just explicitly stating the source files.

Okay, so we defined our sources. Let's now specify that our target requires C++17 support from the compiler:

```
target_compile_features(customer PRIVATE cxx_std_17)
```

The `PRIVATE` keyword specifies that this is an internal requirement, that is, just visible to this specific target and not to any targets that will depend on it. If you were writing a library that provided a user with a C++17 API, you could use the `INTERFACE` keyword. To specify both the interface and internal requirements, you could use the `PUBLIC` keyword. When the consumer links to our target, CMake will then automatically require C++17 support for it as well. If you were writing a target that is not built (that is, a header-only library or an imported target), using the `INTERFACE` keyword is usually enough.

You should also note that specifying that our target wants to use C++17 features doesn't enforce the C++ standard or disallow compiler extensions for our target. To do so, you should instead call the following:

```
set_target_properties(customer PROPERTIES
    CXX_STANDARD 17
    CXX_STANDARD_REQUIRED YES
    CXX_EXTENSIONS NO
)
```

If you want to have a set of compiler flags to pass to each target, you can store them in a variable and call the following if you want to create a target that has those flags set as `INTERFACE` and doesn't have any source and uses this target in `target_link_libraries`:

```
target_compile_options(customer PRIVATE ${BASE_COMPILE_FLAGS})
```

The command automatically propagates include directories, options, macros, and other properties, aside from just adding a linker flag. Speaking of linking, let's create a library that we shall link with:

```
add_library(libcustomer lib.cpp)
add_library(domifair::libcustomer ALIAS libcustomer)
set_target_properties(libcustomer PROPERTIES OUTPUT_NAME customer)
# ...
target_link_libraries(customer PRIVATE libcustomer)
```

`add_library` can be used to create static, shared, object, and interface (think header-only) libraries, as well as defining any imported libraries.

The `ALIAS` version of it creates a namespaced target, which helps debug many CMake issues and is a recommended Modern CMake practice.

Because we gave our target a `lib` prefix already, we set the output name to have `libcustomer.a` instead of `liblibcustomer.a`.

Finally, we link our executable with the added library. Try to always specify the `PUBLIC`, `PRIVATE`, or `INTERFACE` keyword for the `target_link_libraries` command as this is crucial for CMake to effectively manage the transitivity of the target dependencies.

Specifying the output directories

Once you build your code using commands such as `cmake --build .`, you might want to know where to find the build artifacts. By default, CMake will create them in a directory matching the source directory they were defined in. For instance, if you have a `src/CMakeLists.txt` file with an `add_executable` directive, then the binary will land in your build directory's `src` subdirectory by default. We can override this using code such as the following:

```
set(CMAKE_RUNTIME_OUTPUT_DIRECTORY ${PROJECT_BINARY_DIR}/bin)
set(CMAKE_ARCHIVE_OUTPUT_DIRECTORY ${PROJECT_BINARY_DIR}/lib)
set(CMAKE_LIBRARY_OUTPUT_DIRECTORY ${PROJECT_BINARY_DIR}/lib)
```

This way, the binaries and DLL files will land in the `bin` subdirectory of your project's build directory, while static and shared Linux libraries will be placed in the `lib` subdirectory.

Using generator expressions

Setting compile flags in a way to support both single- and multi-configuration generators can be tricky, as CMake executes `if` statements and many other constructs at configure time, not at build/install time.

This means that the following is a CMake antipattern:

```
if(CMAKE_BUILD_TYPE STREQUAL Release)
   target_compile_definitions(libcustomer PRIVATE RUN_FAST)
endif()
```

Instead, generator expressions are the proper way to achieve the same goal, as they're being processed at a later time. Let's see an example of their use in practice. Assuming you want to add a preprocessor definition just for your Release configuration, you could write the following:

```
target_compile_definitions(libcustomer PRIVATE
"$<$<CONFIG:Release>:RUN_FAST>")
```

This will resolve to RUN_FAST only when building that one selected configuration. For others, it will resolve to an empty value. It works for both single- and multi-configuration generators. That's not the only use case for generator expressions, though.

Some aspects of our targets may vary when used by our project during builds and by other projects when the target is installed. A good example is **include directories**. A common way to deal with this in CMake is as follows:

```
target_include_directories(
    libcustomer PUBLIC $<INSTALL_INTERFACE:include>
                       $<BUILD_INTERFACE:${PROJECT_SOURCE_DIR}/include>)
```

In this case, we have two generator expressions. The first one tells us that when installed, the include files can be found in the include directory, relative to the install prefix (the root of the installation). If we're not installing, this expression will become an empty one. This is why we have another expression for building. This one will resolve as the include subdirectory of the directory where the last used project() was found.

 Don't use target_include_directories with a path outside of your module. If you do, you're **stealing** someone's headers instead of explicitly declaring a library/target dependency. This is a CMake antipattern.

CMake defines many generator expressions that you can use to query the compiler and platform, as well as the targets (such as full name, the list of object files, any property values, and so on). Aside from these, there are expressions that run Boolean operations, if statements, string comparisons, and more.

Now, for a more complex example, assuming you'd like to have a set of compile flags that you use across your targets and that depend on the compiler used, you could define it as follows:

```
list(
    APPEND
    BASE_COMPILE_FLAGS
    "$<$<OR:$<CXX_COMPILER_ID:Clang>,$<CXX_COMPILER_ID:AppleClang>,$<CXX_COMPIL
ER_ID:GNU>>:-Wall;-Wextra;-pedantic;-Werror>"
    "$<$<CXX_COMPILER_ID:MSVC>:/W4;/WX>")
```

This will append one set of flags if the compiler is Clang or AppleClang or GCC and another one if MSVC is being used instead. Note that we separate the flags with a semicolon because that's how CMake separates elements on a list.

Let's now see how we could add external code for our projects to use.

Using external modules

There are several ways for you to fetch the external projects you depend on. For instance, you could add them as a Conan dependency, use CMake's `find_package` to look for a version provided by the OS or installed in another way, or fetch and compile the dependency yourself.

The key message of this section is: if you can, you should use Conan. This way, you'll end up using one version of the dependency that matches your project's and its dependencies' requirements.

If you're aiming to support multiple platforms, or even multiple versions of the same distribution, using Conan or compiling everything yourself are the ways to go. This way, you'll use the same dependency version regardless of the OS you compile on.

Let's discuss a few ways of grabbing your dependencies offered by CMake itself, and then jump to using the multi-platform package manager named Conan.

Fetching dependencies

One of the possible ways to prepare your dependencies from the source is to use CMake's built-in `FetchContent` module. It will download your dependencies and then build them for you as a regular target.

The feature arrived in CMake 3.11. It's a replacement for the `ExternalProject` module, which had many flaws. One of them was that it cloned the external repository during build time, so CMake couldn't reason about the targets that the external project defined, as well as about their dependencies. This made many projects resort to manually defining the `include` directories and library paths of such external targets and ignoring their required interface compilation flags and dependencies completely. Ouch. `FetchContent` doesn't have such issues, so it's recommended you use it instead.

 Before we show how to use it, you must know that both `FetchContent` and `ExternalProject` (as well as using Git submodules and similar methods) have one important flaw. If you have many dependencies using the same third-party library themselves, you might end up with having multiple versions of the same project, such as a few versions of Boost. Using package managers such as Conan can help you avoid such issues.

For the sake of an example, let's demonstrate how to integrate **GTest** into your project using the aforementioned `FetchContent` feature. First, create a `FetchGTest.cmake` file and put it in the `cmake` directory in our source tree. Our `FetchGTest` script will be defined as follows:

```
include(FetchContent)

FetchContent_Declare(
  googletest
  GIT_REPOSITORY https://github.com/google/googletest.git
  GIT_TAG dcc92d0ab6c4ce022162a23566d44f673251eee4)

FetchContent_GetProperties(googletest)
if(NOT googletest_POPULATED)
  FetchContent_Populate(googletest)
  add_subdirectory(${googletest_SOURCE_DIR} ${googletest_BINARY_DIR}
                   EXCLUDE_FROM_ALL)
endif()

message(STATUS "GTest binaries are present at ${googletest_BINARY_DIR}")
```

First, we include the built-in `FetchContent` module. Once the module is loaded, we declare the dependency using `FetchContent_Declare`. Now, let's name our dependency and specify the repository that CMake will clone, along with the revision that it will check out.

Now, we can read the properties of our external library and populate (that is, check it out) it if that wasn't done already. Once we have the sources, we can process them using `add_subdirectory`. The `EXCLUDE_FROM_ALL` option will tell CMake to not build those targets if they're not needed by other targets when we run a command such as `make all`. After successfully processing the directory, our script will print a message denoting the directory in which GTests libraries will land after being built.

If you're not fond of building your dependencies together with your project, perhaps the next way of integrating your dependencies will be more suitable for you.

Using find scripts

Assuming your dependency is available somewhere on your host, you can just call `find_package` to try to search for it. If your dependency provides a config or targets files (more on those later), then just writing this one simple command is all you need. That is, of course, assuming that the dependencies are already available on your machine. If not, it's your responsibility to install them before running CMake for your project.

To create the preceding files, your dependency would need to use CMake, which is not always the case. How could you deal with those libraries that don't use CMake? If the library is popular, chances are someone already created a find script for you to use. The Boost libraries in versions older than 1.70 were a common example of this approach. CMake comes with a `FindBoost` module that you can execute by just running `find_package(Boost)`.

To find Boost using the preceding module, you would first need to install it on your system. After that, in your CMake lists, you should set any options that you find reasonable. For instance, to use dynamic and multi-threaded Boost libraries, not linked statically to the C++ runtime, specify the following:

```
set(Boost_USE_STATIC_LIBS OFF)
set(Boost_USE_MULTITHREADED ON)
set(Boost_USE_STATIC_RUNTIME OFF)
```

Then, you need to actually search for the library, as shown next:

```
find_package(Boost 1.69 EXACT REQUIRED COMPONENTS Beast)
```

Here, we specified that we want to just use Beast, a great networking library that comes as part of Boost. Once found, you could link it to your target as follows:

```
target_link_libraries(MyTarget PUBLIC Boost::Beast)
```

Now that you know how to properly use a find script, let's learn how to write one on your own.

Writing find scripts

If your dependency is neither providing config and target files nor has anyone written a find module for it, you can always write such a module yourself.

This is not something you'll do very often, so we'll try to just skim the topic. For an in-depth description, you should also read the guidelines in the official CMake documentation (linked in the *Further reading* section) or just look at a few find modules installed with CMake (usually in a directory such as /usr/share/cmake-3.17/Modules on Unix systems). For simplicity, we assume there's just one configuration of your dependency that you'd like to find, but it's possible to find Release and Debug binaries separately. This will result in different targets with different associated variables being set.

The script name determines the argument you'll pass to find_package; for example, if you wish to end up with find_package(Foo), then your script should be named FindFoo.cmake.

A good practice is to start your script with a reStructuredText section describing what your script will actually do, which variables it will set, and so on. An example of such a description could be as follows:

```
#.rst:
# FindMyDep
# ----------
#
# Find my favourite external dependency (MyDep).
#
# Imported targets
# ^^^^^^^^^^^^^^^^
#
# This module defines the following :prop_tgt:`IMPORTED` target:
#
# ``MyDep::MyDep``
#    The MyDep library, if found.
#
```

Usually, you'll also want to describe the variables your script will set:

```
# Result variables
# ^^^^^^^^^^^^^^^^
#
```

```
# This module will set the following variables in your project:
#
# ``MyDep_FOUND``
#    whether MyDep was found or not
# ``MyDep_VERSION_STRING``
#    the found version of MyDep
```

If `MyDep` has any dependencies itself, now is the time to find them:

```
find_package(Boost REQUIRED)
```

Now we can start our search for the library. A common way to do so is to use `pkg-config`:

```
find_package(PkgConfig)
pkg_check_modules(PC_MyDep QUIET MyDep)
```

If `pkg-config` has information on our dependency, it will set some variables we can use to find it.

A good idea might be to have a variable that the user of our script can set to point us to the location of the library. As per CMake conventions, it should be named `MyDep_ROOT_DIR`. To provide CMake with this variable, the user can either invoke CMake with `-DMyDep_ROOT_DIR=some/path`, modify the variable in `CMakeCache.txt` in their build directory, or use the `ccmake` or `cmake-gui` programs.

Now, we can actually search for the headers and libraries of our dependency using the aforementioned paths:

```
find_path(MyDep_INCLUDE_DIR
    NAMES MyDep.h
    PATHS "${MyDep_ROOT_DIR}/include" "${PC_MyDep_INCLUDE_DIRS}"
    PATH_SUFFIXES MyDep
)

find_library(MyDep_LIBRARY
    NAMES mydep
    PATHS "${MyDep_ROOT_DIR}/lib" "${PC_MyDep_LIBRARY_DIRS}"
)
```

Then, we need to also set the found version, as we promised in the header of our script. To use the one found from `pkg-config`, we could write the following:

```
set(MyDep_VERSION ${PC_MyDep_VERSION})
```

Alternatively, we can just manually extract the version either from the contents of the header file, from components of the library path, or using any other means. Once this is done, let's leverage CMake's built-in scripts to decide whether the library was successfully found while handling all the possible parameters to the `find_package` invocation:

```
include(FindPackageHandleStandardArgs)

find_package_handle_standard_args(MyDep
        FOUND_VAR MyDep_FOUND
        REQUIRED_VARS
        MyDep_LIBRARY
        MyDep_INCLUDE_DIR
        VERSION_VAR MyDep_VERSION
        )
```

As we decided to provide a target and not just a bunch of variables, now it's time to define it:

```
if(MyDep_FOUND AND NOT TARGET MyDep::MyDep)
     add_library(MyDep::MyDep UNKNOWN IMPORTED)
     set_target_properties(MyDep::MyDep PROPERTIES
             IMPORTED_LOCATION "${MyDep_LIBRARY}"
             INTERFACE_COMPILE_OPTIONS "${PC_MyDep_CFLAGS_OTHER}"
             INTERFACE_INCLUDE_DIRECTORIES "${MyDep_INCLUDE_DIR}"
             INTERFACE_LINK_LIBRARIES Boost::boost
             )
endif()
```

Finally, let's hide our internally used variables with users who don't want to deal with them:

```
mark_as_advanced(
  MyDep_INCLUDE_DIR
  MyDep_LIBRARY
  )
```

Now, we have a complete find module that we can use in the following way:

```
find_package(MyDep REQUIRED)
target_link_libraries(MyTarget PRIVATE MyDep::MyDep)
```

This is how you can write the find module yourself.

 Don't write `Find\*.cmake` modules for your own packages. Those are meant for packages that don't support CMake. Instead, write a `Config\*.cmake` module (as described later in this chapter).

Let's now show how to use a proper package manager instead of doing the heavy lifting yourself.

Using the Conan package manager

Conan is an open source, decentralized package manager for native packages. It supports multiple platforms and compilers. It can also integrate with multiple build systems.

If a package has not already been built for your environment, Conan will handle building it on your machine instead of downloading the already-built version. Once built, you can upload it to either the public repositories, your own `conan_server` instance, or an Artifactory server.

Preparing Conan profiles

If this is the first time you're running Conan, it will create a default profile based on your environment. You might want to modify some of its settings either by creating a new profile or by updating the default one. Assuming we're using Linux and want to compile everything using GCC 9.x, we could run the following:

```
conan profile new hosacpp
conan profile update settings.compiler=gcc hosacpp
conan profile update settings.compiler.libcxx=libstdc++11 hosacpp
conan profile update settings.compiler.version=10 hosacpp
conan profile update settings.arch=x86_64 hosacpp
conan profile update settings.os=Linux hosacpp
```

If our dependencies come from other repositories than the default ones, we can add those using `conan remote add <repo> <repo_url>`. You might want to use this to configure your company's one, for instance.

Now that we've set Conan up, let's show how to grab our dependencies using Conan and integrate all of this into our CMake scripts.

Specifying Conan dependencies

Our project relies on the C++ REST SDK. To tell this to Conan, we need to create a file called `conanfile.txt`. In our case, it will contain the following:

```
[requires]
cpprestsdk/2.10.18
```

```
[generators]
CMakeDeps
```

You can specify as many dependencies as you want here. Each of them can have either a fixed version, a range of the fixed versions, or a tag such as **latest**. After the @ sign, you can find the company that owns the package and the channel that allows you to select a specific variant of the package (usually stable and testing).

The **generators** section is where you specify what build systems you want to use. For CMake projects, you should use CMakeDeps. You can also generate lots of others, including ones for generating compiler arguments, CMake toolchain files, Python virtual environments, and many more.

In our case, we don't specify any additional options, but you could easily add this section and configure variables for your packages and for their dependencies. For instance, to compile our dependency as a static library, we could write the following:

```
[options]
cpprestsdk:shared=False
```

Once we have conanfile.txt in place, let's tell Conan to use it.

Installing Conan dependencies

To use our Conan packages in CMake code, we must first install them. In Conan, this means downloading the sources and building them or downloading prebuilt binaries, as well as creating configuration files that we'll use in CMake. To make Conan handle this for us after we have created our build directory, we should cd into it and simply run the following:

```
conan install path/to/directory/containing/conanfile.txt --build=missing -s
build_type=Release -pr=hosacpp
```

By default, Conan wants to download all the dependencies as prebuilt binaries. If the server doesn't have them prebuilt, Conan will build them instead of bailing out as we passed the --build=missing flag. We tell it to grab the release versions built using the same compiler and environment as we have in our profile. You can install packages for more than one build type by simply invoking another commands with build_type set to other CMake build types. This can help you quickly switch between them if needed. If you want to use the default profile (the one Conan can detect for you automatically), just don't pass the -pr flag.

If the CMake generator we plan to use was not specified in `conanfile.txt`, we can append it to the preceding command. For instance, to use the `compiler_args` generator, we should append `--generator compiler_args`. Later you could use what it produced by passing `@conanbuildinfo.args` to your compiler invocation.

Using Conan targets from CMake

Once Conan finishes downloading, building, and configuring our dependencies, we need to tell CMake to use them.

If you're using Conan with the `CMakeDeps` generator, be sure to specify a `CMAKE_BUILD_TYPE` value. In other cases, CMake will be unable to use the packages configured by Conan. An example invocation (from the same directory you ran Conan) could be as follows:

```
cmake path/to/directory/containing/CMakeLists.txt -
DCMAKE_BUILD_TYPE=Release
```

This way, we would build our project in release mode; we must use one of the types we installed using Conan. To find our dependencies, we can just use CMake's `find_package`:

```
list(APPEND CMAKE_PREFIX_PATH "${CMAKE_BINARY_DIR}")
find_package(cpprestsdk CONFIG REQUIRED)
```

First, we add the root build directory to the path CMake will try to find package config files in. Then, we find the package config files generated by Conan.

To pass Conan-defined targets as our targets' dependencies, it's best to use the namespaced target name:

```
target_link_libraries(libcustomer PUBLIC cpprestsdk::cpprest)
```

This way, we'll get an error during CMake's configuration when the package is not found. Without the alias, we'd get an error when trying to link.

Now that we have compiled and linked our targets just the way we wanted, it's time to put them to the test.

Adding tests

CMake has its own test driver program named CTest. It's easy to add new test suites to it from your CMakeLists either on your own or using the many integrations provided by testing frameworks. Later in the book, we'll discuss testing in depth, but let's first show how to quickly and cleanly add unit tests based on the GoogleTest, or GTest, testing framework.

Usually, to define your tests in CMake, you'll want to write the following:

```
if(CMAKE_PROJECT_NAME STREQUAL PROJECT_NAME)
  include(CTest)
  if(BUILD_TESTING)
    add_subdirectory(test)
  endif()
endif()
```

The preceding snippet will first check whether we are the main project that's being built or not. Usually, you just want to run tests for your project and omit even building the tests for any third-party components you use. This is why the project name is checked.

If we are to run our tests, we include the CTest module. This loads the whole testing infrastructure CTest offers, defines its additional targets, and calls a CMake function called enable_testing, which will, among other things, enable the BUILD_TESTING flag. This flag is cached, so you can disable all testing when building your project by simply passing a -DBUILD_TESTING=OFF argument to CMake when generating the build system.

All such cached variables are actually stored in a text file named CMakeCache.txt in your build directory. Feel free to modify the variables there to change what CMake does; it won't overwrite the settings there until you remove the file. You can do so using ccmake, cmake-gui, or just by hand.

If BUILD_TESTING is true, we simply process the CMakeLists.txt file in our test directory. It could look like so:

```
include(FetchGTest)
include(GoogleTest)

add_subdirectory(customer)
```

The first include calls the script for providing us GTest that we described previously. After fetching GTest, our current CMakeLists.txt loads some helper function defined in the GoogleTest CMake module by invoking include(GoogleTest). This will enable us to integrate our tests into CTest more easily. Finally, let's tell CMake to dive into a directory that contains some tests by calling add_subdirectory(customer).

The test/customer/CMakeLists.txt file will simply add an executable with tests that is compiled with our predefined set of flags and links to the tested module and GTest. Then, we call the CTest helper function that discovers the defined tests. All of this is just four lines of CMake code:

```
add_executable(unittests unit.cpp)
target_compile_options(unittests PRIVATE ${BASE_COMPILE_FLAGS})
target_link_libraries(unittests PRIVATE domifair::libcustomer gtest_main)
gtest_discover_tests(unittests)
```

Voilà!

You can now build and execute your tests by simply going to the build directory and calling the following:

```
cmake --build . --target unittests
ctest # or cmake --build . --target test
```

You can pass a -j flag for CTest. It works just like with Make or Ninja invocations – parallelizes the test execution. If you want to have a shorter command for building, just run your build system, that is, by invoking make.

 In scripts, it's usually better to use the longer form of the command; this will make your scripts independent of the build system used.

Once your tests have passed, we can now think about providing them to a wider audience.

Reusing quality code

CMake has built-in utilities that can come a long way when it comes to distributing the results of your builds. This section will describe installing and exporting utilities and the differences between them. Later sections will show you how to package your code using CPack, and how to do it using Conan.

Installing and exporting is not that important for microservices per se, but it's very useful if you're delivering libraries for others to reuse.

Installing

If you have written or used Makefiles, you've most probably invoked `make install` at one point and seen how the deliverables of a project were installed either in the OS directories or in another directory of your choosing. If you're using `make` with CMake, using the steps from this section will allow you to install the deliverables in the same way. If not, you'll still be able to call the install target, of course. Aside from that, in both cases, you will then have an easy way to leverage CPack for creating packages based on your installation commands.

If you're on Linux, it's probably a good idea to preset some installation directories based on the conventions of the OS by calling the following:

```
include(GNUInstallDirs)
```

This will make the installer use a directory structure made of `bin`, `lib`, and similar other directories. Such directories can be also set manually using a few CMake variables.

Creating an install target consists of a few more steps. First and foremost is to define the targets we want to install, which in our case will be the following:

```
install(
    TARGETS libcustomer customer
    EXPORT CustomerTargets
    LIBRARY DESTINATION ${CMAKE_INSTALL_LIBDIR}
    ARCHIVE DESTINATION ${CMAKE_INSTALL_LIBDIR}
    RUNTIME DESTINATION ${CMAKE_INSTALL_BINDIR})
```

This tells CMake to expose our library and executable defined earlier in this chapter as `CustomerTargets`, using the directories we set earlier.

If you plan to install different configurations of your library to different folders, you could use a few invocations of the preceding command, like so:

```
install(TARGETS libcustomer customer
        CONFIGURATIONS Debug
        # destinations for other components go here...
        RUNTIME DESTINATION Debug/bin)
install(TARGETS libcustomer customer
        CONFIGURATIONS Release
        # destinations for other components go here...
```

```
    RUNTIME DESTINATION Release/bin)
```

You can notice that we specify the directories for executables and libraries, but not for include files. We need to provide them in another command, like so:

```
install(DIRECTORY ${PROJECT_SOURCE_DIR}/include/
        DESTINATION include)
```

This means that the top-level include directory's contents will be installed in the include directory under the installation root. The slash after the first path fixes some path issues, so take note to use it.

So, we have our set of targets; now we need to generate a file that another CMake project could read to understand our targets. This can be done in the following way:

```
install(
    EXPORT CustomerTargets
    FILE CustomerTargets.cmake
    NAMESPACE domifair::
    DESTINATION ${CMAKE_INSTALL_LIBDIR}/cmake/Customer)
```

This command takes our target set and creates a `CustomerTargets.cmake` file that will contain all the info about our targets and their requirements. Each of our targets will get prefixed with a namespace; for example, `customer` will become `domifair::customer`. The generated file will get installed in a subdirectory of the library folder in our installation tree.

To allow dependant projects to find our targets using CMake's `find_package` command, we need to provide a `CustomerConfig.cmake` file. If your target doesn't have any dependencies, you can just export the preceding targets directly to that file instead of the `targets` file. Otherwise, you should write your own config file that will include the preceding `targets` file.

In our case, we want to reuse some CMake variables, so we need to create a template and use the `configure_file` command to fill it in:

```
configure_file(${PROJECT_SOURCE_DIR}/cmake/CustomerConfig.cmake.in
               CustomerConfig.cmake @ONLY)
```

Our `CustomerConfig.cmake.in` file will begin by dealing with our dependencies:

```
include(CMakeFindDependencyMacro)

find_dependency(cpprestsdk 2.10.18 REQUIRED)
```

The `find_dependency` macro is a wrapper for `find_package` that is meant to be used in config files. Although we relied on Conan to provide us with the C++ REST SDK 2.10.18 as defined in `conanfile.txt`, here we need to specify the dependency once more. Our package can be used on another machine, so we require that our dependency is installed there too. If you want to use Conan on the target machine, you can install the C++ REST SDK as follows:

```
conan install cpprestsdk/2.10.18
```

After dealing with the dependencies, our config file template will include the `targets` file that we created earlier:

```
if(NOT TARGET domifair::@PROJECT_NAME@)
    include("${CMAKE_CURRENT_LIST_DIR}/@PROJECT_NAME@Targets.cmake")
endif()
```

When `configure_file` executes, it will replace all those `@VARIABLES@` with the contents of their matching `${VARIABLES}` defined in our project. This way, based on our `CustomerConfig.cmake.in` file template, CMake will create a `CustomerConfig.cmake` file.

When finding a dependency using `find_package`, you'll often want to specify a version of the package to find. To support that in our package, we must create a `CustomerConfigVersion.cmake` file. CMake offers us a helper function that will create this file for us. Let's use it as follows:

```
include(CMakePackageConfigHelpers)
write_basic_package_version_file(
    CustomerConfigVersion.cmake
    VERSION ${PACKAGE_VERSION}
    COMPATIBILITY AnyNewerVersion)
```

The `PACKAGE_VERSION` variable will get populated according to the `VERSION` argument we passed when calling `project` at the top of our top-level `CMakeLists.txt` file.

`AnyNewerVersion` `COMPATIBILITY` means our package will be accepted by any package search if it is newer or the same as the requested version. Other options include `SameMajorVersion`, `SameMinorVersion`, and `ExactVersion`.

Once we have created our config and config version files, let's tell CMake that they should be installed along with the binaries and our target file:

```
install(FILES ${CMAKE_CURRENT_BINARY_DIR}/CustomerConfig.cmake
              ${CMAKE_CURRENT_BINARY_DIR}/CustomerConfigVersion.cmake
        DESTINATION ${CMAKE_INSTALL_LIBDIR}/cmake/Customer)
```

One last thing we should install is the license for our project. We'll leverage CMake's command for installing files to put them in our documentation directory:

```
install(
    FILES ${PROJECT_SOURCE_DIR}/LICENSE
    DESTINATION ${CMAKE_INSTALL_DOCDIR})
```

That's all you need to know to successfully create an install target in the root of your OS. You may ask how to install the package into another directory, such as just for the current user. To do so, you would need to set the CMAKE_INSTALL_PREFIX variable, for example, when generating the build system.

Note that if we don't install into the root of our Unix tree, we'll have to provide the dependent project with a path to the installation directory, such as by setting CMAKE_PREFIX_PATH.

Let's now look at yet another way you could reuse what you just built.

Exporting

Exporting is a technique to add information about a package that you built locally to CMake's package registry. This is useful when you want your targets to be visible right from their build directories, even without installation. A common use for exporting is when you have several projects checked out on your development machine and you build them locally.

It's quite easy to add support for this mechanism from your CMakeLists.txt files. In our case, it can be done in this way:

```
export(
    TARGETS libcustomer customer
    NAMESPACE domifair::
    FILE CustomerTargets.cmake)

set(CMAKE_EXPORT_PACKAGE_REGISTRY ON)
export(PACKAGE domifair)
```

This way, CMake will create a targets file similar to the one from the *Installing* section, defining our library and executable targets in the namespace we provided. From CMake 3.15, the package registry is disabled by default, so we need to enable it by setting the appropriate preceding variable. Then, we can put the information about our targets right into the registry by exporting our package.

Note that we now have a `targets` file without a matching config file. This means that if our targets depend on any external libraries, they must be found before our package is found. In our case, the calls must be ordered in the following way:

```
find_package(cpprestsdk 2.10.18)
find_package(domifair)
```

First, we find the C++ REST SDK, and only afterward do we look for our package that depends on it. That's all you need to know to start exporting your targets. Much easier than installing them, isn't it?

Let's now move on to a third way of exposing your targets to the external world.

Using CPack

In this section, we'll describe how to use CPack, the packaging tool that comes with CMake.

CPack allows you to easily create packages in various formats, ranging from ZIP and TGZ archives through to DEB and RPM packages, and even installation wizards such as NSIS or a few OS X-specific ones. Once you have your installation logic in place, it's not hard to integrate the tool. Let's show how to use CPack to package our project.

First, we need to specify variables that CPack will use when creating the packages:

```
set(CPACK_PACKAGE_VENDOR "Authors")
set(CPACK_PACKAGE_CONTACT "author@example.com")
set(CPACK_PACKAGE_DESCRIPTION_SUMMARY
    "Library and app for the Customer microservice")
```

We need to give some information by hand, but some variables can be filled based on our project version specified when we defined our project. There are many more CPack variables and you can read about all of them in the CPack link in the *Further reading* section at the end of the chapter. Some of them are common for all package generators, while some are specific to a few of them. For instance, if you plan to use the installers, you could set the following two:

```
set(CPACK_RESOURCE_FILE_LICENSE "${PROJECT_SOURCE_DIR}/LICENSE")
set(CPACK_RESOURCE_FILE_README "${PROJECT_SOURCE_DIR}/README.md")
```

Once you've set all the interesting variables, it's time to choose the generators for CPack to use. Let's start with putting some basic ones in CPACK_GENERATOR, a variable CPack relies on:

```
list(APPEND CPACK_GENERATOR TGZ ZIP)
```

This will cause CPack to generate those two types of archives based on the installation steps we defined earlier in the chapter.

You can select different package generators based on many things, for example, the tools available on the machine you're running on. An example would be to create Windows installers when building on Windows and a DEB or RPM package if building on Linux with the appropriate tools installed. For instance, if you're running Linux, you could check whether dpkg is installed and if so, create DEB packages:

```
if(UNIX)
   find_program(DPKG_PROGRAM dpkg)
   if(DPKG_PROGRAM)
     list(APPEND CPACK_GENERATOR DEB)
     set(CPACK_DEBIAN_PACKAGE_DEPENDS "${CPACK_DEBIAN_PACKAGE_DEPENDS}
libcpprest2.10 (>= 2.10.2-6)")
     set(CPACK_DEBIAN_PACKAGE_SHLIBDEPS ON)
   else()
     message(STATUS "dpkg not found - won't be able to create DEB
packages")
   endif()
```

We used the CPACK_DEBIAN_PACKAGE_DEPENDS variable to make the DEB package require the C++ REST SDK to be installed first.

For RPM packages, you could manually check for rpmbuild:

```
   find_program(RPMBUILD_PROGRAM rpmbuild)
    if(RPMBUILD_PROGRAM)
      list(APPEND CPACK_GENERATOR RPM)
      set(CPACK_RPM_PACKAGE_REQUIRES "${CPACK_RPM_PACKAGE_REQUIRES} cpprest
>= 2.10.2-6")
    else()
      message(STATUS "rpmbuild not found - won't be able to create RPM
packages")
    endif()
  endif()
```

Nifty, right?

These generators offer a plethora of other useful variables, so feel free to look at CMake's documentation if you need anything more than those basic needs described here.

One last thing when it comes variables – you can also use them to avoid accidentally packaging undesired files. This can be done by using the following:

```
set(CPACK_SOURCE_IGNORE_FILES /.git /dist /.*build.* /\\\\.DS_Store)
```

Once we have all that in place, we can include CPack itself from our CMake lists:

```
include(CPack)
```

Remember to always do this as the last step, as CMake won't propagate any variables you used later to CPack.

To run it, directly invoke either just `cpack` or the longer form that will also check whether anything needs rebuilding first: `cmake --build . --target package`. You can easily override the generators if you just need to rebuild one type of package using the `-G` flag, for example, `-G DEB` to build just the DEB package, `-G WIX -C Release` to pack a release MSI executable, or `-G DragNDrop` to obtain a DMG installer.

Let's now discuss a more barbaric way of building packages.

Packaging using Conan

We already showed how to install our dependencies using Conan. Now, let's dive into creating our own Conan packages.

Let's create a new top-level directory in our project, simply named `conan`, where we will store the files needed for packaging using this tool: a script for building our package and an environment to test it.

Creating the conanfile.py script

The most important file required for all Conan packages is `conanfile.py`. In our case, we'll want to fill in some of its details using CMake variables, so let's create a `conanfile.py.in` file instead. We'll use it to create the former file by adding the following to our `CMakeLists.txt` files:

```
configure_file(${PROJECT_SOURCE_DIR}/conan/conanfile.py.in
               ${CMAKE_CURRENT_BINARY_DIR}/conan/conanfile.py @ONLY)
```

Our file will begin with some boring Python imports, such as those required by Conan for CMake projects:

```
import os
from conans import ConanFile, CMake
```

Now we need to create a class that defines our package:

```
class CustomerConan(ConanFile):
    name = "customer"
    version = "@PROJECT_VERSION@"
    license = "MIT"
    author = "Authors"
    description = "Library and app for the Customer microservice"
    topics = ("Customer", "domifair")
```

First, we start with a bunch of generic variables, taking the project version from our CMake code. Usually, the description will be a multi-line string. The topics are useful for finding our library on sites such as JFrog's Artifactory and can tell the readers what our package is about. Let's now go through other variables:

```
    homepage = "https://example.com"
    url =
"https://github.com/PacktPublishing/Hands-On-Software-Architecture-with-Cpp
/"
```

`homepage` should point to, well, the home page of your project: where the docs, tutorials, FAQs, and similar stuff are placed. The `url` one, on the other hand, is where the package repository is placed. Many open source libraries have their code in one repo and the packaging code in another. A common case is when the package is being built by the central Conan package server. In this case, `url` should point to `https://github.com/conan-io/conan-center-index`.

Going forward, we can now specify how our package is being built:

```
settings = "os", "compiler", "build_type", "arch"
options = {"shared": [True, False], "fPIC": [True, False]}
default_options = {"shared": False, "fPIC": True}
generators = "CMakeDeps"
keep_imports = True  # useful for repackaging, e.g. of licenses
```

settings will determine whether the package needs to be built or an already-built version can be downloaded.

options and the default_options values can be whatever you like. shared and fPIC are the two that most packages provide, so let's follow this convention.

Now that we have defined our variables, let's start writing methods that Conan will use to package our software. First, we specify our libraries that consumers of our package should link against:

```
def package_info(self):
    self.cpp_info.libs = ["customer"]
```

The self.cpp_info object allows setting much more than that, but this is the bare minimum. Feel free to take a look at other properties in Conan's documentation.

Next, let's specify what other packages requires:

```
def requirements(self):
    self.requires.add('cpprestsdk/2.10.18')
```

This time, we grab the C++ REST SDK directly from Conan instead of specifying what packages the OS's package manager should depend on. Now, let's specify how (and where) CMake should generate our build system:

```
def _configure_cmake(self):
    cmake = CMake(self)
    cmake.configure(source_folder="@CMAKE_SOURCE_DIR@")
    return cmake
```

In our case, we simply point it to the source directory. Once the build system is configured, we will need to actually build our project:

```
def build(self):
    cmake = self._configure_cmake()
    cmake.build()
```

Conan also supports non-CMake-based build systems. After building our package, it's packaging time, which requires us to provide yet another method:

```
def package(self):
    cmake = self._configure_cmake()
    cmake.install()
    self.copy("license*", ignore_case=True, keep_path=True)
```

Note how we're using the same `_configure_cmake()` function to both build and package our project. Aside from installing binaries, we also specify where the licenses should be deployed. Finally, let's tell Conan what it should copy when installing our package:

```
def imports(self):
    self.copy("license*", dst="licenses", folder=True,
ignore_case=True)

        # Use the following for the cmake_multi generator on Windows
and/or Mac OS to copy libs to the right directory.
        # Invoke Conan like so:
        #   conan install . -e CONAN_IMPORT_PATH=Release -g cmake_multi
        dest = os.getenv("CONAN_IMPORT_PATH", "bin")
        self.copy("*.dll", dst=dest, src="bin")
        self.copy("*.dylib*", dst=dest, src="lib")
```

The preceding code specifies where to unpack the license files, as well as libraries, and executables when installing the library.

Now that we know how to build a Conan package, let's also see how to test whether it works as desired.

Testing our Conan package

Once Conan builds our package, it should test whether it was properly built. In order to do so, let's start by creating a `test_package` subdirectory in our `conan` directory.

It will also contain a `conanfile.py` script, but this time a shorter one. It should start as follows:

```
import os

from conans import ConanFile, CMake, tools
```

```
class CustomerTestConan(ConanFile):
    settings = "os", "compiler", "build_type", "arch"
    generators = "CMakeDeps"
```

Nothing too fancy here. Now, we should provide the logic to build the test package:

```
def build(self):
    cmake = CMake(self)
    # Current dir is "test_package/build/<build_id>" and
    # CMakeLists.txt is in "test_package"
    cmake.configure()
    cmake.build()
```

We'll write our `CMakeLists.txt` file in a sec. But first, let's write two more things: the `imports` method and the `test` method. The `imports` method can be written as follows:

```
def imports(self):
    self.copy("*.dll", dst="bin", src="bin")
    self.copy("*.dylib*", dst="bin", src="lib")
    self.copy('*.so*', dst='bin', src='lib')
```

Then we have the heart of our package testing logic – the `test` method:

```
def test(self):
    if not tools.cross_building(self.settings):
        self.run(".%sexample" % os.sep)
```

We want to run it only if we're building for our native architecture. Otherwise, we would most probably be unable to run the compiled executable.

Let's now define our `CMakeLists.txt` file:

```
cmake_minimum_required(VERSION 3.12)
project(PackageTest CXX)

list(APPEND CMAKE_PREFIX_PATH "${CMAKE_BINARY_DIR}")

find_package(customer CONFIG REQUIRED)

add_executable(example example.cpp)
target_link_libraries(example customer::customer)


# CTest tests can be added here
```

Simple as that. We link to all the Conan libraries provided (in our case, just our Customer library).

Finally, let's write our `example.cpp` file with just enough logic to check whether the package was successfully created:

```
#include <customer/customer.h>

int main() { responder{}.prepare_response("Conan"); }
```

Before we start running all this, there are a few small changes that we need to make in our main tree of CMake lists. Let's now see how to export Conan targets from our CMake file properly.

Adding Conan packaging code to our CMakeLists

Remember that installation logic we wrote in the *Reusing quality code* section? If you're relying on Conan for packaging, you probably don't need to run the bare CMake exporting and installation logic. Assuming you want to only export and install if Conan is not used, you need to modify the section of your `CMakeLists` described in the *Installing* subsection previously to look similar to this:

```
if(NOT CONAN_EXPORTED)
  install(
    EXPORT CustomerTargets
    FILE CustomerTargets.cmake
    NAMESPACE domifair::
    DESTINATION ${CMAKE_INSTALL_LIBDIR}/cmake/Customer)

  configure_file(${PROJECT_SOURCE_DIR}/cmake/CustomerConfig.cmake.in
                 CustomerConfig.cmake @ONLY)

  include(CMakePackageConfigHelpers)
  write_basic_package_version_file(
    CustomerConfigVersion.cmake
    VERSION ${PACKAGE_VERSION}
    COMPATIBILITY AnyNewerVersion)

  install(FILES ${CMAKE_CURRENT_BINARY_DIR}/CustomerConfig.cmake
                ${CMAKE_CURRENT_BINARY_DIR}/CustomerConfigVersion.cmake
          DESTINATION ${CMAKE_INSTALL_LIBDIR}/cmake/Customer)
endif()

install(
  FILES ${PROJECT_SOURCE_DIR}/LICENSE
```

```
        DESTINATION
    $<IF:$<BOOL:${CONAN_EXPORTED}>,licenses,${CMAKE_INSTALL_DOCDIR}>)
```

Adding an if statement and a generator expression is a reasonable price for having clean packages, and that's all we needed to do.

One last thing to make our lives easier – a target that we could **build** in order to create the Conan package. We can define it as follows:

```
add_custom_target(
    conan
    COMMAND
      ${CMAKE_COMMAND} -E copy_directory
${PROJECT_SOURCE_DIR}/conan/test_package/
      ${CMAKE_CURRENT_BINARY_DIR}/conan/test_package
    COMMAND conan create . customer/testing -s build_type=$<CONFIG>
    WORKING_DIRECTORY ${CMAKE_CURRENT_BINARY_DIR}/conan
    VERBATIM)
```

Now, when we run `cmake --build . --target conan` (or `ninja conan` if we're using that generator and want a short invocation), CMake will copy our `test_package` directory to the `build` folder, build our Conan package, and test it using the copied files.

All done!

 One last remark: what we described here is just the tip of the iceberg when it comes to creating Conan packages. For more information, please refer to Conan's documentation. You can find a link in the *Further reading* section.

Summary

In this chapter, you've learned a lot about building and packaging your code. You're now able to write faster-building template code, know how to choose the tools to compile your code faster (you'll learn more about tooling in the next chapter), and know when to use forward declarations instead of #include directives.

Aside from that, you can now define your build targets and test suites using Modern CMake, manage external dependencies using find modules and FetchContent, create packages and installers in various formats, and last but not least, use Conan to install your dependencies and create your own artifacts.

In the next chapter, we will look at how to write code that would be easy to test. Continuous integration and continuous deployment are useful only if you have good test coverage. Continuous deployment without comprehensive testing will allow you to introduce new bugs to production much quicker. This is not our goal when we design software architecture.

Questions

1. What's the difference between installing and exporting your targets in CMake?
2. How do you make your template code compile faster?
3. How do you use multiple compilers with Conan?
4. What do you do if you'd like to compile your Conan dependencies with the pre-C++11 GCC ABI?
5. How to ensure we force a specific C++ standard in CMake?
6. How would you build documentation in CMake and ship it along with your RPM package?

Further reading

- List of compiler books on GCC's wiki: `https://gcc.gnu.org/wiki/ListOfCompilerBooks`
- *Type Based Template Metaprogramming is Not Dead*, a lecture by Odin Holmes, C++Now 2017: `https://www.youtube.com/watch?v=EtU4RDCCsiU`
- The Modern CMake online book: `https://cliutils.gitlab.io/modern-cmake`
- Conan documentation: `https://docs.conan.io/en/latest/`
- CMake documentation on creating find scripts: `https://cmake.org/cmake/help/v3.17/manual/cmake-developer.7.html?highlight=find#a-sample-find-module`

Section 3: Architectural Quality Attributes

3

This section focuses more on high-level concepts that together make a software project a success. Where possible, we will also show tooling that helps in maintaining the high quality we want to achieve.

This section contains the following chapters:

- Chapter 8, *Writing Testable Code*
- Chapter 9, *Continuous Integration and Continuous Deployment*
- Chapter 10, *Security in Code and Deployment*
- Chapter 11, *Performance*

8
Writing Testable Code

The ability to test code is the most important quality of any software product. Without proper testing, it is prohibitively expensive to refactor the code or to improve any other part of it, such as its security, scalability, or performance. In this chapter, we'll learn how to design and manage automated tests and how to correctly use fakes and mocks when it is necessary to do so.

The following topics will be covered in this chapter:

- Why do you test code?
- Introducing testing frameworks
- Understanding mocks and fakes
- Test-driven class design
- Automating tests for continuous integration/continuous deployment

Technical requirements

The sample code for this chapter can be found at `https://github.com/PacktPublishing/Software-Architecture-with-Cpp/tree/master/Chapter08`.

The software that we will be using in this chapter's examples is as follows:

- GTest 1.10+
- Catch2 2.10+
- CppUnit 1.14+
- Doctest 2.3+
- Serverspec 2.41+
- Testinfra 3.2+
- Goss 0.3+

- CMake 3.15+
- Autoconf
- Automake
- Libtool

Why do you test code?

Software engineering and software architecture is a very complex matter, and the natural way to deal with uncertainties is to insure yourself against potential risks. We do it all the time with life insurance, health insurance, and car insurance. Yet when it comes to software development, we tend to forget about all the safety precautions and just hope for an optimistic outcome.

Knowing that things not only may but *will* go wrong, it is unbelievable that the topic of testing software is still a controversial one. Whether it's from having a lack of skill or from a lack of budget, there are still projects that lack even some of the most basic tests. And when the client decides to change the requirements, a simple correction may result in endless reworks and firefights.

The time that's saved from not implementing proper testing is lost when the first rework happens. If you think this rework will not happen very soon, you are most probably very mistaken. In the agile environment we live in nowadays, reworks are a part of our daily life. Our knowledge about the world and our customers' changes means that the requirements change, and with that comes making changes to our code.

Therefore, testing's main purpose is to protect your precious time later in the project. Sure, it's an investment early on when you have to implement various tests instead of focusing solely on the features, but it's an investment you won't regret. Like an insurance policy, testing takes a little from your budget when things go according to plan, but when things go bad, you'll get a generous payout.

The testing pyramid

There are different types of testing you may encounter when designing or implementing a software system. Each of the classes serves a slightly different purpose. They can be categorized as follows:

- Unit testing: Code
- Integration testing: Design

- System testing: Requirements
- Acceptance testing (**end-to-end** or **E2E**): Client needs

This distinction is arbitrary and you may often see other layers of the pyramid, as follows:

- Unit testing
- Service testing
- UI testing (**end-to-end** or **E2E**)

Here, unit testing refers to the same layer as in the previous example. Service testing refers to a combination of integration testing and system testing. On the other hand, UI testing refers to acceptance testing. The following diagram shows the testing pyramid:

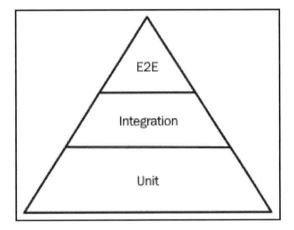

Figure 8.1 – Testing pyramid

It's worth noting that unit tests are not only the cheapest to build but that they also execute pretty quickly and can often run in parallel. This means they make for a great continuous integration gating mechanism. Not only that, but they also often provide the best feedback about the health of your system. Higher-level tests are not only harder to write properly, but they also may be less robust. This can lead to flickering test results, with one in every few test runs failing. If the failure in the higher-level test is not correlated with any failure at the unit test level, chances are that the problem may be with the test itself and not in the system under test.

We don't want to say that the higher-level tests are entirely useless and that you should only focus on writing unit tests. That's not the case. The pyramid has its shape because there should be a solid base covered by unit tests. On that base, however, you should also have all the higher-level tests in an appropriate proportion. After all, it is not very hard to imagine a system where all the unit tests are passing, but the system itself doesn't provide any value to the customer. An extreme example would be a perfectly working backend without any user interface (be it graphical or in the form of an API) present. Sure, it passes all the unit tests, but that's no excuse!

As you may imagine, the opposite of the testing pyramid is known as an ice cone, and it is an antipattern. Violating the testing pyramid often leads to fragile code and hard to trace bugs. This makes debugging much more expensive and doesn't introduce savings in test development either.

Non-functional testing

What we've already covered are so-called functional tests. Their aim is to check whether the system under test fulfills the functional requirements. But there are also other types of requirements besides functional ones that we may want to control. Some of them are as follows:

- **Performance**: Your application may behave according to requirements in terms of functionality but still be unusable for end users due to weak performance. We will focus more on improving performance in Chapter 11, *Performance.*
- **Endurance**: Even if your system can be really performant, it doesn't mean it can survive a continuously high workload. And when it does, can it survive some of the malfunctionings of the components? When we embrace the idea that every piece of software is vulnerable and may break at any given moment, we start designing systems that can be failure-resistant. This is a concept that the Erlang ecosystem embraces, but the concept itself is not limited to that environment alone. In Chapter 13, *Designing Microservices,* and Chapter 15, *Cloud-Native Design,* we will mention a bit more about designing systems that are fault-tolerant and the role of chaos engineering.
- **Security**: Nowadays, there should be no need to repeat that security is crucial. But since it still isn't treated with all the seriousness the matter requires, we will bore you with saying this yet again. Every system that is connected to the network can – and most probably will – be broken. Performing security tests early on during development gives the same benefits as other kinds of tests: you can catch problems before they are too expensive to fix.

- **Availability**: Whereas poor performance may discourage your end users from using your product, poor availability may prevent them from even accessing said product. While availability problems may arise due to performance overload, there are also other causes of lost availability.
- **Integrity**: Your customers' data should not only be safe from outside attackers. It should also be safe from any alterations or losses due to software malfunction. Protection against bit rot, snapshotting, and backups are ways to prevent integrity loss. By comparing the current version with previously recorded snapshots, you can make sure if the difference resulted only from the action that was taken or whether it was caused by errors.
- **Usability**: Even a product that ticks all of the previous boxes may still be unsatisfactory for the users if it has a clunky interface and unintuitive interaction. Usability tests are mostly performed manually. It's important to perform a usability assessment each time the UI or the workflow of the system changes.

Regression testing

Regression tests are usually end-to-end tests that should prevent you from making the same mistake twice. When you (or your QA team or customers) discover a bug in a production system, it is not sufficient to apply a hotfix and forget all about it.

One of the things you need to do is write a regression test that should prevent the same error from ever entering the production system again. Good regression tests can even prevent the same *class* of errors from entering production. After all, once you know what you did wrong, you can imagine other ways to mess things up. Another thing you can do is perform root cause analysis.

Root cause analysis

Root cause analysis is a process that helps you uncover what the original source of the problem was, not only its manifestation. The most common way to perform root cause analysis is to use the method of *5 Whys*, which was made famous by the Toyota company. This method consists of peeling off all the superficial layers of the problem's manifestation to uncover the root cause hidden underneath. You do this by asking "why" at each layer until you find the root cause you are looking for.

Let's look at an example of this method in action.

The problem: We didn't get payments for some of the transactions:

1. *Why?* The system didn't send the appropriate emails to the customers.

2. *Why?* The email sending system doesn't support special characters in customers' names.

3. *Why?* The email sending system wasn't tested properly.

4. *Why?* There was no time for proper testing due to a need to develop new features.

5. *Why?* Our time estimates for the features were incorrect.

In this example, the problem with time estimates may be the root cause of the bug that was found in the production system. But it may as well be another layer to peel. The framework gives you a heuristic that should work most of the time, but if you don't feel entirely sure that what you got is what you are looking for, you can keep on peeling additional layers until you find what caused all the trouble.

Given that many bugs result from the exact same and often repeatable root causes, finding the root cause is extremely beneficial because you can protect yourself from making the same mistake in the future *on several different levels*. This is the principle of defense in depth when it's applied to software testing and problem-solving.

The groundwork for further improvement

Having your code tested protects you from making accidental errors. But it also opens up different possibilities. When your code is covered by test cases, you don't have to fear refactoring. Refactoring is the process of transforming code that does its job into code that is functionally similar, except it has better internal organization. You may be wondering why you need to change the code's organization. There are several reasons for this.

First of all, your code may no longer be readable, which means every modification takes too much time. Second, fixing a bug you are about to fix will make some other features behave incorrectly as the code gathered too many workarounds and special cases over time. Both of those reasons can be summed up as productivity improvements. They will make maintenance cheaper in the long run.

But apart from productivity, you may also want to improve performance. This can mean either runtime performance (how the application behaves in production) or compile-time performance (which is basically another form of productivity improvement).

You can refactor for runtime performance by replacing the current suboptimal algorithms with more efficient ones or by changing the data structures that are used through the module you are refactoring.

Refactoring for compile-time performance usually consists of moving parts of code to different compilation units, reorganizing headers, or reducing dependencies.

No matter what your end goal is, refactoring is generally a risky business. You take something that mostly works correctly and can end up either with a better version or a worse one. How would you know which case is yours? Here, testing comes to the rescue.

If the current feature set is thoroughly covered and you want to fix the recently uncovered bug, all you need to do is add another test case that will fail at that time. The moment your entire test suite starts passing again means your refactoring efforts were successful.

The worst-case scenario is that you have to abort the refactoring process in case you cannot satisfy all the test cases in a specified timeframe. You would undertake a similar procedure if you wanted to improve performance, but instead of unit tests (or end-to-end tests), you would focus on performance testing.

With the recent rise of automated tools that aid in refactoring (such as ReSharper C++: `https://www.jetbrains.com/resharper-cpp/features/ReSharper C++:`) and code maintenance, you can even go as far as outsourcing a part of coding solely to the external software services. Services such as Renovate (`https://renovatebot.com/`), Dependabot (`https://dependabot.com`), and Greenkeeper (`https://greenkeeper.io/`) may soon support C++ dependencies. Having solid test coverage will let you use them without the fear of breaking your application during dependency updates.

Since keeping your dependencies up to date in terms of security vulnerabilities is something you should always consider, such services can reduce the burden significantly. Therefore, testing not only protects you from making mistakes, but it reduces the effort necessary to introduce new features. It can also help you improve your code base and keep it stable and secure!

Now that we understand the need for testing, we want to start writing our own tests. It is possible to write tests without any external dependencies. However, we'd like to focus just on the testing logic. We're not interested in the details of managing test results and reporting. Therefore, we will select a testing framework to handle this tedious job for us. In the next section, we will introduce some of the most popular testing frameworks.

Introducing testing frameworks

As for the frameworks, the current de facto standard is Google's GTest. Together with its counterpart GMock, they form a small suite of tools that allow you to follow the best practices of testing in C++.

Other popular alternatives to GTest/GMock duo are Catch2, CppUnit, and Doctest. CppUnit has been available for a long time, but its lack of recent releases means we don't recommend it for fresh projects. Both Catch2 and Doctest support the modern C++ standards – in particular, C++14, C++17, and C++20.

To compare these testing frameworks, we will use the same codebase that we want to test. Using it as a basis, we will then implement tests in each of the frameworks.

GTest examples

Here is an example test for our customer library written in GTest:

```
#include "customer/customer.h"

#include <gtest/gtest.h>

TEST(basic_responses,
given_name_when_prepare_responses_then_greets_friendly) {
  auto name = "Bob";
  auto code_and_string = responder{}.prepare_response(name);
  ASSERT_EQ(code_and_string.first, web::http::status_codes::OK);
  ASSERT_EQ(code_and_string.second, web::json::value("Hello, Bob!"));
}
```

Most of the tasks that are commonly done during testing have been abstracted. We're mostly focused on providing the action we want to test (`prepare_response`) and the desired behavior (both `ASSERT_EQ` lines).

Catch2 examples

Here is an example test for our customer library written in Catch2:

```
#include "customer/customer.h"

#define CATCH_CONFIG_MAIN // This tells Catch to provide a main() - only do
                          // this in one cpp file
#include "catch2/catch.hpp"
```

```
TEST_CASE("Basic responses",
          "Given Name When Prepare Responses Then Greets Friendly") {
  auto name = "Bob";
  auto code_and_string = responder{}.prepare_response(name);
  REQUIRE(code_and_string.first == web::http::status_codes::OK);
  REQUIRE(code_and_string.second == web::json::value("Hello, Bob!"));
}
```

It looks pretty similar to the previous one. Some keywords differ (TEST and TEST_CASE) and there's a slightly different way to check the results (REQUIRE(a == b) instead of ASSERT_EQ(a,b)). Both are pretty compact and readable anyway.

CppUnit examples

Here is an example test for our customer library written in CppUnit. We will split it into several snippets.

The following code block prepares us to use the constructs from the CppUnit library:

```
#include <cppunit/BriefTestProgressListener.h>
#include <cppunit/CompilerOutputter.h>
#include <cppunit/TestCase.h>
#include <cppunit/TestFixture.h>
#include <cppunit/TestResult.h>
#include <cppunit/TestResultCollector.h>
#include <cppunit/TestRunner.h>
#include <cppunit/XmlOutputter.h>
#include <cppunit/extensions/HelperMacros.h>
#include <cppunit/extensions/TestFactoryRegistry.h>
#include <cppunit/ui/text/TextTestRunner.h>

#include "customer/customer.h"

using namespace CppUnit;
using namespace std;
```

Next, we must define the test class and implement the method that will execute our test case. After that, we must register the class so that we can use it in our test runner:

```
class TestBasicResponses : public CppUnit::TestFixture {
  CPPUNIT_TEST_SUITE(TestBasicResponses);
  CPPUNIT_TEST(testBob);
  CPPUNIT_TEST_SUITE_END();

  protected:
  void testBob();
```

```
  };

  void TestBasicResponses::testBob() {
    auto name = "Bob";
    auto code_and_string = responder{}.prepare_response(name);
    CPPUNIT_ASSERT(code_and_string.first == web::http::status_codes::OK);
    CPPUNIT_ASSERT(code_and_string.second == web::json::value("Hello,
Bob!"));
  }


  CPPUNIT_TEST_SUITE_REGISTRATION(TestBasicResponses);
```

Finally, we must provide the behavior of our test runner:

```
  int main() {
    CPPUNIT_NS::TestResult testresult;

    CPPUNIT_NS::TestResultCollector collectedresults;
    testresult.addListener(&collectedresults);

    CPPUNIT_NS::BriefTestProgressListener progress;
    testresult.addListener(&progress);

    CPPUNIT_NS::TestRunner testrunner;
  testrunner.addTest(CPPUNIT_NS::TestFactoryRegistry::getRegistry().makeTest(
));
    testrunner.run(testresult);

    CPPUNIT_NS::CompilerOutputter compileroutputter(&collectedresults,
std::cerr);
    compileroutputter.write();

    ofstream xmlFileOut("cppTestBasicResponsesResults.xml");
    XmlOutputter xmlOut(&collectedresults, xmlFileOut);
    xmlOut.write();

    return collectedresults.wasSuccessful() ? 0 : 1;
  }
```

Compared to the previous two examples, there's a lot of boilerplate in here. The test itself, however, looks pretty similar to the previous example.

Doctest examples

Here is an example test for our customer library written in Doctest:

```
#include "customer/customer.h"

#define DOCTEST_CONFIG_IMPLEMENT_WITH_MAIN
#include <doctest/doctest.h>

TEST_CASE("Basic responses") {
  auto name = "Bob";
  auto code_and_string = responder{}.prepare_response(name);
  REQUIRE(code_and_string.first == web::http::status_codes::OK);
  REQUIRE(code_and_string.second == web::json::value("Hello, Bob!"));
}
```

Once again, it's quite clean and easy to understand. The main selling point of Doctest is that it's the fastest both at compile-time and at runtime compared to the other similarly-featured alternatives.

Testing compile-time code

Template metaprogramming allows us to write C++ code that is executed during compile-time as opposed to the usual execution time. The constexpr keyword, which was added in C++11, allows us to use even more compile-time code, and consteval keyword from C++20 aims to give us greater control over the way the code is evaluated.

One of the problems with compile-time programming is that there is no easy way to test it. While unit testing frameworks for execution time code are abundant (as we just saw), there are not that many resources regarding compile-time programming. Part of this may stem from the fact that compile-time programming is still considered complicated and only aimed at experts.

Just because something isn't easy doesn't mean it is impossible, though. Just like execution time tests rely on assertions being checked during runtime, you can check your compile-time code for correct behavior using static_assert, which was introduced alongside constexpr in C++11.

The following is a simple example of using static_assert:

```
#include <string_view>

constexpr int generate_lucky_number(std::string_view name) {
  if (name == "Bob") {
```

```
        number = number * 7 + static_cast<int>(letter);
    }
    return number;
}

static_assert(generate_lucky_number("Bob") == 808);
```

Since we can compute each value tested here during compile time, we can effectively use the compiler as our testing framework.

Understanding mocks and fakes

As long as you are testing functions that do not interact too much with the outside world, things are pretty easy. The problems start when the units you are testing interface with third-party components such as databases, HTTP connections, and specific files.

On one hand, you want to see how your code behaves due to various circumstances. On the other hand, you don't want to wait for the database to boot, and you definitely don't want to have several databases containing different versions of data so that you can check all the necessary conditions.

How can we deal with such cases? The idea is not to execute the actual code that triggers all those side effects but instead use test doubles. Test doubles are constructions in code that mimic the actual API, except they don't perform actions of the mimicked functions or objects.

The most common test doubles are mocks, fakes, and stubs. Many people tend to mistake one for another as they are similar, though not the same.

Different test doubles

Mocks are test doubles that register all the received calls but do nothing more than that. They do not return any value and they do not change state in any way. They are useful when we have a third-party framework that is supposed to call our code. By using mocks, we can observe all the calls and are thus able to verify that the framework behaves as expected.

Stubs are a bit more complicated when it comes to their implementation. They return values, but those values are predefined. It may seem surprising that the `StubRandom.randomInteger()` method always returns the same value (for example, 3), but it may be a sufficient stub implementation when we are testing the type of the returned value or the fact that it does return a value at all. The exact value may not be that important.

Finally, fakes are objects that have a working implementation and behave mostly like the actual production implementation. The main difference is that fakes may take various shortcuts, such as avoiding calling the production database or filesystem.

When implementing the **Command Query Separation (CQS)** design pattern, you will usually want to double queries with stubs and commands with mocks.

Other uses for test doubles

Fakes can also be used, to a limited extent, outside of testing. In-memory processing data without resorting to database access can also be great for prototyping or when you're hitting performance bottlenecks.

Writing test doubles

To write test doubles, we typically use an external library, just as we do with unit tests. Some of the most popular solutions are as follows:

- GoogleMock (also known as gMock), which is now a part of the GoogleTest library: `https://github.com/google/googletest`.
- Trompeloeil, which focuses on C++14, integrates well with many testing libraries, such as Catch2, doctest, and GTest: `https://github.com/rollbear/trompeloeil`.

The code in the following sections will show you how to use both GoogleMock and Trompeloeil.

GoogleMock example

Since GoogleMock is part of GoogleTest, we will present them together:

```
#include "merchants/reviews.h"

#include <gmock/gmock.h>
```

```
#include <merchants/visited_merchant_history.h>

#include "fake_customer_review_store.h"

namespace {

class mock_visited_merchant : public i_visited_merchant {
 public:
  explicit mock_visited_merchant(fake_customer_review_store &store,
                                 merchant_id_t id)
      : review_store_{store},
        review_{store.get_review_for_merchant(id).value()} {
    ON_CALL(*this, post_rating).WillByDefault([this](stars s) {
      review_.rating = s;
      review_store_.post_review(review_);
    });
    ON_CALL(*this, get_rating).WillByDefault([this] { return
review_.rating; });
  }

  MOCK_METHOD(stars, get_rating, (), (override));
  MOCK_METHOD(void, post_rating, (stars s), (override));

 private:
  fake_customer_review_store &review_store_;
  review review_;
};

} // namespace

class history_with_one_rated_merchant : public ::testing::Test {
 public:
  static constexpr std::size_t CUSTOMER_ID = 7777;
  static constexpr std::size_t MERCHANT_ID = 1234;
  static constexpr const char *REVIEW_TEXT = "Very nice!";
  static constexpr stars RATING = stars{5.f};

 protected:
  void SetUp() final {
    fake_review_store_.post_review(
        {CUSTOMER_ID, MERCHANT_ID, REVIEW_TEXT, RATING});

    // nice mock will not warn on "uninteresting" call to get_rating
    auto mocked_merchant =
        std::make_unique<::testing::NiceMock<mock_visited_merchant>>(
            fake_review_store_, MERCHANT_ID);

    merchant_index_ = history_.add(std::move(mocked_merchant));
```

```
    }

    fake_customer_review_store fake_review_store_{CUSTOMER_ID};
    history_of_visited_merchants history_{};
    std::size_t merchant_index_{};
};

TEST_F(history_with_one_rated_merchant,
        when_user_changes_rating_then_the_review_is_updated_in_store) {
    const auto &mocked_merchant = dynamic_cast<const mock_visited_merchant
&>(
        history_.get_merchant(merchant_index_));
    EXPECT_CALL(mocked_merchant, post_rating);

    constexpr auto new_rating = stars{4};
    static_assert(RATING != new_rating);
    history_.rate(merchant_index_, stars{new_rating});
}

TEST_F(history_with_one_rated_merchant,
    when_user_selects_same_rating_then_the_review_is_not_updated_in_store) {
    const auto &mocked_merchant = dynamic_cast<const mock_visited_merchant
&>(
        history_.get_merchant(merchant_index_));
    EXPECT_CALL(mocked_merchant, post_rating).Times(0);

    history_.rate(merchant_index_, stars{RATING});
}
```

GTest is the most popular C++ testing framework at the time of writing this book. Its integration with GMock means that GMock is probably already available for you in your project. This combination is intuitive to use and fully-featured, so there's no reason to look for alternatives if you're already invested in GTest.

Trompeloeil example

To contrast this example with the previous one, this time, we are using Trompeloeil for test doubles and Catch2 as a testing framework:

```
#include "merchants/reviews.h"

#include "fake_customer_review_store.h"

// order is important
#define CATCH_CONFIG_MAIN
#include <catch2/catch.hpp>
```

```cpp
#include <catch2/trompeloeil.hpp>

#include <memory>

#include <merchants/visited_merchant_history.h>

using trompeloeil::_;

class mock_visited_merchant : public i_visited_merchant {
 public:
  MAKE_MOCK0(get_rating, stars(), override);
  MAKE_MOCK1(post_rating, void(stars s), override);
};

SCENARIO("merchant history keeps store up to date", "[mobile app]") {
  GIVEN("a history with one rated merchant") {
    static constexpr std::size_t CUSTOMER_ID = 7777;
    static constexpr std::size_t MERCHANT_ID = 1234;
    static constexpr const char *REVIEW_TEXT = "Very nice!";
    static constexpr stars RATING = stars{5.f};

    auto fake_review_store_ = fake_customer_review_store{CUSTOMER_ID};
    fake_review_store_.post_review(
        {CUSTOMER_ID, MERCHANT_ID, REVIEW_TEXT, RATING});

    auto history_ = history_of_visited_merchants{};
    const auto merchant_index_ =
        history_.add(std::make_unique<mock_visited_merchant>());

    auto &mocked_merchant = const_cast<mock_visited_merchant &>(
        dynamic_cast<const mock_visited_merchant &>(
            history_.get_merchant(merchant_index_)));

    auto review_ = review{CUSTOMER_ID, MERCHANT_ID, REVIEW_TEXT, RATING};
    ALLOW_CALL(mocked_merchant, post_rating(_))
        .LR_SIDE_EFFECT(review_.rating = _1;
                        fake_review_store_.post_review(review_););
    ALLOW_CALL(mocked_merchant, get_rating()).LR_RETURN(review_.rating);

    WHEN("a user changes rating") {
      constexpr auto new_rating = stars{4};
      static_assert(RATING != new_rating);

      THEN("the review is updated in store") {
        REQUIRE_CALL(mocked_merchant, post_rating(_));
        history_.rate(merchant_index_, stars{new_rating});
      }
    }
```

```
        WHEN("a user selects same rating") {
          THEN("the review is not updated in store") {
            FORBID_CALL(mocked_merchant, post_rating(_));
            history_.rate(merchant_index_, stars{RATING});
          }
        }
      }
    }
```

One of the great features of Catch2 is that it makes it easy to write behavior-driven development-style tests, such as the one shown here. If you prefer this style, then Catch2 with Trompeloeil would be a good choice as they integrate very well.

Test-driven class design

It's not enough to distinguish between different types of tests and learn a particular testing framework (or several). When you start testing your actual code, you will soon notice that not all classes can be tested easily. Sometimes, you may feel the need to access private attributes or methods. Resist this urge if you want to maintain the principles of good architecture! Instead, consider either testing the business requirements that are available through the type's public API or refactoring the type so that there's another unit of code you can test.

When tests and class design clash

The problem you may be facing is not that the testing frameworks are inadequate. Usually, what you encounter is inappropriately designed classes. Even though your classes may behave correctly and may look correct unless they allow for testing, they are not designed correctly.

However, this is good news. It means that you can repair the problem before it's inconvenient to do so. The class design will probably haunt you later on when you start building a class hierarchy based on it. Fixing the design during test implementation will simply reduce the possible technological debt.

Defensive programming

Unlike its name may suggest, defensive programming is not a security feature. Its name comes from defending your classes and functions from being used contrary to their original intention. It's not directly related to testing, but it's a great design pattern to use since it improves your code's quality, making your project future-proof.

Defensive programming starts with static typing. If you create a function that handles a custom-defined type as a parameter, you must make sure nobody will call it with some accidental value. A user will have to consciously check what the function expects and prepare the input accordingly.

In C++, we can also leverage type-safety features when we're writing template code. When we're creating a container for our customers' reviews, we could accept a list of any type and copy from it. To get nicer errors and well-crafted checks, we could write the following:

```cpp
class CustomerReviewStore : public i_customer_review_store {
 public:
  CustomerReviewStore() = default;
  explicit CustomerReviewStore(const std::ranges::range auto
&initial_reviews) {
    static_assert(is_range_of_reviews_v<decltype(initial_reviews)>,
                  "Must pass in a collection of reviews");
    std::ranges::copy(begin(initial_reviews), end(initial_reviews),
                      begin(reviews_));
  }
  // ...
 private:
  std::vector<review> reviews_;
};
```

The `explicit` keyword protects us from unwanted implicit casts. By specifying that our input parameter satisfies the `range` concept, we ensure that we're only going to compile with a valid container. Thanks to using concepts, we can get clearer error messages from our defense against invalid use. Using `static_assert` in our code is also a great defensive measure as it allows us to provide a nice error message if needed. Our `is_range_of_reviews` check could be implemented as follows:

```cpp
template <typename T>
constexpr bool is_range_of_reviews_v =
    std::is_same_v<std::ranges::range_value_t<T>, review>;
```

This way, we ensure that the range we got actually contains reviews of the type we desire.

Static typing will not prevent invalid runtime values from being passed to the function. That's why the next form of defensive programming is checking preconditions. This way, your code will fail as soon as the first sign of a problem arises, which is always better than returning an invalid value that propagates to other parts of the system. Until we have contracts in C++, we can use the GSL library we mentioned in earlier chapters to check the pre- and post-conditions of our code:

```
void post_review(review review) final {
    Expects(review.merchant);
    Expects(review.customer);
    Ensures(!reviews_.empty());

    reviews_.push_back(std::move(review));
}
```

Here, by using the `Expects` macro, we're checking that our incoming review actually has the IDs of the merchant and reviewer set. Aside from the cases where it doesn't, we are also defending ourselves against cases where adding a review to our storage failed when we use the `Ensures` post-condition macro.

When it comes to runtime checks, one of the first things that comes to mind is checking whether one or more attributes is not a `nullptr`. The best way to guard yourself against this problem is to distinguish nullable resources (those that can take `nullptr` as value) from non-nullable ones. There's a great tool you can use for this, and is available in the standard library from C++17: `std::optional`. If you can, use it in all the APIs that you design.

The boring refrain – write your tests first

This has been said many times, yet many people tend to "forget" this rule. When you actually write your tests, the first thing you must do is reduce the risk of creating classes that are hard to test. You start with API usage and need to bend the implementation to best serve the API. This way, you usually end up with APIs that are both more pleasant to use and easier to test. When you're implementing **test-driven development** (**TDD**) or writing tests before code, you'll also end up implementing dependency injection, which means your classes can be more loosely coupled.

Doing this the other way around (writing your classes first and only then adding unit tests to them) may mean that you up with code that is easier to write but harder to test. And when testing gets harder, you may feel the temptation to skip it.

Automating tests for continuous integration/continuous deployment

In the next chapter, we will focus on **continuous integration** and **continuous deployment** (**CI/CD**). For a CI/CD pipeline to work properly, you need to have a set of tests that catch the bugs before they enter production. It is up to you and your team to make sure all the business requirements are properly expressed as tests.

Tests are useful on several levels. With behavior-driven development, which we mentioned in the previous section, business requirements form a basis for automated tests. But the system you are building doesn't consist solely of business requirements. You want to make sure all the third-party integrations are working as expected. You want to make sure all your subcomponents (such as microservices) can actually interface with each other. Finally, you want to make sure that the functions and classes you are building are free of any bugs you could have imagined.

Each test that you can automate is a candidate for a CI/CD pipeline. Each of them also has its place somewhere in this pipeline. For example, end-to-end tests make the most sense after the deployment as acceptance tests. On the other hand, unit tests make the most sense when they're executed directly after compilation. After all, our aim is to break the circuit as soon as we find any possible divergence from the specification.

You don't have to run all the tests that you have automated each time you run a CI/CD pipeline. It's better if the runtime of each pipeline is relatively short. Ideally, it should finish within a couple of minutes from the commit. How can we make sure everything is properly tested, then, if we want to keep the runtime minimal?

One answer is to prepare different suites of tests for different purposes. For example, you can have minimal tests for commits to a feature branch. With many commits coming to feature branches every day, this means they will only be tested briefly and that the answer will be available fast. Merging feature branches to the shared development branch then requires a slightly larger set of test cases. This way, we make sure we haven't broken anything that other team members will be using. Finally, a more extensive set of cases will be run for merges to production branches. After all, we want the production branches to be tested thoroughly, even if the testing takes quite a long time.

Another answer is to use the trimmed-down set of test cases for CI/CD purposes and have an additional continuous testing process. This process runs regularly and performs in-depth checks on the current state of a particular environment. The tests can go as far as security tests and performance tests and may thus assess the eligibility of the environment to be promoted.

Promotion occurs when we select an environment and acknowledge that this environment has all the qualities to become a more mature environment. For example, that development environment can become the next staging environment, or that staging environment can become the next production environment. If this promotion happens automatically, it is also a good practice to provide automatic rollback in case the subtle differences (such as in terms of domain name or traffic) make the freshly promoted environment no longer pass the tests.

This also presents another important practice: to always run tests on the production environment. Such tests have to be the least intrusive, of course, but they should tell you that your system is performing correctly at any given time.

Testing the infrastructure

If you want to incorporate the concepts of configuration management, Infrastructure as Code, or immutable deployments into the software architecture of your application, you should also consider testing the infrastructure itself. There are several tools you can use to do this, including Serverspec, Testinfra, Goss, and Terratest, which are among some of the more popular ones.

These tools slightly differ in scope, as stated here:

- Serverspec and Testinfra focus more on testing the actual state of the servers that are configured via configuration management, such as Salt, Ansible, Puppet, and Chef. They're written in Ruby and Python, respectively, and they plug into the languages' testing engines. This means RSPec for Serverspec and Pytest for Testinfra.
- Goss is a bit different both in terms of scope and form. Besides testing the servers, you can also use Goss to test the containers you use in your project with the dgoss wrapper. As for its form, it doesn't use the imperative code you would see in Serverspec or Testinfra. Rather, similar to Ansible or Salt, it uses a YAML file to describe the desired state we want to check for. If you're already using a declarative approach to configuration management (such as the aforementioned Ansible or Salt), Goss may be more intuitive and thus a much better fit for testing.
- Finally, Terratest is a tool that allows you to test the output of Infrastructure as Code tools such as Packer and Terraform (hence the name). Just like Serverspec and Testinfra use their language testing engines to write tests for servers, Terratest leverages Go's testing package to write the appropriate test cases.

Let's see how can we use each of these tools to validate that the deployment went on according to plan (at least from the infrastructure's point of view).

Testing with Serverspec

The following is an example of a test for Serverspec that checks the availability of Git in a specific version and the Let's Encrypt configuration file:

```
# We want to have git 1:2.1.4 installed if we're running Debian
describe package('git'), :if => os[:family] == 'debian' do
  it { should be_installed.with_version('1:2.1.4') }
end
# We want the file /etc/letsencrypt/config/example.com.conf to:
describe file('/etc/letsencrypt/config/example.com.conf') do
  it { should be_file } # be a regular file
  it { should be_owned_by 'letsencrypt' } # owned by the letsencrypt user
  it { should be_mode 600 } # access mode 0600
  it { should contain('example.com') } # contain the text example.com
                                        # in the content
end
```

The Ruby DSL syntax should be readable even by those who do not use Ruby daily. You may need to get used to writing the code.

Testing with Testinfra

The following is an example of a test for Testinfra that checks the availability of Git in a specific version and the Let's Encrypt configuration file:

```
# We want Git installed on our host
def test_git_is_installed(host):
    git = host.package("git")
    # we test if the package is installed
    assert git.is_installed
    # and if it matches version 1:2.1.4 (using Debian versioning)
    assert git.version.startswith("1:2.1.4")
# We want the file /etc/letsencrypt/config/example.com.conf to:
def test_letsencrypt_file(host):
    le = host.file("/etc/letsencrypt/config/example.com.conf")
    assert le.user == "letsencrypt" # be owned by the letsencrypt user
    assert le.mode == 0o600 # access mode 0600
    assert le.contains("example.com") # contain the text example.com in the
contents
```

Testinfra uses plain Python syntax. It should be readable, but just like Serverspec, you may need some training to confidently write tests in it.

Testing with Goss

The following is an example of a YAML file for Goss that checks the availability of Git in a specific version and the Let's Encrypt configuration file:

```
# We want Git installed on our host
package:
  git:
    installed: true # we test if the package is installed
  versions:
  - 1:2.1.4 # and if it matches version 1:2.1.4 (using Debian versioning)
file:
  # We want the file /etc/letsencrypt/config/example.com.conf to:
  /etc/letsencrypt/config/example.com.conf:
    exists: true
  filetype: file # be a regular file
  owner: letsencrypt # be owned by the letsencrypt user
  mode: "0600" # access mode 0600
  contains:
  - "example.com" # contain the text example.com in the contents
```

YAML's syntax will probably require the least preparation both to read it and write it. However, if your project already uses Ruby or Python, you may want to stick to Serverspec or Testinfra when it comes to writing more complicated tests.

Summary

This chapter focused both on the architectural and technical aspects of testing different parts of the software. We looked at the testing pyramid to understand how different kinds of tests contribute to the overall health and stability of a software project. Since testing can be both functional and non-functional, we saw some examples of both these types.

One of the most important things to remember from this chapter is that tests are not the end stage. We want to have them not because they bring immediate value, but because we can use them to check for known regressions, when refactoring, or when we're changing the behavior of existing parts of the system. Tests can also prove useful when we want to perform root cause analysis as they can quickly verify different hypotheses.

Having established the theoretical requirements, we showed examples of the different testing frameworks and libraries we can use to write test doubles. Even though writing tests first and their implementation later requires some practice, it has an important benefit. This benefit is a better class design.

Finally, to highlight that modern architecture is something more than just software code, we also looked at a few tools for testing infrastructure and deployment. In the next chapter, we will see how continuous integration and continuous deployment bring better service quality and robustness to the applications you will architect.

Questions

1. What is the base layer of the testing pyramid?
2. What kinds of non-functional tests are there?
3. What is the name of the famous method for root cause analysis?
4. Is it possible to test the compile-time code in C++?
5. What should you use when you're writing unit tests for code with external dependencies?
6. What is the role of unit tests in continuous integration/continuous deployment?
7. What are some tools that allow you to test infrastructure code?
8. Is it a good idea to access the class's private attributes and methods in a unit test?

Further reading

Testing C++ Code: https://www.packtpub.com/application-development/modern-c-programming-cookbook

Test Doubles: https://martinfowler.com/articles/mocksArentStubs.html

Continuous Integration/Continuous Deployment: https://www.packtpub.com/virtualization-and-cloud/hands-continuous-integration-and-delivery and https://www.packtpub.com/virtualization-and-cloud/cloud-native-continuous-integration-and-delivery

9

Continuous Integration and Continuous Deployment

In one of the previous chapters on building and packaging, we learned about different build systems and different packaging systems that our application can use. **Continuous Integration** (CI) and **Continuous Deployment** (CD) allow us to use knowledge of building and packaging to improve service quality and the robustness of the application we are developing.

Both CI and CD rely on good test coverage. CI uses mostly unit tests and integration tests, whereas CD depends more on smoke tests and end-to-end tests. You learned more about the different aspects of testing in `Chapter 8`, *Writing Testable Code*. With this knowledge, you are ready to build a CI/CD pipeline.

In this chapter, we'll cover the following topics:

- Understanding CI
- Reviewing code changes
- Exploring test-driven automation
- Managing deployment as code
- Building deployment code
- Building a CD pipeline
- Using immutable infrastructure

Technical requirements

The sample code of this chapter can be found at `https://github.com/PacktPublishing/Software-Architecture-with-Cpp/tree/master/Chapter09`.

To understand the concepts explained in this chapter, you'll require the following installations:

- A free GitLab account
- Ansible version 2.8+
- Terraform version 0.12+
- Packer version 1.4+

Understanding CI

CI is the process of shortening the integration cycles. Whereas in traditional software, many different features could have been developed separately and only integrated prior to release, in projects developed with CI, integration can occur several times a day. Usually, each change a developer makes is tested and integrated at the same time as it is committed to the central repository.

Since testing occurs just after development, the feedback loop is much quicker. This lets developers fix bugs more easily (as they usually still remember what was changed). In contrast to the traditional approach of testing just prior to release, CI saves a lot of work and improves the quality of software.

Release early, release often

Have you ever heard the saying "release early, release often"? This is a software development philosophy that emphasizes the importance of short release cycles. Short release cycles, in turn, provide a much shorter feedback loop between planning, development, and validation. When something breaks, it should break as early as possible so that the costs of fixing the problem are relatively small.

This philosophy was popularized by Eric S. Raymond (also known as ESR) in his 1997 essay entitled *The Cathedral and the Bazaar*. There's also a book with the same title that contains this and other essays by the author. Considering ESR's activity within open source movements, the "release early, release often" mantra became synonymous with how open source projects operated.

Some years later, the same principle moved beyond just open source projects. With the rising interest in Agile methodologies, such as Scrum, the "release early, release often" mantra became synonymous with development sprints that end with a product increment. This increment is, of course, a software release, but usually, there are many other releases that happened during the sprint.

How can you achieve such short release cycles? One answer is to rely on automation as much as possible. Ideally, every commit to the code repository should end as a release. Whether this release ends up facing the customers is another matter. What's important is that every code change can result in a usable product.

Of course, building and releasing every single commit to the public would be a tedious job for any developer. Even when everything is scripted, this can add unnecessary overhead to the usual chores. This is why you would want to set up a CI system to automate the releases for you and your development team.

Merits of CI

CI is the concept of integrating the work of several developers, at least daily. As already discussed, sometimes it can mean several times a day. Every commit that enters the repository is integrated and validated separately. The build system checks whether the code can be built without errors. The packaging system may create a package that is ready to be saved as an artifact or even deployed later on when CD is used. Finally, the automated tests check that no known regression occurred in relation to the change. Let's now see its merits in detail:

- CI allows for the rapid solving of problems. If one of the developers forgot a semicolon at the end of the line, the compiler on the CI system will catch that error right away before this incorrect code reaches other developers, thereby impeding their work. Of course, developers should always build the changes and test them before committing the code, but minor typos can go unnoticed on the developer's machine and enter the shared repository anyway.
- Another benefit of using CI is that it prevents the common "works on my machine" excuse. If a developer forgets to commit a necessary file, the CI system will fail to build the changes, yet again preventing them from spreading further and causing mischief to the whole team. The special configuration of one developer's environment also stops being an issue. If a change builds on two machines, the developer's computer and the CI system, we are safe to assume that it should build on other machines as well.

Gating mechanism

If we want CI to bring value beyond simply building packages for us, we need a gating mechanism. This gating mechanism will allow us to discern good code changes from bad ones, thus keeping our application safe from modifications that would render it useless. For this to happen, we need a comprehensive suite of tests. Such a suite allows us to automatically recognize when a change is problematic, and we're able to do it quickly.

For individual components, unit tests play the role of a gating mechanism. A CI system can discard any changes that do not pass unit tests or any changes that do not reach a certain code coverage threshold. At the time of building individual components, a CI system may also use integration tests to further ensure that the changes are stable, not only by themselves but also are acting properly together.

Implementing the pipeline with GitLab

Throughout this chapter, we will use popular open source tools to build a full CI/CD pipeline consisting of gating mechanisms, automated deployment, and also showing the concepts of infrastructure automation.

The first such tool is GitLab. You may have heard about it as a Git hosting solution, but in reality, it's much more than that. GitLab comes in several distributions, namely, the following:

- An open source solution that you can host on your own premises
- Self-hosted paid versions that offer additional features over the open source community edition
- And finally, a **Software-as-as-Service (SaaS)** managed offer hosted under `https://gitlab.com`

For the requirements of this book, each of the distributions has all the necessary features. We will, therefore, focus on the SaaS version, as this requires the least amount of preparation.

Although `https://gitlab.com` is mainly targeted at open source projects, you can also create private projects and repositories if you don't feel like sharing your work with the entire world. This allows us to create a new private project in GitLab and populate it with the code we have already demonstrated in Chapter 7, *Building and Packaging*.

A lot of modern CI/CD tools could work instead of GitLab CI/CD. Examples include GitHub Actions, Travis CI, CircleCI, and Jenkins. We've chosen GitLab as it can be used both in SaaS form and on-premises, so should accommodate a lot of different use cases.

We will then use our previous build system to create a simple CI pipeline in GitLab. These pipelines are described in the YAML file as a series of steps and metadata. An example pipeline building all the requirements, as well as the sample project from Chapter 7, *Building and Packaging*, would look like the following:

```yaml
# We want to cache the conan data and CMake build directory
cache:
  key: all
  paths:
    - .conan
    - build

# We're using conanio/gcc10 as the base image for all the subsequent
commands
default:
  image: conanio/gcc10

stages:
  - prerequisites
  - build

before_script:
  - export CONAN_USER_HOME="$CI_PROJECT_DIR"

# Configure conan
prerequisites:
  stage: prerequisites
  script:
    - pip install conan==1.34.1
    - conan profile new default || true
    - conan profile update settings.compiler=gcc default
    - conan profile update settings.compiler.libcxx=libstdc++11 default
    - conan profile update settings.compiler.version=10 default
    - conan profile update settings.arch=x86_64 default
    - conan profile update settings.build_type=Release default
    - conan profile update settings.os=Linux default
    - conan remote add trompeloeil
https://api.bintray.com/conan/trompeloeil/trompeloeil || true

# Build the project
build:
  stage: build
  script:
```

```
- sudo apt-get update && sudo apt-get install -y docker.io
- mkdir -p build
- cd build
- conan install ../ch08 --build=missing
- cmake -DBUILD_TESTING=1 -DCMAKE_BUILD_TYPE=Release ../ch08/customer
- cmake --build .
```

Saving the preceding file as `.gitlab-ci.yml` in the root directory of your Git repository will automatically enable CI in GitLab and run the pipeline with each subsequent commit.

Reviewing code changes

Code reviews can be used both with CI systems and without them. Their main purpose is to double-check each change introduced to the code to make sure that it is correct, that it fits the application's architecture, and that it follows the project's guidelines and best practices.

When used without CI systems, it is often the reviewer's task to test the change manually and verify it is working as expected. CI reduces this burden, letting software developers focus on the logical structure of the code.

Automated gating mechanisms

Automated tests are only one example of a gating mechanism. When their quality is high enough, they can guarantee the code works according to design. But there's still a difference between code that works correctly and good code. As you've learned from this book so far, code can be considered good if it fulfills several values. Being functionally correct is just one of them.

There are other tools that can help achieve the desired standard of your code base. Some of them have been covered in previous chapters, so we won't go into the details. Keep in mind that using linters, code formatters, and static analysis in your CI/CD pipeline is a great practice. While static analysis can act as a gating mechanism, you can apply linting and formatting to each commit that enters the central repository to make it consistent with the rest of the code base. You will find more on linters and formatters in the appendix.

Ideally, this mechanism will only have to check whether the code has already been formatted, as the formatting step should be done by developers before pushing the code to the repository. When using Git as a version control system, the mechanism of Git Hooks can prevent committing code without running the necessary tools on it.

But automated analysis can only get you so far. You can check that the code is functionally complete, that it is free of known bugs and vulnerabilities, and that it fits within the coding standard. This is where manual inspection comes in.

Code review – the manual gating mechanism

Manual inspection of a code change is often known as a code review. The aim of the code review is to identify problems, both with the implementation of specific subsystems and adherence to the overall architecture of the application. Automated performance tests may or may not discover potential problems with a given function. Human eyes, on the other hand, can usually spot a sub-optimal solution to the problem. Whether it is the wrong data structure or an algorithm with unnecessarily high computational complexity, a good architect should be able to pinpoint the problem.

But it isn't just the architect's role to perform code reviews. Peer reviews, that is, code reviews performed by peers of the author, also have their place in the development process. Such reviews are valuable not just because they allow colleagues to find bugs in each other's code. The more important aspect is the fact that many teammates are suddenly aware of what everybody else is doing. This way, when there is an absence in the team (whether because of a long meeting, vacation, or job rotation), another team member can substitute for the missing one. Even if they're not an expert on the topic, every other member at least knows where the interesting code is located and everyone should be able to remember the last changes to the code. This means both the time when they happened and the scope and content of those changes.

With more people aware of how the insides of your application appear, it is also more probable that they can figure out a correlation between recent changes in one component and a freshly discovered bug. Even though every person on your team probably has different experience, they can pool their resources when everyone knows the code quite thoroughly.

So code reviews can check whether the change fits within the desired architecture and whether its implementation is correct. We call such a code review an architectural review, or an expert's review.

Another type of code review, the peer review, not only helps uncover bugs, but also raises awareness within the team about what other members are working on. If necessary, you can also perform a different kind of expert review when dealing with changes that integrate with external services.

As each interface is a source of potential problems, changes close to the interface level should be treated as especially dangerous. We advise you to supplement the usual peer review with an expert coming from the other side of the interface. For example, if you are writing a producer's code, ask a consumer for a review. This way, you ensure you won't miss some vital use case that you may consider very improbable, but that the other side uses constantly.

Different approaches to a code review

You will most often conduct code reviews asynchronously. This means that the communication between the author of the change under review and the reviewers does not happen in real time. Instead, each of the actors posts their comments and suggestions at any given time. Once there are no more comments, the author reworks the original change and once again puts it under review. This can take as many rounds as necessary until everyone agrees that no further corrections are necessary.

When a change is particularly controversial and an asynchronous code review takes too much time, it is beneficial to conduct a code review synchronously. This means a meeting (in-person or remotely) to resolve any opposing views on the way forward. This will happen in particular when a change contradicts one of the initial decisions due to the new knowledge acquired while implementing the change.

There are some dedicated tools aimed solely at code reviews. More often, you will want to use a tool that is built into your repository server, which includes services such as the following:

- GitHub
- Bitbucket
- GitLab
- Gerrit

All of the preceding offer both Git hosting and code review. Some of them go even further, providing a whole CI/CD pipeline, issue management, wiki, and much more.

When you use the combined package of code hosting and code review, the default workflow is to push the changes as a separate branch and then ask the project's owner to merge the changes in a process known as a pull request (or a merge request). Despite the fancy name, the pull request or merge request informs the project owner that you have code that you wish to merge with the main branch. This means that the reviewers should review your changes to make sure everything is in order.

Using pull requests (merge requests) for a code review

Creating pull requests or merge requests with systems such as GitLab is very easy. First of all, when we push a new branch to the central repository from the command line, we can observe the following message:

```
remote:
remote: To create a merge request for fix-ci-cd, visit:
remote:
https://gitlab.com/hosacpp/continuous-integration/merge_requests/new?merge_
request%5Bsource_branch%5D=fix-ci-cd
remote:
```

If you previously had CI enabled (by adding the `.gitlab-ci.yml` file), you'll also see that the newly pushed branch has been subjected to the CI process. This occurs even before you open a merge request, and it means you can postpone tagging your colleagues until you get information from CI that every automated check has passed.

The two main ways to open a merge request are as follows:

- By following the link mentioned in the push message
- By navigating to merge requests in the GitLab UI and selecting the **Create merge request** button or the **New merge request** button

When you submit the merge request, having completed all the relevant fields, you will see that the status of the CI pipeline is also visible. If the pipeline fails, merging the change wouldn't be possible.

Exploring test-driven automation

CI mainly focuses on the integration part. It means building the code of different subsystems and making sure it works together. While tests are not strictly required to achieve this purpose, running CI without them seems like a waste. CI without automated tests makes it easier to introduce subtle bugs to code while giving a false sense of security.

That's one of the reasons why CI often goes hand in hand with continuous testing, which we'll cover in this next section.

Behavior-driven development

So far, we have managed to set up a pipeline that we can call continuous building. Each change we make to the code ends up being compiled, but we don't test it any further. Now it's time to introduce the practice of continuous testing. Testing on a low level will also act as a gating mechanism to automatically reject all the changes that do not satisfy requirements.

How can you check whether a given change satisfies requirements? This is best achieved by writing tests based on these requirements. One of the ways to do this is by following **Behavior-Driven Development (BDD)**. The concept of BDD is to encourage deeper collaboration between the different actors in an Agile project.

Unlike the traditional approach, where tests are written either by developers or the QA team, with BDD, the tests are created collaboratively by the following individuals:

- Developers
- QA engineers
- Business representatives.

The most common way to specify tests for BDD is to use the Cucumber framework, which uses plain English phrases to describe the desired behavior of any part of the system. These sentences follow a specific pattern that can then be turned into working code, integrating with the testing framework of choice.

There is official support for C++ in the Cucumber framework and it's based on CMake, Boost, GTest, and GMock. After specifying the desired behavior in the cucumber format (which uses a domain-specific language known as Gherkin), we also need to provide the so-called step definitions. Step definitions are the actual code corresponding to the actions described in the cucumber specification. For example, consider the following behavior expressed in Gherkin:

```
# language: en
Feature: Summing
In order to see how much we earn,
Sum must be able to add two numbers together

Scenario: Regular numbers
  Given I have entered 3 and 2 as parameters
  When I add them
  Then the result should be 5
```

We can save it as a `sum.feature` file. In order to generate a valid C++ code with tests, we would use the appropriate step definitions:

```cpp
#include <gtest/gtest.h>
#include <cucumber-cpp/autodetect.hpp>

#include <Sum.h>

using cucumber::ScenarioScope;

struct SumCtx {
  Sum sum;
  int a;
  int b;
  int result;
};

GIVEN("^I have entered (\\d+) and (\\d+) as parameters$", (const int a,
const int b)) {
    ScenarioScope<SumCtx> context;

    context->a = a;
    context->b = b;
}

WHEN("^I add them") {
    ScenarioScope<SumCtx> context;

    context->result = context->sum.sum(context->a, context->b);
}

THEN("^the result should be (.*)$", (const int expected)) {
    ScenarioScope<SumCtx> context;

    EXPECT_EQ(expected, context->result);
}
```

When building an application from scratch, it's a good idea to follow the BDD pattern. This book aims to show the best practices you can use in such a greenfield project. But it doesn't mean you can't try our examples in an existing project. CI and CD can be added at any given time during the life cycle of the project. Since it's always a good idea to run your tests as often as possible, using a CI system just for the purpose of continuous testing is almost always a good idea.

If you don't have behavior tests, you shouldn't need to worry. You can add them later and, for the moment, just focus on those tests you already have. Whether they are unit tests or end-to-end tests, anything that helps you assess the state of your application is a good candidate for the gating mechanism.

Writing tests for CI

For CI, it's best to focus on unit tests and integration tests. They work on the lowest possible level, which means they're usually quick to execute and have the smallest requirements. Ideally, all unit tests should be self-contained (no external dependencies like a working database) and able to run in parallel. This way, when the problem appears on the level where unit tests are able to catch it, the offending code would be flagged in a matter of seconds.

There are some people who say that unit tests only make sense in interpreted languages or languages with dynamic typing. The argument goes that C++ already has testing built-in by means of the type system and the compiler checking for erroneous code. While it's true that type checking can catch some bugs that would require separate tests in dynamically typed languages, this shouldn't be used as an excuse not to write unit tests. After all, the purpose of unit tests isn't to verify that the code can execute without any problems. We write unit tests to make sure our code not only executes, but also fulfills all the business requirements we have.

As an extreme example, take a look at the following two functions. Both of them are syntactically correct and they use proper typing. However, just by looking at them, you can probably guess which one is correct and which isn't. Unit tests help to catch this kind of misbehavior:

```
int sum (int a, int b) {
 return a+b;
}
```

The preceding function returns a sum of the two arguments provided. The following one returns just the value of the first argument:

```
int sum (int a, int b) {
   return a;
}
```

Even though the types match and the compiler won't complain, this code wouldn't perform its task. To distinguish useful code from erroneous code, we use tests and assertions.

Continuous testing

Having already established a simple CI pipeline, it is very easy to extend it with testing. Since we are already using CMake and CTest for the building and testing process, all we need to do is add another step to our pipeline that will execute the tests. This step may look like this:

```
# Run the unit tests with ctest
test:
  stage: test
  script:
    - cd build
    - ctest .
```

An entire pipeline will therefore appear as follows:

```
cache:
  key: all
  paths:
    - .conan
    - build

default:
  image: conanio/gcc9

stages:
  - prerequisites
  - build
  - test # We add another stage that tuns the tests

before_script:
  - export CONAN_USER_HOME="$CI_PROJECT_DIR"

prerequisites:
  stage: prerequisites
  script:
    - pip install conan==1.34.1
    - conan profile new default || true
    - conan profile update settings.compiler=gcc default
    - conan profile update settings.compiler.libcxx=libstdc++11 default
    - conan profile update settings.compiler.version=10 default
    - conan profile update settings.arch=x86_64 default
    - conan profile update settings.build_type=Release default
    - conan profile update settings.os=Linux default
    - conan remote add trompeloeil
https://api.bintray.com/conan/trompeloeil/trompeloeil || true
```

```
build:
  stage: build
  script:
    - sudo apt-get update && sudo apt-get install -y docker.io
    - mkdir -p build
    - cd build
    - conan install ../ch08 --build=missing
    - cmake -DBUILD_TESTING=1 -DCMAKE_BUILD_TYPE=Release ../ch08/customer
    - cmake --build .

# Run the unit tests with ctest
test:
  stage: test
  script:
    - cd build
    - ctest .
```

This way, each commit will not only be subjected to the build process, but also to testing. If one of the steps fails, we will be notified which one was the source of the failure and we could see in the dashboard which steps were successful.

Managing deployment as code

With changes tested and approved, now it's time to deploy them to one of the operating environments.

There are many tools to help with deployment. We decided to provide examples with Ansible as this doesn't require any setup on the target machines besides a functional Python installation (which the majority of UNIX systems already have anyway). Why Ansible? It is very popular in the configuration management space and it's backed up by a trustworthy open source company (Red Hat).

Using Ansible

Why not use something that's already available, such as Bourne shell script or PowerShell? For simple deployments, shell scripts may be a better approach. But as our deployment process becomes more complex, it is much harder to handle every possible initial state using the shell's conditional statements.

Dealing with differences between initial states is actually something Ansible is especially good at. Unlike traditional shell scripts, which use the imperative form (move this file, edit that file, run a particular command), Ansible playbooks, as they are called, use the declarative form (make sure the file is available in this path, make sure the file contains specified lines, make sure the program is running, make sure the program completes successfully).

This declarative approach also helps to achieve idempotence. Idempotence is a feature of a function that means applying the function several times over will have exactly the same results as a single application. If the first run of an Ansible playbook introduces some changes to the configuration, each subsequent run will already start in the desired state. This prevents Ansible from performing any additional changes.

In other words, when you invoke Ansible, it will first assess the current state of all the machines you wish to configure:

- If any of them requires any changes, Ansible will only run the tasks required to achieve the desired state.
- If there's no need to modify a particular thing, Ansible won't touch it. Only when the desired and actual states differ will you see Ansible taking action to converge the actual state toward the desired one described by the contents of the playbook.

How Ansible fits with the CI/CD pipeline

Ansible's idempotence makes it a great target to use in CI/CD pipelines. After all, there's no risk in running the same Ansible playbook multiple times even if nothing changes between the two runs. If you use Ansible for your deployment code, creating a CD is just a matter of preparing appropriate acceptance tests (such as smoke tests or end-to-end tests).

The declarative approach may require changing the way you think about deployments, but the gains are well worth it. Besides running playbooks, you can also use Ansible to perform one-off commands on remote machines, but we won't cover this use case as it doesn't really help with deployments.

Everything you can do with a shell you can do with Ansible's `shell` module. That's because, in the playbooks, you write tasks specifying which modules they use and their respective parameters. One such module is the aforementioned `shell` module, which simply executes the provided parameters in a shell on a remote machine. But what makes Ansible not only convenient but also cross-platform (at least when different UNIX distributions are concerned) is the availability of modules to manipulate common concepts such as user administration, package management, and similar instances.

Using components to create deployment code

In addition to the regular modules provided in the standard library, there are also third-party components to allow for code reuse. You can test such components individually, which also makes your deployment code more robust. Such components are called roles. They contain a set of tasks to make a machine fit to take on a specific role, such as `webserver`, `db`, or `docker`. While some roles prepare the machine to provide particular services, other roles may be more abstract, such as the popular `ansible-hardening` role. This has been created by the OpenStack team and it makes it much harder to break into a machine secured by using this role.

When you start to understand the language Ansible uses, all the playbooks cease to be just the scripts. In turn, they will become the documentation of the deployment process. You can either use them verbatim by running Ansible, or you can read the described tasks and perform all the operations manually, for example, on an offline machine.

There is one risk related to using Ansible for deployment in your team. Once you start using it, you have to make sure that everyone on the team is able to use it and modify the relevant tasks. DevOps is a practice the whole team has to follow; it cannot be implemented only partially. When the application's code changes considerably, requiring appropriate changes on the deployment side, the person responsible for changes in the application should also supply the changes in the deployment code. Of course, this is something that your tests can verify, so the gating mechanism can reject the changes that are incomplete.

One noteworthy aspect of Ansible is that it can run both in a push and pull model:

- The push model is when you run Ansible on your own machine or in the CI system. Ansible then connects to the target machine, for example, over an SSH connection, and performs the necessary steps on the target machine.
- In the pull model, the whole process is initiated by the target machine. Ansible's component, `ansible-pull`, runs directly on the target machine and checks the code repository to establish whether there's been any update to the particular branch. After refreshing the local playbook, Ansible performs all the steps as usual. This time, both the controlling component and the actual execution happen on the same machine. Most of the time, you will want to run `ansible-pull` periodically, for example, from within a cron job.

Building deployment code

In its simplest form, deployment with Ansible may consist of copying a single binary to the target machine and then running that binary. We can achieve this with the following Ansible code:

```
tasks:
    # Each Ansible task is written as a YAML object
    # This uses a copy module
    - name: Copy the binaries to the target machine
      copy:
        src: our_application
        dest: /opt/app/bin/our_application
    # This tasks invokes the shell module. The text after the `shell:` key
    # will run in a shell on target machine
    - name: start our application in detached mode
      shell: cd /opt/app/bin; nohup ./our_application </dev/null >/dev/null
2>&1 &
```

Every single task starts with a hyphen. For each of the tasks, you need to specify the module it uses (such as the `copy` module or the `shell` module), along with its parameters (if applicable). A task may also have a `name` parameter, which makes it easier to reference the task individually.

Building a CD pipeline

We have reached the point when we can safely build a CD pipeline using the tools we learned about in this chapter. We already know how CI operates and how it helps to reject changes that are unsuitable for release. The section on test automation presented different ways of making the rejection process more robust. Having smoke tests or end-to-end tests allows us to go beyond CI and to check whether the whole deployed service satisfies requirements. And with deployment code, we can not only automate the process of deployment, but also prepare a rollback when our tests begin to fail.

Continuous deployment and continuous delivery

By a funny coincidence, the abbreviation CD can mean two different things. The concepts of continuous delivery and Continuous deployment are pretty similar, but they have some subtle differences. Throughout the book, we are focusing on the concept of continuous deployment. This is the automated process that originates when a person pushes a change into the central repository and finishes with the change successfully deployed to the production environment with all the tests passing. We can therefore say that this is an end-to-end process as the developer's work travels all the way to the customer without manual intervention (following the code review, of course). You may have heard the term GitOps to relate to such an approach. As all operations are automated, pushing to a specified branch in Git triggers the deployment scripts.

Continuous delivery doesn't go that far. Like CD, it features a pipeline able to release the final product and test it, but the final product is never automatically delivered to the customers. It can be delivered to the QA first or to the business for internal use. Ideally, the delivered artifact is ready to be deployed in the production environment as soon as the internal clients accept it.

Building an example CD pipeline

Let's put all of these skills together once again using the GitLab CI as an example to build our pipeline. Following the testing step, we will add two more steps, one that creates the package and another one that uses Ansible to deploy this package.

All we need for the packaging step is the following:

```
# Package the application and publish the artifact
package:
  stage: package
  # Use cpack for packaging
  script:
    - cd build
    - cpack .
  # Save the deb package artifact
  artifacts:
    paths:
      - build/Customer*.deb
```

When we add the package step containing artifacts definitions, we'll be able to download them from the dashboard.

With this, we can invoke Ansible as part of the deployment step:

```
# Deploy using Ansible
deploy:
  stage: deploy
  script:
    - cd build
    - ansible-playbook -i localhost, ansible.yml
```

The final pipeline would then look like the following:

```
cache:
  key: all
  paths:
    - .conan
    - build

default:
  image: conanio/gcc9

stages:
  - prerequisites
  - build
  - test
  - package
  - deploy

before_script:
  - export CONAN_USER_HOME="$CI_PROJECT_DIR"

prerequisites:
  stage: prerequisites
  script:
    - pip install conan==1.34.1
    - conan profile new default || true
    - conan profile update settings.compiler=gcc default
    - conan profile update settings.compiler.libcxx=libstdc++11 default
    - conan profile update settings.compiler.version=10 default
    - conan profile update settings.arch=x86_64 default
    - conan profile update settings.build_type=Release default
    - conan profile update settings.os=Linux default
    - conan remote add trompeloeil
https://api.bintray.com/conan/trompeloeil/trompeloeil || true

build:
```

```
    stage: build
    script:
      - sudo apt-get update && sudo apt-get install -y docker.io
      - mkdir -p build
      - cd build
      - conan install ../ch08 --build=missing
      - cmake -DBUILD_TESTING=1 -DCMAKE_BUILD_TYPE=Release ../ch08/customer
      - cmake --build .

test:
  stage: test
  script:
    - cd build
    - ctest .

# Package the application and publish the artifact
package:
  stage: package
  # Use cpack for packaging
  script:
    - cd build
    - cpack .
  # Save the deb package artifact
  artifacts:
    paths:
      - build/Customer*.deb

# Deploy using Ansible
deploy:
  stage: deploy
  script:
    - cd build
    - ansible-playbook -i localhost, ansible.yml
```

To see the whole example, go to the repository from the *Technical requirements* section for the original sources.

Using immutable infrastructure

If you are sufficiently confident with your CI/CD pipeline, you may go one step further. Instead of deploying artifacts of the application, you can deploy artifacts of the *system*. What's the difference? We will come to know about this in the following sections.

What is immutable infrastructure?

Previously, we focused on how to make your application's code deployable on the target infrastructure. The CI system created software packages (such as containers) and those packages were then deployed by the CD process. Each time the pipeline ran, the infrastructure stayed the same, but the software differed.

The point is, if you are using cloud computing, you can treat infrastructure just like any other artifact. Instead of deploying a container, you can deploy an entire **Virtual Machine (VM)**, for example, as an AWS EC2 instance. You can build such a VM image upfront as yet another element of your CI process. This way, versioned VM images, as well as the code required to deploy them, become your artifacts, and not the containers themselves.

There are two tools, both authored by HashiCorp, that deal with precisely this scenario. Packer helps to create VM images in a repeatable way, storing all the instructions as code, usually in the form of a JSON file. Terraform is an Infrastructure as Code tool, which means it's used to provision all the necessary infrastructure resources. We will use the output from Packer as input for Terraform. This way, Terraform will create an entire system consisting of the following:

- Instance groups
- Load balancers
- VPCs
- Other cloud elements while using the VMs containing our own code

The title of this section may confuse you. Why is it called **immutable infrastructure** while we are clearly advocating to change the entire infrastructure after every commit? The concept of immutability may be clearer to you if you've studied functional languages.

A mutable object is one whose state we can alter. In infrastructure, this is pretty easy to understand: you can log in to the VM and download a more recent version of the code. The state is no longer the same as it was prior to your intervention.

An immutable object is one whose state we cannot alter. It means we have no means of logging in to the machines and changing things. Once we deploy a VM from an image, it stays like that until we destroy it. This may sound terribly cumbersome, but in fact, it solves a few problems of software maintenance.

The benefits of immutable infrastructure

First of all, immutable infrastructure makes the concept of configuration drift obsolete. There is no configuration management so there can also be no drift. The upgrade is much safer as well because we cannot end up in a half-baked state. That is the state that's neither the previous version nor the next version, but something in between. The deployment process provides binary information: either the machine is created and operational or it isn't. There's no other way.

For immutable infrastructure to work without affecting uptime, you also need the following:

- Load balancing
- Some degree of redundancy

After all, the upgrade process consists of taking down an entire instance. You cannot rely on this machine's address or anything that's particular to that one machine. Instead, you need to have at least a second one that will handle the workload while you replace the other one with the more recent version. When you finish upgrading the one machine, you can repeat the same process with another one. This way, you will have two upgraded instances without losing the service. Such a strategy is known as the rolling upgrade.

As you can realize from the process, immutable infrastructure works best when dealing with stateless services. When your service has some form of persistence, things become tougher to implement properly. In that case, you usually have to split the persistence level into a separate object, for example, an NFS volume containing all of the application data. Such volumes can be shared across all the machines in an instance group and each new machine that comes up can access the common state left by the previous running applications.

Building instance images with Packer

Considering our example application is already stateless, we can proceed with building an immutable infrastructure on top of it. Since the artifacts Packer generates are VM images, we have to decide on the format and the builder we would like to use.
Let's focus our example on Amazon Web Services, while keeping in mind that a similar approach will also work with other supported providers. A simple Packer template may look like this:

```
{
  "variables": {
    "aws_access_key": "",
```

```
      "aws_secret_key": ""
  },
  "builders": [{
    "type": "amazon-ebs",
    "access_key": "{{user `aws_access_key`}}",
    "secret_key": "{{user `aws_secret_key`}}",
    "region": "eu-central-1",
    "source_ami": "ami-0f1026b68319bad6c",
    "instance_type": "t2.micro",
    "ssh_username": "admin",
    "ami_name": "Project's Base Image {{timestamp}}"
  }],
  "provisioners": [{
    "type": "shell",
    "inline": [
      "sudo apt-get update",
      "sudo apt-get install -y nginx"
    ]
  }]
}
```

The preceding code will build an image for Amazon Web Services using the EBS builder. The image will reside in `eu-central-1` region and will be based on `ami-5900cc36`, which is a Debian Jessie image. We want the builder to be a `t2.micro` instance (that's a VM size in AWS). To prepare our image, we run the two `apt-get` commands.

We can also reuse the previously defined Ansible code and, instead of using Packer to provision our application, we can substitute Ansible as the provisioner. Our code will appear as follows:

```
{
  "variables": {
    "aws_access_key": "",
    "aws_secret_key": ""
  },
  "builders": [{
    "type": "amazon-ebs",
    "access_key": "{{user `aws_access_key`}}",
    "secret_key": "{{user `aws_secret_key`}}",
    "region": "eu-central-1",
    "source_ami": "ami-0f1026b68319bad6c",
    "instance_type": "t2.micro",
    "ssh_username": "admin",
    "ami_name": "Project's Base Image {{timestamp}}"
  }],
  "provisioners": [{
    "type": "ansible",
```

```
      "playbook_file": "./provision.yml",
      "user": "admin",
      "host_alias": "baseimage"
    }],
    "post-processors": [{
      "type": "manifest",
      "output": "manifest.json",
      "strip_path": true
    }]
  }
```

The changes are in the provisioners block and also a new block, post-processors, is added. This time, instead of shell commands, we are using a different provisioner that runs Ansible for us. The post-processor is here to produce the results of the build in a machine-readable format. Once Packer finishes building the desired artifact, it returns its ID and also saves it in manifest.json. For AWS, this would mean an AMI ID that we can then feed to Terraform.

Orchestrating the infrastructure with Terraform

Creating an image with Packer is the first step. After that, we would like to deploy the image to use it. We can build an AWS EC2 instance based on the image from our Packer template using Terraform.

Example Terraform code would look like the following:

```
# Configure the AWS provider
provider "aws" {
  region = var.region
  version = "~> 2.7"
}

# Input variable pointing to an SSH key we want to associate with the
# newly created machine
variable "public_key_path" {
  description = <<DESCRIPTION
Path to the SSH public key to be used for authentication.
Ensure this keypair is added to your local SSH agent so provisioners can
connect.
Example: ~/.ssh/terraform.pub
DESCRIPTION

  default = "~/.ssh/id_rsa.pub"
}
```

```
# Input variable with a name to attach to the SSH key
variable "aws_key_name" {
  description = "Desired name of AWS key pair"
  default = "terraformer"
}

# An ID from our previous Packer run that points to the custom base image
variable "packer_ami" {
}

variable "env" {
  default = "development"
}

variable "region" {
}

# Create a new AWS key pair cotaining the public key set as the input
# variable
resource "aws_key_pair" "deployer" {
  key_name = var.aws_key_name

  public_key = file(var.public_key_path)
}

# Create a VM instance from the custom base image that uses the previously
created key
# The VM size is t2.xlarge, it uses a persistent storage volume of 60GiB,
# and is tagged for easier filtering
resource "aws_instance" "project" {
  ami = var.packer_ami

  instance_type = "t2.xlarge"

  key_name = aws_key_pair.deployer.key_name

  root_block_device {
    volume_type = "gp2"
    volume_size = 60
  }

  tags = {
    Provider = "terraform"
    Env = var.env
    Name = "main-instance"
  }
}
```

This creates a key pair and an EC2 instance using this key pair. The EC2 instance is based on AMI provided as a variable. When calling Terraform, we will set this variable to point to the image generated by Packer.

Summary

By now, you should have learned how implementing CI at the beginning of the project can help you save time in the long run. It can also reduce work in progress, especially when paired with CD. In this chapter, we've presented useful tools that can help you implement both of the processes.

We've shown how GitLab CI allows us to write pipelines in YAML files. We've discussed the importance of code review and explained the differences between the various forms of code review. We've introduced Ansible, which assists in configuration management and the creation of deployment code. Finally, we tried Packer and Terraform to move our focus from creating applications to creating systems.

The knowledge in this chapter is not unique to the C++ language. You can use it in projects written in any language using any technology. The important thing that you should keep in mind is this: all applications require testing. A compiler or a static analyzer is not enough to validate your software. As an architect, you would also have to take into account not only your project (the application itself), but also the product (the system your application will work in). Delivering working code is no longer sufficient. Understanding the infrastructure and the process of deployment is crucial as they are the new building blocks of modern systems.

The next chapter is focused on the security of the software. We will cover the source code itself, the operating system level, and the possible interactions with external services as well as with end users.

Questions

1. In what ways does CI save time during development?
2. Do you require separate tools to implement CI and CD?
3. When does it make sense to perform a code review in a meeting?
4. What tools can you use to assess the quality of your code during CI?
5. Who participates in specifying the BDD scenarios?
6. When would you consider using immutable infrastructure? When would you

rule it out?

7. How would you characterize the differences between Ansible, Packer, and Terraform?

Further reading

- Continuous integration/continuous deployment/continuous delivery:

    ```
    https://www.packtpub.com/virtualization-and-cloud/hands-continuous
    -integration-and-delivery
    ```

    ```
    https://www.packtpub.com/virtualization-and-cloud/cloud-native-
    continuous-integration-and-delivery
    ```

- Ansible:

    ```
    https://www.packtpub.com/virtualization-and-cloud/mastering-
    ansible-third-edition
    ```

    ```
    https://www.packtpub.com/application-development/hands-
    infrastructure-automation-ansible-video
    ```

- Terraform:

    ```
    https://www.packtpub.com/networking-and-servers/getting-started-
    terraform-second-edition
    ```

    ```
    https://www.packtpub.com/big-data-and-business-intelligence/hands-
    infrastructure-automation-terraform-aws-video
    ```

- Cucumber:

    ```
    https://www.packtpub.com/web-development/cucumber-cookbook
    ```

- GitLab:

    ```
    https://www.packtpub.com/virtualization-and-cloud/gitlab-quick-
    start-guide
    ```

    ```
    https://www.packtpub.com/application-development/hands-auto-
    devops-gitlab-ci-video
    ```

10
Security in Code and Deployment

After establishing the proper tests, it is necessary to perform a security audit to make sure our application will not be used for malicious purposes. This chapter describes how to assess the security of the code base, including both the internally developed software as well as third-party modules. It will also show how to improve existing software both at the code level and at the operating system level.

You'll learn how to design applications with a focus on security at each level, starting with code, through to dependencies, architecture, and deployment.

The following topics will be covered in this chapter:

- Checking the code security
- Checking whether the dependencies are secure
- Hardening your code
- Hardening your environment

Technical requirements

Some of the examples used in this chapter require the compilers with the minimal versions of the following:

- GCC 10+
- Clang 3.1+

The code present in the chapter has been placed on GitHub at `https://github.com/PacktPublishing/Software-Architecture-with-Cpp/tree/master/Chapter10`.

Checking the code security

In this chapter, we provide information on how to check your code, your dependencies, and your environment for potential threats. Keep in mind, though, that following every step outlined within this chapter won't necessarily protect you against all possible problems. Our aim is to show you some possible dangers and the ways to deal with them. Given this, you should always be conscious of the security of your system and make audits a routine event.

Before the internet became ubiquitous, software authors weren't too concerned about the security of their designs. After all, if the user presented malformed data, the user could crash their own computer at most. In order to use software vulnerabilities to access protected data, the attacker had to obtain physical access to the machines holding the data.

Even in software that was designed to be used within networks, security was often an afterthought. Take the **Hypertext Transfer Protocol (HTTP)** as an example. Even though it allows the password protection of some assets, all of the data is transferred in plain text. This means everyone on the same network can eavesdrop on the data being transferred.

Today, we should embrace security right from the first stages of design and keep it in mind at every stage of software development, operations, and maintenance. Most of the software we produce every day is meant to, in one way or another, connect with other existing systems.

By omitting security measures, we open up not only ourselves but also our partners to potential attacks, data leaks, and, eventually, lawsuits. Keep in mind that failure to protect personal data can result in a fine of several million US dollars.

Security-conscious design

How can we design an architecture for security? The best way to do this is to think like a potential attacker. There are many ways in which you can break a box open but usually, you will look for the cracks where different elements connect. (In the case of a box, this may be between the lid and the bottom of the box.)

In software architecture, connections between elements are called interfaces. Since their main role is to interact with the external world, they are the most vulnerable part of the entire system. Making sure your interfaces are protected, intuitive, and robust will solve the most obvious ways in which your software can be broken.

Making interfaces easy to use and hard to misuse

To design interfaces in a way that would be both easy to use and hard to misuse, consider the following exercise. Imagine you are a customer of your interface. You want to implement an e-commerce store that uses your payment gateway, or maybe you want to implement a VR application that connects with the Customer API of the example system we've used throughout this book.

As a general rule regarding interface design, avoid the following traits:

- Too many parameters passed to the function/method
- Ambiguous names of parameters
- Using output parameters
- Parameters depending on other parameters

Why are these traits considered problematic?

- The first one makes it hard to memorize not only the meaning but also the order of the parameters. This can lead to errors in usage, which, in turn, may lead to crashes and security issues.
- The second trait has similar consequences to the first one. By making it less intuitive to use your interface, you make it easier for the user to make mistakes.
- The third trait is a variant of the second one but with an added twist. Not only does the user have to remember which parameters are input and which are output, but it is also necessary for the user to remember how the output should be treated. Who manages the creation and deletion of the resources? How is this achieved? What is the memory management model behind it?

  With modern C++, it's easier than ever to return a value that contains all of the necessary data. With pairs, tuples, and vectors, there is no excuse to use the output parameters. Besides all of this, returning the value helps embrace the practice of not modifying the state of an object. This, in turn, reduces concurrency-related problems.

- Finally, the last trait introduces unnecessary cognitive load, which, as in the previous examples, can result in mistakes and eventually failures. Such code is also harder to test and maintain as each change introduced has to take into account all the possible combinations already available. Failure to properly handle any combination is a potential threat to the system.

The preceding rules apply to the external part of the interfaces. You should also apply similar measures to the internal part by validating the inputs, making sure the values are correct and sensible and preventing unwanted use of the services the interface provides.

Enabling automatic resource management

System instability may also result from memory leaks, data races, and deadlocks. All of these symptoms are manifestations of poor resource management. Even though resource management is a hard topic, there is a mechanism that can help you reduce the number of problems. One such mechanism is automatic resource management.

In this context, a resource is something you gain access to via the operating system and you have to make sure you use it correctly. This may mean using dynamically allocated memory, open files, sockets, processes, or threads. All of these require specific actions to be taken when you acquire them and when you release them. Some of them also require specific actions during their lifetime. Failure to release such resources at the right time leads to leaks. Since the resources are usually finite, in the long run, leaks will turn to unexpected behavior when no new resources can be created.

Resource management is so important in C++ because, unlike many other high-level languages, there is no garbage collection in C++ and the software developers are responsible for the life cycle of the resources. Understanding this life cycle helps create secure and stable systems.

The most common idiom of resource management is **Resource Acquisition Is Initialization** (**RAII**). Although it originated in C++, it has also been used in other languages, such as Vala and Rust. This idiom uses the object's constructor and destructor to allocate and free up resources, respectively. This way, we can guarantee that the resource in use will be properly freed when the object that holds it goes out of scope.

Some examples of using this idiom in the standard library are the `std::unique_ptr` and `std::shared_ptr` smart pointer types. Other examples include mutexes – `std::lock_guard`, `std::unique_lock`, and `std:shared_lock` – or files – `std::ifstream` and `std::ofstream`.

The **Guidelines Support Library** (**GSL**), which we'll discuss at length shortly, also implements a particularly useful guideline for automated resource management. By using the `gsl::finally()` function in our code, we create a `gsl::final_action()` object with some code attached to it. This code will be executed when the object's destructor is called. This means the code will be executed both upon a successful return from the function as well as when the stack unwinding happens during an exception.

This approach shouldn't be used too often as it is generally a better idea to design your classes with RAII in mind. But if you're interfacing with a third-party module and you want to ensure the safety of your wrapper, `finally()` can help you get there.

As an example, consider that we have a payment operator that allows only a single concurrent login per account. If we don't want to block the user from making future payments, we should always log out as soon as we finish processing the transaction. This is not a problem when we are on a happy path and everything goes according to our design. But in the event of an exception, we also want to be safe and release the resource. Here's how we could do it using `gsl::finally()`:

```
TransactionStatus processTransaction(AccountName account, ServiceToken
token,
Amount amount)
{
  payment::login(account, token);
  auto _ = gsl::finally([] { payment::logout(); });
  payment::process(amount); // We assume this can lead to exception

  return TransactionStatus::TransactionSuccessful;
}
```

Regardless of what happens during the call to `payment::process()`, we can at least guarantee that we log the user out as soon as we go out of `processTransaction()`'s scope.

In short, using RAII makes you think more about the resource management during the class design phase while you have full control of the code and think less about when you (or other parties) use the interface when your intentions may no longer be as clear.

Drawbacks of concurrency and how to deal with it

While concurrency improves performance and resource utilization, it also makes your code much harder to design and debug. This is because, unlike in a single-threaded flow, the timing of operations cannot be determined upfront. In single-threaded code, you either write to the resource or read from it, but you always know the order of the operations and can, therefore, predict the state of the object.

With concurrency, several threads or processes can be either reading from an object or modifying it at the same time. If the modifications aren't atomic, we can reach one of the variants of the common update problem. Consider the following code:

```
TransactionStatus chargeTheAccount(AccountNumber acountNumber, Amount
amount)
```

```
{
  Amount accountBalance = getAcountBalance(accountNumber);
  if (accountBalance > amount)
  {
    setAccountBalance(accountNumber, accountBalance - amount);
    return TransactionStatus::TransactionSuccessful;
  }
  return TransactionStatus::InsufficientFunds;
}
```

When calling the `chargeTheAccount` function from a non-concurrent code, everything will end up well. Our program will check the account balance and charge it if possible. The concurrent execution, however, can lead to a negative balance. This is because two threads can one after another call `getAccountBalance()`, which will return the same amount, such as `20`. After performing that call, both threads check whether the current balance is higher than the available amount. Finally, after the check, they modify the account balance. Supposing both transactions are for the amount of `10`, each thread will set the balance to be 20 – 10 = 10. After *both* operations, the account has a balance of 10, even though it should be 0!

To mitigate a similar class of problems, we can use solutions such as mutexes and critical sections, atomic operations provided by CPU, or concurrency-safe data structures.

Mutexes, critical sections, and other similar concurrency design patterns prevent more than one thread from modifying (or reading) the data. Even though they are useful when designing concurrent applications, there is a trade-off associated with them. They effectively make parts of your code single-threaded. This is because code guarded by mutexes allows only a single thread to execute it; all of the others have to wait until the mutex is released. And since we introduce waiting, we can make our code less performant even though our original aim was to make it more performant.

Atomic operations mean using a single CPU instruction to get the desired effect. The term can mean any high-level operation that transforms into a single CPU instruction. They are particularly interesting when that single instruction achieves *more* than would be normally possible. For example, **compare-and-swap (CAS)** is an instruction that compares the memory location with a given value and modifies the contents of this location to the new value only if the comparison proved successful. Since C++11, there's a `<std::atomic>` header available that contains several atomic data types and operations. CAS, for instance, is implemented as a `compare_and_exchange_*` set of functions.

Finally, concurrency-safe data structures (also known as concurrent data structures) provide safe abstractions for data structures that would otherwise require some sort of synchronization. For example, the Boost.Lockfree (`https://www.boost.org/doc/libs/1_66_0/doc/html/lockfree.html`) library provides concurrent queues and stacks for use with multiple producers and multiple consumers. libcds (`https://github.com/khizmax/libcds`) also offers ordered lists, sets, and maps, but it hasn't been updated in a few years as of the time of writing this book.

Useful rules to keep in mind when designing concurrent processing are as follows:

- Consider whether you need concurrency in the first place.
- Pass data by value rather than by pointer or reference. This prevents modifications of the value when other threads are reading it.
- If the size of the data makes it impractical to share by value, use `shared_ptr`. This way, it's easier to avoid resource leaks.

Secure coding, the guidelines, and GSL

The Standard C++ Foundation released a set of guidelines to document the best practices for building C++ systems. It is a Markdown document released on GitHub under `https://github.com/isocpp/CppCoreGuidelines`. It is an evolving document without a release schedule (unlike the C++ standard itself). The guidelines are aimed at modern C++, which basically means code bases that implement at least C++11 features.

Many of the rules presented in the guidelines cover the topics that we present in this chapter. For example, there are rules related to interface design, resource management, and concurrency. The editors of the guidelines are Bjarne Stroustrup and Herb Sutter, both respected members of the C++ community.

We won't go into detail describing the guidelines. We encourage you to read them yourself. This book is inspired by many of the rules presented there and we follow them in our examples.

To ease the use of these rules in various code bases, Microsoft released the **Guidelines Support Library (GSL)** as an open source project hosted on `https://github.com/microsoft/GSL`. It is a header-only library that you can include in your project to use the defined types. You can either include the whole GSL or selectively use only some of the types you plan on using.

What's also interesting about the library is the fact that it uses CMake for building, Travis for continuous integration, and Catch for unit testing. It is, therefore, a good example of the topics we've covered in Chapter 7, *Building and Packaging*, and Chapter 8, *Writing Testable Code*, and Chapter 9, *Continuous Integration and Continuous Deployment*.

Defensive coding, validating everything

In a previous chapter on testability, we mentioned the method of defensive programming. Even though this method is not strictly a security feature, it happens to help with creating a robust interface. Such interfaces, in turn, increase the overall security of your system.

As a good heuristic, you can treat all the external data as unsafe. What we mean by external data is every input coming to the system via some interface (either a programming interface or user interface). To denote this, you can go as far as prefixing the appropriate types as Unsafe, as follows:

```
RegistrationResult registerUser(UnsafeUsername username, PasswordHash
passwordHash)
{
  SafeUsername safeUsername = username.sanitize();
  try
  {
    std::unique_ptr<User> user = std::make_unique<User>(safeUsername,
passwordHash);
    CommitResult result = user->commit();
    if (result == CommitResult::CommitSuccessful)
    {
      return RegistrationResult::RegistrationSuccessful;
    }
    else
    {
      return RegistrationResult::RegistrationUnsuccessful;
    }
  }
  catch (UserExistsException _)
  {
    return RegistrationResult::UserExists;
  }
}
```

If you have already read the guidelines, you will know that you should generally avoid using the C API directly. Some of the functions in the C API can be used in an unsafe way and require special care to use them defensively. It is much better to instead use respective concepts from C++ that ensure better type safety as well as protection (for example, against buffer overflow).

Another facet of defensive programming is the intelligent reuse of the existing code. Each time you try to implement some technique, ensure nobody else has implemented it before you. Writing a sorting algorithm yourself may be a fun challenge to do when you're learning a new programming language, but for production code, it's much better to use the sorting algorithms available in the standard library. The same goes for password hashing. No doubt you can find some clever way to calculate the password hashes and store them in a database but it is generally wiser to go with the tried and true (and don't forget peer-reviewed!) bcrypt. Keep in mind that intelligent code reuse assumes you check and audit the third-party solutions with the same due diligence as you would your own code. We will dive deeper into this topic in the next section, *Are my dependencies secure?*.

It's worth noting that defensive programming shouldn't turn into paranoid programming. Checking user input is a sane thing to do, while asserting whether an initialized variable is still equal to the original value just after the initialization is going too far. You want to control the integrity of your data and algorithms and the integrity of third-party solutions. You don't want to verify the correctness of your compiler by embracing language features.

In short, it's a good idea from both a security and readability point of view to use Expects() and Ensures() as presented in C++ Core Guidelines and to distinguish between unsafe and safe data through typing and conversions.

The most common vulnerabilities

To check whether your code is safe against the most common vulnerabilities, you should first learn about the said vulnerabilities. After all, a defense is only possible when you know what the offense looks like. The **Open Web Application Security Project (OWASP)** has cataloged the most common vulnerabilities and has published them at https://www.owasp.org/index.php/Category:OWASP_Top_Ten_Project. At the moment of writing this book, those vulnerabilities are as follows:

- **Injection**: Commonly known as SQL injection. It is not limited to SQL; this vulnerability occurs when untrusted data is passed directly to an interpreter (such as a SQL database, NoSQL database, shell, or eval function). The attacker may this way gain access to parts of the system that should be protected.

- **Broken Authentication**: If authentication is improperly implemented, attackers may use flaws to either compromise secret data or impersonate other users.
- **Sensitive Data Exposure**: The lack of encryption and proper access rights may lead to sensitive data being exposed publicly.
- **XML External Entities (XXE)**: Some XML processors may disclose the contents of the server's filesystem or allow remote code execution.
- **Broken Access Control**: When access control is not enforced properly, attackers may gain access to files or data that should be restricted.
- **Security Misconfiguration**: Using insecure defaults and improper care with configuration are the most common sources of vulnerabilities.
- **Cross-Site Scripting (XSS)**: Including and executing untrusted external data, especially with JavaScript, that allows control of the user's web browser.
- **Insecure Deserialization**: Some flawed parsers may fall prey to denial of services attacks or remote code execution.
- **Using Components with Known Vulnerabilities**: A lot of the code in modern applications comes as third-party components. These components should be regularly audited and updated as known security flaws in a single dependency can result in your entire application and data being compromised. Fortunately, there are tools that help automate this.
- **Insufficient Logging & Monitoring**: If your system is under attack and your logging and monitoring is not very thorough, the attacker may obtain deeper access and still become unnoticed.

We won't go into detail regarding each of the mentioned vulnerabilities. What we want to highlight here is that you can prevent injection, XML external entities, and insecure deserialization by following the defensive programing techniques we mentioned before. By treating all external data as unsafe, you can first sanitize it by removing all the unsafe content before you start the actual processing.

When it comes to insufficient logging and monitoring, we will go into detail in Chapter 15, *Cloud-Native Design*. There we will present some possible approaches to observability, including logging, monitoring, and distributed tracing.

Checking whether the dependencies are secure

In the early days of computers, all programs were monoliths without any external dependencies. Ever since the dawn of operating systems, any non-trivial software is rarely free from dependencies. Those dependencies can come in two forms: external dependencies and internal ones:

- External dependencies are those that should be present in the environment that we run our application. Examples can include the aforementioned operating systems, dynamically linked libraries, and other applications (such as a database).
- Internal dependencies are modules we want to reuse, so this will usually mean static libraries or header-only libraries.

Both kinds of dependencies provide potential security risks. As each line of code increases the risk of vulnerability, the more components you have, the higher the chance your system may be susceptible to attack. In the following sections, we'll see how to check whether your software is indeed susceptible to known vulnerabilities.

Common Vulnerabilities and Exposures

The first place to check for known security issues within software is the **Common Vulnerabilities and Exposures** (**CVE**) list available at `https://cve.mitre.org/`. The list is constantly updated by several institutions known as **CVE Numbering Authorities** (**CNAs**). These institutions include vendors and projects, vulnerability researchers, national and industry CERTs, and bug bounty programs.

The website also presents a search engine. With this, you can use several methods to learn about the vulnerabilities:

- You can enter the vulnerability number. These are prefixed by `CVE` with examples including CVE-2014-6271, the infamous ShellShock, or CVE-2017-5715, also known as Spectre).
- You can enter the vulnerability common name, such as the previously mentioned ShellShock or Spectre.
- You can enter the name of the software you want to audit, such as Bash or Boost.

For each search result, you can see the description as well as a list of references to other bug trackers and related resources. The description usually lists versions affected by the vulnerability, so you can check whether the dependency you are planning to use has been already patched.

Automated scanners

There are tools that can help you to audit your list of dependencies. One such tool is OWASP Dependency-Check (`https://www.owasp.org/index.php/OWASP_Dependency_Check`). Although it only supports Java and .NET officially, it has experimental support for Python, Ruby, Node.js, and C++ (when used with CMake or `autoconf`). Besides working as a standalone tool, it has integrations for **Continuous Integration/Continuous Deployment (CI/CD)** software such as Jenkins, SonarQube, and CircleCI.

Another tool that allows checking dependencies for known vulnerabilities is Snyk. This is a commercial product with several levels of support. It also does more than the OWASP Dependency-Check as Snyk can also audit container images and license compliance issues. It also offers more integrations with third-party solutions.

Automated dependency upgrade management

Monitoring your dependencies for vulnerabilities is only the first step in making sure your project is secure. After that, you need to take action and update the compromised dependencies manually. As you might have expected, there are also automated solutions just for that. One of them is Dependabot, which scans your source code repository and issues a pull request whenever there's a security-related update available. At the moment of writing this book, Dependabot does not support C++ yet. It can, however, be used with other languages that your application may use. Other than that, it can scan Docker containers for vulnerabilities found in base images.

Automated dependency management requires mature test support. Switching dependency versions without tests may lead to instabilities and bugs. One protection against problems related to dependency upgrades is using wrappers to interface with third-party code. Such wrappers may have their own suite of tests that instantly tells us when an interface is broken during an upgrade.

Hardening your code

You can reduce the number of common security vulnerabilities in your own code by using modern C++ constructions as opposed to older C equivalents. Yet, there are always cases when even more secure abstractions prove to be vulnerable as well. It is not enough to choose the more secure implementation and decide you've done your best. Most of the time, there are ways to further harden your code.

But what is code hardening? According to the definition, it is the process of reducing the system's surface of vulnerability. Often, this means turning off the features you won't be using and aiming for a simpler system over a complicated one. It may also mean using tools to increase the robustness of the already-available functions.

Such tools may mean kernel patches, firewalls, and **Intrusion Detection Systems (IDSes)** when applied at the operating system level. At the application level, it may mean various buffer overrun and underflow protection mechanisms, using containers and **Virtual Machines (VMs)** for privilege separation and process isolation, or enforcing encrypted communication and storage.

In this section, we'll focus on some examples from the application level, while the next section will focus on the operating system level.

Security-oriented memory allocator

If you are serious about protecting your application from heap-related attacks, such as heap overflow, use-after-free, or double free, you may consider replacing your standard memory allocator with a security-oriented version. Two projects that may be of interest are as follows:

- FreeGuard, available at `https://github.com/UTSASRG/FreeGuard` and described in a paper at `https://arxiv.org/abs/1709.02746`
- `hardened_malloc` from the GrapheneOS project, available at `https://github.com/GrapheneOS/hardened_malloc`

FreeGuard was released in 2017 and it hasn't seen much change since then other than sporadic bug fixes. `hardened_malloc`, on the other hand, is actively developed. Both allocators are designed to act as drop-in replacements for the standard `malloc()`. You can use them without modifying your application simply by setting the `LD_PRELOAD` environment variable or adding the library to the `/etc/preload.so` configuration file. While FreeGuard targets Linux with the Clang compiler on 64-bit x86 systems, `hardened_malloc` aims at broader compatibility, though at the moment supports mostly Android's Bionic, `musl`, and `glibc`. `hardened_malloc` is also based on OpenBSD's `alloc`, with OpenBSD being the security-focused project itself.

Instead of replacing the memory allocator, you can replace the collections you use for their safer equivalents. The SaferCPlusPlus (`https://duneroadrunner.github.io/SaferCPlusPlus/`) project provides substitutes for `std::vector<>`, `std::array<>`, and `std::string` that can be used as drop-in replacements in the existing code. The project also includes substitutes for basic types that guard against uninitialized use or sign mismatch, concurrent data types, and replacements for pointers and references.

Automated checks

There are tools that can be especially helpful to ensure the security of the system you are building. We will cover them in the following section.

Compiler warnings

While not necessarily a tool in itself, compiler warnings can be used and tweaked to achieve even better output from the one tool every C++ developer will be using: the C++ compiler.

Since the compiler can already do some deeper checks than those required by the standard, it is advised to take advantage of this possibility. When using a compiler such as GCC or Clang, the recommended setting involves `-Wall -Wextra` flags. This will generate much more diagnostics and result in warnings when your code doesn't follow the diagnostics. If you want to be really strict, you can also enable `-Werror`, which will turn all the warnings into errors and prevent the compilation of code that doesn't pass the enhanced diagnostics. If you want to keep strictly to the standards, there are the `-pedantic` and `-pedantic-errors` flags that will look for conformance against the standards.

When using CMake for building, you can use the following function to enable these flags during compilation:

```
add_library(customer ${SOURCES_GO_HERE})
target_include_directories(customer PUBLIC include)
target_compile_options(customer PRIVATE -Werror -Wall -Wextra)
```

This way, the compilation will fail unless you fix all the warnings (turned errors) reported by the compiler.

You can also find suggested settings for toolchain hardening in these articles from OWASP (`https://www.owasp.org/index.php/C-Based_Toolchain_Hardening`) and Red Hat (`https://developers.redhat.com/blog/2018/03/21/compiler-and-linker-flags-gcc/`).

Static analysis

One class of tools that can help with making your code more secure is the so-called **Static Application Security Testing** (**SAST**) tools. They are a variant of static analysis tools only focused on security aspects.

SAST tools integrate well into CI/CD pipelines as they are simply reading your source code. The output is usually suitable for CI/CD as well since it highlights problems found in particular places in the source code. On the other hand, static analysis may omit many types of problems that cannot be found automatically or cannot be found solely with static analysis. These tools are also oblivious to issues related to configuration, as configuration files aren't represented in the source code itself.

Examples of C++ SAST tools include the following open source solutions:

- Cppcheck (`http://cppcheck.sourceforge.net/`), which is a general-purpose static analysis tool focused on the low number of false positives
- Flawfinder (`https://dwheeler.com/flawfinder/`), which doesn't seem to be actively maintained
- LGTM (`https://lgtm.com/help/lgtm/about-lgtm`), supporting several different languages and featuring automated analysis of pull requests
- SonarQube (`https://www.sonarqube.org/`), which has great CI/CD integration and language coverage, and offers a commercial version as well

There are also commercial solutions available:

- Checkmarx CxSAST (`https://www.checkmarx.com/products/static-application-security-testing/`), which promises zero configuration and road language coverage
- CodeSonar (`https://www.grammatech.com/products/codesonar`), which focuses on in-depth analysis and finding the most flaws
- Klocwork (`https://www.perforce.com/products/klocwork`), which focuses on accuracy
- Micro Focus Fortify (`https://www.microfocus.com/en-us/products/static-code-analysis-sast/overview`), with broad language support and integration of other tools by the same manufacturer
- Parasoft C/C++test (`https://www.parasoft.com/products/ctest`), which is an integrated solution for static and dynamic analysis, unit testing, tracing, and more
- Polyspace Bug Finder from MathWorks (`https://www.mathworks.com/products/polyspace-bug-finder.html`), with the integration of Simulink models
- Veracode Static Analysis (`https://www.veracode.com/products/binary-static-analysis-sast`), which is a SaaS solution for static analysis
- WhiteHat Sentinel Source (`https://www.whitehatsec.com/platform/static-application-security-testing/`), which also focuses on eliminating false positives

Dynamic analysis

Just like static analysis is performed on the source code, dynamic analysis is performed on the resulting binaries. The "dynamic" in the name refers to the observation of the code in action processing the actual data. When focused on security, this class of tools can also be called **Dynamic Application Security Testing (DAST)**.

Their main advantage over their SAST counterparts is that they can find many flows that cannot be seen from the source code analysis point of view. This, of course, introduces the drawback that you have to run your application in order to perform the analysis. And as we know, running an application can be both time- and memory-consuming.

DAST tools usually focus on web-related vulnerabilities such as XSS, SQL (and other) injection, or disclosed sensitive information. We will focus more on one of the more general-purpose dynamic analysis tools, Valgrind, in the next subsection.

Valgrind and Application Verifier

Valgrind is mostly known as a memory leak debugging tool. It is, in fact, an instrumentation framework that helps to build dynamic analysis tools not necessarily related to memory problems. Besides the memory error detector, the suite of tools currently consists of a thread error detector, a cache and branch prediction profiler, and a heap profiler. It's supported on various platforms on Unix-like operating systems (including Android).

Essentially, Valgrind acts as a VM, first translating the binary into a simpler form called intermediate representation. Instead of running the program on an actual processor, it gets executed under this VM so each call can be can be analyzed and validated.

If you're developing on Windows, you can use **Application Verifier (AppVerifier)** instead of Valgrind. AppVerifier can help you detect stability and security issues. It can monitor running applications and user-mode drivers to look for memory issues such as leaks and heap corruption, threading and locking issues, invalid use of handles, and more.

Sanitizers

Sanitizers are dynamic testing tools that are based on compile-time instrumentation of code. They can help with the overall stability and security of the system, as well as avoiding undefined behavior. At `https://github.com/google/sanitizers`, you can find implementations for LLVM (which Clang is based on) and GCC. They address problems with memory access, memory leaks, data races and deadlocks, uninitialized memory use, and undefined behavior.

AddressSanitizer (ASan) protects your code against issues related to memory addressing, such as global-buffer-overflow, use-after-free, or stack-use-after-return. Even though it's one of the fastest solutions of its kind, it still slows down the process about two times. It's best to use it when running tests and doing development but turn it off in production builds. You can turn it on for your builds by adding the `-fsanitize=address` flag to Clang.

AddressSanitizerLeakSanitizer (LSan) integrates with ASan to find memory leaks. It is enabled by default on x86_64 Linux and x86_64 macOS. It requires setting an environment variable, `ASAN_OPTIONS=detect_leaks=1`. LSan performs leak detection at the end of the process. LSan can also be used as a standalone library without AddressSanitizer, but this mode is much less tested.

ThreadSanitizer (TSan), as we previously mentioned, detects problems with concurrency such as data races and deadlocks. You can enable it with the `-fsanitize=thread` flag to Clang.

MemorySanitizer (MSan) focuses on bugs related to access to uninitialized memory. It implements some of the features of Valgrind that we covered in the previous subsection. MSan supports 64-bit x86, ARM, PowerPC, and MIPS platforms. You can enable it with the `-fsanitize=memory -fPIE -pie` flag to Clang (which also turns on position-independent executables, a concept we'll discuss later on).

Hardware-Assisted Address Sanitizer (HWASAN) is similar to the regular ASan. The main difference is the use of hardware assistance when possible. This feature is, for now, available only on 64-bit ARM architectures.

UndefinedBehaviorSanitizer (UBSan) looks for other possible causes of undefined behavior, such as integer overflow, division by zero, or improper bit shift operations. You can enable it with the `-fsanitize=undefined` flag to Clang.

Even though sanitizers can help you uncover many potential problems, they are only as good as the tests that you run them against. When using the sanitizers, keep in mind to keep the code coverage of your tests high because otherwise, you may get a false sense of security.

Fuzz-testing

A subcategory of DAST tools, fuzz-testing checks the behavior of your application when confronted with invalid, unexpected, random, or maliciously formed data. Such checks can be especially useful when used against the interfaces that cross the trust boundary (such as end user file upload forms or inputs).

Some interesting tools from this category include the following:

- Peach Fuzzer: `https://www.peach.tech/products/peach-fuzzer/`
- PortSwigger Burp: `https://portswigger.net/burp`
- The OWASP Zed Attack Proxy project: `https://www.owasp.org/index.php/OWASP_Zed_Attack_Proxy_Project`
- Google's ClusterFuzz: `https://github.com/google/clusterfuzz` (and OSS-Fuzz: `https://github.com/google/oss-fuzz`)

Process isolation and sandboxing

If you want to run unverified software in your own environment, you may want to isolate it from the rest of your system. Some ways to sandbox the executed code is via VMs, containers, or micro VMs such as Firecracker (`https://firecracker-microvm.github.io/`) used by AWS Lambda.

This way, the crashes, leaks, and security problems of one application won't propagate to the entire system, rendering it either useless or compromised. As each process will have its own sandbox, the worst-case scenario would be the loss of only this one service.

For C and C++ code, there is also **Sandboxed API (SAPI**; `https://github.com/google/sandboxed-api`) an open source project led by Google. It allows building sandboxes not for entire processes but for libraries. It is used by Google's own Chrome and Chromium web browsers, among others.

Even though VMs and containers can be a part of the process isolation strategy, don't confuse them with microservices, which often use similar building blocks. Microservices are an architectural design pattern and they don't automatically equal better security.

Hardening your environment

Even if you take the necessary precautions to ensure that your dependencies and code are free from known vulnerabilities, there still exists an area that can compromise your security strategy. All applications need an execution environment and this can mean either a container, VMs, or an operating system. Sometimes, this can also mean the underlying infrastructure as well.

It's not enough to make your application hardened to the maximum when the operating system it runs on has open access. This way, instead of targeting your application, the attacker can gain unauthorized access to the data directly from the system or infrastructure level.

This section will focus on some techniques of hardening that you can apply at this lowest level of execution.

Static versus dynamic linking

Linking is the process that occurs after compilation when the code you've written is brought together with its various dependencies (such as the standard library). Linking can occur at build time, at load time (when the operating system executes the binary), or at runtime, as is the case with plugins and other dynamic dependencies. The last two use cases are only possible with dynamic linking.

So, what is the difference between dynamic and static linking? With static linking, the contents of all the dependencies are copied to the resulting binary. When the program is loaded, the operating system places this single binary in the memory and executes it. Static linking is performed by programs called linkers as the last step of the build process.

Because each executable has to contain all the dependencies, statically linked programs tend to be big. This has its upside as well; since everything needed to execute the problem is already available in a single place, the execution can be faster and it always takes the same amount of time to load the program into memory. Any changes in the dependencies require recompilation and relinking; there is no way to upgrade one dependency without changing the resulting binary.

In dynamic linking, the resulting binary contains the code you've written, but instead of the contents of the dependencies, there are only references to the actual libraries that need to be loaded separately. During load time, it is the task of the dynamic loader to find the appropriate libraries and load them to memory alongside your binary. When several applications are running simultaneously and each of them is using similar dependencies (such as a JSON parsing library or JPEG processing library), the dynamically liked binaries will result in lower memory usage. This is due to the fact that only a single copy of a given library can be loaded into memory. In contrast, with statically linked binaries, the same libraries would be loaded over and over again as part of the resulting binaries. When you need to upgrade one of your dependencies, you can do so without touching any other component of your system. The next time your application is loaded into memory, it will reference the newly upgraded component automatically.

Static and dynamic linking also have security implications. It is easier to gain unauthorized access to dynamically linked applications. This can be achieved by substituting a compromised dynamic library in place of a regular one or by preloading certain libraries into each newly executed process.

When you combine static linking with containers (explained in detail in a later chapter), you get small, secure, sandboxed execution environments. You may even go further and use such containers with microkernel-based VMs that reduce the attack surface considerably.

Address space layout randomization

Address Space Layout Randomization (**ASLR**) is a technique used to prevent memory-based exploits. It works by replacing the standard memory layout of the program and data with a randomized one. This means an attacker cannot reliably jump to a particular function that would otherwise be present on a system without ASLR.

This technique can be made even more effective when combined with **no-execute** (**NX**) bit support. The NX bit marks certain pages in the memory, such as the heap and stack, as containing only data that cannot be executed. NX bit support has been implemented in most mainstream operating systems and can be used whenever hardware supports it.

DevSecOps

To deliver software increments on a predictable basis, it is best to embrace the DevOps philosophy. In short, DevOps means breaking the traditional model by encouraging communication between business, software development, software operations, quality assurance, and clients. DevSecOps is a form of DevOps that also emphasizes the need to design with security in mind at each step of the process.

This means that the application you are building has observability built-in from the beginning, leverages CI/CD pipelines, and is scanned for vulnerabilities on a regular basis. DevSecOps gives developers a voice in the design of the underlying infrastructure, and it gives operations experts a voice in the design of the software packages that make up the application. Since every increment represents a working system (albeit not fully functional), security audits are performed regularly and therefore take less time than normal. This results in faster and more secure releases and allows for quicker reactions to security incidents.

Summary

In this chapter, we discussed different aspects of a secure system. Since security is a complex topic, you cannot approach it only from the angle of your own application. All applications nowadays function in some environment and it is important to either control this environment and shape it according to your requirements or to shield yourself from the environment by sandboxing and isolating the code.

Having read this chapter, you are now ready to search for the vulnerabilities in your dependencies and in your own code. You know how to design systems for increased security and what tools to use in order to find possible flaws. Maintaining security is a constant process but a good design can reduce the work further down the road.

The next chapter will deal with scalability and the various challenges that we may face when growing our system.

Questions

1. Why is security important in modern systems?
2. What are some challenges of concurrency?
3. What are the C++ Core Guidelines?
4. What's the difference between secure coding and defensive coding?
5. How can you check whether your software contains known vulnerabilities?
6. What's the difference between static and dynamic analysis?
7. What's the difference between static and dynamic linking?
8. How you can use the compiler to fix security problems?
9. How can you implement security awareness in your CI pipeline?

Further reading

Cybersecurity in general:

- https://www.packtpub.com/eu/networking-and-servers/hands-cybersecurity-architects
- https://www.packtpub.com/eu/networking-and-servers/information-security-handbook
- https://www.owasp.org/index.php/Main_Page
- https://www.packtpub.com/eu/networking-and-servers/practical-security-automation-and-testing

Concurrency:

- https://www.packtpub.com/eu/application-development/concurrent-patterns-and-best-practices
- https://www.packtpub.com/eu/application-development/mastering-c-multithreading

Operating system hardening:

- https://www.packtpub.com/eu/networking-and-servers/mastering-linux-security-and-hardening

11
Performance

One of the most common reasons to choose C++ as a key programming language for a project is due to performance requirements. C++ has a clear edge over the competition when it comes to performance, but achieving the best results requires understanding relevant problems. This chapter focuses on increasing the performance of C++ software. We'll start by showing you tools for measuring performance. We'll show you a few techniques for increasing single-threaded compute speed. Then we'll discuss how to make use of parallel computing. Finally, we'll show how you can use C++20's coroutines for non-preemptive multitasking.

The following topics will be covered in this chapter:

- Measuring performance
- Helping the compiler generate performant code
- Parallelizing computations
- Using coroutines

First, let's specify what you'll need to run the examples in this chapter.

Technical requirements

To replicate the examples from this chapter, you should install the following:

- CMake 3.15+
- A compiler supporting C++20's ranges and coroutines, for instance, GCC 10+

The source code snippets from the chapter can be found at `https://github.com/PacktPublishing/Software-Architecture-with-Cpp/tree/master/Chapter11`.

Measuring performance

To effectively improve the performance of your code, you must start by measuring how it performs. Without knowing where the actual bottlenecks are, you will end up optimizing the wrong places, losing time, and getting surprised and frustrated that your hard work gave little to no gains. In this section, we'll show how to properly measure performance using benchmarks, how to successfully profile your code, and how to gain insights into performance in distributed systems.

Performing accurate and meaningful measurements

For accurate and repeatable measurements, you might also want to put your machine into performance mode instead of the usual default power-saving one. If you require low latency from your system, you might want to disable power saving permanently on both the machines you benchmark on and in your production environment. Many times this may mean going into BIOS and configuring your server properly. Note that this may not be possible if you use a public cloud provider. If you have root/admin permissions on your machine, the OS can often steer some of the settings too. For instance, you can force your CPU to run with its maximum frequency on a Linux system by running the following:

```
sudo cpupower frequency-set --governor performance
```

Moreover, to obtain meaningful results, you might want to perform measurements on a system that as closely resembles your production environment as possible. Aside from configuration, aspects such as the different speeds of RAM, the number of CPU caches, and the microarchitecture of your CPUs can also skew your results and lead you to incorrect conclusions. The same goes for the hard drive setup and even the network topology and hardware used. The software you build on also plays a crucial role: from the firmware used, through the OS and kernel, all the way up the software stack to your dependencies. It's best to have a second environment that's identical to your production one and governed using the same tools and scripts.

Now that we have a solid environment for taking measurements, let's see what we can actually measure.

Leveraging different types of measuring tools

There are several ways to measure performance, each focusing on a different scope. Let's go through them one by one.

Benchmarks can be used to time the speed of your system in a pre-made test. Usually, they result in either a time to finish or another performance metric such as orders processed per second. There are several types of benchmarks:

- **Microbenchmarks,** which you can use to measure the execution of a small code fragment. We'll cover them in the next section.
- **Simulations,** which are synthetic tests on a larger scale with artificial data. They can be useful if you don't have access to the target data or your target hardware. For instance, when you are planning to check the performance of hardware that you're working on, but it doesn't exist yet, or when you plan to handle incoming traffic, but can only assume how the traffic will look.
- **Replays,** which can be a very accurate way of measuring performance under the real-life workload. The idea is to record all the requests or workloads coming into the production system, often with timestamps. Such dumps can then later be "replayed" into the benchmarked system, respecting the time differences between them, to check how it performs. Such benchmarks can be great to see how potential changes to code or the environment can influence the latency and throughput of your system.
- **Industry-standard**, which is a good way to see how our product performs compared to its competitors. Examples of such benchmarks include SuperPi for CPUs, 3D Mark for graphic cards, and ResNet-50 for artificial intelligence processors.

Aside from benchmarking, another type of tool that is invaluable when it comes to measuring performance is profilers. Instead of just giving you overall performance metrics, profilers allow you to examine what your code is doing and look for bottlenecks. They're useful for catching unexpected things that slow your system down. We'll cover them in more detail later in this chapter.

The last way to grasp your system's performance is tracing. Tracing is essentially a way to log your system's behavior during execution. By monitoring how long it takes for a request to complete various steps of processing (such as being handled by different types of microservices), you can gain insight into what parts of your system need to improve their performance, or how well your system deals with different kinds of requests: either different types or those that get accepted or rejected. We'll cover tracing later in this chapter – right after profiling.

Let's now say a few more words on microbenchmarks.

Using microbenchmarks

Microbenchmarks are used to measure how fast a "micro" fragment of code can perform. If you're wondering how to implement a given functionality or how fast different third-party libraries deal with the same task, then they're the perfect tool for the job. While they're not representative of a realistic environment, they're well suited to perform such small experiments.

Let's show how to run such experiments using one of the most commonly used frameworks to create microbenchmarks in C++: Google Benchmark.

Setting up Google Benchmark

Let's start by introducing the library into our code by using Conan. Put the following in your `conanfile.txt`:

```
[requires]
benchmark/1.5.2

[generators]
CMakeDeps
```

We're going to use the CMakeDeps generator as it's the recommended CMake generator in Conan 2.0. It relies on CMake's `find_package` feature to use the packages installed by our barbaric dependency manager. To install the dependencies in their release versions, run the following:

```
cd <build_directory>
conan install <source_directory> --build=missing -s build_type=Release
```

If you're using a custom Conan profile, remember to add it here as well.

Using it from your `CMakeLists.txt` file is also pretty straightforward, as shown next:

```
list(APPEND CMAKE_PREFIX_PATH "${CMAKE_BINARY_DIR}")
find_package(benchmark REQUIRED)
```

First, we add our build directory to `CMAKE_PREFIX_PATH` so that CMake can find the config and/or target files produced by Conan. Next, we just use them to find our dependency.

As we're going to create several microbenchmarks, we could use a CMake function to help us with defining them:

```
function(add_benchmark NAME SOURCE)
  add_executable(${NAME} ${SOURCE})
  target_compile_features(${NAME} PRIVATE cxx_std_20)
  target_link_libraries(${NAME} PRIVATE benchmark::benchmark)
endfunction()
```

The function will be able to create single-translation-unit microbenchmarks, each using C++20 and linked to the Google Benchmark library. Let's now use it to create our first microbenchmark executable:

```
add_benchmark(microbenchmark_1 microbenchmarking/main_1.cpp)
```

Now we're ready to put some code in our source file.

Writing your first microbenchmark

We'll try to benchmark how much faster a lookup takes when it's done using bisection in a sorted vector as compared to just going through it linearly. Let's start with code that will create the sorted vector:

```
using namespace std::ranges;

template <typename T>
auto make_sorted_vector(std::size_t size) {
  auto sorted = std::vector<T>{};
  sorted.reserve(size);

  auto sorted_view = views::iota(T{0}) | views::take(size);
  std::ranges::copy(sorted_view, std::back_inserter(sorted));
  return sorted;
}
```

Our vector will contain size elements with all the numbers from 0 to size - 1 in ascending order. Let's now specify the element we're looking for and the container size:

```
constexpr auto MAX_HAYSTACK_SIZE = std::size_t{10'000'000};
constexpr auto NEEDLE = 2137;
```

As you can see, we'll benchmark how long it takes to find a needle in a haystack. The simple linear search can be implemented as follows:

```
void linear_search_in_sorted_vector(benchmark::State &state) {
  auto haystack = make_sorted_vector<int>(MAX_HAYSTACK_SIZE);
  for (auto _ : state) {
    benchmark::DoNotOptimize(find(haystack, NEEDLE));
  }
}
```

Here, we can see the first use of Google Benchmark. Each microbenchmark should accept `State` as an argument. This special type does the following:

- Contains information about the iterations performed and the time spent on the measured computation
- Counts the bytes processed if wanted
- Can return other state information, such as the need to run further (through the `KeepRunning()` member function)
- Can be used to pause and resume the timing of an iteration (through the `PauseTiming()` and `ResumeTiming()` member functions, respectively)

The code in our loop will be measured, making as many iterations as desired, based on the total allowed time to run this particular benchmark. The creation of our haystack is outside the loop and won't be measured.

Inside the loop, there's a sink helper named `DoNotOptimize`. Its purpose is to ensure the compiler doesn't get rid of our computations as it can prove that they are irrelevant outside of this scope. In our case, it will mark the result of `std::find` necessary, so the actual code to find the needle is not optimized away. Using tools such as objdump or sites such as Godbolt and QuickBench allows you to peek if the code you want to run wasn't optimized out. QuickBench has the additional advantage of running your benchmarks in the cloud and sharing their results online.

Back to our task at hand, we have a microbenchmark for the linear search, so let's now time the binary search in another microbenchmark:

```
void binary_search_in_sorted_vector(benchmark::State &state) {
  auto haystack = make_sorted_vector<int>(MAX_HAYSTACK_SIZE);
```

```
  for (auto _ : state) {
    benchmark::DoNotOptimize(lower_bound(haystack, NEEDLE));
  }
}
```

Our new benchmark is pretty similar. It only differs in the function used: `lower_bound` will perform a binary search. Note that similar to our base example, we don't even check if the iterator returned points to a valid element in the vector, or to its end. In the case of `lower_bound`, we could check if the element under the iterator is actually the one we're looking for.

Now that we have the microbenchmark functions, let's create actual benchmarks out of them by adding the following:

```
BENCHMARK(binary_search_in_sorted_vector);
BENCHMARK(linear_search_in_sorted_vector);
```

If the default benchmark settings are okay with you, that's all you need to pass. As the last step, let's add a `main()` function:

```
BENCHMARK_MAIN();
```

Simple as that! Alternatively, you can link our program with `benchmark_main` instead. Using Google Benchmark's `main()` function has the advantage of providing us with some default options. If you compile our benchmark and run it passing `--help` as a parameter, you'll see the following:

```
benchmark [--benchmark_list_tests={true|false}]
          [--benchmark_filter=<regex>]
          [--benchmark_min_time=<min_time>]
          [--benchmark_repetitions=<num_repetitions>]
          [--benchmark_report_aggregates_only={true|false}]
          [--benchmark_display_aggregates_only={true|false}]
          [--benchmark_format=<console|json|csv>]
          [--benchmark_out=<filename>]
          [--benchmark_out_format=<json|console|csv>]
          [--benchmark_color={auto|true|false}]
          [--benchmark_counters_tabular={true|false}]
          [--v=<verbosity>]
```

This is a nice set of features to use. For example, when designing experiments, you can use the `benchmark_format` switch to get a CSV output for easier plotting on a chart.

Let's now see our benchmark in action by running the compiled executable with no command-line arguments. A possible output from running `./microbenchmark_1` is as follows:

```
2021-02-28T16:19:28+01:00
Running ./microbenchmark_1
Run on (8 X 2601 MHz CPU s)
Load Average: 0.52, 0.58, 0.59
-------------------------------------------------------------------------
Benchmark                             Time            CPU    Iterations
-------------------------------------------------------------------------
linear_search_in_sorted_vector      984 ns          984 ns        746667
binary_search_in_sorted_vector     18.9 ns         18.6 ns      34461538
```

Starting with some data about the running environment (the time of benchmarking, the executable name, the server's CPUs, and the current load), we get to the results of each benchmark we defined. For each benchmark, we get the average wall time per iteration, the average CPU time per iteration, and the number of iterations that the benchmark harness ran for us. By default, the longer a single iteration, the fewer iterations it will go through. Running more iterations ensures you get more stable results.

Passing arbitrary arguments to a microbenchmark

If we were to test more ways of dealing with our problem at hand, we could look for a way to reuse the benchmark code and just pass it to the function used to perform the lookup. Google Benchmark has a feature that we could use for that. The framework actually lets us pass any arguments we want to the benchmark by adding them as additional parameters to the function signature.

Let's see how a unified signature for our benchmark could look with this feature:

```
void search_in_sorted_vector(benchmark::State &state, auto finder) {
  auto haystack = make_sorted_vector<int>(MAX_HAYSTACK_SIZE);
  for (auto _ : state) {
    benchmark::DoNotOptimize(finder(haystack, NEEDLE));
  }
}
```

You can notice the new `finder` parameter to the function, which is used in the spot where we previously called either `find` or `lower_bound`. We can now make our two microbenchmarks using a different macro than we did last time:

```
BENCHMARK_CAPTURE(search_in_sorted_vector, binary, lower_bound);
BENCHMARK_CAPTURE(search_in_sorted_vector, linear, find);
```

The BENCHMARK_CAPTURE macro accepts the function, a name suffix, and the arbitrary number of parameters. If we wanted more, we could just pass them here. Our benchmark function could be a regular function or a template – both are supported. Let's now see what we get when running the code:

```
--------------------------------------------------------------------
Benchmark                               Time           CPU   Iterations
--------------------------------------------------------------------
search_in_sorted_vector/binary        19.0 ns       18.5 ns   28000000
search_in_sorted_vector/linear         959 ns        952 ns     640000
```

As you can see the arguments passed to the functions are not part of the name, but the function name and our suffix are.

Let's now see how we can further customize our benchmarks.

Passing numeric arguments to a microbenchmark

A common need when designing experiments like ours is to check it on different sizes of arguments. Such needs can be addressed in Google Benchmark in a number of ways. The simplest is to just add a call to Args() on the object returned by the BENCHMARK macros. This way, we can pass a single set of values to use in a given microbenchmark. To use the passed value, we'd need to change our benchmark function as follows:

```
void search_in_sorted_vector(benchmark::State &state, auto finder) {
  const auto haystack = make_sorted_vector<int>(state.range(0));
  const auto needle = 2137;
  for (auto _ : state) {
    benchmark::DoNotOptimize(finder(haystack, needle));
  }
}
```

The call to state.range(0) will read the 0-th argument passed. An arbitrary number can be supported. In our case, it's used to parameterize the haystack size. What if we wanted to pass a range of value sets instead? This way, we could see how changing the size influences the performance more easily. Instead of calling Args, we could call Range on the benchmark:

```
constexpr auto MIN_HAYSTACK_SIZE = std::size_t{1'000};
constexpr auto MAX_HAYSTACK_SIZE = std::size_t{10'000'000};

BENCHMARK_CAPTURE(search_in_sorted_vector, binary, lower_bound)
    ->RangeMultiplier(10)
    ->Range(MIN_HAYSTACK_SIZE, MAX_HAYSTACK_SIZE);
BENCHMARK_CAPTURE(search_in_sorted_vector, linear, find)
```

```
  ->RangeMultiplier(10)
  ->Range(MIN_HAYSTACK_SIZE, MAX_HAYSTACK_SIZE);
```

We specify the range boundaries using a predefined minimum and maximum. We then tell the benchmark harness to create the ranges by multiplying by 10 instead of the default value. When we run such benchmarks, we could get the following results:

```
---------------------------------------------------------------------
Benchmark                                   Time        CPU     Iterations
---------------------------------------------------------------------
search_in_sorted_vector/binary/1000         0.2 ns     19.9 ns   34461538
search_in_sorted_vector/binary/10000        24.8 ns    24.9 ns   26352941
search_in_sorted_vector/binary/100000       26.1 ns    26.1 ns   26352941
search_in_sorted_vector/binary/1000000      29.6 ns    29.5 ns   24888889
search_in_sorted_vector/binary/10000000     25.9 ns    25.7 ns   24888889
search_in_sorted_vector/linear/1000         482 ns      474 ns    1120000
search_in_sorted_vector/linear/10000        997 ns     1001 ns     640000
search_in_sorted_vector/linear/100000       1005 ns    1001 ns     640000
search_in_sorted_vector/linear/1000000      1013 ns    1004 ns     746667
search_in_sorted_vector/linear/10000000     990 ns     1004 ns     746667
```

When analyzing those results, you might be wondering why the linear search doesn't show us linear growth. That's because we look for a constant value of the needle that can be spotted at a constant position. If the haystack contains our needle, we need the same number of operations to find it regardless of the haystack size, so the execution time stops growing (but can still be subject to small fluctuations).

Why not play with the needle position as well?

Generating the passed arguments programmatically

Generating both the haystack sizes and needle positions might be the easiest when done in a simple function. Google Benchmark allows such scenarios, so let's show how they work in practice.

Let's first rewrite our benchmark function to use two parameters passed in each iteration:

```
void search_in_sorted_vector(benchmark::State &state, auto finder) {
  const auto needle = state.range(0);
  const auto haystack = make_sorted_vector<int>(state.range(1));
  for (auto _ : state) {
    benchmark::DoNotOptimize(finder(haystack, needle));
  }
}
```

As you can see, `state.range(0)` will mark our needle position, while `state.range(1)` will be the haystack size. This means we need to pass two values each time. Let's create a function that generates them:

```
void generate_sizes(benchmark::internal::Benchmark *b) {
  for (long haystack = MIN_HAYSTACK_SIZE; haystack <= MAX_HAYSTACK_SIZE;
       haystack *= 100) {
    for (auto needle :
         {haystack / 8, haystack / 2, haystack - 1, haystack + 1}) {
      b->Args({needle, haystack});
    }
  }
}
```

Instead of using `Range` and `RangeMultiplier`, we write a loop to generate the haystack sizes, this time increasing them by 100 each time. When it comes to the needles, we use three positions in proportionate positions of the haystack and one that falls outside of it. We call `Args` on each loop iteration, passing both the generated values.

Now, let's apply our generator function to the benchmarks we define:

```
BENCHMARK_CAPTURE(search_in_sorted_vector, binary,
lower_bound)->Apply(generate_sizes);
BENCHMARK_CAPTURE(search_in_sorted_vector, linear,
find)->Apply(generate_sizes);
```

Using such functions makes it easy to pass the same generator to many benchmarks. Possible results of such benchmarks are as follows:

```
---------------------------------------------------------------------------
Benchmark                                             Time      CPU   Iterations
---------------------------------------------------------------------------
search_in_sorted_vector/binary/125/1000            20.0 ns  20.1 ns   37333333
search_in_sorted_vector/binary/500/1000            19.3 ns  19.0 ns   34461538
search_in_sorted_vector/binary/999/1000            20.1 ns  19.9 ns   34461538
search_in_sorted_vector/binary/1001/1000           18.1 ns  18.0 ns   40727273
search_in_sorted_vector/binary/12500/100000        35.0 ns  34.5 ns   20363636
search_in_sorted_vector/binary/50000/100000        28.9 ns  28.9 ns   24888889
search_in_sorted_vector/binary/99999/100000        31.0 ns  31.1 ns   23578947
search_in_sorted_vector/binary/100001/100000       29.1 ns  29.2 ns   23578947
// et cetera
```

Now we have a pretty well-defined experiment for performing the searches. As an exercise, run the experiment on your own machine to see the complete results and try to draw some conclusions from the results.

Choosing what to microbenchmark and optimize

Running such experiments can be educative and even addictive. However, keep in mind that microbenchmarks shouldn't be the only type of performance testing in your project. As Donald Knuth famously said:

We should forget about small efficiencies, say about 97% of the time: premature optimization is the root of all evil

This means that you should microbenchmark only code that matters, especially code on your hot path. Larger benchmarks, along with tracing and profiling, can be used to see where and when to optimize instead of guessing and optimizing prematurely. First, understand how your software executes.

 NOTE: There's one more point we want to make regarding the quote above. It doesn't mean you should allow premature *pessimization*. Poor choice of data structures or algorithms, or even small inefficiencies that spread all your code, can sometimes influence the overall performance of your system. For instance, performing unnecessary dynamic allocations, although it might not look that bad at first, can lead to heap fragmentation over time and cause you serious trouble if your app should run for long periods of time. Overuse of node-based containers can lead to more cache misses too. Long story short, if it's not a big effort to write efficient code instead of less efficient code, go for it.

Let's now learn what to do if your project has spots that need to maintain good performance over time.

Creating performance tests using benchmarks

Similar to having unit tests for precise testing and functional tests for larger-scale testing of your code's correctness, you can use microbenchmarks and larger benchmarks to test your code's performance.

If you have tight constraints on the execution time for certain code paths, having a test that ensures the limit is met can be very useful. Even if you don't have such specific constraints, you might be interested in monitoring how the performance changes across code changes. If after a change your code runs slower than before by a certain threshold, the test could be marked as failed.

Although also a useful tool, remember that such tests are prone to the boiling frog effect: degrading the performance slowly over time can go unnoticed, so be sure to monitor the execution times occasionally. When introducing performance tests to your CI, be sure to always run them in the same environment for stable results.

Let's now discuss the next type of tools in our performance shed.

Profiling

While benchmarks and tracing can give you an overview and specific numbers for a given scope, profilers can help you analyze where those numbers came from. They are an essential tool if you need to gain insight into your performance and improve it.

Choosing the type of profiler to use

There are two types of profilers available: instrumentation profilers and sampling ones. One of the better-known instrumentation profilers is Callgrind, part of the Valgrind suite. Instrumentation profilers have lots of overhead because they need to, well, instrument your code to see what functions you call and how much each of them takes. This way, the results they produce contain even the smallest functions, but the execution times can be skewed by this overhead. It also has the drawback of not always catching **input/output (I/O)** slowness and jitters. They slow down the execution, so while they can tell you how often you call a particular function, they won't tell you if the slowness is due to waiting on a disk read to finish.

Due to the flaws of instrumentation profilers, it's usually better to use sampling profilers instead. Two worth mentioning are the open source perf for profiling on Linux systems and Intel's proprietary tool called VTune (free for open source projects). Although they can sometimes miss key events due to the nature of sampling, they should usually give you a much better view of where your code spends time.

If you decide to use perf, you should know that you can either use it by invoking `perf stat`, which gives you a quick overview of statistics like CPU cache usage, or `perf record -g` and `perf report -g` to capture and analyze profiling results.

If you want a solid overview of perf, please watch Chandler Carruth's video, which shows the tool's possibilities and how to use it, or take a look at its tutorial. Both are linked in the *Further reading* section.

Preparing the profiler and processing the results

When analyzing profiling results, you may often want to perform some preparation, cleanup, and processing. For instance, if your code mostly spends time spinning around, you might want to filter that out. Before even starting the profiler, be sure to compile or download as many debug symbols as you can, both for your code, your dependencies, even the OS libraries, and kernel. Also, it's essential you disable frame pointer optimizations. On GCC and Clang, you can do so by passing the `-fno-omit-frame-pointer` flag. It won't affect performance much but will give you much more data about the execution of your code. When it comes to post-processing of the results, when using perf, it's usually a good idea to create flame graphs from the results. Brendan Gregg's tool from the *Further reading* section is great for that. Flame graphs are a simple and effective tool to see where the execution takes too much time, as the width of each item on the graph corresponds to the resource usage. You can have flame graphs for CPU usage, as well as for resources such as memory usage, allocations, and page faults, or the time spent when the code is not executing such as staying blocked during system calls, on mutexes, I/O operations, and the like. There are also ways to perform diffs on the generated flame graphs.

Analyzing the results

Keep in mind that not all performance issues will show up on such graphs and not all can be found using profilers. While with some experience you'll be able to see that you could benefit from setting affinity to your threads or changing which threads execute on specific NUMA nodes, it might not always be that obvious to see that you've forgotten to disable power-saving features or would benefit from enabling or disabling hyper-threading. Information about the hardware you're running on is useful, too. Sometimes you might see the SIMD registers of your CPU being used, but the code still doesn't run at its full speed: you might be using SSE instructions instead of AVX ones, AVX instead of AVX2, or AVX2 instead of AVX512. Knowing what specific instructions your CPU is capable of running can be golden when you analyze the profiling results.

Solving performance issues also requires a bit of experience. On the other hand, sometimes experience can lead you to false assumptions. For instance, in many cases, using dynamic polymorphism will hurt your performance; there are cases where it doesn't slow down your code. Before jumping to conclusions, it might be worth profiling the code and gaining knowledge about the various ways a compiler can optimize code and the limits of those techniques. Talking specifically about virtualization, it's often beneficial to mark your classes of virtual member functions as final when you don't want other types to inherit and override them, respectively. This tends to help the compilers in lots of cases.

Compilers can also optimize much better if they "see" what type the object is: if you create a type in scope and call its virtual member function, the compiler should be able to deduce which function should be called. GCC tends to devirtualize better than other compilers. For more information on this, you can refer to Arthur O'Dwyer's blog post from the *Further reading* section.

As with other types of tools presented in this section, try not to rely only on your profiler. Improvements in profiling results are not a guarantee that your system got faster. A better-looking profile can still not tell you the whole story. And the better performance of one component doesn't necessarily mean the whole system's performance improved. This is where our last type of tool can come in use.

Tracing

The last technique we'll discuss in this section is meant for distributed systems. When looking at the overall system, often deployed in the cloud, profiling your software on one box won't tell you the whole story. In such a scope, your best bet would be to trace the requests and responses flowing through your system.

Tracing is a way to log the execution of your code. It's often used when a request (and sometimes its response) has to flow through many parts of your system. Usually, such messages are being traced along the route, with timestamps being added at interesting points of execution.

Correlation IDs

One common addition to timestamps is correlation IDs. Basically, they're unique identifiers that get assigned to each traced message. Their purpose is to correlate the logs produced by different components of your system (like different microservices) during the processing of the same incoming request and sometimes for the events it caused, too. Such IDs should be passed with the message everywhere it goes, for example, by appending to its HTTP header. Even when the original request is gone, you could add its correlation ID to each of the responses produced.

By using correlation IDs, you can track how messages for a given request propagate through the system and how long it took for different parts of your system to process it. Often you'll want additional data to be gathered along the way, like the thread that was used to perform the computation, the type, and count of responses produced for a given request, or the names of the machines it went through.

Tools like Jaeger and Zipkin (or other OpenTracing alternatives) can help you to add tracing support to your system fast.

Let's now tackle a different subject and say a few words about code generation.

Helping the compiler generate performant code

There are many things that can help your compiler generate efficient code for you. Some boil down to steering it properly, others require writing your code in a compiler-friendly way.

It's also important to know what you need to do on your critical path and to design it efficiently. For instance, try to avoid virtual dispatch there (unless you can prove it's being devirtualized), and try not to allocate new memory on it. Often, the clever design of code to avoid locking (or at least using lock-free algorithms) is helpful. Generally speaking, everything that can worsen your performance should be kept outside your hot path. Having both your instruction and data caches hot is really going to pay out. Even attributes such as `[[likely]]` and `[[unlikely]]` that hint to the compiler which branch it should expect to be executed can sometimes change a lot.

Optimizing whole programs

An interesting way to increase the performance of many C++ projects is to enable **link-time optimization (LTO)**. During compilation, your compiler doesn't know how the code will get linked with other object files or libraries. Many opportunities to optimize arise only at this point: when linking, your tools can see the bigger picture of how the parts of your program interact with each other. By enabling LTO, you can sometimes grab a significant improvement in performance with very little cost. In CMake projects, you can enable LTO by setting either the global `CMAKE_INTERPROCEDURAL_OPTIMIZATION` flag or by setting the `INTERPROCEDURAL_OPTIMIZATION` property on your targets.

One drawback of using LTO is that it makes the building process longer. Sometimes a lot longer. To mitigate this cost for developers, you may want to only enable this optimization for builds that undergo performance testing or are meant to be released.

Optimizing based on real-world usage patterns

Another interesting way to optimize your code is to use **Profile-Guided Optimization (PGO)**. This optimization is actually a two-step one. In the first step, you need to compile your code with additional flags that cause the executable to gather special profiling information during runtime. You should then execute it under the expected production load. Once you're done with it, you can use the gathered data to compile the executable a second time, this time passing a different flag that instructs the compiler to use the gathered data to generate code better suited for your profile. This way, you'll end up with a binary that's prepared and tuned to your specific workload.

Writing cache-friendly code

Both those types of optimization can be of use, but there's one more important thing that you need to keep in mind when working on performant systems: cache friendliness. Using flat data structures instead of node-based ones means that you need to perform less pointer chasing at runtime, which helps your performance. Using data that's contiguous in memory, regardless of whether you're reading it forward or backward, means your CPU's memory prefetcher can load it before it's used, which can often make a huge difference. Node-based data structures and the mentioned pointer chasing cause random memory access patterns that can "confuse" the prefetcher and make it impossible for it to prefetch correct data.

If you want to see some performance results, please refer to the *C++ Containers Benchmark* linked in the *Further reading* section. It compares various usage scenarios of `std::vector`, `std::list`, `std::deque`, and `plf::colony`. If you don't know that last one, it's an interesting "bag"-type container with great fast insertion and deletion of large data.

When choosing from associative containers, you'll most often want to use "flat" implementations instead of node-based ones. This means that instead of using `std::unordered_map` and `std::unordered_set`, you might want to try out ones like `tsl::hopscotch_map` or Abseil's `flat_hash_map` and `flat_hash_set`.

Techniques such as putting colder instructions (such as exception handling code) in a non-inline function can help to increase the hotness of your instruction cache. This way, lengthy code for handling rare cases will not be loaded in the instruction cache, leaving space for more code that should be there, which can also improve your performance.

Designing your code with data in mind

If you want to help your caches, another technique that can be helpful is data-oriented design. Often, it's a good idea to store members used more often close to each other in memory. Colder data can often be placed in another struct and just be connected with the hotter data by an ID or a pointer.

Sometimes, instead of the more commonly spotted arrays of objects, using objects of arrays can yield better performance. Instead of writing your code in an object-oriented manner, split your object's data member across a few arrays, each containing data for multiple objects. In other words, take the following code:

```
struct Widget {
    Foo foo;
    Bar bar;
    Baz baz;
};

auto widgets = std::vector<Widget>{};
```

And consider replacing it with the following:

```
struct Widgets {
    std::vector<Foo> foos;
    std::vector<Bar> bars;
    std::vector<Baz> bazs;
};
```

This way, when processing a specific set of data points against some objects, the cache hotness increases and so does the performance. If you don't know whether this will yield more performance from your code, measure.

Sometimes even reordering members of your types can give you better performance. You should take into account the alignment of your types of data members. If performance matters, usually it's a good idea to order them so that the compiler doesn't need to insert too much padding between the members. Thanks to that, the size of your data type can be smaller, so many such objects can fit into one cache line. Consider the following example (let's assume we're compiling for the x86_64 architecture):

```
struct TwoSizesAndTwoChars {
    std::size_t first_size;
    char first_char;
    std::size_t second_size;
    char second_char;
};
static_assert(sizeof(TwoSizesAndTwoChars) == 32);
```

Despite the sizes being 8 bytes each and chars being just 1 byte each, we end up with 32 bytes in total! That's because `second_size` must start on an 8-byte aligned address, so after `first_char`, we get 7 bytes of padding. The same goes for `second_char`, as types need to be aligned with respect to their largest data type member.

Can we do better? Let's try switching the order of our members:

```
struct TwoSizesAndTwoChars {
    std::size_t first_size;
    std::size_t second_size;
    char first_char;
    char second_char;
};
static_assert(sizeof(TwoSizesAndTwoChars) == 24);
```

By simply putting the biggest members first, we were able to cut the size of our structure by 8 bytes, which is 25% of its size. Not bad for such a trivial change. If your goal is to pack many such structs in a contiguous block of memory and iterate through them, you could see a big performance boost of that code fragment.

Let's now talk about another way to improve your performance.

Parallelizing computations

In this section, we'll discuss a few different ways to parallelize computations. We will start with a comparison between threads and processes, after which we'll show you the tools available in the C++ standard, and last but not least, we'll say a few words about the OpenMP and MPI frameworks.

Before we start, let's say a few words on how to estimate the maximum possible gains you can have from parallelizing your code. There are two laws that can help us here. The first is Amdahl's law. It states that if we want to speed up our program by throwing more cores at it, then the part of our code that must remain sequential (cannot be parallelized) will limit our scalability. For instance, if 90% of your code is parallelizable, then even with infinite cores you can still get only up to a 10x speedup. Even if we cut down the time to execute that 90% to zero, the 10% of the code will always remain there.

The second law is Gustafson's law. It states that every large-enough task can be efficiently parallelized. This means that by increasing the size of the problem, we can obtain better parallelization (assuming we have free computing resources to use). In other words, sometimes it's better to add more capabilities to be run in the same time frame instead of trying to reduce the execution time of existing code. If you can cut the time of a task by half by doubling the cores, at some point, doubling them again and again will get you diminishing returns, so their processing power can be better spent elsewhere.

Understanding the differences between threads and processes

To parallelize computations efficiently, you need to also understand when to use processes to perform computation and when threads are the better tool for the job. Long story short, if your only target is to actually parallelize work, then it's best to start with adding extra threads up to the point where they don't bring extra benefits. At such a point, add more processes on other machines in your network, each with multiple threads too.

Why is that? Because processes are more heavyweight than threads. Spawning a process and switching between them takes longer than creating and switching between threads. Each process requires its own memory space, while threads within the same process share their memory. Also, inter-process communication is slower than just passing variables between threads. Working with threads is easier than it is with processes, so the development will be faster too.

Processes, however, also have their uses in the scope of a single application. They're great for isolating components that can independently run and crash without taking down the whole application with them. Having separate memory also means one process can't snoop another one's memory, which is great when you need to run third-party code that could turn out to be malicious. Those two reasons are why they're used in web browsers, among other apps. Aside from that, it's possible to run different processes with different OS permissions or privileges, which you can't achieve with multiple threads.

Let's now discuss a simple way to parallelize work in the scope of a single machine.

Using the standard parallel algorithms

If the computations you perform can be parallelized, there are two ways you can use that to your advantage. One is by replacing your regular calls to standard library algorithms with parallelizable ones. If you're not familiar with parallel algorithms, they were added in C++17 and in essence are the same algorithms, but you can pass each of them an execution policy. There are three execution policies:

- `std::execution::seq`: The sequenced policy for the plain-old execution of an algorithm in a non-parallelized way. This one we know too well.
- `std::execution::par`: A parallel policy that signals that the execution *may* be parallelized, usually using a thread pool under the hood.
- `std::execution::par_unseq`: A parallel policy that signals that the execution *may* be parallelized and vectorized.
- `std::execution::unseq`: A C++20 addition to the family. This policy signals that the execution can be vectorized, but not parallelized.

If the preceding policies are not enough for you, additional ones may be provided by a standard library implementation. Possible future additions may include ones for CUDA, SyCL, OpenCL, or even artificial intelligence processors.

Let's now see the parallel algorithms in action. As an example, to sort a vector in a parallel way, you can write the following:

```
std::sort(std::execution::par, v.begin(), v.end());
```

Simple and easy. Although in many cases this will yield better performance, in some cases you might be better off executing the algorithms in the traditional way. Why? Because scheduling work on more threads requires additional work and synchronization. Also, depending on the architecture of your app, it may influence the performance of other already existing threads and flush their cores' data caches. As always, measure first.

Parallelizing computations using OpenMP and MPI

An alternative to using the standard parallel algorithms would be to leverage OpenMP's pragmas. They're an easy way to parallelize many types of computations by just adding a few lines of code. And if you want to distribute your code across a cluster, you might want to see what MPI can do for you. Those two can also be joined together.

With OpenMP, you can use various pragmas to easily parallelize code. For instance, you can write `#pragma openmp parallel for` before a `for` loop to get it executed using parallel threads. The library can do much more, such as executing computations on GPUs and other accelerators.

Integrating MPI into your project is harder than just adding an appropriate pragma. Here, you'll need to use the MPI API in your code base to send or receive data between processes (using calls such as `MPI_Send` and `MPI_Recv`), or perform various gather and reduce operations (calling `MPI_Bcast` and `MPI_Reduce`, among other functions in this family). Communication can be done point to point or to all clusters using objects called communicators.

Depending on your algorithm implementation, MPI nodes can all execute the same code or it can vary when needed. The node will know how it should behave based on its rank: a unique number assigned when the computations start. Speaking of which, to start a process using MPI, you should run it through a wrapper, like so:

```
$ mpirun --hostfile my_hostfile -np 4 my_command --with some ./args
```

This would read hosts from said file one by one, connect to each of them, and run four instances of `my_command` on each with the args passed.

There are many implementations of MPI. One of the most notable is OpenMPI (don't confuse that with OpenMP). Among some useful features, it offers fault tolerance. After all, it's not uncommon for a node to go down.

The last tool we'd like to mention in this section is GNU Parallel, which you might find useful if you want to easily span processes that perform work by spawning parallel processes. It can be used both on a single machine and across a compute cluster.

Speaking about different ways to execute code, let's now discuss one more big topic from C++20: coroutines.

Using coroutines

Coroutines are functions that can suspend their execution and resume it later on. They allow writing asynchronous code in a very similar manner to how you would write synchronous code. Compared to writing asynchronous code with `std::async`, this allows writing cleaner code that's easier to understand and maintain. There's no need to write callbacks anymore, and no need to deal with the verbosity of `std::async` with promises and futures.

Aside from all that, they can also often provide you with much better performance. `std::async` based code usually has more overhead for switching threads and waiting. Coroutines can resume and suspend very cheaply even compared to the overhead of calling functions, which means they can yield better latency and throughput. Also, one of their design goals was to be highly scalable, even to billions of concurrent coroutines.

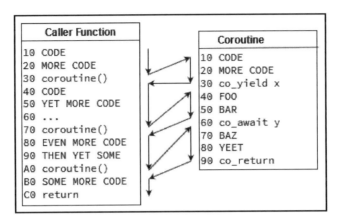

Figure 11.1 – Calling and executing coroutines is different from using regular functions as they can be suspended and resumed

C++ coroutines are stackless, which means their state is not stored on the calling thread's stack. This gives them an interesting property: several different threads can pick up the execution of a coroutine. In other words, even though it looks like the coroutine function body would be executed sequentially, parts of it can be executed in different threads. This makes it possible to leave parts of the function to be executed on dedicated threads. For instance, I/O operations can be done in a dedicated I/O thread.

To check whether a function is a C++ coroutine, you need to look for one of the following keywords in its body:

- `co_await`, which suspends the coroutine.
- `co_yield` for returning a value to the caller and suspending the coroutine. Similar to Python's `yield` keyword used in generators. Allows generating values lazily.
- `co_return`, which returns a value and finishes executing the coroutine. It's a coroutine equivalent of the `return` keyword.

Whenever a function body has one of those keywords, the function automatically becomes a coroutine. Although this means it's an implementation detail, there's one more hint that you can use: coroutine return types must satisfy certain requirements, which we'll discuss later on.

Coroutines are first-class citizens in the C++ world. This means you can get their address, use them as function arguments, return them from functions, and store them in objects.

In C++, you could write coroutines even before C++20. This was possible thanks to libraries such as Boost.Coroutine2, or Bloomberg's Quantum. The latter was even used to implement CoroKafka – a library for efficiently dealing with Kafka streams using coroutines. With the advent of standard C++ coroutines, new libraries started popping up. Now, we're going to show you one of them.

Distinguishing between cppcoro utilities

It's hard to write coroutine-based code from scratch. C++20 only offers the fundamental utilities for writing coroutines, so we need a set of primitives to use when writing our own coroutines. The cppcoro library created by Lewis Baker is one of the most commonly used coroutine frameworks for C++. In this section, we'll showcase the library and demonstrate how to use it when writing coroutine-based code.

Let's start with an overview of the coroutine types the library offers us:

- `task<>`: For scheduling work to be executed later – starts executing when it's `co_awaited` for.
- `shared_task<>`: A task that multiple coroutines can await. It can be copied so that multiple coroutines reference the same result. Doesn't offer any thread-safety on its own.
- `generator`: Produces a sequence of Ts lazily and synchronously. It's effectively a `std::range`: it has a `begin()` returning an iterator and an `end()` returning a sentinel.
- `recursive_generator`: Similar to `generator<T>`, but can yield either a T or `recursive_generator<T>`. Has some extra overhead.
- `async_generator`: Similar to `generator<T>`, but values may be produced asynchronously. This means that, as opposed to generator, asynchronous generators can use `co_await` in their bodies.

You should use those types as return types for your coroutines. Usually, in your generators (coroutines returning one of the preceding generator types), you'd want to return values using `co_yield` (similar to in Python generators). In your tasks, however, usually, you'll want to schedule work with `co_await`.

The library actually offers many more programming abstractions than just the preceding coroutine types. It also provides the following types:

- **Awaitables** types that you can `co_await` on, such as coroutine-flavored events and synchronization primitives: mutexes, latches, barriers, and so on.
- **Cancellation-related utilities**, essentially allowing you to cancel the execution of your coroutines.
- **Schedulers** – objects allowing you to schedule work through them, such as `static_thread_pool`, or ones for scheduling work on a specific thread.
- **I/O and networking utilities**, allowing you to read from and write to files and IP sockets.
- **Meta-functions and concepts**, such as `awaitable_traits`, `Awaitable`, and `Awaiter`.

Aside from the preceding utilities, cppcoro offers us functions – utilities for using other classes and steering execution, such as the following:

- `sync_wait`: Block until the passed awaitable completes.
- `when_all, when_all_ready`: Return an awaitable that completes when all the passed awaitables complete. The difference between those two is in handling failures of the sub-awaitables. `when_all_ready` will complete even in the event of failures and the caller can examine each result, while `when_all` will rethrow an exception if any of the sub-awaitables throws one (it's impossible to know which one did, though). It will also cancel any incomplete tasks.
- `fmap`: Similarly to functional programming, applies a function to an awaitable. You can think of it as transforming a task of one type into a task of another. For example, you can serialize types returned by your coroutines by calling `fmap(serialize, my_coroutine())`.
- `resume_on`: Instructs the coroutine which scheduler to use to continue execution once some work is completed. This enables you to execute certain work in certain execution contexts, such as running I/O-related tasks on a dedicated I/O thread. Note that this means a single C++ function (coroutine) can execute its parts on separate threads. Can be "piped" with computations similarly to `std::ranges`.
- `schedule_on`: Instructs the coroutine which scheduler to use to start some work. Commonly used as `auto foo = co_await schedule_on(scheduler, do_work());`.

Before we start using those utilities together, let's say a few more words about awaitables.

Looking under the hood of awaitables and coroutines

Aside from cppcoro, the standard library offers two more trivial awaitables: `suspend_never` and `suspend_always`. By looking at them, we can see how to implement our own awaitables when needed:

```
struct suspend_never {
    constexpr bool await_ready() const noexcept { return true; }
    constexpr void await_suspend(coroutine_handle<>) const noexcept {}
    constexpr void await_resume() const noexcept {}
};

struct suspend_always {
    constexpr bool await_ready() const noexcept { return false; }
    constexpr void await_suspend(coroutine_handle<>) const noexcept {}
    constexpr void await_resume() const noexcept {}
};
```

When typing `co_await`, you tell the compiler to first call the awaiter's `await_ready()`. If it says the awaiter is ready by returning true, `await_resume()` will get called. The return type of `await_resume()` should be the type the awaiter is actually producing. If the awaiter was not ready, the program will instead execute `await_suspend()`. After it's done, we have three cases:

- `await_suspend` returns `void`: The execution will always suspend afterwards.
- `await_suspend` returns `bool`: The execution will suspend or not depending on the returned value.
- `await_suspend` returns `std::coroutine_handle<PromiseType>`: Another coroutine will get resumed.

There's much more going on with coroutines under the hood. Even though coroutines don't use the `return` keyword, the compiler will generate code under the hood to make them compile and work. When using keywords such as `co_yield`, it will rewrite them to calls to the appropriate member functions of helper types. For instance, a call to `co_yield x` is equivalent to `co_await promise.yield_value(x)`. If you want to learn more about what's happening exactly and write your own coroutine types, refer to the *Your First Coroutine* article from the *Further reading* section.

Okay, let's now use all this knowledge to write our own coroutines. We'll create a simple application that mimics doing meaningful work. It will use a thread pool to fill a vector with some numbers.

Our CMake target will look as follows:

```
add_executable(coroutines_1 coroutines/main_1.cpp)
target_link_libraries(coroutines_1 PRIVATE cppcoro fmt::fmt
Threads::Threads)
target_compile_features(coroutines_1 PRIVATE cxx_std_20)
```

We'll link to the cppcoro library. In our case, we're using Andreas Buhr's fork of cppcoro, as it is a well-maintained fork of Lewis Baker's repository and supports CMake.

We'll also link to the excellent {fmt} library for text formatting. If your standard library offers C++20's string formatting, you can use that instead.

Last but not least, we're going to need a threading library – after all, we want to use multiple threads in a pool.

Let's start our implementation with some constants and a `main` function:

```
inline constexpr auto WORK_ITEMS = 5;

int main() {
   auto thread_pool = cppcoro::static_thread_pool{3};
```

We want to produce five items using three pooled threads. cppcoro's thread pool is a neat way to schedule work. By default, it creates as many threads as your machine has hardware ones. Moving onward, we need to specify our work:

```
fmt::print("Thread {}: preparing work\n", std::this_thread::get_id());
auto work = do_routine_work(thread_pool);

fmt::print("Thread {}: starting work\n", std::this_thread::get_id());
const auto ints = cppcoro::sync_wait(work);
```

We'll sprinkle our code with log messages so you can better see what's going on in which thread. This will help us better understand how coroutines work. We create work by calling a coroutine named `do_routine_work`. It returns us the coroutine, which we run using the `sync_wait` blocking function. A coroutine won't start executing until it is actually being awaited. This means that our actual work will start inside this function call.

Once we have our results, let's log them:

```
fmt::print("Thread {}: work done. Produced ints are: ",
           std::this_thread::get_id());
for (auto i : ints) {
  fmt::print("{}, ", i);
}
fmt::print("\n");
```

No voodoo magic here. Let's define our `do_routine_work` coroutine:

```
cppcoro::task<std::vector<int>>
do_routine_work(cppcoro::static_thread_pool &thread_pool) {
  auto mutex = cppcoro::async_mutex{};
  auto ints = std::vector<int>{};
  ints.reserve(WORK_ITEMS);
```

It returns a task, which produces some integers. Because we're going to use the thread pool, let's use cppcoro's `async_mutex` to synchronize the threads. Let's now start using the pool:

```
fmt::print("Thread {}: passing execution to the pool\n",
           std::this_thread::get_id());

co_await thread_pool.schedule();
```

You might be surprised that the `schedule()` call doesn't pass in any callable to execute. In the coroutine's case, we're actually making our current thread suspend the coroutine and start executing its caller. This means it will now wait for the coroutine to finish (somewhere in the `sync_wait` call).

In the meantime, a thread from our pool will resume the coroutine – simply continuing to execute its body. Here's what we've prepared for it:

```
fmt::print("Thread {}: running first pooled job\n",
           std::this_thread::get_id());

std::vector<cppcoro::task<>> tasks;
for (int i = 0; i < WORK_ITEMS; ++i) {
  tasks.emplace_back(
      cppcoro::schedule_on(thread_pool, fill_number(i, ints, mutex)));
}
co_await cppcoro::when_all_ready(std::move(tasks));
co_return ints;
```

We create a vector of tasks to execute. Each task fills one number in `ints` under the mutex. The `schedule_on` call runs the filling coroutine using another thread from our pool. Finally, we wait for all the results. At this point, our tasks start executing. Finally, as our coroutine is a task, we use `co_return`.

> Don't forget to `co_return` the produced value. If we removed the `co_return ints;` line from our example, we would simply return a default constructed vector. The program would run, happily print the empty vector, and exit with code 0.

Our last step is to implement the coroutine that will produce a number:

```
cppcoro::task<> fill_number(int i, std::vector<int> &ints,
                            cppcoro::async_mutex &mutex) {
  fmt::print("Thread {}: producing {}\n", std::this_thread::get_id(), i);
  std::this_thread::sleep_for(
      std::chrono::milliseconds((WORK_ITEMS - i) * 200));
```

This one is a task that doesn't return any value. Instead, it will add it to our vector. Its hard work will actually be done by dozing off for a number of milliseconds. After the wake-up, the coroutine will continue with more productive endeavors:

```
{
   auto lock = co_await mutex.scoped_lock_async();
   ints.emplace_back(i);
}
```

It will lock the mutex. In our case, it's just an `await`. When the mutex is locked, it will add a number to our vector – the same number it was called with.

> NOTE: Remember to `co_await`. If you forget and your awaitable allows that (perhaps because its okay to not consume each awaitable), then you might skip some essential computations. In our example, this could mean not locking a mutex.

Let's finish the coroutine's implementation now:

```
fmt::print("Thread {}: produced {}\n", std::this_thread::get_id(), i);
co_return;
```

Just a simple `status print` and a `co_return` to mark the coroutine as complete. Once it returns, the coroutine frame can be destroyed, freeing the memory occupied by it.

That's all. Let's now run our code and see what happens:

```
Thread 140471890347840: preparing work
Thread 140471890347840: starting work
Thread 140471890347840: passing execution to the pool
Thread 140471890282240: running first pooled job
Thread 140471890282240: producing 4
Thread 140471881828096: producing 1
Thread 140471873373952: producing 0
Thread 140471890282240: produced 4
Thread 140471890282240: producing 3
Thread 140471890282240: produced 3
Thread 140471890282240: producing 2
Thread 140471881828096: produced 1
Thread 140471873373952: produced 0
Thread 140471890282240: produced 2
Thread 140471890347840: work done. Produced ints are: 4, 3, 1, 0, 2,
```

Our main thread was used to fire up the work on the pool and then waited for the results to come. Then, our three threads from the pool were producing numbers. The last task scheduled was actually the first one that ran, producing the number 4. This is because it was the one that continued executing `do_routine_work` all the time: first, it scheduled all other tasks on the pool, then started performing the first task when `when_all_ready` was called. Later on, the execution continued with the first free thread taking the next task scheduled on the pool until the whole vector was filled. Finally, the execution returned to our main thread.

This concludes our short example. And with it, we conclude our last section of this chapter. Let's now summarize what we've learned.

Summary

In this chapter, we've learned what types of tools can help us achieve better performance with our code. We learned how to perform experiments, write performance tests, and look for performance bottlenecks. You're now able to write microbenchmarks using Google Benchmark. Moreover, we discussed how to profile your code and how (and why) to implement distributed tracing of your system. We also discussed parallelizing your computations using both standard library utilities and external solutions. Last but not least, we introduced you to coroutines. You now know what C++20 brings to the coroutine table, as well as what you can find in the cppcoro library. You've also learned how to write your own coroutines.

The most important lesson from this chapter is: when it comes to performance, measure first and optimize later. This will help you maximize the impact of your work.

That's it for performance – the last of quality attributes we wanted to discuss in our book. In the next chapter, we'll start moving into the world of services and the cloud. We'll start by discussing service-oriented architecture.

Questions

1. What can we learn from the performance results from this chapter's microbenchmarks?
2. Is how we traverse a multi-dimensional array important for performance? Why/why not?
3. In our coroutines example, why can't we create our thread pool inside the `do_routine_work` function?
4. How can we rework our coroutine example so it uses a generator instead of just tasks?

Further reading

- When can the C++ compiler devirtualize a call?, blog post, Arthur O'Dwyer, `https://quuxplusone.github.io/blog/2021/02/15/devirtualization/`
- CppCon 2015: Chandler Carruth "Tuning C++: Benchmarks, and CPUs, and Compilers! Oh My!", YouTube video, `https://www.youtube.com/watch?v=nXaxk27zwlk`
- Tutorial, Perf Wiki, `https://perf.wiki.kernel.org/index.php/Tutorial`
- CPU Flame Graphs, Brendan Gregg, `http://www.brendangregg.com/FlameGraphs/cpuflamegraphs.html`
- C++ Containers Benchmark, blog post, Baptiste Wicht, `https://baptiste-wicht.com/posts/2017/05/cpp-containers-benchmark-vector-list-deque-plf-colony.html`
- Your First Coroutine, blog post, Dawid Pilarski, `https://blog.panicsoftware.com/your-first-coroutine`

Section 4: Cloud-Native Design Principles

4

This section focuses on the modern architectural style that originated with distributed systems and within cloud environments. It shows concepts such as service-oriented architecture, microservices including containers, and various messaging systems.

This section contains the following chapters:

- Chapter 12, *Service-Oriented Architecture*
- Chapter 13, *Designing Microservices*
- Chapter 14, *Containers*
- Chapter 15, *Cloud-Native Design*

12
Service-Oriented Architecture

A very common architecture for distributed systems is **Service-Oriented Architecture** (**SOA**). It's not a new invention, as this architectural style is almost as old as computer networking. There are many aspects of SOA ranging from an **Enterprise Service Bus** (**ESB**) to cloud-native microservices.

If your applications include web, mobile, or **Internet-of-Things** (**IoT**) interfaces, this chapter will help you understand how they can be built with a focus on modularity and maintainability. As most of the current systems work in a client-server (or other network topology) manner, learning about SOA principles will help you design and improve such systems.

The following topics will be covered in this chapter:

- Understanding SOA
- Adopting messaging principles
- Using web services
- Leveraging managed services and cloud providers

Technical requirements

Most of the examples presented in this chapter do not require any specific software. For an AWS API example, you will need the **AWS SDK for C++**, which can be found at https://aws.amazon.com/sdk-for-cpp/.

The code present in the chapter has been placed on GitHub at https://github.com/PacktPublishing/Software-Architecture-with-Cpp/tree/master/Chapter12.

Understanding Service-Oriented Arcitecture

Service-Oriented Architecture is an example of a software design that features loosely coupled components that provide services to each other. The components use a shared communication protocol, usually over a network. In this design, services mean units of functionality that can be accessed outside of the originating component. An example of a component could be a mapping service that provides a map of the area in response to geographical coordinates.

According to the definition, a service has four properties:

- It is a representation of business activity with a defined outcome.
- It is self-contained.
- It is opaque to its users.
- It may be composed of other services.

Implementation approaches

Service-Oriented Architecture does not regulate how to approach the service orientation. It's a term that may be applied to many different implementations. There are discussions on whether some approaches actually should be considered to be Service-Oriented Architecture. We don't want to take part in these discussions, only to highlight some of the approaches that often are mentioned as SOA approaches.

Let's compare some of them.

Enterprise Service Bus

ESB is often the first association when someone says Service-Oriented Architecture. It's one of the oldest approaches to implementing SOA.

ESB draws an analogy from computer hardware architecture. Hardware architecture uses computer buses such as PCI to achieve modularity. This way, third-party providers are able to implement modules (such as graphic cards, sound cards, or I/O interfaces) independently of the motherboard manufacturer as long as everyone is adhering to the standards required by the bus.

Much like the PCI, the ESB architecture aims to build a standard, general-purpose way to allow for the interaction of loosely coupled services. Such services are expected to be developed and deployed independently. It should also be possible to combine heterogeneous services.

As with SOA itself, ESB is not defined by any global standard. To implement ESB, it is necessary to establish an additional component in the system. This component is the bus itself. The communication over ESB is event-driven and often achieved with the means of message-oriented middleware and message queues, which we'll discuss in later chapters.

The Enterprise Service Bus component serves the following roles:

- Controlling the deployment and versioning of services
- Maintaining service redundancy
- Routing messages between services
- Monitoring and controlling the message exchange
- Resolving contention between the components
- Providing common services, such as event handling, encryption, or message queuing
- Enforcing Quality of Service (**QOS**)

There are both proprietary commercial products as well as open source ones that implement the Enterprise Service Bus functionality. Some of the most popular open source products are the following:

- Apache Camel
- Apache ServiceMix
- Apache Synapse
- JBoss ESB
- OpenESB
- Red Hat Fuse (based on Apache Camel)
- Spring Integration

The most popular commercial products are the following:

- IBM Integration Bus (replacing IBM WebSphere ESB)
- Microsoft Azure Service Bus
- Microsoft BizTalk Server
- Oracle Enterprise Service Bus
- SAP Process Integration

As with all the patterns and products that we present in this book, you will have to consider the strengths and weaknesses before deciding to go with a particular architecture. Some of the benefits of introducing Enterprise Service Bus are as follows:

- Better scalability of services
- Distributed workload
- Can focus on configuration rather than implementing custom integration in services
- An easier way to design loosely coupled services
- Services are replaceable
- Built-in redundancy capability

The disadvantages, on the other hand, mostly revolve around the following:

- A single point of failure – the ESB component's failure means the outage of an entire system.
- The configuration is more complex, which impacts maintenance.
- Message queuing, message translation, and other services provided by ESB may reduce performance or even become a bottleneck.

Web services

Web services are another popular implementation of Service-Oriented Architecture. By their definition, web services are services offered by one machine to another machine (or operator) where communication occurs over World Wide Web protocols. Even though W3C, the governing body concerning the World Wide Web, allows the use of other protocols such as FTP or SMTP, web services typically use HTTP as transport.

Although it is possible to implement web services using proprietary solutions, most implementations are based on open protocols and standards. Although many of the approaches are often referred to as web services, they are fundamentally different from each other. Later in the chapter, we will describe the various approaches in detail. For now, let's focus on their common features.

Benefits and disadvantages of web services

The benefits of web services are as follows:

- Using popular web standards
- A lot of tooling
- Extensibility

Given next are the disadvantages:

- A lot of overhead.
- Some implementations are too complex (for example, SOAP/WSDL/UDDI specifications).

Messaging and streaming

We've mentioned message queues and message brokers already when covering the Enterprise Service Bus architecture. Other than as part of an ESB implementation, messaging systems may also be standalone architectural elements.

Message queues

Message queues are components used for **Inter-Process Communication (IPC)**. As the name suggests, they use the queue data structure to pass messages between different processes. Usually, message queues are a part of **Message-Oriented Middleware (MOM)** designs.

On the lowest level, message queues are available in UNIX specifications, both in System V and in POSIX. While they are interesting when implementing IPC on a single machine, we would like to focus on message queues that are suitable for distributed computing.

There are currently three standards used in open source software that are related to message queuing:

1. **Advanced Message Queuing Protocol (AMQP)**, a binary protocol operating on the application layer of the 7-Layer OSI model. Popular implementations include the following:

    - Apache Qpid
    - Apache ActiveMQ
    - RabbitMQ

- Azure Event Hubs
- Azure Service Bus

2. **Streaming Text Oriented Messaging Protocol (STOMP)**, a text-based protocol similar to HTTP (uses verbs such as CONNECT, SEND, SUBSCRIBE). Popular implementations include the following:

   - Apache ActiveMQ
   - RabbitMQ
   - syslog-ng

3. **MQTT**, a lightweight protocol aimed at embedded devices. Popular implementations include home automation solutions such as the following:

   - OpenHAB
   - Adafruit IO
   - IoT Guru
   - Node-RED
   - Home Assistant
   - Pimatic
   - AWS IoT
   - Azure IoT Hub

Message brokers

Message brokers deal with the translation, validation, and routing of messages in a messaging system. Like message queues, they are parts of MOM.

Using message brokers, you can minimize the application's awareness regarding other parts of the system. This leads to designing loosely coupled systems, as message brokers take all the burden related to common operations on messages. It is known as a **Publish-Subscribe (PubSub)** design pattern.

Brokers typically manage message queues for receivers but are also able to perform additional functions, such as the following:

- Translating messages from one representation to another
- Validating the message sender, receiver, or contents
- Routing messages to one or more destinations

- Aggregating, decomposing, and recomposing messages in transit
- Retrieving data from external services
- Augmenting and enriching messages through interaction with external services
- Handling and responding to errors and other events
- Providing different routing patterns, such as PubSub

Popular implementations of message brokers are the following:

- Apache ActiveMQ
- Apache Kafka
- Apache Qpid
- Eclipse Mosquitto MQTT Broker
- NATS
- RabbitMQ
- Redis
- AWS ActiveMQ
- AWS Kinesis
- Azure Service Bus

Cloud computing

Cloud computing is a broad term with a lot of different meanings. Initially, the term **cloud** referred to a layer of abstraction that the architecture shouldn't be too worried about. This could, for example, mean servers and network infrastructure managed by a dedicated operations team. Later, service providers started applying the term cloud computing to their own products that abstracted the underlying infrastructure with all its complexities. Instead of having to configure each piece of infrastructure individually, it was possible to use a simple **Application Programming Interface (API)** to set up all the necessary resources.

Nowadays, cloud computing has grown to include many novel approaches to application architecture. It may consist of the following:

- Managed services, such as databases, cache layers, and message queues
- Scalable workload orchestration
- Container deployment and orchestration platforms
- Serverless computing platforms

The most important thing to remember when considering cloud adoption is that hosting your application in the cloud requires an architecture designed specifically for the cloud. Most often, it also means architecture designed specifically for the given cloud provider.

This means choosing a cloud provider is not just a decision about whether one choice is better than another at a given moment in time. It means that the future cost of switching a provider may be too big to warrant the move. Migration between providers requires architectural changes and for a working application, they may outweigh the savings expected from the migration.

There is also another consequence of cloud architecture design. For legacy applications, it means that in order to take advantage of the cloud benefits, the applications would first have to be rearchitected and rewritten. Migration to the cloud is not just a matter of copying binary and configuration files from on-premises hosting to virtual machines managed by a cloud provider. Such an approach would only mean a waste of money as cloud computing is only cost-effective if your applications are scalable and cloud-aware.

Cloud computing doesn't necessarily mean using external services and leasing machines from third-party providers. There are also solutions such as OpenStack that run on-premises, which allow you to leverage the benefits of cloud computing using the servers you already own.

We will cover managed services later in this chapter. Containers, cloud-native design, and serverless architecture will have their own dedicated chapters later in the book.

Microservices

There is some debate regarding whether microservices are a part of SOA or not. Most of the time, the term SOA is pretty much equivalent to the ESB design. Microservices are in many respects the opposite of ESB. This leads to opinions that microservices are a distinct pattern from SOA, being the next step in the evolution of software architecture.

We believe that they are, in fact, a modern approach to SOA that aims to eliminate some of the problems featured in ESB. After all, microservices fit within the definition of Service-Oriented Architecture very well.

Microservices are the subject of the next chapter.

Benefits of Service-Oriented Architecture

Splitting the system's functionality over multiple services has several benefits. First of all, each service can be maintained and deployed separately. This helps the team focus on a given task, without the need to understand every possible interaction within the system. It also enables agile development as tests only have to cover a particular service, not the entire system.

The second benefit is that the modularity of the services helps create a distributed system. With a network (usually based on the Internet Protocol) as a means of communication, services can be split between different machines to provide scalability, redundancy, and better resource usage.

Implementing new features and maintaining the existing software is a difficult task when there are many producers and many consumers for each service. This is why SOA encourages the use of documented and versioned APIs.

Another way to make it easier for both service producers and consumers to interact is by using established protocols that describe how to pass data and metadata between different services. These protocols may include SOAP, REST, or gRPC.

The use of APIs and standard protocols makes it easy to create new services that provide added value over the existing ones. Considering we have a service, A, that returns our geographical location and another service, B, that provides the current temperature for a given location, we can invoke A and use its response in a request to B. This way, we get the current temperature for the current location without implementing the entire logic on our own.

All of the complexity and implementation details of both services are unknown to us and we treat them as **black boxes**. The maintainers of both services may also introduce new functionality and release new versions of the services without the need to inform us about it.

Testing and experimenting with Service-Oriented Architecture is also easier than with monolithic applications. A small change in a single place doesn't require the recompilation of an entire code base. It is often possible to invoke services in an ad hoc manner using client tools.

Let's return to our example with the weather and geographical location service. If both services are exposing a REST API, we are able to build a prototype using nothing more than a cURL client to send appropriate requests manually. When we confirm that the response is satisfactory, we may then start writing code that will automate the entire operation and possibly expose the results as another service.

To get the benefits of SOA, we need to remember that all of the services have to be loosely coupled. If services depend on each other's implementation, it means they are no longer loosely coupled and are tightly coupled instead. Ideally, any given service should be replaceable by a different analogous service without impacting the operation of the entire system.

In our weather and location example, this means that reimplementing a location service in a different language (say, switching from Go to C++) should not affect the downstream consumers of that service as long as they use the established API.

It is possible to still introduce breaking changes in the API by releasing a new API version. A client connecting to version 1.0 would observe the legacy behavior while clients connecting to 2.0 would benefit from bugfixes, better performance, and other improvements that come at the cost of compatibility.

For services relying on HTTP, API versioning usually occurs at the URI level. So a version 1.0, 1.1, or 1.2 API can be accessed when calling `https://service.local/v1/customer` while the version 2.0 API resides at `https://service.local/v2/customer`. An API gateway, HTTP proxy, or a load balancer is then able to route the requests to appropriate services.

Challenges with SOA

Introducing an abstraction layer always comes at a cost. The same rule applies to Service-Oriented Architecture. It's easy to see the abstraction costs when looking at Enterprise Service Bus, web services, or message queues and brokers. What may be less obvious is that microservices also come at a cost. Their cost is related to the **Remote Procedure Call (RPC)** frameworks they use and the resource consumption related to service redundancy and duplication of their functionality.

Another target of criticism related to SOA is the lack of uniform testing frameworks. Individual teams that develop the services of an application may use tooling unknown to other teams. Other issues related to testing are that the heterogeneous nature and interchangeability of components mean there is a huge set of combinations to test. Some combinations may introduce edge cases that are not typically observed.

As the knowledge about particular services is mostly concentrated in a single team, it is much harder to understand how an entire application works.

When the SOA platform is developed during the lifetime of an application, it may introduce the need for all the services to update their version to target the recent platform development. This means that instead of introducing new features, developers would be focused on making sure their application functions correctly after the changes to the platform. In an extreme case, maintenance costs may rise drastically for those services that don't see new releases and are constantly patched to adhere to platform requirements.

Service-Oriented Architecture follows Conway's law, described in `Chapter 2`, *Architectural Styles*.

Adopting messaging principles

As we've mentioned previously in this chapter, messaging has many different use cases, ranging from IoT and sensor networks to microservices-based distributed applications running in the cloud.

One of the benefits of messaging is that it is a neutral way to connect services implemented using different technologies. When developing an SOA, each service is typically developed and maintained by a dedicated team. Teams may choose the tools they feel comfortable with. This applies to programming languages, third-party libraries, and build systems.

Maintaining a uniform set of tools may be counter-productive as different services may have different needs. For example, a kiosk application may require a **Graphical User Interface (GUI)** library such as Qt. A hardware controller that is a part of the same application will have other requirements, possibly linking to the hardware manufacturer's third-party components. These dependencies may then impose some restrictions that cannot be satisfied for both components simultaneously (for example, a GUI application may require a recent compiler, while the hardware counterpart may be pinned to an older one). Using messaging systems to decouple these components lets them have separate life cycles.

Some use cases for messaging systems include the following:

- Financial operations
- Fleet monitoring
- Logistics capturing
- Processing sensor
- Data order fulfillment
- Task queuing

The following sections focus on the messaging systems designed for low overhead and message systems with brokers used for distributed systems.

Low-overhead messaging systems

Low-overhead messaging systems are typically used in environments that either require a small footprint or low latency. These are usually sensor networks, embedded solutions, and IoT devices. They are less common in cloud-based and distributed services, but it's still possible to use them in such solutions.

MQTT

MQTT stands for **Message Queuing Telemetry Transport**. It is an open standard both under OASIS and ISO. MQTT uses the PubSub model usually over TCP/IP, but it can also work with other transport protocols.

As the name suggests, MQTT's design goals are a low-code footprint and the possibility of running in low-bandwidth locations. There is a separate specification called **MQTT-SN**, which stands for **MQTT for Sensor Networks**. It focuses on battery-powered embedded devices without the TCP/IP stack.

MQTT uses a message broker that receives all the messages from the client and routes those messages to their destinations. QoS is provided on three levels:

- At most once delivery (no guarantee)
- At least once delivery (acknowledged delivery)
- Exactly once delivery (assured delivery)

It should be no surprise that MQTT is especially popular with various IoT applications. It's supported by OpenHAB, Node-RED, Pimatic, Microsoft Azure IoT Hub, and Amazon IoT. It's also popular with instant messaging, being used in ejabberd and Facebook Messanger. Other use cases include carsharing platforms, logistics, and transportation.

The two most popular C++ libraries supporting this standard are Eclipse Paho and mqtt_cpp based on C++14 and Boost.Asio. For Qt applications, there's also qmqtt.

ZeroMQ

ZeroMQ is a brokerless messaging queue. It supports common messaging patterns, such as PubSub, client/server, and several others. It is independent of a particular transport and may be used with TCP, WebSockets, or IPC.

The main idea, contained in the name, is that ZeroMQ requires zero brokers and zero administration. It is also advocated as providing zero latency, which means no latency is added coming from the presence of a broker.

The low-level library is written in C, and it has implementations for various popular programming languages, including C++. The most popular implementation for C++ is cppzmq, which is a header-only library targeting C++11.

Brokered messaging systems

The two most popular messaging systems that don't focus on low overhead are AMQP-based RabbitMQ and Apache Kafka. Both are mature solutions that are extremely popular in a lot of different designs. Many articles focus on superiority in a particular area of either RabbitMQ or Apache Kafka.

This is a slightly incorrect point of view as both messaging systems are based on different paradigms. Apache Kafka focuses on streaming vast amounts of data and storing the stream in persistent memory to allow future replay. RabbitMQ, on the other hand, is often used as a message broker between different microservices or a task queue to handle background jobs. For this reason, routing in RabbitMQ is much more advanced than the one present in Apache Kafka. Kafka's primary use cases are data analysis and real-time processing.

While RabbitMQ uses the AMQP protocol (and supports other protocols as well, such as MQTT and STOMP), Kafka uses its own protocol based on TCP/IP. This means that RabbitMQ is interoperable with other existing solutions based on these supported protocols. If you write an application that uses AMQP to interact with RabbitMQ, it should be possible to migrate it later to use Apache Qpid, Apache ActiveMQ, or managed solutions from AWS or Microsoft Azure.

The scaling concerns could also drive the choice of one message broker over another. The architecture of Apache Kafka allows for easy horizontal scaling, which means adding more machines to the existing pool of workers. RabbitMQ, on the other hand, was designed with vertical scaling in mind, which means adding more resources to the existing machine, rather than adding more machines of similar sizes.

Using web services

As mentioned earlier in the chapter, the common characteristic of web services is that they are based on standard web technologies. Most of the time, this will mean the **Hypertext Transfer Protocol (HTTP)** and this is the technology we will focus on. Although it is possible to implement web services based on different protocols, such services are extremely rare and therefore out of our scope.

Tools for debugging web services

One of the major benefits of using HTTP as transport is the wide availability of tools. For the most part, testing and debugging a web service may be performed using nothing more than a web browser. Apart from that, there are a lot of additional programs that may be helpful in automation. These include the following:

- The standard Unix file downloader `wget`
- The modern HTTP client `curl`
- Popular open source libraries such as libcurl, curlpp, C++ REST SDK, cpr (C++ HTTP requests library), and NFHTTP
- Testing frameworks such as Selenium or Robot Framework
- Browser extensions such as Boomerang
- Standalone solutions such as Postman and Postwoman
- Dedicated testing software including SoapUI and Katalon Studio

HTTP-based web services work by returning an HTTP response to an HTTP request that uses appropriate HTTP verbs (such as GET, POST, and PUT). The semantics of how the request and the response should look and what data they should convey differs from implementation to implementation.

Most implementations fall into one of two categories: XML-based web services and JSON-based web services. JSON-based web services are currently displacing XML-based ones, but it is still common to find services that use XML formats.

For dealing with data encoded with either JSON or XML, additional tools such as xmllint, xmlstarlet, jq, and libxml2 may be required.

XML-based web services

The first web services that gained traction were primarily based on XML. **XML** or **eXtensible Markup Language** was at the time the interchange format of choice in distributed computing and in the web environment. There were several different approaches to designing services with an XML payload.

It is possible that you may want to interact with existing XML-based web services that are developed either internally within your organization or externally. However, we advise you to implement new web services using more lightweight methods, such as JSON-based web services, RESTful web services, or gRPC.

XML-RPC

One of the first standards that emerged was called XML-RPC. The idea behind the project was to provide an RPC technology that would compete with the then prevalent **Common Object Model** (**COM**), and CORBA. The aim was to use HTTP as a transport protocol and make the format human-readable and human-writable as well as parsable to machines. To achieve that, XML was chosen as the data encoding format.

When using XML-RPC, the client that wants to perform a remote procedure call sends an HTTP request to the server. The request may have multiple parameters. The server answers with a single response. The XML-RPC protocol defines several data types for parameters and results.

Although SOAP features similar data types, it uses XML schema definitions, which make the messages much less readable than the ones in XML-RPC.

Relationship to SOAP

Since XML-RPC is no longer actively maintained, there aren't any modern C++ implementations for the standard. If you want to interact with XML-RPC web services from modern code, the best way may be to use the gSOAP toolkit that supports XML-RPC and other XML web service standards.

The main criticism of XML-RPC was that it didn't give much value over sending plain XML requests and responses while making the messages significantly larger.

As the standard evolved, it became SOAP. As SOAP it formed the basis for the W3C web services stack of protocols.

SOAP

The original abbreviation of **SOAP** stood for **Simple Object Access Protocol**. The abbreviation was dropped in version 1.2 of the standard. It's an evolution of the XML-RPC standard.

SOAP consists of three parts:

- **The SOAP envelope**, defining the message's structure and processing rules
- **The SOAP header** rules defining application-specific data types (optional)
- **The SOAP body**, which carries remote procedure calls and responses

Here's an example SOAP message using HTTP as transport:

```
POST /FindMerchants HTTP/1.1
Host: www.domifair.org
Content-Type: application/soap+xml; charset=utf-8
Content-Length: 345
SOAPAction: "http://www.w3.org/2003/05/soap-envelope"

<?xml version="1.0"?>
<soap:Envelope xmlns:soap="http://www.w3.org/2003/05/soap-envelope">
 <soap:Header>
 </soap:Header>
 <soap:Body xmlns:m="https://www.domifair.org">
    <m:FindMerchants>
      <m:Lat>54.350989</m:Lat>
      <m:Long>18.6548168</m:Long>
      <m:Distance>200</m:Distance>
    </m:FindMerchants>
  </soap:Body>
</soap:Envelope>
```

The example uses standard HTTP headers and the POST method to call a remote procedure. One header that is unique to SOAP is the `SOAPAction`. It points to a URI identifying the intent of the action. It is up to the clients to decide how to interpret this URI.

`soap:Header` is optional so we leave it empty. Together with `soap:Body`, it is contained within `soap:Envelope`. The main procedure call takes place within `soap:Body`. We introduce our own XML namespace that is specific to the Dominican Fair application. The namespace points to the root of our domain. The procedure we call is `FindMerchants` and we provide three arguments: latitude, longtitude, and distance.

As SOAP was designed to be extensible, transport-neutral, and independent of the programming model, it also led to the creation of other accompanying standards. This means it is usually necessary to learn all the related standards and protocols before using SOAP.

This is not a problem if your application makes extensive use of XML and your development team is familiar with all the terms and specifications. However, if all you want is to expose an API for a third party, a much easier approach would be to build a REST API as it is much easier to learn for both producers and consumers.

WSDL

Web Services Description Language (WSDL) provides a machine-readable description of how services can be called and how messages should be formed. Like the other W3C web services standards, it is encoded in XML.

It is often used with SOAP to define interfaces that the web service offers and how they may be used.

Once you define your API in WSDL, you may (and should!) use automated tooling to help you create code out of it. For C++, one framework with such tools is gSOAP. It comes with a tool named `wsdl2h`, which will generate a header file out of the definition. You can then use another tool, `soapcpp2`, to generate bindings from the interface definition to your implementation.

Unfortunately, due to the verbosity of the messages, the size and bandwidth requirements for SOAP services are generally huge. If this is not an issue, then SOAP can have its uses. It allows for both synchronous and asynchronous calls, as well as stateful and stateless operations. If you require rigid, formal means of communication, SOAP can provide them. Just make sure to use version 1.2 of the protocol due to the many improvements it introduces. One of them is the enhanced security of the services. Another is the improved definition of services themselves, which aids interoperability, or the ability to formally define the means of transportation (allowing for the usage of message queues), to name just a few.

UDDI

The next step after documenting the web service interfaces is service discovery, which allows applications to find and connect to the services implemented by other parties.

Universal Description, Discovery, and Integration (UDDI) is a registry for WSDL files that may be searched manually or automatically. As with the other technologies discussed in this section, UDDI uses an XML format.

UDDI registry may be queried with SOAP messages for automated service discovery. Even though UDDI provided the logical extensions of WSDL, its adoption in the open was disappointing. It is still possible to find UDDI systems used internally by companies.

SOAP libraries

Two of the most popular libraries for SOAP are **Apache Axis** and **gSOAP**.

Apache Axis is suitable for implementing both SOAP (including WSDL) and REST web services. It's worth noting that the library hasn't seen a new release for over a decade.

gSOAP is a toolkit that allows for creating and interacting with XML-based web services with a focus on SOAP. It handles data binding, SOAP and WSDL support, JSON and RSS parsing, UDDI APIs, and several other related web services standards. Although it doesn't use modern C++ features, it is still actively maintained.

JSON-based web services

JSON stands for **JavaScript Object Notation**. Contrary to what the name suggests, it is not limited to JavaScript. It is language-independent. Parsers and serializers for JSON exist in most programming languages. JSON is much more compact than XML.

Its syntax is derived from JavaScript as it was based on a JavaScript subset.

Supported data types for JSON are the following:

- Number: The exact format may vary between implementations; defaults to the double-precision floating-point in JavaScript.
- String: Unicode-encoded.
- Boolean: Using `true` and `false` values.
- Array: May be empty.
- Object: A map with key-value pairs.
- `null`: Representing an empty value.

The `Packer` configuration presented in `Chapter` 9, *Continuous Integration/Continuous Deployment*, is an example of a JSON document:

```json
{
  "variables": {
    "aws_access_key": "",
    "aws_secret_key": ""
  },
  "builders": [{
    "type": "amazon-ebs",
    "access_key": "{{user `aws_access_key`}}",
    "secret_key": "{{user `aws_secret_key`}}",
    "region": "eu-central-1",
    "source_ami": "ami-5900cc36",
    "instance_type": "t2.micro",
    "ssh_username": "admin",
    "ami_name": "Project's Base Image {{timestamp}}"
  }],
  "provisioners": [{
    "type": "ansible",
    "playbook_file": "./provision.yml",
    "user": "admin",
    "host_alias": "baseimage"
  }],
  "post-processors": [{
    "type": "manifest",
    "output": "manifest.json",
    "strip_path": true
  }]
}
```

One of the standards using JSON as a format is the JSON-RPC protocol.

JSON-RPC

JSON-RPC is a JSON-encoded remote procedure call protocol similar to XML-RPC and SOAP. Unlike its XML predecessor, it requires little overhead. It is also very simple while maintaining the human-readability of XML-RPC.

This is how our previous example expressed in a SOAP call will look with JSON-RPC 2.0:

```json
{
  "jsonrpc": "2.0",
  "method": "FindMerchants",
  "params": {
    "lat": "54.350989",
```

```
      "long": "18.6548168",
      "distance": 200
   },
   "id": 1
}
```

This JSON document still requires proper HTTP headers, but even with the headers, it is still considerably smaller than the XML counterpart. The only metadata present is the file with the JSON-RPC version and the request ID. The `method` and `params` fields are pretty much self-explanatory. The same can't always be said about SOAP.

Even though the protocol is lightweight, easy to implement, and easy to use, it hasn't seen widespread adoption when compared to both SOAP and REST web services. It was released much later than SOAP and around the same time that REST services started to get popular. While REST quickly rose to success (possibly due to its flexibility), JSON-RPC failed to get similar traction.

Two useful implementations for C++ are libjson-rpc-cpp and json-rpc-cxx. json-rpc-cxx is a modern reimplementation of the previous library.

REpresentational State Transfer (REST)

An alternative approach to web services is **REpresentional State Transfer (REST).** Services that conform to this architectural style are often called RESTful services. The main difference between REST and SOAP or JSON-RPC is that REST is based almost entirely on HTTP and URI semantics.

REST is an architectural style defining a set of constraints when implementing web services. Services that conform to this style are called RESTful. These constraints are as follows:

- Must use a client-server model.
- Statelessness (neither the client nor the server needs to store the state related to their communication).
- Cacheability (responses should be defined as cacheable or non-cacheable to benefit from standard web caching to improve scalability and performance).
- Layered system (proxies and load balancers should by no means affect the communication between the client and server).

REST uses HTTP as the transport protocol with URIs representing resources and HTTP verbs that manipulate the resources or invoke operations. There is no standard regarding how each HTTP method should behave, but the semantics most often agreed on are the following:

- POST – Create a new resource.
- GET – Retrieve an existing resource.
- PATCH – Update an existing resource.
- DELETE – Delete an existing resource.
- PUT – Replace an existing resource.

Due to reliance on web standards, RESTful web services can reuse existing components such as proxies, load balancers, and the cache. Thanks to the low overhead, such services are also very performant and efficient.

Description languages

Just like with XML-based web services, RESTful services can be described in both a machine and human-readable way. There are a few competing standards available, with OpenAPI being the most popular.

OpenAPI

OpenAPI is a specification overseen by the OpenAPI Initiative, part of the Linux Foundation. It used to be known as the Swagger Specification as it used to be a part of the Swagger framework.

The specification is language agnostic. It uses JSON or YAML input to generate documentation of methods, parameters, and models. This way, using OpenAPI helps to keep the documentation and source code up to date.

There is a good selection of tools compatible with OpenAPI, such as code generators, editors, user interfaces, and mock servers. The OpenAPI generator can generate code for C++ using either cpp-restsdk or Qt 5 for client implementation. It can also generate server code using Pistache, Restbed, or Qt 5 QHTTPEngine. There's also a convenient OpenAPI editor available online: `https://editor.swagger.io/`.

An API documented with OpenAPI would look like the following:

```json
{
  "openapi": "3.0.0",
  "info": {
    "title": "Items API overview",
    "version": "2.0.0"
  },
  "paths": {
    "/item/{itemId}": {
      "get": {
        "operationId": "getItem",
        "summary": "get item details",
        "parameters": [
          "name": "itemId",
          "description": "Item ID",
          "required": true,
          "schema": {
            "type": "string"
          }
        ],
        "responses": {
          "200": {
            "description": "200 response",
            "content": {
              "application/json": {
                "example": {
                  "itemId": 8,
                  "name", "Kürtőskalács",
                  "locationId": 5
                }
              }
            }
          }
        }
      }
    }
  }
}
```

The first two fields (`openapi` and `info`) are metadata describing the document. The `paths` field contains all of the possible paths that correspond to the resources and methods of the REST interface. In the preceding example, we are only documenting a single path (`/item`) and a single method (`GET`). This method takes `itemId` as a required parameter. We provide a single possible response code, which is `200`. A 200 response contains a body that is a JSON document itself. The value associated with the `example` key is the example payload of a successful response.

RAML

A competing specification, **RAML**, stands for **RESTful API Modeling Language**. It uses YAML for description and enables discovery, code reuse, and pattern-sharing.

The rationale behind establishing RAML was that while OpenAPI is a great tool to document existing APIs, it was not, at the time, the best way to design new APIs. Currently, the specification is being considered to become a part of the OpenAPI Initiative.

A RAML document may be converted to OpenAPI to make use of the available tooling.

Here's an example of an API documented with RAML:

```
#%RAML 1.0

title: Items API overview
version: 2.0.0

annotationTypes:
  oas-summary:
    type: string
    allowedTargets: Method

/item:
  get:
    displayName: getItem
    queryParameters:
      itemId:
        type: string
    responses:
      '200':
        body:
          application/json:
            example: |
              {
                "itemId": 8,
                "name", "Kürtőskalács",
                "locationId": 5
              }
        description: 200 response
      (oas-summary): get item details
```

This example describes the same interface documented previously with OpenAPI. When serialized in YAML, both OpenAPI 3.0 and RAML 2.0 look very similar. The main difference is that OpenAPI 3.0 requires the use of JSON schema for documenting structures. With RAML 2.0, you can reuse the existing **XML Schema Definition (XSD)**, which makes it easier to migrate from XML-based web services or to include external resources.

API Blueprint

API Blueprint presents a different approach to the preceding two specifications. Instead of relying on either JSON or YAML, it uses Markdown to document data structures and endpoints.

Its approach is similar to the test-driven development methodology, as it encourages designing contracts before implementing features. This way, it is easier to test whether the implementation actually fulfills the contract.

Just like with RAML, it is possible to convert the API Blueprint specification to OpenAPI as well as the other way round. There is also a command-line interface and a C++ library for parsing API Blueprints, called Drafter, which you can use in your code.

An example of a simple API documented with API Blueprint looks like the following:

```
FORMAT: 1A

# Items API overview

# /item/{itemId}

## GET

+ Response 200 (application/json)

        {
            "itemId": 8,
            "name": "Kürtőskalács",
            "locationId": 5
        }
```

In the preceding, we see that a `GET` method directed at the `/item` endpoint should result in a response code of `200`. Below that is the JSON message that corresponds to the one our service will typically return.

API Blueprint allows for more natural documentation. The main disadvantage is that it is the least popular of the formats described so far. This means both the documentation and tooling are nowhere near the quality of OpenAPI.

RSDL

Similar to WSDL, **RSDL** (or **RESTful Service Description Language**), is an XML description for web services. It is language-independent and designed to be both human- and machine-readable.

It's much less popular than the previously presented alternatives. It is also much harder to read, especially compared to API Blueprint or RAML.

Hypermedia as the Engine of Application State

Although providing a binary interface such as a *gRPC-based* one can give you great performance, in many cases, you'll still want to have the simplicity of a RESTful interface. **Hypermedia as the Engine of Application State (HATEOAS)** can be a useful principle to implement if you want an intuitive REST-based API.

Just as you would open a web page and navigate based on the hypermedia shown, you can write your services with HATEOAS to achieve the same thing. This promotes the decoupling of server and client code and allows a client to quickly know what requests are valid to send, which is often not the case with binary APIs. The discovery is dynamic and based on the hypermedia provided.

If you take a typical RESTful service, when executing an operation, you get JSON with data such as an object's state. With HATEOAS, aside from that, you would get a list of links (URLs) showing you the valid operations you can run on said object. The links (hypermedia) are the engine of the application. In other words, the available actions are determined by the state of the resources. While the term hypermedia may sound strange in this context, it basically means linking to the resources, including text, images, and video.

For example, if we have a REST method allowing us to add an item by using the PUT method, we could add a return parameter that links to the resource created that way. If we use JSON for serialization, this could take the following form:

```
{
    "itemId": 8,
    "name": "Kürtőskalács",
    "locationId": 5,
    "links": [
        {
            "href": "item/8",
            "rel": "items",
            "type" : "GET"
        }
    ]
}
```

There is no universally accepted method of serializing HATEOAS hypermedia. On the one hand, it makes it easier to implement regardless of the server implementation. On the other hand, the client needs to know how to parse the response to find the relevant traversal data.

One of the benefits of HATEOAS is that it makes it possible to implement the API changes on the server side without necessarily breaking the client code. When one of the endpoints gets renamed, the new endpoint is referenced in subsequent responses, so the client is informed where to direct further requests.

The same mechanism may provide features such as paging or make it easy to discover methods available for a given object. Getting back to our item example, here's a possible response we could receive after making a GET request:

```
{
    "itemId": 8,
    "name": "Kürtőskalács",
    "locationId": 5,
    "stock": 8,
    "links": [
        {
            "href": "item/8",
            "rel": "items",
            "type" : "GET"
        },
        {
            "href": "item/8",
            "rel": "items",
            "type" : "POST"
        },
        {
            "href": "item/8/increaseStock",
            "rel": "increaseStock",
            "type" : "POST"
        },
        {
            "href": "item/8/decreaseStock",
            "rel": "decreaseStock",
            "type" : "POST"
        }
    ]
}
```

Here, we got links to two methods responsible for modifying the stock. If the stock is no longer available, our response will look like this (note that one of the methods is no longer advertised):

```
{
    "itemId": 8,
    "name": "Kürtőskalács",
    "locationId": 5,
    "stock": 0,
    "links": [
        {
            "href": "items/8",
            "rel": "items",
            "type" : "GET"
        },
        {
            "href": "items/8",
            "rel": "items",
            "type" : "POST"
        },
        {
            "href": "items/8/increaseStock",
            "rel": "increaseStock",
            "type" : "POST"
        }
    ]
}
```

One of the significant problems related to HATEOAS is that the two design principles seem to be at odds with each other. Adding traversable hypermedia would be much easier to consume if it were always presented in the same format. The freedom of expression here makes it harder to write clients unaware of the server's implementation.

Not all RESTful APIs can benefit from introducing this principle – by introducing HATEOAS you commit to writing clients in a specific manner so that they're able to benefit from this API style.

REST in C++

Microsoft's C++ REST SDK is currently one of the best ways to implement RESTful APIs in C++ applications. Also known as cpp-restsdk, it is the library that we're using in this book to illustrate various examples.

GraphQL

A recent alternative to REST web services is GraphQL. The **QL** in the name stands for **Query Language**. Rather than relying on the server to serialize and present the necessary data, in GraphQL clients query and manipulate the data directly. Apart from the reversal of responsibility, GraphQL also features mechanisms that make it easier to work with data. Typing, static validation, introspection, and schemas are all parts of the specification.

There are server implementations of GraphQL available for a lot of languages including C++. One of the popular implementations is cppgraphqlgen from Microsoft. There are also many tools that help with development and debugging. What's interesting is that you can use GraphQL to query the database directly thanks to products such as Hasura or PostGraphile, which add the GraphQL API on top of a Postgres database.

Leveraging managed services and cloud providers

Service-Oriented Architecture may be extended to the current cloud computing trend. While Enterprise Service Bus features services usually developed in-house, with cloud computing it is possible to use the services provided by one or more cloud providers.

While designing an application architecture for cloud computing, you should always consider the managed services offered by the provider before implementing any alternatives. For example, before you decide that you want to host your own PostgreSQL database with selected plugins, make sure you understand the trade-offs and costs when compared to a managed database hosting offered by your provider.

The current cloud landscape provides a lot of services designed to handle popular use cases such as the following:

- Storage
- Relational databases
- Document (NoSQL) databases
- In-memory cache
- Email
- Message queues
- Container orchestration
- Computer vision

- Natural language processing
- Text-to-speech and speech-to-text
- Monitoring, logging, and tracing
- Big data
- Content delivery networks
- Data analytics
- Task management and scheduling
- Identity management
- Key and secret management

Due to the huge choice of available third-party services, it is clear how cloud computing fits within Service-Oriented Architecture.

Cloud computing as an extension of SOA

Cloud computing is an extension of virtual machine hosting. What differentiates cloud computing providers from traditional VPS providers is two things:

- Cloud computing is available via an API, which makes it a service in itself.
- Besides virtual machine instances, cloud computing offers additional services such as storage, managed databases, programmable networking, and many others. All of them are also available via an API.

There are several ways you can use the cloud provider's API to feature in your application, which we will now present.

Using API calls directly

If your cloud provider offers an API accessible in your language of choice, you can interact with the cloud resources directly from your application.

Example: you have an application that allows users to upload their own pictures. This application uses the Cloud API to create a storage bucket for each newly registered user:

```
#include <aws/core/Aws.h>
#include <aws/s3/S3Client.h>
#include <aws/s3/model/CreateBucketRequest.h>

#include <spdlog/spdlog.h>
```

```
const Aws::S3::Model::BucketLocationConstraint region =
    Aws::S3::Model::BucketLocationConstraint::eu_central_1;

bool create_user_bucket(const std::string &username) {
  Aws::S3::Model::CreateBucketRequest request;

  Aws::String bucket_name("userbucket_" + username);
  request.SetBucket(bucket_name);

  Aws::S3::Model::CreateBucketConfiguration bucket_config;
  bucket_config.SetLocationConstraint(region);
  request.SetCreateBucketConfiguration(bucket_config);

  Aws::S3::S3Client s3_client;
  auto outcome = s3_client.CreateBucket(request);

  if (!outcome.IsSuccess()) {
    auto err = outcome.GetError();
    spdlog::error("ERROR: CreateBucket: {}: {}",
                  err.GetExceptionName(),
                  err.GetMessage());
    return false;
  }

  return true;
}
```

In this example, we have a C++ function that creates an AWS S3 bucket named after the username provided in the parameter. This bucket is configured to reside in a given region. If the operation fails, we want to get the error message and log it using `spdlog`.

Using API calls through a CLI tool

Some operations don't have to be performed during the runtime of your application. They are typically run during the deployment and therefore may be automated in shell scripts, for example. One such use case is invoking a CLI tool to create a new VPC:

```
gcloud compute networks create database --description "A VPC to access the
database from private instances"
```

We use the gcloud CLI tool from Google Cloud Platform to create a network called `database` that will be used to handle traffic from the private instances to the database.

Using third-party tools that interact with the Cloud API

Let's look at an example of running HashiCorp Packer to build a virtual machine instance image that is preconfigured with your application:

```
{
    variables : {
      do_api_token : {{env `DIGITALOCEAN_ACCESS_TOKEN`}} ,
      region : fra1 ,
      packages : "customer"
      version : 1.0.3
    },
    builders : [
      {
        type : digitalocean ,
        api_token : {{user `do_api_token`}} ,
        image : ubuntu-20-04-x64 ,
        region : {{user `region`}} ,
        size : 512mb ,
        ssh_username : root
      }
    ],
    provisioners: [
      {
        type : file ,
        source : ./{{user `package`}}-{{user `version`}}.deb ,
        destination : /home/ubuntu/
      },
      {
        type : shell ,
        inline :[
          dpkg -i /home/ubuntu/{{user `package`}}-{{user `version`}}.deb
        ]
      }
    ]
}
```

In the preceding code, we provide the required credentials and region and employ a builder to prepare an instance from the Ubuntu image for us. The instance we are interested in needs to have 512 MB RAM. Then, we provide the instance first by sending a .deb package to it, and then by executing a shell command to install this package.

Accessing the cloud API

Accessing cloud computing resources via an API is one of the most important features that distinguish it from traditional hosting. Using an API means you are able to create and delete instances at will without the intervention of an operator. This way, it becomes very easy to implement features such as load-based autoscaling, advanced deployments (Canary releases or Blue-Green), and automated development and testing environments for an application.

Cloud providers usually expose their APIs as RESTful services. On top of that, they often also provide client libraries for several programming languages. While all of the three most popular providers support C++ as a client library, the support from smaller vendors may vary.

If you're thinking about deploying your C++ application to the cloud and plan on using the Cloud API, make sure your provider has released a C++ **Software Development Kit (SDK)**. It is still possible to use the Cloud API without an official SDK, for example, using the CPP REST SDK library, but keep in mind this would require a lot more work to implement.

To access the **Cloud SDK**, you will also need access control. Typically, there are two ways your application can be authenticated to use the Cloud API:

- **By providing an API token**

  The API token should be secret and never stored as part of the version control system or inside a compiled binary. To prevent theft, it should also be encrypted at rest.

  One of the ways to pass the API token securely to the application is by means of a security framework such as HashiCorp Vault. It is programmable secret storage with built-in lease time management and key rotation.

- **By being hosted on an instance with appropriate access rights**

  Many cloud providers allow giving access rights to particular virtual machine instances. This way, an application hosted on such an instance doesn't have to authenticate using a separate token. Access control is then based on the instance the cloud API request originates from.

  This approach is easier to implement since it doesn't have to factor in the need for secret management. The downside is that when the instance becomes compromised, the access rights will be available to all of the applications running there, not just the application you've deployed.

Using the cloud CLI

The Cloud CLI is typically used by human operators to interact with the Cloud API. Alternatively, it may be used for scripting or using the Cloud API with languages that are officially unsupported.

As an example, the following Bourne Shell script creates a resource group in the Microsoft Azure cloud and then creates a virtual machine belonging to that resource group:

```
#!/bin/sh
RESOURCE_GROUP=dominicanfair
VM_NAME=dominic
REGION=germanynorth

az group create --name $RESOURCE_GROUP --location $REGION

az vm create --resource-group $RESOURCE_GROUP --name $VM_NAME --image
UbuntuLTS --ssh-key-values dominic_key.pub
```

When looking for documentation on how to manage cloud resources, you will encounter a lot of examples using the Cloud CLI. Even if you wouldn't normally use the CLI, instead preferring a solution such as Terraform, having the Cloud CLI at hand may help you with debugging infrastructure problems.

Using tools that interact with the Cloud API

You have already learned about the dangers of vendor lock-in when using products from cloud providers. Typically, each cloud provider will offer a different API and a different CLI to all the others. There are cases where smaller providers offer abstraction layers that allow accessing their products via an API similar to that of the well-known providers. This approach aims to help with migrating the application from one platform to another.

Such instances are rare, though, and in general, tools used to interact with services from one provider are incompatible with those from another provider. This is a problem not only when you consider migration from one platform to the next. It may also be problematic if you want to host your application on a variety of providers.

For this purpose, there's a new set of tools, collectively known as **Infrastructure as Code (IaC)** tools, that offer an abstraction layer on top of different providers. These tools are not necessarily limited to cloud providers either. They're usually general-purpose and help to automate many different layers of your application's architecture.

In Chapter 9, *Continuous Integration and Continuous Deployment*, we briefly covered some of them.

Cloud-native architecture

New tools allow architects and developers to abstract the infrastructure even more and build, first and foremost, with the cloud in mind. Popular solutions such as Kubernetes and OpenShift are driving this trend, but the landscape consists of a lot of smaller players as well. The last chapter of this book is dedicated to cloud-native design and describes this modern approach to building applications.

Summary

In this chapter, we have learned about different approaches to implementing Service-Oriented Architecture. Since a service may interact with its environment in different ways, there are many architectural patterns to choose from. We've learned about the benefits and disadvantages of the most popular ones.

We have focused on the architectural and implementational aspects of some of the widely popular approaches: message queues, web services including REST, and using managed services and cloud platforms. Other approaches that we will dig even deeper into will be presented in the standalone chapters, such as microservices and containers.

In the next chapter, we'll look into microservices.

Questions

1. What are the properties of a service in Service-Oriented Architecture?
2. What are some benefits of web services?
3. When are microservices not a good choice?
4. What are some of the use cases of message queues?
5. What are some of the benefits of choosing JSON over XML?
6. How does REST build on web standards?
7. How do cloud platforms differ from traditional hosting?

Further reading

- *SOA Made Simple*: `https://www.packtpub.com/product/soa-made-simple/9781849684163`
- *SOA Cookbook*: `https://www.packtpub.com/product/soa-cookbook/9781847195487`

13 Designing Microservices

With the increasing popularity of microservices, we would like to dedicate to them an entire chapter of this book. When discussing architecture, you will probably at some point hear, "Should we use microservices for that?" This chapter will show you how to migrate an existing application to a microservices architecture and how to build a new application that leverages microservices.

The following topics will be covered in this chapter:

- Diving into microservices
- Building microservices
- Observing microservices
- Connecting microservices
- Scaling microservices

Technical requirements

Most of the examples presented in this chapter do not require any specific software. For the `redis-cpp` library, check https://github.com/tdv/redis-cpp.

The code present in the chapter has been placed on GitHub at https://github.com/PacktPublishing/Software-Architecture-with-Cpp/tree/master/Chapter13.

Diving into microservices

While microservices are not tied to any particular programming language or technology, a common choice when implementing microservices has been the Go language. That does not mean that other languages are not suitable for microservices development – quite the contrary. The low computational and memory overhead of C++ makes it an ideal candidate for microservices.

But first, we will start with a detailed view of some of the pros and cons of microservices. After that, we'll focus on design patterns that are often associated with microservices (as opposed to the general design patterns covered in Chapter 4, *Architectural and System Design*).

The benefits of microservices

You may often hear about microservices in superlatives. It is true that they can bring some benefits and here are some of them.

Modularity

Since the entire application is split into many relatively small modules, it is easier to understand what each microservice does. The natural consequence of this understanding is that it is also easier to test individual microservices. Testing is also aided by the fact that each microservice typically has a limited scope. After all, it's easier to test just the calendar application than to test the entire **Personal Information Management (PIM)** suite.

This modularity, however, comes at some cost. Your teams may have a much better understanding of individual microservices, but at the same time they may find it harder to grasp how the entire application is composed. While it shouldn't be necessary to learn all the internal details of the microservices that form an application, the sheer number of relationships between components presents a cognitive challenge. It's good practice to use microservices contracts when using this architectural approach.

Scalability

It is easier to scale applications that are limited in scope. One reason for that is that there are fewer potential bottlenecks.

Scaling smaller pieces of a workflow is also more cost-effective. Imagine a monolithic application responsible for managing a trade fair. Once the system starts showing performance issues, the only way to scale is to bring in a bigger machine for the monolith to run on. This is called vertical scaling.

With microservices, the first advantage is that you can scale horizontally, that is, bring in more machines instead of a bigger machine (which is usually cheaper). The second advantage comes from the fact that you only need to scale those parts of the application that are having performance issues. This also contributes to money saved on infrastructure.

Flexibility

Microservices, when properly designed, are less susceptible to vendor lock-in. When you decide you want to switch one of the third-party components, you don't have to do the entire painful migration all at once. Microservices design takes into account that you need to use interfaces, so the only part that requires modification is the interface between your microservice and the third-party component.

The components may also migrate one by one, some still using the software from the old provider. This means you can separate the risk of introducing breaking changes in many places at once. What's more, you can combine this with the canary deployments pattern to manage risk with even more granularity.

This flexibility is not related just to single services. It may also mean different databases, different queueing and messaging solutions, or even entirely different cloud platforms. While different cloud platforms typically offer different services and APIs to use them, with a microservices architecture, you can start migrating your workload piece by piece and test it independently on a new platform.

When rewrites are necessary due to performance issues, scalability, or available dependencies, it is much faster to rewrite a microservice than a monolith.

Integration with legacy systems

Microservices are not necessarily an all-or-nothing approach. If your application is well-tested and migration to microservices may create a lot of risks, there's no pressure to dismantle the working solution altogether. It is even better to split only the parts that require further development and introduce them as microservices that the original monolith will use.

By following this approach, you will gain the benefits of the agile release cycle associated with microservices, while at the same time avoiding creating a new architecture from scratch and basically rebuilding an entire application. If something is already working well, it's better to focus on how to add new features without breaking the good parts, rather than starting from scratch. Be careful here, as starting from scratch is often used as an ego boost!

Distributed development

The times of development teams being small and colocated are long gone. Remote work and distributed development are a fact even in traditional office-based companies. Giants such as IBM, Microsoft, and Intel have people from different locations working together on a single project.

Microservices allow for smaller and more agile teams, which makes distributed development much easier. When it's no longer necessary to facilitate communication between a group of 20 or more people, it's also easier to build self-organized teams that require less external management.

Disadvantages of microservices

Even if you think you may need microservices due to their benefits, keep in mind that they also have some serious drawbacks. In short, they are definitely not for everyone. Larger companies can generally offset these drawbacks, but smaller companies often don't have this luxury.

Reliance on a mature DevOps approach

Building and testing microservices should be much faster than performing similar operations on big, monolithic applications. But in order to achieve agile development, this building and testing would need to be performed much more often.

While it may be sensible to deploy the application manually when you are dealing with a monolith, the same approach will lead to a lot of problems if applied to microservices.

In order to embrace the microservices in your development, you have to ensure that your team has a DevOps mindset and understands the requirements of both building and running the microservice. It's not enough to simply hand the code to someone else and forget about it.

The DevOps mindset will help your team to automate as much as possible. Developing microservices without a continuous integration/continuous delivery pipeline is probably one of the worst possible ideas in software architecture. Such an approach will bring all the other disadvantages of microservices without enabling most of the benefits.

Harder to debug

Microservices require introducing observability. Without it, when something breaks, you're never sure where to start looking for the potential root cause. Observability is a way to deduce the state of your application without the need to run a debugger or log to the machines your workload is running on.

A combination of log aggregation, application metrics, monitoring, and distributed tracing is a prerequisite to manage microservices-based architecture. This is especially true once you consider that autoscaling and self-healing may even prevent you from accessing individual services if they start crashing.

Additional overhead

Microservices should be lean and agile. And that's usually true. However, microservices-based architecture usually requires additional overhead. The first layer of overhead is related to the additional interfaces used for microservices communication. RPC libraries and API providers and consumers have to be multiplied not only by the number of microservices but also by the number of their replicas. Then there are auxiliary services, such as databases, message queues, and so on. Those services also include observability facilities that usually consist of both storage facilities and individual collectors that gather data.

The costs that you optimize with better scaling may be outweighed by the costs required to run the entire fleet of services that don't bring immediate business value. What's more, it may be hard for you to justify these costs (both in terms of infrastructure and development overhead) to the stakeholders.

Design patterns for microservices

A lot of general design patterns apply to microservices as well. There are also some design patterns that are typically associated with microservices. The patterns presented here are useful for both greenfield projects as well as migration from monolithic applications.

Decomposition patterns

These patterns relate to the ways in which microservices are decomposed. We want to ensure the architecture is stable and the services are loosely coupled. We also want to make sure that services are cohesive and testable. Finally, we want autonomous teams to fully own one or more services.

Decomposition by business capability

One of the decomposition patterns requires decomposition by business capability. Business capability relates to what a business does in order to produce value. Examples of business capabilities are merchant management and customer management. Business capabilities are often organized in a hierarchy.

The main challenge when applying this pattern is to correctly identify the business capabilities. This requires an understanding of the business itself and may benefit from cooperation with a business analyst.

Decomposition by subdomain

A different decomposition pattern is related to the **Domain-Driven Design (DDD)** approach. To define services, it is necessary to identify DDD subdomains. Just like business capability, identifying subdomains requires knowledge of the business context.

The main difference between the two approaches is that with decomposing by business capability, the focus is more on the organization of the business (its structure), whereas with decomposing by subdomain, the focus is on the problems that the business tries to solve.

Database per service pattern

Storing and handling data is a complex issue in every software architecture. Wrong choices may impact scalability, performance, or maintenance costs. With microservices, there's an added complexity coming from the fact that we want the microservices to be loosely coupled.

This leads to a design pattern where each microservice connects to its own database so it is independent of any changes introduced by the other services. While this pattern adds some overhead, its additional benefit is that you can optimize the schema and indexes for each microservice individually.

Since databases tend to be pretty huge pieces of infrastructure, this approach may not be feasible, so sharing a database between microservices is an understandable trade-off.

Deployment strategies

With microservices running on multiple hosts, you will probably wonder which is the better way to allocate resources. Let's compare the two possible approaches.

Single service per host

Using this pattern, we allow each host to only serve a particular type of microservice. The main benefit is that you can tweak the machine to better fit the desired workload and services are well isolated. When you provide extra-large memory or fast storage, you'll be sure that it is used only for the microservice that needs it. The service is also unable to consume more resources than provisioned.

The downside of this approach is that some of the hosts may be under-utilized. One possible workaround is to use the smallest possible machines that still satisfy the microservice requirements and scale them when necessary. This workaround, however, does not solve the issue of additional overhead on the host itself.

Multiple services per host

An opposite approach is hosting multiple services per host. This helps to optimize the utilization of the machines but it also comes with some drawbacks. First of all, different microservices may require different optimizations, so hosting them on a single host will still be impossible. What's more, with this approach, you lose control of the host allocation, so the problems in one microservice may cause outages in a colocated microservice even if the latter would be otherwise unaffected.

Another problem is the dependency conflict between the microservices. When the microservices are not isolated from one another, the deployment has to take into account different possible dependencies. This model is also less secure.

Observability patterns

In the previous section, we mentioned that microservices come at a price. This price includes the requirement to introduce observability or risk losing the ability to debug your applications. Here are some patterns related to observability.

Log aggregation

Microservices use logging just like monolithic applications. Instead of storing the logs locally, the logs are aggregated and forwarded to a central facility. This way, the logs are available even if the service itself is down. Storing logs in a centralized manner also helps correlate data coming from different microservices.

Application metrics

To make decisions based on data, you first need some data to act on. Collecting application metrics helps to understand the application behavior as used by the actual users, and not in synthetic tests. The approaches to collect those metrics are push (where an application actively calls the performance monitoring service) and pull (where the performance monitoring service regularly checks the configured endpoints).

Distributed tracing

Distributed tracing helps not only to investigate performance issues but also to gain better insight into the application behavior under real-world traffic. Unlike logging, which collects pieces of information from a single point, tracing is concerned with the entire life cycle of a single transaction, starting at the point where it originates from a user action.

Health check APIs

Since microservices are often targets of automation, they need to have the ability to communicate their internal state. Even if the process is present in the system, it doesn't mean the application is operational. The same goes for an open network port; the application may be listening, but it is not yet able to respond. Health check APIs provide a way for external services to determine whether the application is ready to process the workload. Self-healing and autoscaling use health checks to determine when an intervention is needed. The base premise is that a given endpoint (such as /health) returns an HTTP code 200 when the application behaves as expected and a different code (or does not return at all) if any problem is found.

Now that all the pros, cons, and patterns are known to you, we'll show you how you can split the monolithic application and turn it into microservices part by part. The presented approaches are not limited to just microservices; they may be useful in other cases as well, including monolithic applications.

Building microservices

There are a lot of opinions concerning monolithic applications. Some architects believe that monoliths are inherently evil because they don't scale well, are tightly coupled, and are hard to maintain. There are others who claim that the performance benefits coming from monoliths counterbalance their shortcomings. It's a fact that tightly coupled components require much less overhead in terms of networking, processing power, and memory than their loosely coupled counterparts.

As each application has unique business requirements and operates in a unique environment when it comes to stakeholders, there is no universal rule regarding which approach is better suited. Even more confusing is the fact that after the initial migration from monoliths to microservices, some companies started consolidating microservices into macroservices. This was because the burden of maintaining thousands of separate software instances proved to be too big to handle.

The choice of one architecture over another should always come from the business requirements and careful analysis of different alternatives. Putting ideology before pragmatism usually results in a lot of waste within an organization. When a team tries to adhere to a given approach at all costs, without considering different solutions or diverse external opinions, that team is no longer fulfilling its obligations to deliver the right tools for the right job.

If you are developing or maintaining a monolith, you may consider improving its scalability. The techniques presented in this section aim to solve this problem while also making your application easier to migrate to microservices if you decide so.

The three primary causes of bottlenecks are as follows:

- Memory
- Storage
- Computing

We will show you how to approach each of them to develop scalable solutions based on microservices.

Outsourcing memory management

One of the ways to help microservices scale is to outsource some of their tasks. One such task that may hinder scaling efforts is memory management and caching data.

For a single monolithic application, storing cached data directly in the process memory is not a problem as the process will be the only one accessing the cache anyway. But with several replicas of a process, this approach starts to show some problems.

What if one replica has already computed a piece of a workload and stored it in a local cache? The other replica is unaware of this fact and has to compute it again. This way, your application wastes both computational time (as the same task has to be performed multiple times) and memory (as the results are also stored with each replica separately).

To mitigate such challenges, consider switching to an external in-memory store rather than managing the cache internally within an application. Another benefit of using an external solution is that the life cycle of your cache is no longer tied to the life cycle of your application. You can restart and deploy new versions of your application and the values already stored in the cache are preserved.

This may also result in shorter startup times as your application no longer needs to perform the computing during startup. Two popular solutions for in-memory cache are Memcached and Redis.

Memcached

Memcached, released in 2003, is the older product of the two. It's a general-purpose, distributed key-value store. The original goal of the project was to offload databases used in web applications by storing the cached values in memory. Memcached is distributed by design. Since version 1.5.18, it is possible to restart the Memcached server without losing the contents of the cache. This is possible through the use of RAM disk as a temporary storage space.

It uses a simple API that can be operated via telnet or netcat or using bindings for many popular programming languages. There aren't any bindings specifically for C++, but it's possible to use the C/C++ `libmemcached` library.

Redis

Redis is a newer project than Memcached with the initial version released in 2009. Since then, Redis has replaced the usage of Memcached in many cases. Just like Memcached, it is a distributed, general-purpose, in-memory key-value store.

Unlike Memcached, Redis also features optional data durability. While Memcached operates on keys and values being simple strings, Redis also supports other data types, such as the following:

- Lists of strings
- Sets of strings
- Sorted sets of strings
- Hash tables where keys and values are strings
- Geospatial data (since Redis 3.2)
- HyperLogLogs

The design of Redis makes it a great choice for caching session data, caching web pages, and implementing leaderboards. Apart from that, it may also be used for message queueing. The popular distributed task queue library for Python, Celery, uses Redis as one of the possible brokers, along with RabbitMQ and Apache SQS.

Microsoft, Amazon, Google, and Alibaba all offer Redis-based managed services as part of their cloud platforms.

There are many implementations of a Redis client in C++. Two interesting ones are the `redis-cpp` library (https://github.com/tdv/redis-cpp) written using C++17 and QRedisClient (https://github.com/uglide/qredisclient) using the Qt toolkit.

The following example of `redis-cpp` usage taken from the official documentation illustrates how to use it to set and get some data in the store:

```
#include <cstdlib>
#include <iostream>

#include <redis-cpp/execute.h>
#include <redis-cpp/stream.h>

int main() {
  try {
    auto stream = rediscpp::make_stream("localhost", "6379");

    auto const key = "my_key";

    auto response = rediscpp::execute(*stream, "set", key,
                                "Some value for 'my_key'", "ex",
                                "60");

    std::cout << "Set key '" << key << "': "
              << response.as<std::string>()
```

```
                         << std::endl;

        response = rediscpp::execute(*stream, "get", key);
        std::cout << "Get key '" << key << "': "
                  << response.as<std::string>()
                  << std::endl;
    } catch (std::exception const &e) {
        std::cerr << "Error: " << e.what() << std::endl;
        return EXIT_FAILURE;
    }
    return EXIT_SUCCESS;
}
```

As you can see, the library handles processing different data types. The example sets the value to a list of strings.

Which in-memory cache is better?

For most applications, Redis would be a better choice nowadays. It has a better user community, a lot of different implementations, and is well-supported. Other than that, it features snapshots, replication, transactions, and the pub/sub model. It is possible to embed Lua scripts with Redis and the support for geospatial data makes it a great choice for geo-enabled web and mobile applications.

However, if your main goal is to cache the results of database queries in web applications, Memcached is a simpler solution with much less overhead. This means it should use the resources better as it doesn't have to store type metadata or perform conversions between different types.

Outsourcing storage

Another possible limitation when introducing and scaling microservices is storage. Traditionally, local block devices have been used for storing objects that don't belong to the database (such as static PDF files, documents, or images). Even nowadays, block storage is still very popular with both local block devices and network filesystems such as NFS or CIFS.

While NFS and CIFS are the domain of **Network-Attached Storage (NAS)**, there are also protocols related to a concept operating on a different level: **Storage Area Network (SAN)**. Some of the popular ones are iSCSI, **Network Block Device (NBD)**, ATA over Ethernet, Fibre Channel Protocol, and Fibre Channel over Ethernet.

A different approach features clustered filesystems designed for distributed computing: GlusterFS, CephFS, or Lustre. All of these, however, operate as block devices exposing the same POSIX file API to the user.

A fresh point of view on storage has been proposed as part of Amazon Web Services. Amazon **Simple Storage Service** (S3) is object storage. An API provides access to objects stored in buckets. This is different from the traditional filesystem as there is no distinction between files, directories, or inodes. There are buckets and keys that point to objects and objects are binary data stored by the service.

Outsourcing computing

One of the principles of microservices is that a process should only be responsible for doing a single piece of the workflow. A natural step while migrating from monoliths to microservices would be to define possible long-running tasks and split them into individual processes.

This is the concept behind task queues. Task queues handle the entire life cycle of managing tasks. Instead of implementing threading or multiprocessing on your own, with task queues, you delegate the task to be performed, which is then asynchronously handled by the task queue. The task may be performed on the same machine as the originating process but it may also run on a machine with dedicated requirements.

The tasks and their results are asynchronous, so there is no blocking in the main process. Examples of popular task queues in web development are Celery for Python, Sidekiq for Ruby, Kue for Node.js, and Machinery for Go. All of them can be used with Redis as a broker. Unfortunately, there aren't any similar mature solutions available for C++.

If you are seriously considering taking this route, one possible approach would be to implement a task queue directly in Redis. Redis and its API provide the necessary primitives to support such a behavior. Another possible approach is to use one of the existing task queues, such as Celery, and invoke them by directly calling Redis. This, however, is not advised, as it depends on the implementation details of the task queue rather than the documented public API. Yet another approach is to interface the task queue using bindings provided by SWIG or similar methods.

Observing microservices

Each microservice you build needs to follow the general architectural design patterns. The main distinction between microservices and traditional applications is the need for implementing observability for the former.

This section focuses on some approaches to observability. We describe here several open source solutions that you might find useful when designing your system.

Logging

Logging is a topic that should be familiar to you even if you've never designed microservices. Logs (or log files) store the information about the events happening in a system. The system may mean your application, the operating system your application runs on, or the cloud platform you use for deployment. Each of these components may provide logs.

Logs are stored as separate files because they provide a permanent record of all the events taking place. When the system becomes unresponsive, we want to query the logs and figure out the possible root cause of the outage.

This means that logs also provide an audit trail. Because the events are recorded in chronological order, we are able to understand the state of the system by examining the recorded historical state.

To help with debugging, logs are usually human-readable. There are binary formats for logs, but such formats are rather rare when using files to store the logs.

Logging with microservices

This approach to logging itself doesn't differ much from the traditional approach. Rather than using text files to store the logs locally, microservices usually print logs to `stdout`. A unified logging layer is then used to retrieve the logs and process them. To implement logging, you need a logging library that you can configure to suit your needs.

Logging in C++ with spdlog

One of the popular and fast logging libraries for C++ is `spdlog`. It's built using C++11 and can be used either as a header-only library or as a static library (which reduces compile time).

Some interesting features of `spdlog` include the following:

- Formatting
- Multiple sinks:
  - Rotating files
  - Console
  - Syslog
  - Custom (implemented as a single function)
- Multi-threaded and single-threaded versions
- Optional asynchronous mode

One feature that might be missing from `spdlog` is the direct support for Logstash or Fluentd. If you want to use one of these aggregators, it is still possible to configure `spdlog` with file sink output and use Filebeat or Fluent Bit to forward the file contents to the appropriate aggregator.

Unified logging layer

Most of the time, we won't be able to control all of the microservices that we use. Some of them will use one logging library, while others would use a different one. On top of that, the formats will be entirely different and so will their rotation policies. To make things worse, there are still operating system events that we want to correlate with application events. This is where the unified logging layer comes into play.

One of the unified logging layer's purposes is to collect logs from different sources. Such unified logging layer tools provide many integrations and understand different logging formats and transports (such as file, HTTP, and TCP).

The unified logging layer is also capable of filtering the logs. We may want filtering to satisfy compliance, anonymize the personal details of our customers, or protect the implementation details of our services.

To make it easier to query the logs at a later time, the unified logging layer can also perform translation between formats. Even if the different services that you use store the logs in JSON, CSV, and the Apache format, the unified logging layer solution is able to translate them all to JSON to give them structure.

The final task of the unified logging layer is forwarding the logs to their next destination. Depending on the complexity of the system, the next destination may be a storage facility or another filtering, translation, and forwarding facility.

Here are some interesting components that let you build the unified logging layer.

Logstash

Logstash is one of the most popular unified logging layer solutions. Currently, it is owned by Elastic, the company behind Elasticsearch. If you've heard of the ELK stack (now known as the Elastic Stack), Logstash is the "L" in the acronym.

Logstash was written in Ruby and then has been ported to JRuby. This unfortunately means that it is rather resource-intensive. For this reason, it is not advisable to run Logstash on each machine. Rather, it is meant to be used mainly as a log forwarder with lightweight Filebeat deployed to each machine and performing just the collection.

Filebeat

Filebeat is part of the Beats family of products. Their aim is to provide a lightweight alternative to Logstash that may be used directly with the application.

This way, Beats provide low overhead that scales well, whereas a centralized Logstash installation performs all the heavy lifting, including translation, filtering, and forwarding.

Apart from Filebeat, the other products from the Beats family are as follows:

- Metricbeat for performance
- Packetbeat for network data
- Auditbeat for audit data
- Heartbeat for uptime monitoring

Fluentd

Fluentd is the main competitor of Logstash. It is also the tool of choice of some cloud providers.

Thanks to its modular approach with the use of plugins, you can find plugins for data sources (such as Ruby applications, Docker containers, SNMP, or MQTT protocols), data outputs (such as Elastic Stack, SQL Database, Sentry, Datadog, or Slack), and several other kinds of filters and middleware.

Fluentd should be lighter on resources than Logstash, but it is still not a perfect solution for running at scale. The counterpart to Filebeat that works with Fluentd is called Fluent Bit.

Fluent Bit

Fluent Bit is written in C and provides a faster and lighter solution that plugs into Fluentd. As a log processor and forwarder, it also features many integrations for inputs and outputs.

Besides log collection, Fluent Bit can also monitor CPU and memory metrics on Linux systems. It might be used together with Fluentd or it can forward directly to Elasticsearch or InfluxDB.

Vector

While Logstash and Fluentd are stable, mature, and tried solutions, there are also newer propositions in the unified logging layer space.

One of them is Vector, which aims to handle all of the observability data in a single tool. To differentiate from the competition, it focuses on performance and correctness. This is also reflected in the choice of technology. Vector uses Rust for the engine and Lua for scripting (as opposed to the custom domain-specific languages used by Logstash and Fluentd).

At the moment of writing, it hasn't yet reached a stable 1.0 version, so at this point, it shouldn't be considered production-ready.

Log aggregation

Log aggregation solves another problem that arises from too much data: how to store and access the logs. While the unified logging layer makes logs available even in the event of machine outage, it is the task of log aggregation to help us quickly find the information that we are looking for.

The two possible products that allow storing, indexing, and querying huge amounts of data are Elasticsearch and Loki.

Elasticsearch

Elasticsearch is the most popular solution for self-hosted log aggregation. This is the "E" in the (former) ELK Stack. It features a great search engine based on Apache Lucene.

As the de facto standard in its niche, Elasticsearch has a lot of integrations and has great support both from the community and as a commercial service. Some cloud providers offer Elasticsearch as a managed service, which makes it easier to introduce Elasticsearch in your application. Other than that, Elastic, the company that makes Elasticsearch, offers a hosted solution that is not tied to any particular cloud provider.

Loki

Loki aims to address some of the shortcomings found in Elasticsearch. The focus area for Loki is horizontal scalability and high availability. It's built from the ground up as a cloud-native solution.

The design choices for Loki are inspired by both Prometheus and Grafana. This shouldn't be a surprise since it is developed by the team responsible for Grafana.

While Loki should be a stable solution, it is not as popular as Elasticsearch, which means some integrations might be missing and the documentation and community support won't be on the same level as for Elasticsearch. Both Fluentd and Vector have plugins that support Loki for log aggregation.

Log visualization

The last piece of the logging stack we want to consider is log visualization. This helps us to query and analyze the logs. It presents the data in an accessible way so it can be inspected by all the interested parties, such as operators, developers, QA, or business.

Log visualization tools allow us to create dashboards that make it even easier to read the data we are interested in. With that, we are able to explore the events, search for correlations, and find outlying data from a simple user interface.

There are two major products dedicated to log visualization.

Kibana

Kibana is the final element of the ELK Stack. It provides a simpler query language on top of Elasticsearch. Even though you can query and visualize different types of data with Kibana, it is mostly focused on logs.

Like the rest of the ELK Stack, it is currently the de facto standard when it comes to visualizing logs.

Grafana

Grafana is another data visualization tool. Until recently, it was mostly focused on time-series data from performance metrics. However, with the introduction of Loki, it may now also be used for logs.

One of its strengths is that it's built with pluggable backends in mind, so it's easy to switch the storage to fit your needs.

Monitoring

Monitoring is the process of collecting performance-related metrics from the system. When paired with alerting, monitoring helps us understand when our system behaves as expected and when an incident happens.

The three types of metrics that would interest us the most are as follows:

- Availability, which lets us know which of our resources are up and running, and which of them have crashed or became unresponsive.
- Resource utilization gives us insight into how the workload fits into the system.
- Performance, which shows us where and how to improve service quality.

The two models of monitoring are push and pull. In the former, each monitored object (a machine, an application, and a network device) pushes data to the central point periodically. In the latter, the objects present the data at the configured endpoints and the monitoring agent scrapes the data regularly.

The pull model makes it easier to scale. This way, multiple objects won't be clogging the monitoring agent connection. Instead, multiple agents may collect the data whenever ready, thus better utilizing the available resources.

Two monitoring solutions that feature C++ client libraries are Prometheus and InfluxDB. Prometheus is an example of a pull-based model and it focuses on collecting and storing time-series data. InfluxDB by default uses a push model. Besides monitoring, it is also popular for the Internet of Things, sensor networks, and home automation.

Both Prometheus and InfluxDB are typically used with Grafana for visualizing data and managing dashboards. Both have alerting built-in, but they can also integrate with the external alerting system through Grafana.

Tracing

Traces provide information that is generally lower-level to that of event logs. Another important distinction is that traces store the ID of every single transaction so it is easy to visualize the entire workflow. This ID is commonly known as the trace ID, transaction ID, or correlation ID.

Unlike event logs, traces are not meant to be human-readable. They are processed by a tracer. When implementing tracing, it is necessary to use a tracing solution that integrates with all the possible elements of the system: frontend applications, backend applications, and databases. This way, tracing helps to pinpoint the exact cause of lagging performance.

OpenTracing

One of the standards in distributed tracing is OpenTracing. This standard was proposed by the authors of Jaeger, one of the open-source tracers.

OpenTracing supports many different tracers apart from Jaeger and it supports many different programming languages. The most important ones include the following:

- Go
- C++
- C#
- Java
- JavaScript
- Objective-C
- PHP
- Python
- Ruby

The most important feature of OpenTracing is that it is vendor-neutral. This means that once we instrument our application, we won't need to modify the entire codebase to switch to a different tracer. This way, it prevents vendor lock-in.

Jaeger

Jaeger is a tracer that can be used with various backends, including Elasticsearch, Cassandra, and Kafka.

It is natively compatible with OpenTracing, which shouldn't be a surprise. Since it is a Cloud Native Computing Foundation-graduated project, it has great community support, which also translates to good integration with other services and frameworks.

OpenZipkin

OpenZipkin is the main competitor for Jaeger. It has been on the market for a longer time. Although this should mean it is a more mature solution, its popularity is fading when compared to Jaeger. Particularly, the C++ in OpenZipkin isn't actively maintained, which may cause future problems with maintenance.

Integrated observability solutions

If you don't want to build the observability layer on your own, there are some popular commercial solutions that you might consider. They all operate in a software-as-a-service model. We won't go into a detailed comparison here, as their offerings may change drastically after the writing of this book.

These services are as follows:

- Datadog
- Splunk
- Honeycomb

In this section, you have seen implementing observability in Microservices. Next, we'll move on to learn how to connect microservices.

Connecting microservices

Microservices are so useful because they can be connected in many different ways with other services, thus creating new value. However, as there is no standard for microservices, there is not a single way to connect to them.

This means that most of the time when we want to use a particular microservice, we have to learn how to interact with it. The good news is that although it is possible to implement any communication method in microservices, there are a few popular approaches that most microservices follow.

How to connect microservices is just one of the relevant questions when designing architecture around them. The other is what to connect with and where. This is where service discovery comes into play. With service discovery, we let the microservices use automated means of discovering and connecting to other services within our application.

These three questions, how, what, and where, will be our next topic. We will introduce some of the most popular methods of communication and discovery used by modern microservices.

Application programming interfaces (APIs)

Just like software libraries, microservices often expose APIs. These APIs make it possible to communicate with the microservices. Since the typical manner of communication utilizes computer networking, the most popular form of an API is the web API.

In the previous chapter, we already covered some possible approaches with web services. Nowadays, microservices typically use web services based on **REpresentational State Transfer (REST)**.

Remote procedure calls

While web APIs such as REST allow easy debugging and great interoperability, there's a lot of overhead related to data translation and using HTTP for transport.

This overhead may be too much for some microservices, which is the reason for lightweight **Remote Procedure Calls (RPCs)**.

Apache Thrift

Apache Thrift is an interface description language and binary communication protocol. It is used as an RPC method that allows creating distributed and scalable services built in a variety of languages.

It supports several binary protocols and transport methods. Native data types are used for each programming language, so it is easy to introduce even in an existing codebase.

gRPC

If you really care about performance, often you'll find that text-based solutions don't work for you. REST, however elegant and easily understandable, may turn out to be too slow for your needs. If that's the case, you should try to build your API around binary protocols. One of them, which is growing in popularity, is gRPC.

gRPC, as its name suggests, is an RPC system that was initially developed by Google. It uses HTTP/2 for transport, and Protocol Buffers as an **Interface Description Language (IDL)** for interoperability between multiple programming languages, and for data serialization. It's possible to use alternative technologies for this, for example, FlatBuffers. gRPC can be used both synchronously and in an asynchronous manner and allows creating both simple services and streaming ones.

Assuming you've decided to use `protobufs`, our Greeter service definition can look like this:

```
service Greeter {
  rpc Greet(GreetRequest) returns (GreetResponse);
}

message GreetRequest {
  string name = 1;
}

message GreetResponse {
  string reply = 1;
}
```

Using the `protoc` compiler, you can create data access code from this definition. Assuming you want to have a synchronous server for our Greeter, you can create the service in the following way:

```
class Greeter : public Greeter::Service {
  Status sendRequest(ServerContext *context, const GreetRequest *request,
                     GreetReply *reply) override {
    auto name = request->name();
    if (name.empty()) return Status::INVALID_ARGUMENT;
    reply->set_result("Hello " + name);
    return Status::OK;
  }
};
```

Then, you have to build and run the server for it:

```
int main() {
  Greeter service;
  ServerBuilder builder;
  builder.AddListeningPort("localhost", grpc::InsecureServerCredentials());
  builder.RegisterService(&service);

  auto server(builder.BuildAndStart());
  server->Wait();
}
```

Simple as that. Let's now take a look at a client to consume this service:

```
#include <grpcpp/grpcpp.h>

#include <string>

#include "grpc/service.grpc.pb.h"

using grpc::ClientContext;
using grpc::Status;

int main() {
  std::string address("localhost:50000");
  auto channel =
      grpc::CreateChannel(address, grpc::InsecureChannelCredentials());
  auto stub = Greeter::NewStub(channel);

  GreetRequest request;
  request.set_name("World");

  GreetResponse reply;
  ClientContext context;
  Status status = stub->Greet(&context, request, &reply);

  if (status.ok()) {
    std::cout << reply.reply() << '\n';
  } else {
    std::cerr << "Error: " << status.error_code() << '\n';
  }
}
```

This was a simple, synchronous example. To make it work asynchronously, you'll need to add tags and `CompletionQueue`, as described on gRPC's website.

One interesting feature of gRPC is that it is available for mobile applications on Android and iOS. This means that if you use gRPC internally, you don't have to provide an additional server to translate the traffic from your mobile applications.

In this section, you learned the most popular methods of communication and discovery utilized by microservices. Next, we'll see how microservices can be scaled.

Scaling microservices

One of the significant benefits of microservices is that they scale more efficiently than monoliths. Given the same hardware infrastructure, you could theoretically be able to get more performance out of microservices than monoliths.

In practice, the benefits are not that straightforward. Microservices and related helpers also provide overhead that for smaller-scale applications may be less performant than an optimal monolith.

Remember that even if something looks good "on paper," it doesn't mean it will fly. If you want to base your architectural decisions on scalability or performance, it is better to prepare calculations and experiments. This way, you'll act based on data, not just emotion.

Scaling a single service per host deployment

For a single service per host deployment, scaling a microservice requires adding or removing additional machines that host the microservice. If your application is running on a cloud architecture (public or private), many providers offer a concept known as autoscaling groups.

Autoscaling groups define a base virtual machine image that will run on all grouped instances. Whenever a critical threshold is reached (for example, 80% CPU use), a new instance is created and added to the group. Since autoscaling groups run behind a load balancer, the increasing traffic then gets split between both the existing and the new instances, thus reducing the mean load on each one. When the spike in traffic subsides, the scaling controller shuts down the excess machines to keep the costs low.

Different metrics can act as triggers for the scaling event. The CPU load is one of the easiest to use, but it may not be the most accurate one. Other metrics, such as the number of messages in a queue, may better fit your application.

Here's an excerpt from a Terraform configuration for a scaler policy:

```
autoscaling_policy {
    max_replicas = 5
    min_replicas = 3
    cooldown_period = 60
    cpu_utilization {
      target = 0.8
    }
}
```

It means that at any given time, there will be at least three instances running and at most five instances. The scaler will trigger once the CPU load hits at least an 80% average for all the group instances. When that happens, a new instance is spun up. The metrics from the new machine will only be collected after it has been running for at least 60 seconds (the cooldown period).

Scaling multiple services per host deployment

This mode of scaling is also suitable for multiple services per host deployment. As you can probably imagine, this isn't the most efficient method. Scaling an entire set of services based only on a reduced throughput of a single one is similar to scaling monoliths.

If you're using this pattern, a better way to scale your microservices is to use an orchestrator. If you don't want to use containers, Nomad is a great choice that works with a lot of different execution drivers. For containerized workloads, either Docker Swarm or Kubernetes will help you. Orchestrators are a topic that we'll come back to in the next two chapters.

Summary

Microservices are a great new trend in software architecture. They could be a good fit provided you make sure you know about the hazards and prepare for them. This chapter explained the common design and migration patterns that help to introduce microservices. We've also covered advanced topics such as observability and connectivity that are crucial when establishing microservices-based architectures.

By now, you should be able to design and decompose applications into individual microservices. Each microservice is then capable of processing a single piece of workload.

While microservices are valid on their own, they're especially popular in combination with containers. Containers are the subject of the next chapter.

Questions

1. Why do microservices help you better use the system resources?
2. How can microservices and monoliths coexist (in an evolving system)?
3. Which types of teams benefit the most from microservices?
4. Why is it necessary to have a mature DevOps approach when introducing microservices?
5. What is a unified logging layer?
6. How do logging and tracing differ?
7. Why may REST not be the best choice for connecting microservices?
8. What are the deployment strategies for microservices? What are the benefits of each of them?

Further reading

- *Mastering Distributed Tracing*: https://www.packtpub.com/product/mastering-distributed-tracing/9781788628464
- *Hands-On Microservices with Kubernetes*: https://www.packtpub.com/product/hands-on-microservices-with-kubernetes/9781789805468
- *Microservices* by Martin Fowler: https://martinfowler.com/articles/microservices.html
- Microservice architecture: https://microservices.io/

14
Containers

Transitioning from development to production has always been a painful process. It involves a lot of documentation, hand-offs, installation, and configuration. Since every programming language produces software that behaves slightly differently, the deployment of heterogenous applications is always difficult.

Some of these problems have been mitigated by containers. With containers, the installation and configuration is mostly standardized. There are several ways for how to deal with distribution, but this issue also has some standards to follow. This makes containers a great choice for organizations that want to increase the cooperation between development and operations.

The following topics will be covered in this chapter:

- Building containers
- Testing and integrating containers
- Understanding container orchestration

Technical requirements

The examples listed in this chapter require the following:

- Docker 20.10
- manifest-tool (`https://github.com/estesp/manifest-tool`)
- Buildah 1.16
- Ansible 2.10
- ansible-bender
- CMake 3.15

The code present in the chapter has been placed on GitHub at `https://github.com/PacktPublishing/Software-Architecture-with-Cpp/tree/master/Chapter14`.

Reintroducing containers

Containers are making a lot of buzz recently. One might think they are a brand new technology that was not available before. However, that is not the case. Before the rise of Docker and Kubernetes, the dominating players in the industry at the moment, there were already solutions such as LXC, which offered a lot of similar features.

We can trace the origins of separating one execution environment from another with the chroot mechanism available in UNIX systems since 1979. Similar concepts were also used in FreeBSD jails and Solaris Zones.

The main task of the container is to isolate one execution environment from another. This isolated environment can have its own configuration, different applications, and even different user accounts than the host environment.

Even though the containers are isolated from the host, they usually share the same operating system kernel. This is the main differentiator from virtualized environments. Virtual machines have dedicated virtual resources, which means they are separated at the hardware level. Containers are separated at the process level, which means there is less overhead to run them.

The ability to package and run another operating system that is already optimized and configured for running your application is a strong advantage of containers. Without containers, the build and deploy process usually consists of several steps:

1. The application is built.
2. The example configuration files are provided.
3. Installation scripts and associated documentation is prepared.
4. The application is packaged for a target operating system (such as Debian or Red Hat).
5. The packages are deployed to the target platform.
6. Installation scripts prepare the basis for the application to run.
7. The configuration has to be tweaked to fit the existing system.

When you switch to containers, there is less of a need for a robust installation script. The application will only target a single well-known operating system – the one present in the container. The same goes for configuration: instead of preparing many configurable options, the application is pre-configured for the target operating system and distributed alongside it. The deployment process consists only of unpacking the container image and running the application process inside it.

While containers and microservices are often thought to be the same thing, they are not. Moreover, containers may mean application containers or operating system containers, and only application containers fit well with microservices. The following sections will tell you why. We'll describe the different container types that you can encounter, show you how they relate to microservices, and explain when it's best to use them (and when to avoid them).

Exploring the container types

Of the containers described so far, operating system containers are fundamentally different from the current container trend led by Docker, Kubernetes, and LXD. Instead of focusing on recreating an entire operating system with services such as syslog and cron, application containers focus on running a single process within a container – just the application.

Proprietary solutions replace all the usual OS-level services. These solutions provide a unified way to manage the applications within a container. For example, instead of using syslog to handle logs, the standard output of the process with PID 1 is considered as application logs. Instead of using a mechanism such as `init.d` or systemd, the application container's lifecycle is handled by the runtime application.

Since Docker is at the moment the dominant solution for application containers, we will mostly use it as an example throughout this book. To make the picture complete, we will present viable alternatives, as they may be better suited to your needs. Since the project and specification are open source, these alternatives are compatible with Docker and can be used as replacements.

Later in this chapter, we will explain how to use Docker to build, deploy, run, and manage application containers.

The rise of microservices

The success of Docker coincided with the rise of the adoption of microservices. It is no surprise since microservices and application containers fit together naturally.

Without application containers, there was no easy and unified way to package, deploy, and maintain microservices. Even though individual companies developed some solutions to fix these problems, none was popular enough to approach being an industry standard.

Without microservices, the application containers were pretty limited. The software architecture focused on building entire systems explicitly configured for the given set of services running there. Replacing one service with another required a change of the architecture.

When brought together, application containers provide a standard way for the distribution of microservices. Each microserver comes with its own configuration embedded, so operations such as autoscaling or self-healing no longer require knowledge about an underlying application.

You can still use microservices without application containers and you can use application containers without hosting microservices in them. For instance, even though neither PostgreSQL databases nor Nginx web servers were designed as microservices, they are typically used in application containers.

Choosing when to use containers

There are several benefits to the container approach. OS containers and application containers also have some different use cases in which their strengths lie.

The benefits of containers

When compared to virtual machines, the other popular way of isolating environments, containers require less overhead during runtime. Unlike virtual machines, there is no need to run a separate version of an operating system kernel and use the hardware or software virtualization techniques. Application containers also do not run other operating system services that are typically found in virtual machines such as syslog, cron, or init. Additionally, application containers offer smaller images as they do not usually have to carry an entire operating system copy. In extreme examples, an application container can consist of a single statically linked binary.

At this point, you may wonder why to bother with containers at all if there is just a single binary inside? There is one particular benefit of having a unified and standardized way to build and run containers. As containers have to follow specific conventions, it is easier to orchestrate them than regular binaries, which can have different expectations regarding logging, configuration, opening ports, and so on.

Another thing is that containers provide a built-in means of isolation. Each container has its own namespace for processes and a namespace for user accounts, among others. This means that the process (or processes) from one container has no notion of the processes on the host or in the other containers. The sandboxing can go even further as you can assign memory and a CPU quota to your containers with the same standard user interface (whether it is Docker, Kubernetes, or something else).

The standardized runtime also means higher portability. Once a container is built, you can typically run it on different operating systems without modifications. This also means what runs in operations is very close or identical to what runs in development. Issue reproduction is more effortless and so is debugging.

The disadvantages of containers

Since there is a lot of pressure nowadays to move workloads to containers, you want to understand all the risks associated with such migration as an architect. The benefits are touted everywhere and you probably already understand them.

The main obstacle to container adoption is that not all applications can be easily migrated to containers. This is especially true of application containers that are designed with microservices in mind. If your application is not based on microservices architecture, putting it into containers may introduce more problems than it will solve.

If your application already scales well, uses TCP/IP-based IPC, and is mostly stateless, the move to containers should not be challenging. Otherwise, each of these aspects would pose a challenge and prompt a rethink of the existing design.

Another problem associated with containers is persistent storage. Ideally, containers should have no persistent storage of their own. This makes it possible to take advantage of fast startups, easy scaling, and flexible scheduling. The problem is that applications providing business value cannot exist without persistent storage.

This drawback is usually mitigated by making most containers stateless and relying on an external non-containerized component to store the data and the state. Such an external component can be either a traditional self-hosted database or a managed database from a cloud provider. Going in either direction requires you to reconsider the architecture and modify it accordingly.

Since application containers follow specific conventions, the application has to be modified to follow these conventions. For some applications, it will be a low-effort task. For others, such as multiprocess components using in-memory **Inter-Process Communication** (**IPC**), it will be complicated.

One point often omitted is that application containers work great as long as the applications inside them are native Linux applications. While Windows containers are supported, they are neither convenient nor as supported as their Linux counterparts. They also require licensed Windows machines running as hosts.

It is easier to enjoy the application containers' benefits if you are building a new application from scratch and can base your design on this technology. Moving an existing application to application containers, especially if it is complicated, will require a lot more work and possibly also a revamp of the entire architecture. In such a case, we advise you to consider all the benefits and disadvantages extra carefully. Making a wrong decision may harm your product's lead time, availability, and budget.

Building containers

Application containers are the focus of this section. While OS containers mostly follow system programming principles, application containers bring new challenges and patterns. Also, they provide specialized build tools to deal with those challenges. The primary tool we will consider is Docker, as it's the current de facto standard for building and running application containers. We will also present some alternative approaches to building application containers.

Unless otherwise noted, whenever we use the word "containers" from now on, it relates to "application containers."

In this section, we will focus on different approaches to using Docker for building and deploying containers.

Container images explained

Before we describe container images and how to build them, it is vital to understand the distinction between containers and container images. There is often confusion between the terms, especially during informal conversations.

The difference between a container and a container image is the same as between a running process and an executable file.

Container images are static: They're snapshots of a particular filesystem and associated metadata. The metadata describes, among other things, what environmental variables are set during runtime or which program to run when the container is created from the image.

Containers are dynamic: They are running a process contained within the container image. We can create containers from the container images and we can also create container images by snapshotting a running container. The container image build process consists, in fact, of creating several containers, executing commands inside them, and snapshotting them after the command finishes.

To distinguish between the data introduced by the container image and the data generated during runtime, Docker uses union mount filesystems to create different filesystem layers. These layers are also present in the container images. Typically, each build step of the container image corresponds to a new layer in the resulting container image.

Using Dockerfiles to build an application

The most common way to build an application container image using Docker is to use a Dockerfile. Dockerfile is an imperative language describing the operations required to produce the resulting image. Some of the operations create new filesystem layers; others operate on metadata.

We will not go into details and specifics related to Dockerfiles. Instead, we will show different approaches to containerizing a C++ application. For this, we need to introduce some syntax and concepts related to Dockerfiles.

Here is an example of a very simple Dockerfile:

```
FROM ubuntu:bionic

RUN apt-get update && apt-get -y install build-essentials gcc

CMD /usr/bin/gcc
```

Typically, we can divide a Dockerfile into three parts:

- Importing the base image (the FROM instruction)
- Performing operations within the container that will result in a container image (the RUN instruction)
- Metadata used during runtime (the CMD command)

The latter two parts may well be interleaved, and each of them may comprise one or more instructions. It is also possible to omit any of the later parts as only the base image is mandatory. This does not mean you cannot start with an empty filesystem. There is a special base image named `scratch` exactly for this purpose. Adding a single statically linked binary to an otherwise empty filesystem could look like the following:

```
FROM scratch

COPY customer /bin/customer

CMD /bin/customer
```

In the first Dockerfile, the steps we take are the following:

1. Import the base Ubuntu Bionic image.
2. Run a command inside the container. The results of the command will create a new filesystem layer inside the target image. This means the packages installed with `apt-get` will be available in all the containers based on this image.
3. Set the runtime metadata. When creating a container based on this image, we want to run `GCC` as the default process.

To build an image from a Dockerfile, you will use the `docker build` command. It takes one required argument, the directory containing the build context, which means the Dockerfile itself and other files you want to copy inside the container. To build a Dockerfile from a current directory, use `docker build`.

This will build an anonymous image, which is not very useful. Most of the time, you want to use named images. There is a convention to follow when naming container images and that's what we'll cover in the next section.

Naming and distributing images

Each container image in Docker has a distinctive name consisting of three elements: the name of the registry, the name of the image, a tag. Container registries are object repositories holding container images. The default container registry for Docker is `docker.io`. When pulling an image from this registry, we may omit the registry name.

Our previous example with `ubuntu:bionic` has the full name of `docker.io/ubuntu:bionic`. In this example, `ubuntu` is the name of the image, while `bionic` is a tag that represents a particular version of an image.

When building an application based on containers, you will be interested in storing all the registry images. It is possible to host your private registry and keep your images there or use a managed solution. Popular managed solutions include the following:

- Docker Hub
- quay.io
- GitHub
- Cloud providers (such as AWS, GCP, or Azure)

Docker Hub is still the most popular one, though some public images are migrating to quay.io. Both are general-purpose and allow the storage of public and private images. GitHub or cloud providers will be mainly attractive to you if you are already using a particular platform and want to keep your images close to the CI pipeline or the deployment targets. It is also helpful if you want to reduce the number of individual services you use.

If none of the solutions appeal to you, hosting your own local registry is also very easy and requires you to run a single container.

To build a named image, you need to pass the `-t` argument to the `docker build` command. For example, to build an image named `dominicanfair/merchant:v2.0.3`, you will use `docker build -t dominicanfair/merchant:v2.0.3 ..`.

Compiled applications and containers

When building container images for applications in interpreted languages (such as Python or JavaScript), the approach is mostly the same:

1. Install dependencies.
2. Copy source files to the container image.
3. Copy the necessary configuration.
4. Set the runtime command.

For compiled applications, however, there's an additional step of compiling the application first. There are several possible ways to implement this step, each of them with their pros and cons.

The most obvious approach is to install all the dependencies first, copy the source files, and then compile the application as one of the container build steps. The major benefit is that we can accurately control the toolchain's contents and configuration and therefore have a portable way to build an application. However, the downside is too big to ignore: the resulting container image contains a lot of unnecessary files. After all, we will need neither source code nor the toolchain during runtime. Due to the way overlay filesystems work, it is impossible to remove the files after being introduced in a previous layer. What is more, the source code in the container may prove to be a security risk if an attacker manages to break into the container.

Here's how it can look:

```
FROM ubuntu:bionic

RUN apt-get update && apt-get -y install build-essentials gcc cmake

ADD . /usr/src

WORKDIR /usr/src

RUN mkdir build && \
    cd build && \
    cmake .. -DCMAKE_BUILD_TYPE=Release && \
    cmake --build . && \
    cmake --install .

CMD /usr/local/bin/customer
```

Another obvious approach, and the one we discussed earlier, is building the application on the host machine and only copying the resulting binaries inside the container image. This requires fewer changes to the current build process when one is already established. The main drawback is that you have to match the same set of libraries on your build machines as you do in your containers. If you're running, for example, Ubuntu 20.04 as your host operating system, your containers will have to be based on Ubuntu 20.04 as well. Otherwise, you risk incompatibilities. With this approach, it is also necessary to configure the toolchain independently of the container.

Just like this:

```
FROM scratch

COPY customer /bin/customer

CMD /bin/customer
```

A slightly more complicated approach is to have a multi-stage build. With multi-stage builds, one stage may be dedicated to setting up the toolchain and compiling the project, while another stage copies the resulting binaries to their target container image. This has several benefits over the previous solutions. First of all, the Dockerfiles now control both the toolchain and the runtime environment, so every step of the build is thoroughly documented. Second of all, it is possible to use the image with the toolchain to ensure compatibility between development and the **Continuous Integration/Continuous Deployment (CI/CD)** pipeline. This way also makes it easier to distribute upgrades and fixes to the toolchain itself. The major downside is that the containerized toolchain may not be as comfortable to use as a native one. Also, build tools are not particularly well-suited to application containers, which require that there's one process running per container. This may lead to unexpected behavior whenever some of the processes crash or are forcefully stopped.

A multi-stage version of the preceding example would look like this:

```
FROM ubuntu:bionic AS builder

RUN apt-get update && apt-get -y install build-essentials gcc cmake

ADD . /usr/src

WORKDIR /usr/src

RUN mkdir build && \
    cd build && \
    cmake .. -DCMAKE_BUILD_TYPE=Release && \
    cmake --build .

FROM ubuntu:bionic

COPY --from=builder /usr/src/build/bin/customer /bin/customer

CMD /bin/customer
```

The first stage, starting at the first FROM command sets up the builder, adds the sources, and builds the binaries. Then, the second stage, starting at the second FROM command, copies the resulting binary from the previous stage without copying the toolchain or the sources.

Targeting multiple architectures with manifests

Application containers with Docker are typically used on x86_64 (also known as AMD64) machines. If you are only targeting this platform, you have nothing to worry about. However, if you are developing IoT, embedded, or edge applications, you may be interested in multi-architecture images.

Since Docker is available on many different CPU architectures, there are several ways to approach image management on multiple platforms.

One way to handle images built for different targets is by using the image tags to describe a particular platform. Instead of `merchant:v2.0.3`, we could have `merchant:v2.0.3-aarch64`. Although this approach may seem to be the easiest to implement, it is, in fact, a bit problematic.

Not only do you have to change the build process to include the architecture in the tagging process. When pulling the images to run them, you will also have to take care to manually append the expected suffix everywhere. If you are using an orchestrator, you won't be able to share the manifests between the different platforms in a straightforward way, as the tags will be platform-specific.

A better way that doesn't require modifying the deployment step is to use `manifest-tool` (`https://github.com/estesp/manifest-tool`). The build process at first looks similar to the one suggested previously. Images are built separately on all the supported architectures and pushed to the registry with a platform suffix in their tags. After all the images are pushed, `manifest-tool` merges the images to provide a single multi-architecture one. This way, each supported platform is able to use the exact same tag.

An example configuration for `manifest-tool` is provided here:

```
image: hosacpp/merchant:v2.0.3
manifests:
  - image: hosacpp/merchant:v2.0.3-amd64
    platform:
      architecture: amd64
      os: linux
  - image: hosacpp/merchant:v2.0.3-arm32
    platform:
      architecture: arm
      os: linux
  - image: hosacpp/merchant:v2.0.3-arm64
    platform:
      architecture: arm64
      os: linux
```

Here, we have three supported platforms, each with their respective suffix
(`hosacpp/merchant:v2.0.3-amd64`, `hosacpp/merchant:v2.0.3-arm32`,
and `hosacpp/merchant:v2.0.3-arm64`). `Manifest-tool` combines the images built for
each platform and produces a `hosacpp/merchant:v2.0.3` image that we can use
everywhere.

Another possibility is to use Docker's built-in feature called Buildx. With Buildx, you can
attach several builder instances, each of which targets a required architecture. What's
interesting is that you don't need to have native machines to run the builds; you can also
use the QEMU emulation or cross-compilation in a multi-stage build. Although it is much
more powerful than the previous approach, Buildx is also quite complicated. At the time of
writing, it requires Docker experimental mode and Linux kernel 4.8 or later. It requires you
to set up and manage builders and not everything behaves in an intuitive way. It's possible
it will improve and become more stable in the near future.

An example code to prepare the build environment and build a multi-platform image may
look like the following:

```
# create two build contexts running on different machines
docker context create \
    --docker host=ssh://docker-user@host1.domifair.org \
    --description="Remote engine amd64" \
    node-amd64
docker context create \
    --docker host=ssh://docker-user@host2.domifair.org \
    --description="Remote engine arm64" \
    node-arm64

# use the contexts
docker buildx create --use --name mybuild node-amd64
docker buildx create --append --name mybuild node-arm64

# build an image
docker buildx build --platform linux/amd64,linux/arm64 .
```

As you can see, this may be a little confusing if you're used to the regular `docker build`
command.

Alternative ways to build application containers

Building container images with Docker requires the Docker daemon to be running. The Docker daemon requires root privileges, which may pose security problems in some setups. Even though the Docker client that does the building may be run by an unprivileged user, it is not always feasible to install the Docker daemon in the build environment.

Buildah

Buildah is an alternative tool to build container images that can be configured to run without root access. Buildah can work with regular Dockerfiles, which we discussed earlier. It also presents its own command-line interface that you can use in shell scripts or other automation you find more intuitive. One of the previous Dockerfiles rewritten as a shell script using the buildah interface will look like this:

```
#!/bin/sh

ctr=$(buildah from ubuntu:bionic)

buildah run $ctr -- /bin/sh -c 'apt-get update && apt-get install -y build-
essential gcc'

buildah config --cmd '/usr/bin/gcc' "$ctr"

buildah commit "$ctr" hosacpp-gcc

buildah rm "$ctr"
```

One interesting feature of Buildah is that it allows you to mount the container image filesystem into your host filesystem. This way, you can use your host's commands to interact with the contents of the image. If you have software you don't want (or can't due to licensing restrictions) put within the container, it's still possible to invoke it outside of the container when using Buildah.

Ansible-bender

Ansible-bender uses Ansible playbooks and Buildah to build container images. All of the configuration, including base images and metadata, is passed as a variable within the playbook. Here is our previous example converted to Ansible syntax:

```
---
- name: Container image with ansible-bender
  hosts: all
```

```
vars:
  ansible_bender:
    base_image: python:3-buster

    target_image:
      name: hosacpp-gcc
      cmd: /usr/bin/gcc
tasks:
- name: Install Apt packages
  apt:
    pkg:
      - build-essential
      - gcc
```

As you see, the `ansible_bender` variable is responsible for all the configuration specific to containers. The tasks presented below are executed inside the container based on `base_image`.

One thing to note is that Ansible requires a Python interpreter present in the base image. This is why we had to change `ubuntu:bionic` used in previous examples to `python:3-buster`. `ubuntu:bionic` is an Ubuntu image without a Python interpreter preinstalled.

Others

There are also other ways to build container images. You can use Nix to create a filesystem image and then put it inside the image using Dockerfile's `COPY` instruction, for example. Going further, you can prepare a filesystem image by any other means and then import it as a base container image using `docker import`.

Choose whichever solution fits your particular needs. Keep in mind that building with a Dockerfile using `docker build` is the most popular approach and hence it is the best-documented one and the best supported. Going with Buildah is more flexible and allows you to better fit creating container images into your build process. Finally, `ansible-bender` may be a good solution if you're already heavily invested in Ansible and you want to reuse already available modules.

Integrating containers with CMake

In this section, we'll demonstrate how to create a Docker image by working with CMake.

Configuring the Dockerfile with CMake

First, and foremost, we'll need a Dockerfile. Let's use yet another CMake input file for this:

```
configure_file(${CMAKE_CURRENT_SOURCE_DIR}/Dockerfile.in
               ${PROJECT_BINARY_DIR}/Dockerfile @ONLY)
```

Note that we're using PROJECT_BINARY_DIR to not overwrite any Dockerfiles created by other projects in the source tree if our project is part of a bigger one.

Our Dockerfile.in file will look as follows:

```
FROM ubuntu:latest
ADD Customer-@PROJECT_VERSION@-Linux.deb .
RUN apt-get update && \
    apt-get -y --no-install-recommends install ./Customer-
@PROJECT_VERSION@-Linux.deb && \
    apt-get autoremove -y && \
    apt-get clean && \
    rm -r /var/lib/apt/lists/* Customer-@PROJECT_VERSION@-Linux.deb
ENTRYPOINT ["/usr/bin/customer"]
EXPOSE 8080
```

First, we specify that we'll take the latest Ubuntu image, install our DEB package on it along with its dependencies, and then tidy up. It's important to update the package manager cache in the same step as installing the package to avoid issues with stale caches due to how layers in Docker work. Cleanup is also performed as part of the same RUN command (in the same layer) so that the layer size is smaller. After installing the package, we make our image run the customer microservice when it is started. Finally, we tell Docker to expose the port that it will be listening on.

Now, back to our CMakeLists.txt file.

Integrating containers with CMake

For CMake-based projects, it is possible to include a build step responsible for building the containers. For that, we need to tell CMake to find the Docker executable and bail out if it doesn't. We can do this using the following:

```
find_program(Docker_EXECUTABLE docker)
 if(NOT Docker_EXECUTABLE)
   message(FATAL_ERROR "Docker not found")
 endif()
```

Let's revisit the example from one of Chapter 7, *Building and Packaging*. There, we built a binary and a Conan package for the customer application. Now, we want to package this application as a Debian archive and build a Debian container image with a pre-installed package for the customer application.

To create our DEB package, we need a helper target. Let's use CMake's add_custom_target functionality for this:

```
add_custom_target(
    customer-deb
    COMMENT "Creating Customer DEB package"
    COMMAND ${CMAKE_CPACK_COMMAND} -G DEB
    WORKING_DIRECTORY ${PROJECT_BINARY_DIR}
    VERBATIM)
 add_dependencies(customer-deb libcustomer)
```

Our target invokes CPack to create just the one package that's interesting for us and omitting the rest. We want the package to be created in the same directory as the Dockerfile for convenience. The VERBATIM keyword is recommended as, with it, CMake will escape problematic characters. If it's not specified, the behavior of your scripts may vary across different platforms.

The add_dependencies call will make sure that before CMake builds the customer-deb target, libcustomer is already built. As we now have our helper target, let's use it when creating the container image:

```
add_custom_target(
    docker
    COMMENT "Preparing Docker image"
    COMMAND ${Docker_EXECUTABLE} build ${PROJECT_BINARY_DIR}
            -t dominicanfair/customer:${PROJECT_VERSION} -t
dominicanfair/customer:latest
    VERBATIM)
 add_dependencies(docker customer-deb)
```

As you can see, we invoke the Docker executable we found earlier in the directory containing our Dockerfile and DEB package, to create an image. We also tell Docker to tag our image as both the latest and with the version of our project. Finally, we ensure the DEB package will be built when we invoke our Docker target.

Building the image is as simple as `make docker` if `make` is the generator you chose. If you prefer the full CMake command (for example, to create generator-agnostic scripts), the invocation is `cmake --build . --target docker`.

Testing and integrating containers

Containers fit very well with CI/CD pipelines. Since they mostly require no further dependencies other than the container runtime itself, they can be easily tested. Worker machines don't have to be provisioned to fulfill the testing needs, so adding more nodes is much easier. What is more, all of them are general-purpose so that they may act both as builders, test runners, and even deployment executors without any prior configuration.

Another great benefit of using containers in **CI/CD** is the fact that they are isolated from one another. This means multiple copies running on the same machine should not interfere. That is true unless the tests require some resources from the host operating system, such as port forwarding or volume mounting. Therefore it's best to design tests so that such resources are not necessary (or at least they don't clash). Port randomization is a helpful technique to avoid clashes, for example.

Runtime libraries inside containers

The choice of containers may influence the choice of a toolchain and, therefore, C++ language features available to the application. Since containers are typically Linux-based, the system compiler available is usually GNU GCC with glibc as a standard library. However, some Linux distributions popular with containers, such as Alpine Linux, are based on a different standard library, musl.

If you are targeting such a distribution, make sure the code you'll be using, whether developed in-house or from third-party providers, is compatible with musl. The main advantage of both musl and Alpine Linux is that it results in much smaller container images. For example, a Python image built for Debian Buster is around 330 MB, the slimmed-down Debian version is around 40 MB, while the Alpine version is only around 16 MB. Smaller images mean less wasted bandwidth (for uploads and downloads) and quicker updates.

Alpine may also introduce some unwanted traits, such as longer build times, obscure bugs, or reduced performance. If you want to use it to reduce the size, run proper tests to make sure the application behaves without problems.

To reduce your images' size even more, you may consider ditching the underlying operating system altogether. What we mean by operating system here is all the userland tools ordinarily present in a container, such as a shell, package manager, and shared libraries. After all, if your application is the only thing that's going to be running, everything else is unnecessary.

It is typical for Go or Rust applications to provide a static build that is self-sufficient and can form a container image. While this might not be as straightforward in C++, it is worth considering.

There are a few drawbacks related to decreasing the image size as well. First of all, if you decide to go with Alpine Linux, keep in mind it is not as popular as, say, Ubuntu, Debian, or CentOS. Although it is often a platform of choice for container developers, it's very unusual for any other purpose.

This means that there might be new compatibility problems, mostly stemming from the fact it's not based on the de facto standard glibc implementation. If you rely on third-party components, the provider may not offer support for this platform.

If you decide to go down the single statically linked binary inside the container image route, there are also some challenges to consider. First of all, you are discouraged from statically linking glibc as it makes internal use of dlopen to handle **Name Service Switch (NSS)** and iconv. If your software relies on DNS resolving or character set conversion, you'll have to provide a copy of glibc and the relevant libraries anyway.

Another point to consider is that shell and package managers are often used for debugging containers that misbehave. When one of your containers is acting strangely, you may start another process inside the container and figure out what is happening inside by using standard UNIX tools such as `ps`, `ls`, or `cat`. To run such an application inside the container, it has to be present in the container image first. Some workarounds allow the operator to inject debugging binaries inside the running container, but none of them are well-supported at the moment.

Alternative container runtimes

Docker is the most popular way to build and run containers, but since the container standard is open, there are also alternative runtimes that you may use. The main replacement for Docker that offers a similar user experience is Podman. Together with Buildah, described in the previous section, they are tools aimed to replace Docker altogether.

The added benefit is that they *don't require an additional daemon running on a host machine, as Docker does*. Both also have support (although it is not yet mature) for rootless operations, which makes them a better fit for security-critical operations. Podman accepts all the commands you would expect the Docker CLI to take, so you can simply use it as an alias this way.

Another approach to containers that aims to provide better security is the **Kata Containers** initiative. Kata Containers uses lightweight virtual machines to leverage the hardware virtualization required for an additional level of isolation between the containers and the host operating system.

Cri-O and containerd are also popular runtimes used by Kubernetes.

Understanding container orchestration

Some of the containers' benefits only become apparent when you are using a container orchestrator to manage them. An orchestrator keeps track of all the nodes that will be running your workload, and it also monitors the health and status of the containers spread across these nodes.

More advanced features, for example, high availability, require the proper setup of the orchestrator, which typically means dedicating at least three machines for the control plane and another three machines for worker nodes. The autoscaling of nodes, in addition to the autoscaling of containers, also requires the orchestrator to have a driver able to control the underlying infrastructure (for example, by using the cloud provider's API).

Here, we will cover some of the most popular orchestrators that you can choose from to base your system on. You will find more practical information on Kubernetes in the next chapter, Chapter 15, *Cloud-Native Design*. Here, we give you an overview of the possible choices.

The presented orchestrators operate on similar objects (services, containers, batch jobs) although each may behave differently. The available features and operating principles vary between them. What they have in common is that you typically write a configuration file that declaratively describes the required resources and then you apply this configuration using a dedicated CLI tool. To illustrate the differences between the tools, we provide an example configuration specifying a web application introduced before (the merchant service) and a popular web server, Nginx, to act as a proxy.

Self-hosted solutions

Whether you are running your application on-premises, in a private cloud, or in a public cloud, you may want to have tight control over the orchestrator of your choice. The following is a collection of self-hosted solutions in this space. Keep in mind that most of them are also available as managed services. However, going with self-hosted helps you prevent vendor lock-in, which may be desirable for your organization.

Kubernetes

Kubernetes is probably the best-known orchestrator of all the ones that we mention here. It is prevalent, which means there is a lot of documentation and community support if you decide to implement it.

Even though Kubernetes uses the same application container format as Docker, this is basically where all the similarities end. It is impossible to use standard Docker tools to interact with Kubernetes clusters and resources directly. There is a new set of tools and concepts to learn when using Kubernetes.

Whereas with Docker, the container is the main object you will operate on, with Kubernetes, the smallest piece of the runtime is called a Pod. A Pod may consist of one or more containers that share mount points and networking resources. Pods in themselves are rarely of interest as Kubernetes also has higher-order concepts such as Replication Controllers, Deployment Controllers, or DaemonSets. Their role is to keep track of the pods and ensure the desired number of replicas is running on the nodes.

The networking model in Kubernetes is also very different from Docker. With Docker, you can forward ports from a container to make it accessible from different machines. With Kubernetes, if you want to access a pod, you typically create a Service resource, which may act as a load balancer to handle the traffic to the pods that form the service's backend. Services may be used for pod-to-pod communication, but they may also be exposed to the internet. Internally, Kubernetes resources perform service discovery using DNS names.

Kubernetes is declarative and eventually consistent. This means that instead of directly creating and allocating resources, you only have to provide the description of the desired end state and Kubernetes will do the work required to bring the cluster to the desired state. Resources are often described using YAML.

Since Kubernetes is highly extensible, there are a lot of associated projects developed under the **Cloud Native Computing Foundation** (**CNCF**), which turn Kubernetes into a provider-agnostic cloud development platform. We will present Kubernetes in more detail in the next chapter, Chapter 15, *Cloud Native Design*.

Here's how the resource definition looks for Kubernetes using YAML (merchant.yaml):

```
apiVersion: apps/v1
kind: Deployment
metadata:
  labels:
    app: dominican-front
  name: dominican-front
spec:
  selector:
    matchLabels:
      app: dominican-front
  template:
    metadata:
      labels:
        app: dominican-front
    spec:
      containers:
        - name: webserver
          imagePullPolicy: Always
          image: nginx
          ports:
            - name: http
              containerPort: 80
              protocol: TCP
      restartPolicy: Always
---
apiVersion: v1
kind: Service
metadata:
  labels:
    app: dominican-front
  name: dominican-front
spec:
  ports:
    - port: 80
      protocol: TCP
```

```
      targetPort: 80
    selector:
      app: dominican-front
    type: ClusterIP
---
apiVersion: apps/v1
kind: Deployment
metadata:
  labels:
    app: dominican-merchant
  name: merchant
spec:
  selector:
    matchLabels:
      app: dominican-merchant
  replicas: 3
  template:
    metadata:
      labels:
        app: dominican-merchant
    spec:
      containers:
        - name: merchant
          imagePullPolicy: Always
          image: hosacpp/merchant:v2.0.3
          ports:
            - name: http
              containerPort: 8000
              protocol: TCP
      restartPolicy: Always
---
apiVersion: v1
kind: Service
metadata:
  labels:
    app: dominican-merchant
  name: merchant
spec:
  ports:
    - port: 80
      protocol: TCP
      targetPort: 8000
  selector:
    app: dominican-merchant
    type: ClusterIP
```

To apply this configuration and orchestrate the containers, use `kubectl apply -f merchant.yaml`.

Docker Swarm

Docker Engine, also required to build and run Docker containers, comes pre-installed with its own orchestrator. This orchestrator is Docker Swarm, and its main feature is high compatibility with existing Docker tools by using the Docker API.

Docker Swarm uses the concept of Services to manage health checks and autoscaling. It supports rolling upgrades of the services natively. Services are able to publish their ports, which will then be served by Swarm's load balancer. It supports storing configs as objects for runtime customization and has basic secret management built in.

Docker Swarm is much simpler and less extensible than Kubernetes. This could be an advantage if you do not want to learn about all the details of Kubernetes. However, the main disadvantage is a lack of popularity, which means it is harder to find relevant material about Docker Swarm.

One of the benefits of using Docker Swarm is that you don't have to learn new commands. If you're already used to Docker and Docker Compose, Swarm works with the same resources. It allows specific options that extend Docker to handle deployments.

Two services orchestrated with Swarm would look like this (`docker-compose.yml`):

```
version: "3.8"
services:
  web:
    image: nginx
    ports:
      - "80:80"
    depends_on:
      - merchant
  merchant:
    image: hosacpp/merchant:v2.0.3
    deploy:
      replicas: 3
    ports:
      - "8000"
```

To apply the configuration, you run `docker stack deploy --compose-file docker-compose.yml dominican`.

Nomad

Nomad is different from the previous two solutions, as it is not focused solely on containers. It is a general-purpose orchestrator with support for Docker, Podman, Qemu Virtual Machines, isolated fork/exec, and several other task drivers. Nomad is a solution worth learning about if you want to gain some of the advantages of container orchestration without migrating your application to containers.

It is relatively easy to set up and integrates well with other HashiCorp products such as Consul for service discovery and Vault for secret management. Like Docker or Kubernetes, Nomad clients can run locally and connect to the server responsible for managing your cluster.

There are three job types available in Nomad:

- **Service**: A long-lived task that should not exit without manual intervention (for example, a web server or a database).
- **Batch**: A shorter-lived task that can complete within as little as a few minutes. If the batch job returns an exit code indicating an error, it is either restarted or rescheduled according to configuration.
- **System**: A task that it is necessary to run on every node in the cluster (for example, logging agent).

Compared to other orchestrators, Nomad is relatively easy to install and maintain. It is also extensible when it comes to task drivers or device plugins (used to access dedicated hardware such as GPUs or FPGAs). It lacks in community support and third-party integrations when compared to Kubernetes. Nomad does not require you to redesign the application's architecture to access the provided benefits, which is often the case with Kubernetes.

To configure the two services with Nomad, we need two configuration files. The first one is `nginx.nomad`:

```
job "web" {
  datacenters = ["dc1"]
  type = "service"
  group "nginx" {
    task "nginx" {
      driver = "docker"
      config {
        image = "nginx"
        port_map {
          http = 80
        }
```

```
          }
          resources {
            network {
              port "http" {
                  static = 80
              }
            }
          }
          service {
            name = "nginx"
            tags = [ "dominican-front", "web", "nginx" ]
            port = "http"
            check {
              type = "tcp"
              interval = "10s"
              timeout = "2s"
            }
          }
        }
      }
    }
  }
```

The second describes the merchant application, so it's called `merchant.nomad`:

```
job "merchant" {
  datacenters = ["dc1"]
  type = "service"
  group "merchant" {
    count = 3
    task "merchant" {
      driver = "docker"
      config {
        image = "hosacpp/merchant:v2.0.3"
        port_map {
          http = 8000
        }
      }
      resources {
        network {
          port "http" {
              static = 8000
          }
        }
      }
      service {
        name = "merchant"
        tags = [ "dominican-front", "merchant" ]
        port = "http"
```

```
        check {
          type = "tcp"
          interval = "10s"
          timeout = "2s"
        }
      }
    }
  }
}
```

To apply the configuration, you run `nomad job run merchant.nomad && nomad job run nginx.nomad`.

OpenShift

OpenShift is Red Hat's commercial container platform built on Kubernetes. It includes a lot of additional components that are useful in the everyday operations of Kubernetes clusters. You get a container registry, a build tool similar to Jenkins, Prometheus for monitoring, Istio for service mesh, and Jaeger for tracing. It is not fully compatible with Kubernetes so it shouldn't be thought of as a drop-in replacement.

It is built on top of existing Red Hat technology such as CoreOS and Red Hat Enterprise Linux. You can use it on-premises, within Red Hat Cloud, on one of the supported public cloud providers (including AWS, GCP, IBM, and Microsoft Azure), or as a hybrid cloud.

There is also an open source community-supported project called OKD, which forms the basis of Red Hat's OpenShift. If you do not require commercial support and other benefits of OpenShift, you may still use OKD for your Kubernetes workflow.

Managed services

As previously mentioned, some of the aforementioned orchestrators are also available as managed services. Kubernetes, for instance, is available as a managed solution in multiple public cloud providers. This section will show you some of the different approaches to container orchestration, which are not based on any of the solutions mentioned above.

AWS ECS

Before Kubernetes released its 1.0 version, Amazon Web Services proposed its own container orchestration technology called **Elastic Container Service (ECS)**. ECS provides an orchestrator that monitors, scales, and restarts your services when needed.

To run containers in ECS, you need to provide the EC2 instances on which the workload will run. You are not billed for the orchestrator's use, but you are billed for all the AWS services that you typically use (the underlying EC2 instances, for example, or an RDS database).

One of the significant benefits of ECS is its excellent integration with the rest of the AWS ecosystem. If you are already familiar with AWS services and invested in the platform, you will have less trouble understanding and managing ECS.

If you do not require many of the Kubernetes advanced features and its extensions, ECS may be a better choice as it's more straightforward and more comfortable to learn.

AWS Fargate

Another managed orchestrator offered by AWS is Fargate. Unlike ECS, it does not require you to provision and pay for the underlying EC2 instances. The only components you are focused on are the containers, the network interfaces attached to them, and IAM permissions.

Fargate requires the least amount of maintenance compared to other solutions and is the easiest to learn. Autoscaling and load-balancing are available out of the box thanks to the existing AWS products in this space.

The main downside here is the premium that you pay for hosting your services when compared to ECS. A straight comparison is not possible as ECS requires paying for the EC2 instances, while Fargate requires paying for the memory and CPU usage independently. This lack of direct control over your cluster may easily lead to high costs once your services start to autoscale.

Azure Service Fabric

The problem with all of the preceding solutions is that they mostly target Docker containers, which are first and foremost Linux-centric. Azure Service Fabric, on the other hand, is a Windows-first product backed by Microsoft. It enables running legacy Windows apps without modifications, which may help you migrate your application if it relies on such services.

As with Kubernetes, Azure Service Fabric is not so much a container orchestrator in itself, but rather a platform on top of which you can build your applications. One of the building blocks happens to be containers, so it works fine as an orchestrator.

With the recent introduction of Azure Kubernetes Service, the managed Kubernetes platform in the Azure cloud, there is less need for using Service Fabric.

Summary

When you are an architect of modern software, you have to take into account modern technologies. Taking them into account doesn't mean following the trends blindly; it means being able to objectively assess whether a particular proposition makes sense in your case or not.

Both microservices, presented in the previous chapters, and containers, presented in this chapter, are worth considering and understanding. Are they worth implementing as well? It depends heavily on what type of product you are designing. If you've read this far, you are ready to make the decision for yourself.

The next chapter is dedicated to cloud-native design. A very interesting but also a complex topic that ties in service-oriented architecture, CI/CD, microservices, containers, and cloud services. As it turns out, the great performance of C++ is a welcome feature for some of the cloud-native building blocks.

Questions

1. How do application containers differ from operating system containers?
2. What are some early examples of sandboxing environments in UNIX systems?
3. Why are containers a good fit for microservices?
4. What are the main differences between containers and virtual machines?
5. When are application containers a bad choice?
6. What are some tools to build multi-platform container images?
7. Besides Docker, what are some other container runtimes?
8. What are some popular orchestrators?

Further reading

- *Learning Docker - Second Edition*: https://www.packtpub.com/product/learning-docker-second-edition/9781786462923
- *Learn OpenShift*: https://www.packtpub.com/product/learn-openshift/9781788992329
- *Docker for Developers*: https://www.packtpub.com/product/docker-for-developers/9781789536058

15
Cloud-Native Design

As the name suggests, cloud-native design describes the application's architecture built, first and foremost, to operate in the cloud. It is not defined by a single technology or language, but rather takes advantage of all that the modern cloud platforms offer.

This may mean a combination of using **Platform-as-a-Service (PaaS)** whenever necessary, multi-cloud deployments, edge computing, **Function-as-a-Service (FaaS)**, static file hosting, microservices, and managed services. It transcends the boundaries of traditional operating systems. Instead of targeting the POSIX API and UNIX-like operating systems, cloud-native developers build on higher-level concepts using libraries and frameworks such as boto3, Pulumi, or Kubernetes.

The following topics will be covered in this chapter:

- Understanding cloud-native
- Using Kubernetes to orchestrate cloud-native workloads
- Connecting services with a service mesh
- Observability in distributed systems
- Going GitOps

By the end of the chapter, you'll have a good understanding of how modern trends in software architecture can be used in your applications.

Technical requirements

Some of the examples in this chapter require Kubernetes 1.18.

The code present in the chapter has been placed on GitHub at `https://github.com/PacktPublishing/Software-Architecture-with-Cpp/tree/master/Chapter15`.

Understanding cloud-native

Whereas it is possible to migrate an existing application to run in the cloud, such migration won't make the application cloud-native. It would be running in the cloud, but the architectural choices would still be based on the on-premises model.

In short, cloud-native applications are distributed by nature, loosely coupled, and are scalable. They're not tied to any particular physical infrastructure and don't require the developers to even think about specific infrastructure. Such applications are usually web-centric.

In this chapter, we'll go over some examples of cloud-native building blocks and describe some cloud-native patterns.

Cloud-Native Computing Foundation

One proponent of cloud-native design is the **Cloud Native Computing Foundation** (**CNCF**), which hosts the Kubernetes project. CNCF is home to various technologies, making it easier to build cloud-native applications independent of the cloud vendor. Examples of such technologies include the following:

- **Fluentd**, a unified logging layer
- **Jaeger**, for distributed tracing
- **Prometheus**, for monitoring
- **CoreDNS**, for service discovery

Cloud-native applications are typically built with application containers, often running on top of the Kubernetes platform. However, this is not a requirement, and it's entirely possible to use many of the CNCF frameworks outside Kubernetes and containers.

Cloud as an operating system

The main trait of cloud-native design is to treat the various cloud resources as the building blocks of your application. Individual **virtual machines** (**VMs**) are seldom used in cloud-native design. Instead of targeting a given operating system running on some instances, with a cloud-native approach, you target either the cloud API directly (for example, with FaaS) or some intermediary solution such as Kubernetes. In this sense, the cloud becomes your operating system, as the POSIX API no longer limits you.

As containers changed the approach to building and distributing software, it is now possible to free yourself from thinking about the underlying hardware infrastructure. Your software is not working in isolation, so it's still necessary to connect different services, monitor them, control their life cycle, store data, or pass the secrets. This is something that Kubernetes provides and it's one of the reasons why it became so popular.

As you can probably imagine, cloud-native applications are web- and mobile-first. Desktop applications can also benefit from having some cloud-native components, but it's a less common use case.

It's still possible to use hardware and other low-level access in cloud-native applications. If your workload requires the use of the GPU, this should not prevent you from going cloud-native. What's more, cloud-native applications can be built on-premises if you want access to custom hardware unavailable elsewhere. The term is not limited to the public cloud, but rather to the way of thinking about different resources.

Load balancing and service discovery

Load balancing is an essential part of distributed applications. It not only spreads the incoming requests across a cluster of services, which is essential for scaling, but can also help the responsiveness and availability of the applications. A smart load balancer can gather metrics to react to patterns in incoming traffic, monitor the state of the servers in its cluster, and forward requests to the less loaded and faster responding nodes – avoiding the currently unhealthy ones.

Load balancing brings more throughput and less downtime. By forwarding requests to many servers, a single point of failure is eliminated, especially if multiple load balancers are used, for example, in an active-passive scheme.

Load balancers can be used anywhere in your architecture: you can balance the requests coming from the web, requests done by web servers to other services, requests to cache or database servers, and whatever else suits your requirements.

 There are a few things to remember when introducing load balancing. One of them is session persistence—make sure all requests from the same customer go to the same server, so the carefully chosen pink stilettos won't disappear from their basket in your e-commerce site. Sessions can get tricky with load balancing: take extra care to not mix sessions, so customers won't suddenly start being logged into each other's profiles – countless companies stumbled upon this error before, especially when adding caching into the mix. It's a great idea to combine the two; just make sure it is done the right way.

Reverse proxies

Even if you want to deploy just one instance of your server, it might be a good idea to add yet another service in front of it instead of the load balancer—a reverse proxy. While a proxy usually acts on behalf of the client sending some requests, a reverse proxy acts on behalf of the servers handling those requests, hence the name.

Why use it, you ask? There are several reasons and uses for such a proxy:

- **Security**: The address of your server is now hidden, and the server can be protected by the proxy's DDoS prevention capabilities.
- **Flexibility and scalability**: You can modify the infrastructure hidden behind the proxy in any way you want and when you want.
- **Caching**: Why bother the server if you already know what answer it will give?
- **Compression**: Compressing data will reduce the bandwidth needed, which may be especially useful for mobile users with poor connectivity. It can also lower your networking costs (but will likely cost you compute power).
- **SSL termination**: Reduce the backend server's load by taking its burden to encrypt and decrypt network traffic.

An example of a reverse proxy is **NGINX**. It also provides load balancing capabilities, A/B testing, and much more. One of its other capabilities is service discovery. Let's see how it can be helpful.

Service Discovery

As the name suggests, **Service Discovery (SD)** allows for automatically detecting instances of specific services in a computer network. Instead of hardcoding a domain name or IP where the service should be hosted, the caller must only be pointed to a service registry. Using this approach, your architecture gets a lot more flexible, as now all the services you use can be easily found. If you design a microservice-based architecture, introducing SD really goes a long way.

There are several approaches to SD. In client-side discovery, the caller contacts the SD instance directly. Each service instance has a registry client, which registers and de-registers the instance, handles heartbeats, and others. While quite straightforward, in this approach, each client has to implement the service discovery logic. Netflix Eureka is an example of a service registry commonly used in this approach.

An alternative is to use server-side discovery. Here, a service registry is also present, along with the registry clients in each service instance. The callers, however, don't contact it directly. Instead, they connect to a load balancer, for example, the AWS Elastic Load Balancer, which, in turn, either calls a service registry or uses its built-in service registry before dispatching the client calls to specific instances. Aside from AWS ELB, NGINX and Consul can be used to provide server-side SD capabilities.

We now know how to find and use our services efficiently, so let's learn how best to deploy them.

Using Kubernetes to orchestrate cloud-native workloads

Kubernetes is an extensible open source platform for automating and managing container applications. It is sometimes referred to as k8s since it starts with 'k,' ends with 's,' and there are eight letters in the middle.

Its design is based on Borg, a system used internally by Google. Some of the features present in Kubernetes are as follows:

- Autoscaling of applications
- Configurable networking
- Batch job execution
- Unified upgrading of applications
- The ability to run highly available applications on top of it
- The declarative configuration

There are different ways to run Kubernetes in your organization. Choosing one over the other requires you to analyze additional costs and benefits related to them.

Kubernetes structure

While it is possible to run Kubernetes on a single machine (for example, using minikube, k3s, or k3d), it is not recommended to do so in production. Single-machine clusters have limited functionality and no failover mechanisms. A typical size for a Kubernetes cluster is six machines or more. Three of the machines then form the control plane. The other three are worker nodes.

The minimum requirement of three machines comes from the fact that this is the minimal number to provide high availability. It is possible to have the control plane nodes also available as worker nodes, although this is not encouraged.

Control plane

In Kubernetes, you rarely interact with individual worker nodes. Instead, all the API requests go to the control plane. The control plane then decides on the actions to take based on the requests, and then it communicates with the worker nodes.

The interaction with the control plane can take several forms:

- Using the kubectl CLI
- Using a web dashboard
- Using the Kubernetes API from inside an application other than kubectl

Control plane nodes usually run the API server, scheduler, a configuration store (etcd), and possibly some additional processes to handle the specific needs. For example, Kubernetes clusters deployed in a public cloud such as Google Cloud Platform have cloud controllers running on control plane nodes. The cloud controller interacts with the cloud provider's API to replace the failed machines, provision load balancers, or assign external IP addresses.

Worker nodes

The nodes that form the control plane and the worker pool are the actual machines the workload will run on. They may be physical servers that you host on-premises, VMs hosted privately, or VMs from your cloud provider.

Every node in a cluster runs at least the three programs as listed follows:

- A container runtime (for example, Docker Engine or cri-o) that allows the machine to handle the application containers
- A kubelet, which is responsible for receiving requests from the control plane and manages the individual containers based on those requests
- A kube-proxy, which is responsible for networking and load balancing on the node level

Possible approaches to deploying Kubernetes

As you may have realized from reading the previous section, there are different possible ways to deploy Kubernetes.

One of them is to deploy it to bare-metal servers hosted on-premises. One of the benefits is that this may be cheaper for large-scale applications than what the cloud providers offer. This approach has one major drawback—you will require an operator to provide the additional nodes whenever necessary.

To mitigate this issue, you can run a virtualization appliance on top of your bare-metal servers. This makes it possible to use the Kubernetes built-in cloud controller to provision the necessary resources automatically. You still have the same control over the costs, but there's less manual work. Virtualization adds some overhead, but in most cases, this should be a fair trade-off.

If you are not interested in hosting the servers yourself, you can deploy Kubernetes to run on top of VMs from a cloud provider. By choosing this route, you can use some of the existing templates for optimal setup. There are Terraform and Ansible modules available to build a cluster on popular cloud platforms.

Finally, there are the managed services available from the major cloud players. You only have to pay for the worker nodes in some of them, while the control plane is free of charge.

Why would you choose self-hosted Kubernetes over the managed services when operating in a public cloud? One of the reasons may be a specific version of Kubernetes that you require. Cloud providers are typically a bit slow when it comes to introducing updates.

Understanding the Kubernetes concepts

Kubernetes introduces some concepts that may sound unfamiliar or be confusing if you hear them for the first time. When you learn their purpose, it should be easier to grasp what makes Kubernetes special. Here are some of the most common Kubernetes objects:

- A *container*, specifically, an application container, is a method of distributing and running a single application. It contains the code and configuration necessary to run the unmodified application anywhere.
- A *Pod* is a basic Kubernetes building block. It is atomic and consists of one or more containers. All the containers inside the pod share the same network interfaces, volumes (such as persistent storage or secrets), and resources (CPU and memory).

- A *deployment* is a higher-level object that describes the workload and its life cycle features. It typically manages a set of pod replicas, allows for rolling upgrades, and manages the rollbacks in case of failure. This is what makes it easy to scale and manage the life cycle of Kubernetes applications.

- A *DaemonSet* is a controller similar to a deployment in that it manages where the pods are distributed. While deployments are concerned with keeping a given number of replicas, DaemonSets spreads the pods across all worker nodes. The primary use case is to run a system-level service, such as a monitoring or logging agent on each node.

- *Jobs* are designed for one-off tasks. Pods in deployments restart automatically when the containers inside them terminate. They are suitable for all the always-on services that listen on network ports for requests. However, deployments are unsuited for batch jobs, such as thumbnail generation, which you want to run only when required. Jobs create one or more pods and watch them until they complete a given task. When a specific number of successful pods terminate, the job is considered complete.

- *CronJobs*, as the name suggests, are the jobs that are run periodically within the cluster.

- *Services* represent a particular function performed within a cluster. They have a network endpoint associated with them (which is usually load balanced). Services may be performed by one or more pods. The life cycle of services is independent of the life cycles of the many pods. Since pods are transient, they may be created and destroyed at any time. Services abstract the individual pods to allow for high availability. Services have their own IP addresses and DNS names for ease of use.

Declarative approach

We've covered the differences between declarative and imperative approaches earlier in Chapter 9, *Continuous Integration/Continuous Deployment*. Kubernetes takes the declarative approach. Instead of giving instructions regarding the steps that need to be taken, you provide the resources that describe your cluster's desired state. It is up to the control plane to allocate internal resources so that they fulfill your needs.

It is possible to add the resources using the command line directly. This can be quick for testing, but you want to have a trail of the resources you created most of the time. Thus, most people work with manifest files, which provide a coded description of the resources required. Manifests are typically YAML files, but it is also possible to use JSON.

Here's an example YAML manifest with a single Pod:

```yaml
apiVersion: v1
kind: Pod
metadata:
  name: simple-server
  labels:
    app: dominican-front
spec:
  containers:
    - name: webserver
      image: nginx
      ports:
        - name: http
          containerPort: 80
          protocol: TCP
```

The first line is mandatory, and it tells which API version will be used in the manifest. Some resources are only available in extensions, so this is the information for the parser on how to behave.

The second line describes what resource we are creating. Next, there is metadata and the specification of the resource.

A name is mandatory in metadata as this is the way to distinguish one resource from another. If we wanted to create another pod with the same name, we would get an error stating that such a resource already exists. The label is optional and useful when writing selectors. For example, if we wanted to create a service that allows connection to the pod, we would use a selector matching label app with a value equal to `dominican-front`.

The specification is also the mandatory part as it describes the actual content of the resource. In our example, we list all the containers that are running inside the pod. To be precise, one container named `webserver` using an image, `nginx`, from Docker Hub. Since we want to connect to the Nginx web server from the outside, we also expose the container port `80` on which the server is listening. The name in the port description is optional.

Kubernetes networking

Kubernetes allows for pluggable network architectures. Several drivers exist that may be used depending on requirements. Whichever driver you select, some concepts are universal. The following are the typical networking scenarios.

Container-to-container communication

A single pod may host several different containers. Since the network interface is tied to the pod and not to the containers, each container operates in the same networking namespace. This means various containers may address one another using localhost networking.

Pod-to-pod communication

Each pod has an internal cluster-local IP address assigned. The address does not persist once the pod has been deleted. One pod can connect to another's exposed ports when it knows the other's address as they share the same flat network. You can think of pods as VMs hosting containers with regard to this communication model. This is rarely used as the preferred method is pod-to-service communication.

Pod-to-service communication

Pod-to-service communication is the most popular use case for communication within the cluster. Each service has an individual IP address and a DNS name assigned to it. When a pod connects to a service, the connection is proxied to one of the pods in the group selected by the service. Proxying is a task of the kube-proxy tool described earlier.

External-to-internal communication

External traffic typically comes to the cluster via the means of load balancers. These are either tied to or handled by specific services or ingress controllers. When the externally exposed services handle the traffic, it behaves like pod-to-service communication. With the ingress controller, you have additional features available that allow for routing, observability, or advanced load balancing.

When is using Kubernetes a good idea?

Introducing Kubernetes within an organization requires some investment. There are many benefits provided by Kubernetes, such as autoscalability, automation, or deployment scenarios. However, these benefits may not justify the necessary investment.

This investment concerns several areas:

- **Infrastructure costs**: The costs associated with running the control plane and the worker nodes may be relatively high. Additionally, the costs may rise if you want to use various Kubernetes expansions, such as GitOps or a service mesh (described later). They also require additional resources to run and provide more overhead on top of your application's regular services. Apart from the nodes themselves, you should also factor in other costs. Some of the Kubernetes features work best when deployed to a supported cloud provider. This means that in order to benefit from those features, you'd have to go down one of the following routes:

  a. Move your workload to the specifically supported cloud.

  b. Implement your own drivers for a cloud provider of your choice.

  c. Migrate your on-premises infrastructure to a virtualized API-enabled environment such as VMware vSphere or OpenStack.

- **Operations costs**: The Kubernetes cluster and associated services require maintenance. Even though you get less maintenance for your applications, this benefit is slightly offset by the cost of keeping the cluster running.
- **Education costs**: Your entire product team has to learn new concepts. Even if you have a dedicated platform team that will provide developers with easy-to-use tools, developers would still require a basic understanding of how the work they do influences the entire system and which API they should use.

Before you decide on introducing Kubernetes, consider first whether you can afford the initial investment it requires.

Observability in distributed systems

Distributed systems such as cloud-native architecture pose some unique challenges. The sheer number of different services working at any given time makes it very inconvenient to investigate how well the components perform.

In monolithic systems, logging and performance monitoring are usually enough. With a distributed system, even logging requires a design choice. Different components produce different log formats. Those logs have to be stored somewhere. Keeping them together with a service that delivers them will make it challenging to get the big picture in an outage case. Besides, since microservices may be short-lived, you will want to decouple the life cycle of logs from the life cycle of a service that provides them or a machine that hosts the service.

In `Chapter 13`, *Designing Microservices*, we described how a unified logging layer helps manage the logs. But logs only show what happens at a given point in the system. To see the picture from a single transaction point of view, you require a different approach.

This is where tracing comes in.

How tracing differs from logging

Tracing is a specialized form of logging. It provides lower-level information than logs. This may include all the function calls, their parameters, their size, and execution time. They also contain the unique ID of the transaction being processed. These details make it possible to reassemble them and see the life cycle of a given transaction as it passes through your system.

Performance information present in tracing helps you with uncovering bottlenecks and sub-optimal components in the system.

While logs are often read by operators and developers, they tend to be human-readable. There are no such requirements for tracing. To view the traces, you will use a dedicated visualization program. This means that even though traces are more detailed, they may also take up less space than logs.

The following diagram is an overview of a single trace:

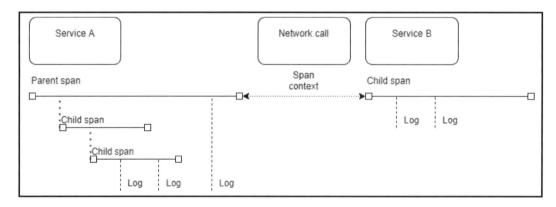

Figure 15.1 – Single trace

Two services communicate over a network. In *Service A*, we have one parent span that contains a child span and a single log. Child spans usually correspond to deeper function calls. A log represents the smallest piece of information. Each of them is timed and may contain additional information.

The network call to *Service B* preserves the span context. Even though *Service B* is executed in a different process on another machine, all of the information can be later reassembled as the transaction ID is preserved.

A piece of bonus information that we get from reassembling traces is the dependency graph between the services in our distributed system. As traces contain the entire call chain, it is possible to visualize this information and inspect unexpected dependencies.

Choosing a tracing solution

There are several possible solutions to choose from when implementing tracing. As you may imagine, there are both self-hosted and managed tools that you can use to instrument your applications. We will briefly describe the managed ones and focus on the self-hosted ones.

Jaeger and OpenTracing

One of the standards in distributed tracing is OpenTracing proposed by the authors of Jaeger. Jaeger is a tracer built for cloud-native applications. It addresses the problems of monitoring distributed transactions and propagating the tracing context. It's useful for the following purposes:

- Performance or latency optimization
- Performing a root cause analysis
- Analyzing the inter-service dependencies

OpenTracing is an open standard presenting an API that is independent of the tracer used. This means that when your application is instrumented using OpenTracing, you avoid lock-in to one particular vendor. If, at some point, you decide to switch from Jaeger to Zipkin, DataDog, or any other compatible tracer, you won't have to modify the entire instrumentation code.

There are many client libraries compatible with OpenTracing. You can also find many resources, including tutorials and articles that explain how to implement the API for your needs. OpenTracing officially supports the following languages:

- Go
- JavaScript
- Java
- Python

- Ruby
- PHP
- Objective-C
- C++
- C#

There are also unofficial libraries available, and specific applications can export OpenTracing data as well. This includes Nginx and Envoy, both popular web proxies.

Jaeger also accepts samples in Zipkin format. We will cover Zipkin in the next section. What it means is that you don't have to rewrite the instrumentation from one format to another if you (or any of your dependencies) already use Zipkin. For all new applications, OpenTracing is the recommended approach.

Jaeger scales well. You can run it as a single binary or a single application container if you want to evaluate it. You may configure Jaeger for production use to use its own backend or a supported external one, such as Elasticsearch, Cassandra, or Kafka.

Jaeger is a CNCF graduated project. This means it has reached a similar level of maturity to Kubernetes, Prometheus, or Fluentd. Because of this, we expect it to gain even more support in other CNCF applications.

Zipkin

The main competitor for Jaeger is Zipkin. It's an older project, which also means it is more mature. Usually, more senior projects are also better supported, but in this case, the endorsement of CNCF plays in Jaeger's favor.

Zipkin uses its proprietary protocol to handle tracing. It has OpenTracing support available, but it may not be at the same maturity and support level as the native Jaeger protocol. As we've mentioned earlier, it is also possible to configure Jaeger to collect traces in Zipkin format. This means the two are, at least to some point, interchangeable.

The project is hosted under the Apache foundation, but is not considered a CNCF project. When developing cloud-native applications, Jaeger is a better alternative. If you are looking instead for an all-purpose tracing solution, it is worth considering Zipkin as well.

One drawback is that Zipkin doesn't have a supported C++ implementation. There are unofficial libraries, but they don't seem to be well-supported. Using a C++ OpenTracing library is the preferred way to instrument the C++ code.

Instrumenting an application with OpenTracing

This section will illustrate how to add instrumentation with Jaeger and OpenTracing to an existing application. We'll use the `opentracing-cpp` and `jaeger-client-cpp` libraries.

First, we want to set up the tracer:

```
#include <jaegertracing/Tracer.h>

void setUpTracer()
{
    // We want to read the sampling server configuration from the
    // environment variables
    auto config = jaegertracing::Config;
    config.fromEnv();
    // Jaeger provides us with ConsoleLogger and NullLogger
    auto tracer = jaegertracing::Tracer::make(
        "customer", config, jaegertracing::logging::consoleLogger());
    opentracing::Tracer::InitGlobal(
        std::static_pointer_cast<opentracing::Tracer>(tracer));
}
```

The two preferred methods for configuring a sampling server are either by using the environment variable, as we did, or by using a YAML configuration file. When using environment variables, we will have to set them up before running the application. The most important ones are as follows:

- JAEGER_AGENT_HOST: The hostname where the Jaeger agent is located
- JAEGER_AGENT_POR: The port on which the Jaeger agent is listening
- JAEGER_SERVICE_NAME: The name of our application

Next, we configure the tracer and supply the logging implementation. It is possible to implement a custom logging solution if the available `ConsoleLogger` is not enough. For container-based applications with a unified logging layer, the ConsoleLogger should be enough.

When we have the tracer set up, we want to add spans to the functions that we want to be instrumented. The following code does just that:

```
auto responder::respond(const http_request &request, status_code status,
                        const json::value &response) -> void {
  auto span = opentracing::Tracer::Global()->StartSpan("respond");
  // ...
}
```

This span may be used later to create child spans within a given function. It may also be propagated to deeper function calls as a parameter. This is how it appears:

```
auto responder::prepare_response(const std::string &name, const
std::unique_ptr<opentracing::Span>& parentSpan)
    -> std::pair<status_code, json::value> {
  auto span = opentracing::Tracer::Global()->StartSpan(
        "prepare_response", { opentracing::ChildOf(&parentSpan->context())
});
  return {status_codes::OK,
          json::value::string(string_t("Hello, ") + name + "!")};
}

auto responder::respond(const http_request &request, status_code status)
    -> void {
  auto span = opentracing::Tracer::Global()->StartSpan("respond");
  // ...
  auto response = this->prepare_response("Dominic", span);
  // ...
}
```

Context propagation happens when we call the `opentracing::ChildOf` function. We may also pass the context over network calls using the `inject()` and `extract()` calls.

Connecting services with a service mesh

Microservices and cloud-native design come with their own set of problems. Communication between different services, observability, debugging, rate limiting, authentication, access control, and A/B testing may be challenging even with a limited number of services. When the number of services rises, so does the complexity of the aforementioned requirements.

That's where a service mesh enters the fray. In short, a service mesh trades off some resources (necessary to run the control plane and sidecars) for an automated and centrally controlled solution to the aforementioned challenges.

Introducing a service mesh

All the requirements we mentioned in the introduction to this chapter used to be coded within the application itself. As it turns out, many may be abstracted as they are shared across many different applications. When your application consists of many services, adding new features to all of them starts to be costly. With a service mesh, you may control these features from a single point instead.

Since a containerized workflow already abstracts some of the runtime and some networking, a service mesh takes the abstraction to another level. This way, the application within a container is only aware of what happens at the application level of the OSI networking model. The service mesh handles lower levels.

Setting up a service mesh allows you to control all network traffic in a new way and gives you better insights into this traffic. The dependencies become visible, as does the flow, shape, and amount of traffic.

Not only is the flow of traffic handled by the service mesh. Other popular patterns, such as circuit breaking, rate limiting, or retries, don't have to be implemented by each application and configured separately. This is also a feature that can be outsourced to the service mesh. Similarly, A/B testing or canary deployments are the use cases that a service mesh is able to fulfill.

One of the benefits of the service mesh, as previously mentioned, is greater control. Its architecture typically consists of a manageable edge proxy for external traffic and internal proxies usually deployed as sidecars along each microservice. This way, the networking policies can be written as code and stored alongside all the other configuration in a single place. Rather than having to switch on mutual TLS encryption for two of the services you want to connect, you only have to enable the feature once in your service mesh configuration.

Next, we'll cover some of the service mesh solutions.

Service mesh solutions

All of the solutions described here are self-hosted.

Istio

Istio is a powerful collection of service mesh tools. It allows you to connect microservices through the deployment of Envoy proxies as sidecar containers. Because Envoy is programmable, the Istio control plane's configuration changes are communicated to all the proxies, which then reconfigure themselves accordingly.

The Envoy proxies are, among other things, responsible for handing encryption and authentication. With Istio, enabling mutual TLS between your services requires a single switch in the configuration for the majority of the time. If you don't want mTLS between all your services, you may also select those that demand this additional protection while allowing unencrypted traffic between everything else.

Istio also helps with observability. First of all, the Envoy proxies export proxy-level metrics compatible with Prometheus. There are also service-level metrics and control plane metrics exported by Istio. Next, there are distributed traces that describe the traffic flow within the mesh. Istio can serve the traces to different backends: Zipkin, Jaeger, Lightstep, and Datadog. Finally, there are Envoy access logs, which show every call in a format similar to Nginx.

It's possible to visualize your mesh using Kiali, an interactive web interface. This way, you can see a graph of your services, including information such as whether the encryption is enabled, what the size of the flow between different services is, or what's the health check status of each of them is.

The authors of Istio claim that this service mesh should be compatible with different technologies. At the time of writing, the best documented, best integrated, and best tested is the integration with Kubernetes. Other supported environments are on-premises, general-purpose clouds, Mesos, and Nomad with Consul.

If you work in an industry concerned with compliance (such as financial institutions), then Istio can help in these aspects.

Envoy

While Envoy is not a service mesh in itself, it is worth mentioning in this section due to its use in Istio.

Envoy is a service proxy that acts much like Nginx or HAProxy. The main difference is that it can be reconfigured on the fly. This happens programmatically via an API and does not require the configuration file to be changed and the daemon to then be reloaded.

Interesting facts regarding Envoy are its performance and popularity. According to tests performed by SolarWinds, Envoy beats the competition when it comes to performance as a service proxy. This competition includes HAProxy, Nginx, Traefik, and AWS Application Load Balancer. Envoy is much younger than the established leaders in this space, such as Nginx, HAProxy, Apache, and Microsoft IIS, but this didn't stop Envoy from entering the top 10 list of most-used web servers, according to Netcraft.

Linkerd

Before Istio became synonymous with a service mesh, this field was represented by Linkerd. There is some confusion regarding the naming, as the original Linkerd project was designed to be platform-agnostic and targeted the Java VM. This meant that it was resource-heavy and often sluggish. The newer version, called Linkerd2, has been rewritten to address these issues. Linkerd2, as opposed to the original Linkerd, is only focused on Kubernetes.

Both Linkerd and Linkerd2 use their own proxy solution instead of relying on an existing project such as Envoy. The rationale for that is that a dedicated proxy (versus a general-purpose Envoy) offers better security and performance. An interesting feature of Linkerd2 is that the company that developed it also offers paid support.

Consul service mesh

A recent addition to the service mesh space is the Consul service mesh. This is a product from HashiCorp, a well-established cloud company known for such tools as Terraform, Vault, Packer, Nomad, and Consul.

Just like the other solutions, it features mTLS and traffic management. It's advertised as a multi-cloud, multi-data center, and multi-region mesh. It integrates with different platforms, data plane products, and observability providers. At the time of writing, the reality is a bit more modest as the main supported platforms are Nomad and Kubernetes, while the supported proxies are either the built-in proxy or Envoy.

If you are considering using Nomad for your application, then the Consul service mesh may be a great choice and a good fit as both are HashiCorp products.

Going GitOps

The last topic that we would like to cover in this chapter is GitOps. Even though the term sounds new and trendy, the idea behind it is not entirely novel. It's an extension of the well-known **Continuous Integration/Continuous Deployment (CI/CD)** pattern. Or maybe an extension is not a good description.

While CI/CD systems usually aim to be very flexible, GitOps seeks to minimize the number of possible integrations. The two main constants are Git and Kubernetes. Git is used for version control, release management, and environment separation. Kubernetes is used as a standardized and programmable deployment platform.

This way, the CI/CD pipeline becomes almost transparent. It's the opposite approach to that of imperative code handling all the stages of the build. To allow such a level of abstraction, you will typically need the following:

- Infrastructure as Code to allow the automated deployment of all the necessary environments
- A Git workflow with feature branches and pull requests or merge requests
- A declarative workflow configuration, which is already available in Kubernetes

The principles of GitOps

Since GitOps is an extension of the established CI/CD pattern, it may not be very clear to distinguish between the two. Here are some of the GitOps principles that differentiate this approach from general-purpose CI/CD.

Declarative description

The main difference between a classical CI/CD system and GitOps lies in the mode of operation. Most CI/CD systems are imperative: they consist of a sequence of steps to be taken in order for a pipeline to succeed.

Even the pipeline's notion is imperative as it implies an object that has an entry, a set of connections, and a sink. Some of the steps may be performed in parallel, but a process has to stop and wait for the depending step to finish whenever there is a dependency.

In GitOps, the configuration is declarative. This refers to the entire state of your system – the applications, their configuration, monitoring, and dashboards. It is all treated as code, giving it the same features as regular application code.

The system's state versioned in Git

Since the state of your system is written in code, you derive some benefits from that fact. Features such as easier auditing, code reviews, and version control are now applicable not just to the application code. The consequence is that in case anything goes wrong, reverting back to a working state requires a single `git revert` command.

You can use the power of Git's signed commits and SSH and GPG keys to give control over different environments. By adding a gating mechanism that makes sure only the commits meeting required standards can be pushed to the repository, you also eliminate many accidental errors that may result from running commands manually using `ssh` or `kubectl`.

Auditable

Everything that you store in your version control systems becomes auditable. Before introducing a new code, you perform a code review. When you notice a bug, you can revert the change that introduced it or get back to the last working version. Your repository becomes the single point of truth regarding your entire system.

It's already useful when applied to the application code. However, extending the ability to audit configuration, helper services, metrics, dashboards, and even deployment strategies makes it even more powerful. You no longer have to ask yourself, "*OK, so why did this configuration end up in production?*" All you have to do is check the Git log.

Integrated with established components

Most CI/CD tools introduce proprietary configuration syntax. Jenkins uses Jenkins DSL. Each of the popular SaaS solutions uses YAML, but the YAML files are incompatible with each other. You can't switch from Travis to CircleCI or from CircleCI to GitLab CI without rewriting your pipelines.

This has two drawbacks. One is the obvious vendor lock-in. The other is the need to learn the configuration syntax to use the given tool. Even if most of your pipeline is already defined elsewhere (shell scripts, Dockerfiles, or Kubernetes manifests), you still need to write some glue code to instruct the CI/CD tool to use it.

It's different with GitOps. Here, you don't write explicit instructions or use proprietary syntax. Instead, you reuse other common standards, such as Helm or Kustomize. There's less to learn, and the migration process is much more comfortable. Also, GitOps tools usually integrate well with other components from the CNCF ecosystem, so you can get your deployment metrics stored in Prometheus and auditable with Grafana.

Configuration drift prevention

Configuration drift happens when a given system's current state differs from the desired state as described in the repository. Multiple causes are contributing to the configuration drift.

For example, let's consider a configuration management tool with a VM-based workload. All of the VMs start in the same state. As the CM runs for the first time, it brings the machines to the desired state. But if an auto-update agent is running on those machines by default, this agent may update some of the packages on its own, without considering the desired state from the CM. Moreover, as network connectivity may be fragile, some of the machines may update to a newer version of a package, while others won't.

One of the updated packages may be incompatible with the pinned package that your application requires in extreme cases. Such a situation will break the entire CM workflow and leave your machine in an unusable state.

With GitOps, an agent is always running inside your system that keeps track of the current state and the desired state of the system. If the current state suddenly differs from the desired one, an agent may fix it or issue an alert regarding configuration drift.

Preventing configuration drift adds another layer of self-healing to your system. If you're running Kubernetes, you already have self-healing on the pod level. Whenever a pod fails, another one is recreated in its place. If you are using a programmable infrastructure underneath (such as a cloud provider or OpenStack on-premises), you also have self-healing capabilities of your nodes. With GitOps, you get the self-healing for workloads and its configuration.

The benefits of GitOps

As you can imagine, the described features of GitOps afford several benefits. Here are some of them.

Increased productivity

CI/CD pipelines already automate a lot of usual tasks. They reduce lead time by helping get more deployments. GitOps adds a feedback loop that prevents configuration drift and allows self-healing. This means that your team can ship quicker and worry less about introducing potential problems as they are easy to revert. This, in turn, means that the development throughput increases and you can introduce new features faster and with more confidence.

Better developer experience

With GitOps, developers don't have to worry about building containers or using kubectl to control the cluster. Deploying new features requires just the use of Git, which is already a familiar tool in most environments.

This also means that onboarding is quicker since new hires don't have to learn a lot of new tools in order to be productive. GitOps uses standard and consistent components, so introducing changes to the operations side should not impact developers.

Higher stability and reliability

Using Git to store the state of your system means you have access to an audit log. This log contains a description of all the changes introduced. If your task tracking system integrates with Git (which is a good practice), you can typically tell which business feature is related to the system's change.

With GitOps, there is less need to allow manual access to the nodes or the entire cluster, which reduces the chance of accidental errors originating from running an invalid command. Those random errors that get into the system are easily fixed by using Git's powerful revert feature.

Recovery from a severe disaster (such as losing the entire control plane) is also a lot easier. All it requires is setting up a new clean cluster, installing a GitOps operator there, and pointing it to the repository with your configuration. After a short while, you have an exact replica of your previous production system, all without manual intervention.

Improved security

A reduced need to give access to the cluster and nodes means improved security. There is less to worry about in terms of lost or stolen keys. You avoid a situation where someone retains access to your production environment even though this person is no longer working on the team (or in the company).

When it comes to access to the system, the single point of truth is handled by the Git repository. Even if a malicious actor decides to introduce a backdoor into your system, the change required will undergo a code review. Impersonating another developer is also more challenging when your repository uses GPG-signed commits with strong verification.

So far, we've mainly covered the benefits from the development and operations point of view. But GitOps also benefits the business. It affords business observability in the system, something that was hard to achieve before.

It's easy to track the features present in a given release as they are all stored in Git. Since Git commits a link to the task tracker, business people can get preview links to see how the application looks in various development stages.

It also gives clarity that allows the following common questions to be answered:

- What's running in production?
- Which tickets have been resolved with the last release?
- Which change might be responsible for service degradations?

The questions for all those answers may even be presented in a friendly dashboard. Naturally, the dashboard itself can be stored in Git as well.

GitOps tools

The GitOps space is a new and growing one. There are already tools that can be considered stable and mature. Here are some of the most popular ones.

FluxCD

FluxCD is an opinionated GitOps operator for Kubernetes. Selected integrations provide core functionality. It uses Helm charts and Kustomize to describe the resources.

Its integration with Prometheus adds observability to the deployment process. To help with maintenance, FluxCD features a CLI.

ArgoCD

Unlike FluxCD, it offers a broader choice of tools to use. This might be useful if you're already using Jsonnet or Ksonnet for your configuration. Like FluxCD, it integrates with Prometheus and features a CLI.

At the time of writing this book, ArgoCD is a more popular solution than FluxCD.

Jenkins X

Contrary to what the name might suggest, Jenkins X doesn't have much in common with the well-known Jenkins CI system. It is backed by the same company, but the entire concepts of Jenkins and Jenkins X are totally different.

While the other two tools are purposefully small and self-contained, Jenkins X is a complex solution with many integrations and a broader scope. It supports the triggering of custom build tasks, making it look like a bridge between a classic CI/CD system and GitOps.

Summary

Congratulations on reaching the end of the chapter! Using modern C++ is not limited to understanding the recently added language features. Your applications will run in production. As an architect, it's also your choice to make sure the runtime environment matches requirements. In the few previous chapters, we described some popular trends in distributed applications. We hope this knowledge will help you decide which one is the best fit for your product.

Going cloud-native brings a lot of benefits and can automate a good chunk of your workflow. Switching custom-made tools to industry standards makes your software more resilient and easier to update. In this chapter, we have covered the pros, cons, and use cases of popular cloud-native solutions.

Some, such as distributed tracing with Jaeger, bring immediate benefits to most projects. Others, such as Istio or Kubernetes, perform best in large-scale operations. After reading this chapter, you should have sufficient knowledge to decide whether introducing cloud-native design into your application is worth the cost.

Questions

1. What's the difference between running your applications in your cloud and making them cloud-native?
2. How can you run cloud-native applications on-premises?
3. What's the minimal highly available cluster size for Kubernetes?
4. Which Kubernetes object represents a microservice that allows network connections?

5. Why is logging not sufficient in distributed systems?
6. How does a service mesh help with building secure systems?
7. How does GitOps increase productivity?
8. What's the standard CNCF project for monitoring?

Further reading

- *Mastering Kubernetes*: https://www.packtpub.com/product/mastering-kubernetes-third-edition/9781839211256
- *Mastering Distributed Tracing*: https://www.packtpub.com/product/mastering-distributed-tracing/9781788628464
- *Mastering Service Mesh*: https://www.packtpub.com/product/mastering-service-mesh/9781789615791

Appendix A

Thank you for coming this far on this journey through software architecture. Our goal in writing this book was to help you make informed decisions regarding the design of your applications and systems. By now, you should feel confident when deciding whether to choose IaaS, PaaS, SaaS, or FaaS.

There are a lot of things we haven't even touched on in this book as they were extensive and out of the scope of the book. Either we had too little experience with the given topic, or we thought that it was too niche. There are also areas that we felt were very important, but we couldn't find the right place for them in the chapters. You'll find them in this appendix.

Designing data storage

Let's now discuss the storage for your application. First let's decide whether you should go with SQL, NoSQL, or something else.

A good rule of thumb is to decide on the technology according to the size of your database. For small databases, say, those whose size will never grow into the terabyte area, going with SQL is a valid approach. If you have a very small database or want to create an in-memory cache, you can try SQLite. If you plan to go into single terabytes, again guaranteeing that the size will never get bigger than that, your best bet would be to go with NoSQL. It's possible in some cases to still stick to SQL databases, but it gets expensive quickly because of the costs of hardware, as you'll need a beast of a server for your master node. Even if it's not an issue, you should measure whether the performance is enough for your needs and be prepared for long maintenance windows. In some cases, it may also suit you to just run a cluster of SQL machines using technologies such as Citus, which is, in essence, a sharded PostgreSQL. However, usually, it's just cheaper and simpler to go with NoSQL in such cases. If the size of your database exceeds 10 TBs or you need to ingest data in real time, consider using a data warehouse instead of NoSQL.

Which NoSQL technology should I use?

The answer to this question depends on several factors. A few are listed here:

- If you want to store time series (save increments at small, regular intervals), then the best option would be to use InfluxDB or VictoriaMetrics.
- If you need something similar to SQL but could live without joins, or in other words, if you plan to store your data in columns, you can try out Apache Cassandra, AWS DynamoDB, or Google's BigTable.
- If that's not the case, then you should think about whether your data is a document without a schema, such as JSON or some kind of application logs. If that's the case, you could go with Elasticsearch, which is great for such flexible data and provides a RESTful API. You could also try out MongoDB, which stores its data in **Binary JSON (BSON)** format and allows MapReduce.

OK, but what if you don't want to store documents? Then you could opt for object storage, especially if your data is large. Usually, going with a cloud provider is OK in this case, which means that using Amazon's S3 or Google's Cloud Storage or Microsoft's Blob storage should help your case. If you want to go with something local, you could use OpenStack's Swift or deploy Ceph.

If file storage is also not what you're looking for, then perhaps your case is just about simple key-value data. Using such storage has its benefits as it's fast. This is why many distributed caches are built using it. Notable technologies include Riak, Redis, and Memcached (this last one is not suitable for persisting data).

Aside from the previously mentioned options, you could consider using a tree-based database such as BerkeleyDB. Those databases are basically specialized key-value storage with path-like access. If trees are too restricting for your case, you might be interested in graph-oriented databases such as Neo4j or OrientDB.

Serverless architecture

While related to cloud-native design, serverless architecture is a popular topic on its own. It gained a lot of popularity since the introduction of FaaS or CaaS products, such as AWS Lambda, AWS Fargate, Google Cloud Run, and Azure Functions.

Serverless is mostly an evolution of PaaS products such as Heroku. It abstracts the underlying infrastructure so that developers can focus on the application and not on infrastructural choices.

An additional benefit of serverless over older PaaS solutions is that you don't have to pay for what you don't use. Rather than paying for a given service level, you typically pay for the actual execution time of the deployed workload with serverless. If you only want to run a given piece of code once a day, you don't need to pay a monthly fee for an underlying server.

While we didn't get into too much detail about serverless, it is rarely used with C++. When it comes to FaaS, only AWS Lambda currently supports C++ as a possible language. Since containers are language-agnostic, you can use C++ applications and functions with CaaS products such as AWS Fargate, Azure Container Instances, or Google Cloud Run.

Serverless functions may still be relevant to you if you want to run non-C++ auxiliary code used along with your C++ application. Maintenance tasks and scheduled jobs are an excellent fit for serverless and they usually don't require the performance or efficiency of C++ binaries.

Communication and culture

The focus of this book is software architecture. Why would we want to mention communication and culture in a book around software, then? If you think about it, all software is written *by* people *for* people. The human aspect is prevalent and yet we often fail to admit it.

As an architect, your role won't be to figure out the best approach to solving a given problem. You'll also have to communicate your proposed solution to your team members. Often, the choices you make will result from previous conversations.

These are the reasons communication and team culture also play a role in software architecture.

In one of the early chapters, we've mentioned Conway's Law. This law states that the architecture of the software system reflects the organization that's working on it. This means that building great products requires building great teams and understanding psychology.

If you want to be a great architect, learning people skills may be as important as learning technical ones.

DevOps

We've used the term DevOps (and DevSecOps) several times within this book. This topic deserves some additional space, in our opinion. DevOps is an approach to building software products that breaks with traditional silo-based development.

In the waterfall model, teams operated on single aspects of work independently of each other. The development team would write code, QA would test and validate the code, and security and compliance would come after that. Eventually, the operations team would take care of maintenance. The teams rarely communicated, and even then, it was usually a very formal process.

Knowledge about particular fields of expertise was only available to the teams responsible for a given piece of the workflow. Developers knew very little about QA and next to nothing about operations. While this setup was very convenient, the modern landscape requires more agility than the waterfall model can provide.

That's why a new model of working was proposed, one that encourages more collaboration, better communication, and lots of knowledge sharing between different stakeholders of a software product. While DevOps refers to bringing together developers and operations, what it means is bringing everyone closer.

Developers start working with QA and security even before they write the first lines of code. Operation engineers are more familiar with the code base. Businesses can easily track the progress of a given ticket and, in some cases, can even do a deployment preview in a self-service manner.

DevOps has become synonymous with using particular tools such as Terraform or Kubernetes. But DevOps is by no means the same as using any specific tools. Your organization can follow the DevOps principles without using Terraform or Kubernetes, and it can use Terraform and Kubernetes while not practicing DevOps.

One of the principles of DevOps is that it encourages improved information flow among the product's stakeholders. With that, it's possible to fulfill another principle: reduce wasteful activities that don't bring value to the end product.

When you're building modern systems, it is worth doing so using modern methodology. Migrating an existing organization to DevOps may require a massive mindset shift, so it is not always possible. It's worth pursuing when starting a greenfield project that you have control over.

Assessments

Chapter 1

1. Why should you care about software architecture?
    - Architecture allows you to achieve and maintain the requisite qualities of software. Being mindful and caring about it prevents a project from having accidental architecture, thereby losing quality, and also prevents software decay.
2. Should the architect be the ultimate decision maker in an Agile team?
    - No. Agile is about empowering the whole team. An architect brings their experience and knowledge to the table, but if a decision has to be accepted by the whole team, the team should own it, not just the architect. Considering the needs of stakeholders is also of great importance here.
3. How does the **Single Responsibility Principle (SRP)** relate to cohesion?
    - Following the SRP leads to better cohesion. If a component starts having multiple responsibilities, usually it becomes less cohesive. In such instances, it's best to just refactor it into multiple components, each having a single responsibility. This way, we increase cohesiveness, so the code becomes easier to understand, develop, and maintain.
4. During what phases of a project's lifetime can benefit be derived from having an architect?
    - An architect can bring value to a project from its inception until the time it goes into maintenance. The most value can be achieved during the early phases of the project's development, as this is where key decisions about how it should look will be taken. However, this doesn't mean that architects cannot be valuable during development. They can keep the project on the right course and on track. By aiding decisions and overseeing the project, they ensure that the code doesn't end up with accidental architecture and is not subject to software decay.

5. What's the benefit of following the SRP?
   - Code that follows the SRP is easier to understand and maintain. This also means that it has fewer bugs.

Chapter 2

1. What are the traits of a RESTful service?
   - Obviously, the use of REST APIs.
   - Statelessness – Each request contains all the data required for its processing. Remember, this doesn't mean that RESTful services cannot use databases, quite the opposite.
   - Using cookies instead of keeping sessions.

2. What toolkit can you use to assist you in creating a resilient distributed architecture?
   - Simian Army by Netflix.

3. Should you use centralized storage for your microservices? Why/why not?
   - Microservices should use decentralized storage. Each microservice should choose the storage type that suits it best, as this leads to increased efficiency and scalability.

4. When should you write a stateful service instead of a stateless one?
   - Only when it's not reasonable to have a stateless one and you won't need to scale. For instance, when the client and service have to keep their state in sync or when the state to send would be enormous.

5. How does a broker differ from a mediator?
   - A mediator "mediates" between services, so it needs to know how to process each request. A broker only knows where to send each request, so it's a lightweight component. It can be used to create a publisher-subscriber (pub-sub) architecture.

6. What is the difference between an N-tier and an N-layer architecture?
   - Layers are logical and specify how you organize your code. Tiers are physical and specify how you run your code. Each tier has to be separated by others, either by being run in a different process, or even on a different machine.

7. How should you approach replacing a monolith with a microservice-based architecture?
    - Incrementally. Carve small microservices out of the monolith. You can use the strangler pattern described in *Chapter 4, Architectural and System Design*, to help you with this.

Chapter 3

1. What are quality attributes?
    - Traits, or qualities, that a system may have. Often called "ilities," as many of them have this postfix in their names, for instance, portability.

2. What sources should you use when gathering requirements?
    - The context of your system, existing documentation, and the system's stakeholders.

3. How should you be able to tell whether a requirement is architecturally significant?
    - **Architecturally significant requirements** (ASRs) often require a separate software component, impact a large part of the system, are hard to achieve, and/or force you to make trade-offs.

4. How should you document graphically the functional requirements various parties may have regarding your system?
    - Prepare a use case diagram.

5. When is development view documentation useful?
    - In cases where you're developing a large system with many modules and need to communicate global constraints and common design choices to all the software teams.

6. How should you automatically check whether your code's API documentation is out of date?
    - Doxygen has built-in checks, like the one that warns you about mismatches between the function signatures and their parameters in comments.

7. How should you show on a diagram that a given operation is handled by different components of the system?
    - Use one of the UML interaction diagrams for this purpose. Sequence diagrams are a good choice, although communication diagrams can be fine in certain scenarios, too.

Chapter 4

1. What is event sourcing?
   - This is an architectural pattern that relies on keeping track of events that change the state of the system instead of keeping track of the state *per se*. It brings benefits such as lower latency, free audit logs, and debugability.

2. What are the practical consequences of the CAP theorem?
   - As network partitions happen, if you want a distributed system, you'll need to choose between consistency and availability. In cases of partitions, you can either return stale data, an error, or risk timeouts.

3. What can you use Netflix's Chaos Monkey for?
   - It can help you prepare for unexpected downtime of your services.

4. Where can caching be applied?
   - Either on your client's side, in front of web servers, databases, or applications, or on a host near your potential client, depending on your needs.

5. How should you prevent your app from going down when an entire data center does?
   - By using geodes.

6. Why should you use an API gateway?
   - To simplify client code, as it doesn't need to hardcode the addresses of your service instances.

7. How can Envoy help you to achieve various architectural goals?
   - It aids your system's fault tolerance by providing backpressure, circuit breaking, automatic retries, and outlier detection.
   - It aids deployability by allowing canary releases and blue-green deployments.
   - It also offers load balancing, tracing, monitoring, and metrics.

Chapter 5

1. How should you ensure each file of our code that's open, will be closed when no longer in use?
   - By using the RAII idiom; for instance, by using `std::unique_ptr`, which will close it in its destructor.

2. When should you use "naked" pointers in C++ code?
   - Only to pass optional (nullable) references.

3. What is a deduction guide?
   - A way of telling the compiler what parameters it should deduce for a template. They can be implicit or user-defined.

4. When should you use `std::optional`, and when should you use `gsl::not_null`?
   - The former is for cases where we want to pass the contained value around. The latter just passes the pointer to it. Also, the former can be empty, while the latter will always point to an object.

5. How do range algorithms differ from views?
   - Algorithms are eager, while views are lazy. Algorithms also allow the use of projections.

6. How should you constrain your type more than just by specifying the concept name when you're defining a function?
   - By using a `requires` clause.

7. How does `import X` differ from `import <X>`?
   - The latter allows macros from the imported X header to be visible.

Chapter 6

1. What are the rules of three, five, and zero?
   - Best practices to follow for writing types with unsurprising semantics and fewer bugs.

2. When should you use niebloids versus hidden friends?
   - Niebloids "disable" ADL, while hidden friends rely on it to be found. The former can therefore speed up compilation (fewer overloads to consider), while the latter can help you implement customization points.

3. How can an `Array` interface be improved to be more production-ready?
   - `begin`, `end`, and their constant and reverse equivalents should be added so it can be used like a proper container. Traits such as `value_type`, `pointer`, and `iterator` can be useful to reuse it in generic code. Sprinkling the members with `constexpr` and `noexcept` could aid safety and performance. The `const` overload for `operator[]` is also missing.

4. What are fold expressions?
    - Expressions that fold, or reduce, a parameter pack over a binary functor. In other words, statements that apply a given operation to all the passed variadic template arguments so that a single value (or `void`) is produced.

5. When shouldn't you use static polymorphism?
    - When you need to provide the consumers of your code with a way to add more types at runtime.

6. How can we save on one more allocation in the winking out example?
    - By avoiding the resizing of the vector when adding elements.

Chapter 7

1. What's the difference between installing and exporting your targets in CMake?
    - Exporting means the targets will be available for other projects that try to find our package, even if our code is not installed. CMake's package registry can be used to store data about locations of the exported targets. The binaries never leave the build directory. Installation requires the targets to be copied somewhere and, if it's not a system directory, setting up paths to the config files or the targets themselves.

2. How should you make your template code compile faster?
    - Follow the Rule of Chiel.

3. How should you use multiple compilers with Conan?
    - Use Conan profiles.

4. What should you do if you'd like to compile your Conan dependencies with the pre-C++11 GCC ABI?
    - Set `compiler.libcxx` to `libstdc++` instead of `libstdc++11`.

5. How should you ensure that you force a specific C++ standard in CMake?
    - By calling `set_target_properties(our_target PROPERTIES CXX_STANDARD our_required_cxx_standard CXX_STANDARD_REQUIRED YES CXX_EXTENSIONS NO)`.

6. How should you build documentation in CMake and ship it along with your RPM package?
    • Create a target to generate the documentation as described in Chapter 3, *Functional and Nonfunctional Requirements*, install it to CMAKE_INSTALL_DOCDIR, and then make sure the path is not specified in the CPACK_RPM_EXCLUDE_FROM_AUTO_FILELIST variable.

Chapter 8

1. What is the base layer of the testing pyramid?
    • Unit tests.

2. What kinds of non-functional tests are there?
    • Performance, endurance, security, availability, integrity, and usability.

3. What is the name of a famous method for root cause analysis?
    • 5 whys

4. Is it possible to test compile-time code in C++?
    • Yes, for example, using static_assert.

5. What should you use when writing unit tests for code with external dependencies?
    • Test doubles such as mocks and fakes.

6. What is the role of unit tests in Continuous Integration/Continuous Deployment?
    • They are the basis of a gating mechanism and act as an early warning feature.

7. Name some tools that allow the testing of infrastructure code.
    • Serverspec, Testinfra, Goss.

8. Is it a good idea to access the class's private attributes and methods in a unit test?
    • You should design classes in such a way that you never have to access their private attributes directly.

Chapter 9

1. In what ways does Continuous Integration save time during development?
   - It allows you to catch bugs earlier and fix them before they enter production.
2. Do you need separate tools to implement Continuous Integration and Continuous Deployment?
   - The pipelines are usually written using a single tool; multiple tools are used for actual testing and deployment.
3. When does it make sense to perform a code review in a meeting?
   - When an asynchronous code review is taking too long.
4. What tools can you use to assess the quality of your code during Continuous Integration?
   - Tests, static analysis.
5. Who participates in specifying BDD scenarios?
   - Developers, QA, the business.
6. When should you consider using immutable infrastructure? When should you rule it out?
   - It is best used with stateless services or services that can outsource storage using a database or a network storage. It is not suitable for stateful services.
7. How would you characterize the differences between Ansible, Packer, and Terraform?
   - Ansible is designed for the configuration management of existing VMs, Packer is for building cloud VM images, and Terraform is for building the cloud infrastructure (such as networks, VMs, and load balancers).

Chapter 10

1. Why is security important in modern systems?
   - Modern systems are typically connected to a network and are therefore potentially vulnerable to external attacks.
2. What are some of the challenges associated with concurrency?
   - Code is harder to design and to debug. Update problems may arise.
3. What are the C++ core guidelines?
   - Best practices that document how to build C++ systems.

4. What's the difference between secure coding and defensive coding?
    - Secure coding offers robustness to end users, whereas defensive coding offers robustness to interface consumers.

5. How should you check whether your software contains known vulnerabilities?
    - By using a CVE database or an automated scanner such as OWASP Dependency-Check or Snyk.

6. What's the difference between static and dynamic analysis?
    - Static analysis is performed on source code without executing it. Dynamic analysis requires execution.

7. What's the difference between static and dynamic linking?
    - With static linking, the executable contains all the code necessary to run the application. With dynamic linking, some parts of the code (the dynamic libraries) are shared between different executables.

8. How can you use the compiler to fix security problems?
    - Modern compilers include sanitizers that check for certain flaws.

9. How can you implement security awareness in your Continuous Integration pipeline?
    - By using automated tools that scan for vulnerabilities and perform all kinds of static and dynamic analysis.

Chapter 11

1. What can we learn from the performance results from this chapter's microbenchmarks?
    - The fact that a binary search is a lot faster than a linear search, even if the number of elements to check is not that high. This means that computational complexity (aka the Big O) matters. Probably on your machine, even the longest search on the biggest dataset for a binary search was still faster than the shortest one for a linear search!
    - Depending on your cache sizes, you may have also noticed how increasing the required memory caused slowdowns when the data could no longer fit in specific cache levels.

2. Is how we traverse a multi-dimensional array important for performance? Why/why not?
    - It's crucial, as we may access the data linearly in memory, which the CPU prefetcher would like and reward us with better performance, or jump through the memory, hindering thereby our performance.

3. In our coroutines example, why can't we create our thread pool inside the `do_routine_work` function?
    - Because of lifetime issues.

4. How can we rework our coroutine example so that it uses a generator instead of just tasks?
    - The body of the generator would need to `co_yield`. Also, the threads from our pool would need to synchronize, probably using an atomic.

Chapter 12

1. What are the properties of a service in service-oriented architecture?
    - It is a representation of business activity with a defined outcome.
    - It is self-contained.
    - It is opaque to its users.
    - It may be composed of other services

2. What are some of the benefits of web services?
    - They are easy to debug using common tools, they work well with firewalls, and they may take advantage of existing infrastructure, such as load balancing, caching, and CDNs.

3. When are microservices not a good choice?
    - When the cost of RPC and redundancy outweighs the benefits.

4. What are some of the use cases of message queues?
    - IPC, transactional services, IoT.

5. What are some of the benefits of choosing JSON over XML?
    - JSON requires lower overhead, is gaining in popularity over XML, and should be easier to read by a human.

6. How does REST build on web standards?
    - It uses HTTP verbs and URLs as building blocks.

7. How do cloud platforms differ from traditional hosting?
    - Cloud platforms offer easy-to-use APIs, meaning the resources can be programmed.

Chapter 13

1. How do microservices help you to use the system's resources better?
    - It is easier to scale just the resources that are lacking instead of entire systems.
2. How can microservices and monoliths coexist (in an evolving system)?
    - New features may be developed as microservices, while some features may be split and outsourced from the monolith.
3. Which types of teams benefit the most from microservices?
    - Cross-functional autonomous teams following DevOps principles.
4. Why is it necessary to have a mature DevOps approach when introducing microservices?
    - Testing and deploying lots of microservices is almost impossible to be effected manually by separate teams.
5. What is a unified logging layer?
    - It is a configurable facility for collecting, processing, and storing logs.
6. How do logging and tracing differ?
    - Logging is usually human-readable and focused on operations, whereas tracing is usually machine-readable and focused on debugging.
7. Why might REST not be the best choice for connecting microservices?
    - It may provide bigger overhead compared to gRPC, for example.
8. What are the deployment strategies for microservices? What are the benefits of each of them?
    - Single service per host – easier to tweak the machines to the workload.
    - Multiple services per host – better utilization of resources.

Chapter 14

1. How do application containers differ from operating system containers?
    - Application containers are designed to host a single process, while operating system containers usually run all the processes typically available in a Unix system.
2. What are some early examples of sandboxing environments in Unix systems?
    - chroot, BSD Jails, Solaris Zones.

3. Why are containers a good fit for microservices?
    - They offer a unified interface to run applications regardless of the underlying technology.

4. What are the main differences between containers and virtual machines?
    - Containers are more lightweight as they don't require a hypervisor, a copy of an operating system kernel, or auxiliary processes, such as an init system or syslog.

5. When are application containers a bad choice?
    - When you want to put a multi-process application in a single container.

6. Name some tools for building multi-platform container images.
    - manifest-tool, docker buildx.

7. Besides Docker, what are some other container runtimes?
    - Podman, containerd, CRI-O.

8. What are some popular orchestrators?
    - Kubernetes, Docker Swarm, Nomad.

Chapter 15

1. What's the difference between running your applications in the cloud and making them cloud-native?
    - Cloud-native design encompasses modern technologies such as containers and serverless that break the dependency on virtual machines.

2. Can you run cloud-native applications on-premises?
    - Yes, it's possible with solutions such as OpenStack, for example.

3. What's the minimum **highly available (HA)** cluster size for Kubernetes?
    - The minimum HA cluster requires three nodes in the control plane and three worker nodes.

4. Which Kubernetes object represents a microservice that allows network connections?
    - Service.

5. Why is logging insufficient in distributed systems?
    - Gathering logs and looking for correlations between them in distributed systems is problematic. Distributed tracing is better suited for certain use cases.

6. How does a service mesh help with building secure systems?
    - A service mesh abstracts connectivity between different systems, which allows encryption and auditing to be applied.

7. How does GitOps increase productivity?
    - It uses a familiar tool, Git, to handle the CI/CD without the need to write dedicated pipelines.

8. What's the standard CNCF project for monitoring?
    - Prometheus.

Packt.com

Subscribe to our online digital library for full access to over 7,000 books and videos, as well as industry leading tools to help you plan your personal development and advance your career. For more information, please visit our website.

Why subscribe?

- Spend less time learning and more time coding with practical eBooks and Videos from over 4,000 industry professionals

- Improve your learning with Skill Plans built especially for you

- Get a free eBook or video every month

- Fully searchable for easy access to vital information

- Copy and paste, print, and bookmark content

Did you know that Packt offers eBook versions of every book published, with PDF and ePub files available? You can upgrade to the eBook version at www.packt.com and as a print book customer, you are entitled to a discount on the eBook copy. Get in touch with us at customercare@packtpub.com for more details.

At www.packt.com, you can also read a collection of free technical articles, sign up for a range of free newsletters, and receive exclusive discounts and offers on Packt books and eBooks.

Other Books You May Enjoy

If you enjoyed this book, you may be interested in these other books by Packt:

C++ High Performance - Second Edition

Björn Andrist , Viktor Sehr

ISBN: 978-1-83921-654-1

- Write specialized data structures for performance-critical code
- Use modern metaprogramming techniques to reduce runtime calculations
- Achieve efficient memory management using custom memory allocators
- Reduce boilerplate code using reflection techniques
- Reap the benefits of lock-free concurrent programming
- Gain insights into subtle optimizations used by standard library algorithms
- Compose algorithms using ranges library
- Develop the ability to apply metaprogramming aspects such as constexpr, constraints, and concepts
- Implement lazy generators and asynchronous tasks using C++20 coroutines

Modern C++ Programming Cookbook - Second Edition
Marius Bancila

ISBN: 978-1-80020-898-8

- Understand the new C++20 language and library features and the problems they solve
- Become skilled at using the standard support for threading and concurrency for daily tasks
- Leverage the standard library and work with containers, algorithms, and iterators
- Solve text searching and replacement problems using regular expressions
- Work with different types of strings and learn the various aspects of compilation
- Take advantage of the file system library to work with files and directories
- Implement various useful patterns and idioms
- Explore the widely used testing frameworks for C++

Packt is searching for authors like you

If you're interested in becoming an author for Packt, please
visit authors.packtpub.com and apply today. We have worked with thousands of
developers and tech professionals, just like you, to help them share their insight with the
global tech community. You can make a general application, apply for a specific hot topic
that we are recruiting an author for, or submit your own idea.

Leave a review - let other readers know what you think

Please share your thoughts on this book with others by leaving a review on the site that you
bought it from. If you purchased the book from Amazon, please leave us an honest review
on this book's Amazon page. This is vital so that other potential readers can see and use
your unbiased opinion to make purchasing decisions, we can understand what our
customers think about our products, and our authors can see your feedback on the title that
they have worked with Packt to create. It will only take a few minutes of your time, but is
valuable to other potential customers, our authors, and Packt. Thank you!

Index

D

data transfer object (DTO) 121
declarative code
  versus imperative code 149
  writing 149, 151
decomposition patterns, for microservices
  by business capability 402
  by subdomain 402
deduction guides 144
defensive programming 270, 271, 312, 313
Dependabot
  reference link 259
dependencies
  automated upgrade management 316
  security, checking 315
dependency inversion principle 23, 26, 27
deployment code
  Ansible, using 290, 291
  Ansible, using in CI/CD pipeline 291
  building 293
  creating, with components 292
  managing 290
deployment strategies, for microservices
  multiple services per host 403
  single service per host 403
deployment view 83, 84
development view 82
DevSecOps 325
distributed computing
  misconceptions 102, 103, 104, 105, 106
  misconceptions, avoiding 102
distributed systems
  characteristics 98
  observability 465
  service models 98
Docker Swarm 448
Dockerfiles
  using, to build applications 431, 432
Doctest
  examples 263
document, views
  about 79, 80
  concurrency view 82
  deployment view 83, 84

development view 82
functional view 80, 81
information view 81
operational view 83, 84
documentation
  diagrams, generating from code 85
  generating 84
documenting requirements
  sections 69
domain-driven design (DDD) 15, 16, 402
don't repeat yourself (DRY) rule 27
drawing tool
  URL 75
dynamic allocations
  reducing, with SSO/SSO 202
Dynamic Application Security Testing (DAST) 320
dynamic polymorphism
  versus static polymorphism 183

E

Easy Approach to Requirements Syntax (EARS) 66
Elasticsearch 414
Elasticsearch, Logstash, Kibana (ELK) 105
Enterprise Service Bus (ESB)
  about 42, 362, 364, 368
  benefits 364
  commercial products 363
  component 363
  disadvantages 364
  source products 363
Envoy 473
event-based architecture
  broker-based topologies 45
  even sourcing 48
  event sourcing 46
  exploring 44
  mediator-based topologies 45
  topologies 45, 46
event-based sagas 108
eventual consistency 106, 107
exception safety levels
  basic exception safety 177
  no guarantee 177
  no-throw guarantee 177

O

P